Lucia Happe

Configurable Software Performance Completions through Higher-Order Model Transformations

The Karlsruhe Series on Software Design and Quality
Volume 8

Chair Software Design and Quality
Faculty of Computer Science
Karlsruhe Institute of Technology

and

Software Engineering Division
Research Center for Information Technology (FZI), Karlsruhe

Editor: Prof. Dr. Ralf Reussner

Configurable Software Performance Completions through Higher-Order Model Transformations

by
Lucia Happe

KIT Scientific Publishing

Dissertation, Karlsruher Institut für Technologie (KIT)
Fakultät für Informatik
Tag der mündlichen Prüfung: 10. November 2011
Referenten: Prof. Dr. Ralf H. Reussner, Assist.-Prof. Petr Hnetynka PhD.

Impressum

KIT Scientific Publishing

Karlsruher Institut für Technologie (KIT)
KIT Scientific Publishing
Straße am Forum 2
D-76131 Karlsruhe

KIT Scientific Publishing is a registered trademark of Karlsruhe Institute of Technology. Reprint using the book cover is not allowed.

www.ksp.kit.edu

Print on Demand 2014

ISSN 1867-0067
ISBN 978-3-86644-990-9

Abstract

Performance is one of the key quality attributes of a software system and is crucial for its success. Software performance engineering (SPE) supports developers and architects in building responsive and resource efficient applications. During early development stages, performance predictions based on architecture models allow the evaluation of design alternatives, capacity planning, and the identification of potential bottlenecks. To provide accurate performance predictions, such models have to include low-level details, for example, about the underlying middleware or design patterns used. Including such low-level details conflicts with the abstract architecture paradigm. It leads to significant modelling effort for software architects and requires detailed knowledge about the modelled system.

Model-Driven Software Development (MDSD) can solve this conflict and include the necessary details using model transformations. However, such transformations have to cope with the complexity of today's architecture models. Additionally, lower levels (infrastructure or implementation) are variable in many cases. The effect of such variability on performance must be captured in the transformations. Current MDSD technologies can support variability of transformations only to a limited extend.

In literature, *completions* allow the inclusion of low-level details into high level prediction models. However, they are not fully automated, are not variable and configurable, and make limited use of MDSD technologies. Related solutions introducing variability in MDSD typically deal with model instances only. As a consequence, model transformations become very complex and hard to understand, develop, and maintain. To overcome this problem, we have to introduce variability to transformations themselves, which is not supported by current transformation languages.

In this thesis, we propose an advanced concept for model transformations closing the gap between abstract architecture models and low-level details. For this purpose, we extend existing MDSD techniques by variability of transformations. Our approach, called CHILIES, moves the management of variability to a higher abstraction level. We enable variability of transformations using generators based on the presented Higher-Order Transformation (HOT) patterns. HOT patterns target different goals, such as template instantiation or transformation fragment composition. We applied our approach to the domain of SPE to complete prediction models. In this thesis, we developed a completion library that allows to reuse expert knowledge and to improve the accuracy of performance predictions.

The validation of our approach addresses the improvement of prediction accuracy by completions and the complexity of their transformations. We evaluated the prediction accuracy of the completions developed in the scope of this thesis in several case studies by comparing performance prediction results to measurements on real implementations. Our results imply that the prediction accuracy can be increased significantly when completions are applied to a software performance model. Furthermore, we compared the complexity of manually implemented transformations to transformations developed with our CHILIES framework. The results suggest that transformations developed using CHILIES are less complex and more focussed as they allow to manage variability more efficiently.

Acknowledgments

I enjoyed the work on my thesis so much especially because of the people who accompanied me. This thesis would not be possible without constant support, guidance and encouragement provided to me by my colleagues, friends and immediate family members. They helped me to overcome daily obstacles during this, sometimes hard, but always enjoyable period of my life.

I want to begin with the most important and very patient witness of my life. Jens, this work would not have been possible without your love and encouradgement you always have for me. I am happy (happe :)) to have such a beautiful family with you and I am very grateful for our little daughter Natalie. I want to mention here as well the unconditional support, love and motivation that my parents gave me. They are accompaning me from the beginning and they are my biggest fans. With you standing behind me nothing can go wrong. Matko, my lovely brother, I want to thank you for your lasting support, love and inspiration. You all make my life worth living. I love you and I am grateful to have you all!

Fundamental for this work and my research was guidance and support from Prof. Dr. Ralf Reussner, who gave me thorough guidance for my dissertation and taught me the principles of good research. Thank you from whole heart for your patience and for being the best advisor I ever met (far beyond PhD thesis). You gave me motivation to accomplish my goals, constructive critic and helpfull feedback. You provoked me to be better and better in everything I do. Moreover, I thank you for the exeptional and stable research enviroment full of team-spirit that you created.

In this environment I could meet my PhD-fellows and visiting researchers who accommpanied my research. Many of you happen to be wonderfull friends and an irreplaceable part of my life far beyond PhD research. Despite the male-dominated profession, I have to mention at first number of women: Bara, who has unfalling endurance in support and fine-tunning research ideas, Anne, who I love to have discussions with, Catia, who brought energy and even more fun in our research. Girls, thank you for the great time we had! When mentioning support and endurance, I'm thinking of Thomas Goldschmidt, who was a grey eminence behind my work and guided my first experiments in the MDSD world. Thomas, thank you for your support!

Moreover, I worked with many great people from various projects at the Charles University in Prague and at the University of Karlsruhe (TH). From the Charles University, I would like to thank all members of D3S Group, in particular, I would like to thank Petr Hnetynka for supervising this thesis and for his detailed and constructive comments. Furthermore, I want to thank Ján Kofroň, Lubomír Bulej, Tomáš Bureš, Petr Tůma and František Plášil for their support and motivating discussions. At the University of Karlsruhe (TH), the people from the SDQ group strongly contributed to this work. Especially, I would like to thank: Heiko Koziolek, Steffen Becker, Klaus Krogmann, Michael Kuperberg, Erik Burger, Jörg Henss, Franz Brosch, Martin Küster, Michael Hauck, Matthias Huber, Andreas Rentschler, Max Kramer und Philipp Merkle for their valuable feedback, constructive discussions and unforgettable collaboration. During the course of this work, I supervised the bachelor or diploma theses of Misha Strittmatter and Christian Vogel whose contributions are also part of this work. Many thanks to both of you! Misha, I really enjoyed, and still enjoy, working with you. I would also like to thank all students I had the pleasure to work with: Georg Hinkel, Christian Heupel, Florian Klein, Christian Harnisch, Christoph Kurrat and Thomas Schuischel.

Furthermore, I have been lucky to work with number of researchers who inspired and motivated me. Big thanks to Raffaela Mirandola, Dorina Petriu, Colin Atkinson and Alberto Avritzer. Alberto, thank you for introducing me into the world of smart-grids and energy distribution, it is pleasure to work with you!

Last but not least, I would like to mention, a german-czekoslovakian collaboration during the Check/Czech evenings with my colleagues Barbora Buhnova, Jan Kofron and Jens Happe who were the main ingredience for the great time we had together.

Karlsruhe, August 2012

Contents

1. Introduction

For successful and effective software development, the ability to predict the impact of design decisions in early development stages is crucial. Design decision can influence quality properties, e.g., performance, of software systems. Using predictions, potential problems, such as bottlenecks and long delays, can be detected early avoiding costly redesigns or re-implementations in later stages. Williams and Smith [170] estimated the financial benefit of software performance prediction for medium sized project on several millions of US dollars.

In model-driven software performance engineering [6], abstract design models are used to predict and evaluate response time, throughput, and resource utilisation of the target system during early development stages.In order to provide accurate predictions, the performance models have to consider the influence of the underlying platform, of the operating system, and even of used design patterns (e.g., concurrency design patterns). The low-level details influence performance metrics and as such are essential for accurate predictions. The problem of missing details was already identified by Woodside et al. [172]:

> *"Performance modelling is effective, but it is often costly;* ***models are approximate, they leave out detail that may be important****, and are difficult to validate."*

Including low-level details in prediction models conflicts with the abstract architecture paradigm and leads to a significant modelling effort for software architects. Moreover, such models are very complex leading to a decreased understandability, reusability and model credibility. For example, the middleware's complexity and the specific knowledge on the implementation, which is required to create the necessary models, would increase the modelling effort dramatically. Since the low-level details can appear in different configurations, it is hardly feasible to create such models manually. This leads to the well known conflict between variability and automation [172]:

> One of the obstacles to the adoption of performance tools is "***a conflict between automation and adaptability*** *in that systems which are highly automated but are difficult to change, and vice versa. As a result no tool does the job the user needs, so the user goes and invents one. Further, various tools all have different forms of output which makes* ***interoperability*** *challenging at best.*"

Woodside et al. in [172] point out the leading research question of this thesis that addresses the problem of automated inclusion of variable low-level details into highly-abstract prediction models. The conflict between the inclusion of low-level details into prediction models and maintaining highly-abstract models can be addressed by Model-Driven Software Development (MDSD). Because of the reconfigurability of the included details, the used MDSD techniques must support variability as well.

However, MDSD approaches lack an applicable and suitable solution for managing variability. Existing variability approaches result in a growing complexity of transformations, limited usage of configurations, and the maintainability of transformations quickly becomes a huge problem. Completion-based approaches described in the literature allow inclusion of low-level details, however, they are not automated, do not support variability of completions, or they are limited to the configuration of attributes only. These approaches suggest only simple annotation models that extend prediction models through parametrization of resource demands using measurements on real systems (e.g., in the case of performance prediction, for example, number of processor cycles needed for particular activity). They concentrate on the properties of the underlying platform and do not consider structural changes in the architecture, such as inclusion of certain design pattern (e.g., Replication, Barrier, Connector patterns etc.).

While most of the implementation details are not known in advance, a rough knowledge about the design patterns that are to be used might be available already very early. This knowledge can be exploited for further analysis, such as performance prediction. One reason why such details are not considered is the high level of variability in the architecture that would be required. It is not feasible to create such models manually. Therefore, automated tool support is crucial to build such detailed models.

In this thesis, we propose a concept of configurable model transformations to close the gap between an abstract model and low-level details required by the modelling purpose (e.g. to provide accurate predictions of performance). The solution, presented in this thesis, is based on the parametrized model completions that include the details of lower levels into high-level architectures. Model completions are realised using and extending existing model-driven technologies. They express low-level details as reconfigurable black-box constructs and, thus, hide the model complexity from software architects. Software architects only have to provide a configuration for the modelled detail. The integration of the configured detail is fully automated.

MDSD allows to create software families specially tailored for a certain domain and sharing common details. The existing techniques to support variability in the software families, however, mostly focus on the variability of models. Hence, the transformations, from a more general family member into a more detailed family member, define already how the model variants look like. Thus, it is not necessary to actually create model variants, it is enough to focus on the variants of transformations generating required models. We take a step back and analyse broader variability scenarios in the MDSD. We shift our attention from the variability of models to the variability of other artefacts, especially transformations.

The model transformations, sharing common parts, need to be customised to integrate different performance-relevant details. Moreover, these details may introduce optional extensions to metamodels. In such situation, we have to handle the variability of metamodels as well. We created an automated support of variable transformations development using pre-processors and generators based on, so called, Higher-Order Transformations (HOTs) [167]. The proposed approach, called CHILIES, presents a set of HOT patterns for different variability scenarios. We use these patterns to build a Software Product Line (SPL) [37] for completion transformations. The CHILIES approach does not require heavy development effort and allows the light weight integration of low-level details into performance prediction methods.

1.1. Research Questions

In the scope of this thesis, we address research challenges from two areas: (i) Model-Driven Software Performance Engineering (MDSPE), and (ii) Model-Driven Software Development (MDSD). More specifically, we work on answering the following research questions:

Q1: *How to include purpose-specific aspects to models in an automated but adaptable manner inheriting its standard mechanisms and facilities, including transformations and tools?*

The goal is to automate the integration of purpose-specific aspects into the models. The model details increase the prediction accuracy as such more detailed models correspond better to the reality. Each aspect is encapsulated in a completion and can be instantiated in different variants added to the model. Potentially, we may use any of these completions and then, using completed models, generate the implementation, e.g. code, or to run analyses. To support, for example, the code generation from any of these models, we have to maintain the same language as the generation chain requires as input. Moreover, the variability of completions results in multiple implementations of transformations, which consist in majority of common parts composed together with customisations based on the configuration. Thus, the second question emerges.

Q2: *How to support configuration-based variability in model transformations?*

In other words, what methodology, technologies, model-driven structures of pre-processors or generators are needed to support variability? The requirement for variability results from different goals and different settings, which results in a different kinds of variability. Some of the required variable artefacts have to be composed together, other are only instantiated in form of templates or added as customisations of more general transformations. Our solution needs to support variability in transformations resulting from these different requirements. The answer to this question overcomes the limitations of current transformation approaches.

Q3: *How to structure the Completion Library to reduce possible conflicts in an application of multiple completions?*

The previous question deals with the management of variability in general. In our application domain, the Model-Driven Performance Engineering (MDSPE), additional factors need to be considered. Especially, in this domain, conflicts in a sequence of completions has an additional dimension, the dimension of quality attribute (i.e., performance). We discuss the application of the proposed method and the structure of the completion library for MDSPE. In this context, we have to consider multiple applications of completions and the conflicts in their application. Furthermore, transformations have certain quality properties themselves, which leads to the last question.

Q4: *How to analyse maintainability of relational transformations?*

The final question deals with the evaluation of quality properties, such as maintainability, ease-of-use or understandability, of resulting transformations. We have to discuss the complexity and understandability of resulting transformations. For this goal, we have to evaluate the metrics to quantify quality properties of transformations.

These research questions resulted in the scientific contributions listed in the following section.

1.2. Scientific Contributions

The following gives details on the particular contributions. The main contributions of this thesis are:

Generalised Model Completions The separation of concerns is essential to avoid construction of large and monolithic models, which are hard to maintain or reuse. Reusability of such models is limited especially because such models are often designed for one purpose, as such they do not consider possible enhancements when the purpose of the model changes and new domain-specific details have to be introduced. For example, a component-based architecture model could be used to predict performance. However, the same model could be used to analyse reliability, as well. Both of these purposes require additional domain-specific details, i.e. performance or reliability specific implementation details.

Existing approaches do not consider model completions in general. The idea of completions introduced by [174, 76], however, only in a form of performance-specific annotations. These approaches do not discuss the role of model completions in MDSD, either provide a support for completions. Especially, they do not discuss the variability of structural changes resulting from completion integration.

In the model-driven world, models are understood as instances conforming to predefined metamodels. Each model is created for certain purpose. Two models could have different levels of detail although they are based on the same metamodel. Models may have even different level of detail in the same domain. Increasing the level of detail of a metamodel to the magnitude that each aspect of the real subject could be expressed by its model would increase complexity of metamodel in a such way that metamodel would be unusable. Additionally, such metamodel does not support separation of concerns by modelling only one detail at the time. Having many metamodels on a different level of detail is also infeasible. It is impossible to foresee all different purposes for which a model could be created and related requirements on such models. This problem cannot be approached on the metamodel level. It is necessary to come up with a solution on the model level that would support the incremental completion of model instances that are in each step conform to the one and the same metamodel. We consider this approach as indirect extension of metamodel by introducing (mini-)domain specific languages for a sub-domain of one completion. This way, we can define model pragmatics, similarly as it is possible for programming languages. Furthermore, the proposed solution should provide support for reuse and reconfiguration of such incremental completions.

We propose a concept of model completions to close the gap between an abstract model and low-level details required by the model's purpose (e.g. to provide accurate predictions of performance). Completions do not change the metamodel, thus, all existing tools built for this modelling-language could be reused. The core idea of this thesis is to introduce model pragmatics that could be used on a model level to increase the level of detail in model instances, without need to extend the metamodel directly. Moreover, the complexity of model enhancements encapsulated in completions is hidden to the developers. They only configure the variant of the completion on an abstract level and the integration of the completion is a black-box operation for them. These completions are highly variable, thus the integration of them is non-trivial task, a lot of effort is needed to implement and to maintain any automated solution realizing them. We use an approach similar to model weaving. Each completion has a DSL for its modelled sub-domain and can be maintained individually. Together with the original metamodel, completions are interconnected into a 'lattice of metamodels' that could be considered as a more complete metamodel. The idea is to allow the use of this more complete metamodel to create model instances and later transform instances to conforming to the original metamodel again, which allows reuse of existing tools. Because, the necessary transformations inherit the high level of variability from completions and the chosen variant is not known in advance, it is a higher-order problem. This challenge is the target of the second contribution in this thesis.

CHILIES Variability Management Method The main contribution of this thesis is a novel approach called CHILIES which automates the management of variability in transformations. The support of variability in the definition of transformations is crucial to support completions. Although, we apply CHILIES to support performance completions, our approach can be used in other domains, as well.

Typically, variability approaches focus on variability of models [154, 70, 89] or propose solutions based on the model annotations [162, 12]. The main problem of such approaches is the complexity of resulting transformations which have to consider each possible combination of configuration options. The main advantage of our variability approach is provided by performing the model transformation configuration automatically based on configuration instead of models. This separation of concerns can achieve high variability and flexibility in the development of software applications.

In this thesis, we created a Software Product Line (SPL) for model transformations using Higher-Order Transformations (HOTs). A HOT compiles a transformation model again into a transformation model. We used these HOTs as pre-processors or generators, at load time of the transformation (e.g. in MDSPE), executed before the actual transformation. In our approach, we use chains of HOTs where each HOT represents a different pre-processing step. We identified different scenarios where the variability of transformations has to be handled and specified model-driven structures using HOTs (called HOT patterns), which can be used to build SPLs for transformations. Based on these patterns, software engineers can build pre-processor chains to generate transformations on demand and integrate them into the existing model-driven process. By formalising these patterns, we build a framework allowing the *reuse* of HOT specifications. The SPL designed to support completions is a composition of three of such HOT patterns: *Routine*, *Composite* and *Template* pattern.

The first one is used for synthesis of a general transformation from a metamodel; the second one for transformation composition based on the structure of the configuration model; the third one for the instantiation of parametrized domain-specific templates as a partial transformation synthesis.

Completion Library for Software Performance Engineering The specification of completions requires a lot of domain-specific expert knowledge (e.g. for performance prediction the knowledge about performance-relevant implementation details). Moreover, the same activities are often repeated, e.g. usage of the same design pattern or integration of the same middleware platform. Therefore, we introduce a library offering reusable completions to developers. This library is structured, as mapping sets of completions to the roles in the development process. Thus, one development role can configure only completions in its responsibility. Building on the separation of concerns among the development roles is already reflected in the design of the metamodel (e.g. in PCM), the responsibility domains of the roles can be mapped on disjunct sets of model elements. Based on this principle, we can reduce conflicts in a sequence of multiple completions.

Moreover, using predefined quality heuristics, we can evaluate if all permutations of a completion sequence are quality equivalent. We introduced a method to reduce and resolve conflicts in the sequence of completions. Considering that a model could require more than one completion to be integrated, our approach can deal with chains of completion transformations.

We formalise this problem and provide a solution based on a stepwise conflict resolution. In the first step, the conflict domain is reduced based on the structure of the underlying metamodel. In the next step, the quality heuristics are applied to resolve the conflict.

In addition, we introduce an initial set of completions, validated for the Palladio Component Model [18], that allow to reuse expert knowledge about modelling of concurrency and serve as illustration of the application of completions. Each completion or combination of completions should increase the prediction accuracy, i.e. reduce the deviation of prediction and observation, to correspond better the reality. Therefore, the creation of a completion is a challenge itself and requires detailed research of the modelled aspect and its validation by comparison to the measurements on a real system. The validation was performed in an end-to-end manner, by using the PCM workbench extensions based on CHILIES introduced in this thesis.

To support completions, CHILIES are integrated in the Palladio Component Model (PCM) tools. The tool takes a complete PCM instance (i.e., a software architecture model including performance specifications) as input and generates a new PCM instance by applying the completions defined and configured in the source model. Such refined models are prepared for further analyses of the performance, reliability, maintainability and cost properties. Additionally, this thesis discusses the support for automated measurements and experiments to collect possible configuration options that should be included in the configuration model. These measurements and experiments are done on real systems [77].

Maintainability Metrics for Model Transformations Furthermore, we discuss the quality of the HOTs and completion transformations. The maintainability of transformations is influenced by various characteristics - as with every programming language artifact. Code metrics are often used to estimate code maintainability. However, most of the established metrics do not apply to declarative transformation languages (such as QVT Relations) since they focus on imperative coding styles. Code metrics are one way to characterize the maintainability of programs. However, the vast majority of these metrics focus on imperative coding styles and thus cannot be reused as-is for transformations written in declarative languages.

In this thesis, we propose a set of quality metrics to evaluate transformations written in the declarative QVT Relations language. We evaluated the transformations' maintainability through this set of automated metrics for model-to-model transformations. In the analysis, the classical parametrized model transformations are compared to the generated transformations by HOTs.

Statefull Model-Driven Software Performance Engineering Integrating rising variability of software systems in performance prediction models is crucial to allow the widespread industrial use of performance prediction. One of such variabilities is the dependency of system performance on the context and history-dependent internal state of the system (or its components). The questions that rise for current prediction models are (i) how to include the state properties in a prediction model, and (ii) how to balance the expressiveness and complexity of created models.

Only a few performance prediction approaches deal with modelling states in component-based systems. Currently, there is neither a consensus in the definition, nor in the method to include the state in prediction models. For these reasons, we have conducted a state-of-the-art survey of existing approaches addressing their expressiveness to model stateful components. Based on the results, we introduce a classification scheme and present the state-defining and state-dependent model parameters. We extend the Palladio Component Model (PCM), a model-based performance prediction approach, with state-modelling capabilities, and study the performance impact of modelled state.

1.3. Structure

After the introduction provided by this chapter, this thesis is structured in eight chapters:

- **Chapter 2** describes the foundations necessary for this thesis. We discuss the basic terms and gives a brief overview on the concepts from the two main areas: Section 2.1 introduces the foundations of MDSD and Section 2.2 the foundation of MDSPE domain.
- **Chapter 3** starts with a motivation and introduction of model completions in general. We locate the model completion concepts in the MDSD and MDSPE domain. After, discussing the consequences of model completions for the MDSD processes (e.g. MDA), we introduce an completion-based MDSPE process in Section 3.3. It provides a running example and illustrates the completion-based MDSPE process using this example. This chapter deals with the research question Q1: *How to include purpose-specific aspects to models in an automated but adaptable manner inheriting its standard mechanisms and facilities, including transformations and tools?*
- **Chapter 4** introduces the CHILIES approach. We discuss the application of HOTs for different goals in Section 4.3. Furthermore, each of the Sections 4.4, 4.5 and 4.6 gives, first, the specification of an one HOT pattern in general and, second, the description of its implementation in the context of performance completions. Furthermore, we introduce the composition of these three patterns providing support for completions in the MDSPE process. The Chapter 4 presents the solution to the research question Q2: *How to support configuration-based variability in model transformations?*
- In **Chapter 5** we apply model completions to the MDSPE approach 'Palladio Component Model (PCM)'. At the beginning of this chapter (cf. Section 5.2.3), we discuss the reduction and resolution of

conflicts in the sequence of completion execution for the PCM meta-model. Later, we introduce an initial library of performance completions for concurrency design patterns in Section 5.3. The chapter introduces the results of the research question Q3: *How to structure the Completion Library to reduce possible conflicts in an application of multiple completions?*

- **Chapter 6** continues to evaluate the proposed variability mechanism for transformations. This chapter introduces a set of quality metrics that can be used to evaluate the maintainability of transformations, especially their complexity, understandability, extendibility and ease-of-use. This chapter answers the research question Q4: *How to analyse maintainability of relational transformations?*

- **Chapter 7** shows on several case studies the validity of the contributions presented in this thesis. Two case studies in Section 7.2.1 demonstrate that predictions made based on completed models reflect the reality in an appropriate and accurate way. In addition, we present a case study based on the realistic Business Reporting Scenario demonstrating the prediction accuracy in a composition of completions. Moreover, we evaluate the method for the conflict resolution in Section 7.2.2. Section 7.2.3 discusses the complexity and maintainability of the HOTs and completion transformations using quality metrics for transformations introduced in the previous chapter.

- **Chapter 8** discusses the current state-of-art in the related areas. The discussion includes work from the areas of model transformation engineering and platform completions for software performance engineering. In addition, we summarize and compare the related approaches to the contributions introduced by this thesis and discuss the resulting deficiencies.

- **Chapter 9** concludes this thesis. We summarize the most important contributions presented in this thesis. Finally, we discuss the open questions and future directions of our research.

The additional contributions of this thesis are discussed in more detail in the Appendix, where we also introduce further HOT patterns. Moreover, we give examples on the implementation of two completion transformations, for the MOM and Procedure Call Connector completion. The most important contribution presented in Appendix is the set of experiments and heuristics building a foundations for stateful SPE.

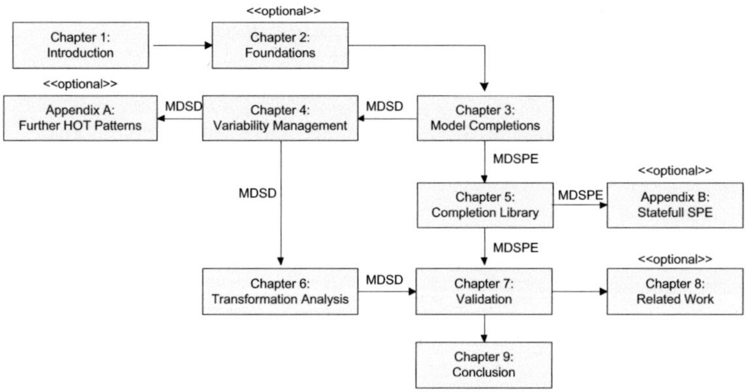

Figure 1.1.: Chapter structure in this thesis.

The dependencies among the chapters are illustrated in Figure 1.1. The `optional` chapters could be safely skipped, if the reader is familiar with the basic MDSD and MDSPE concepts. The further chapters are divided between the two context domains in this thesis, the MDSD and MDSPE domain. The reader interested in the MDSD contributions could follow the reading plan marked by the `MDSD` tag, analogously for the `MDSPE` tag.

2. Foundations

In this chapter, we introduce the concepts and terms from the three different research areas on which this thesis is built on (cf. Figure 2.1). *Software Performance Engineering*(SPE) supports developers to take the right decision about the developed software system to fulfil their performance requirements. Performance prediction methods evaluate response time, throughput, and resource utilisation of the developed systems in early development phases. The application of SPE avoids cost, time and effort intensive redesigns of systems later. In this work, we focus on the SPE for *component-based architectures* (CB-SPE). In the component-based systems, the performance of a whole system is determined by the performance characteristics of individual components and their composition. Components and compositions are described by models specifying software system's structure and properties. These models serve as basis for further generation of implementation skeletons (code), analysis models or simulation code. These different generation scenarios are supported by *Model-Driven Software Development* (MDSD). Because design decisions about the software systems can easily change during the development, model transformations automate creation of different model variants and avoid effort resulting from manual implementation.

We structured this chapter as depicted in Figure 2.1. First, Section 2.1 introduces foundations of MDSD necessary to understand concepts presented in this thesis. Second, Section 2.1.2.2 provides an overview of well-established Generative Programming, Model-Driven Architecture (MDA) and Software Product Line (SPL) concepts and related terms. Third, Section 2.2 discusses MDSPE methods for component-based architectures

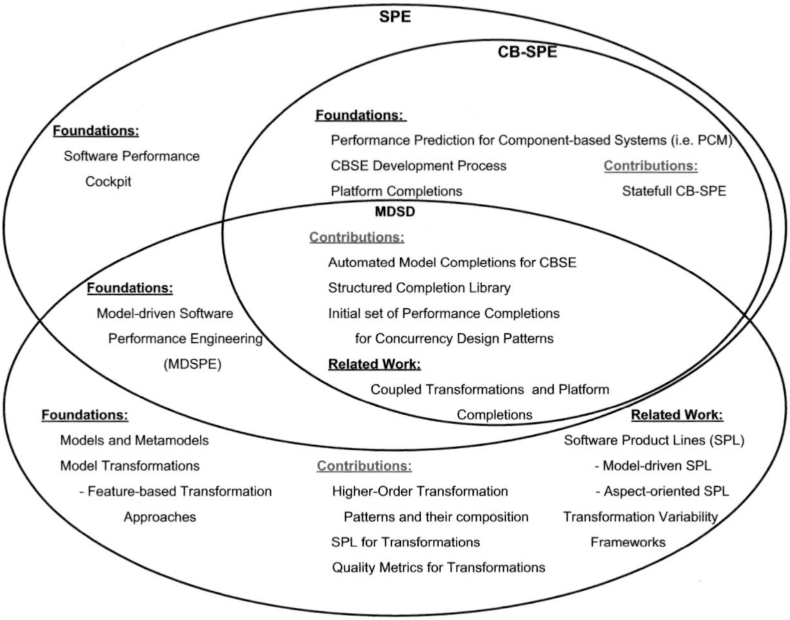

Figure 2.1.: Research areas involved in this thesis.

with special focus on approaches using model transformations to derive performance models. Finally, we provide an overview of the used Software Performance Cockpit in Section 2.2.4.

2.1. Model-driven Software Development

Abstraction plays a central role in Model-Driven Software Development (MDSD): it allows to separate the specification of a software system from its implementation. The ultimate goal of the MDSD is to construct models of higher abstraction and to translate them stepwise into models of lower abstraction until the implementation is generated. In doing so, the implementation task (code writing) is replaced by modelling activities, such as creating model instances, writing model transformations for different purposes, or specifying other problem specific models. The following sections introduce several concepts central to the MDSD. We discuss the main MDSD artefacts in Section 2.1.1. The first subsection shows the definitions of basic terms like model and metamodel. The focus of the following section is on model transformation techniques including discussions on higher-order transformations. Special kinds of transformation methodologies, such as generative programming and software product lines, play central role in later sections. Additionally, Section 2.1.2 discusses details of MDSD generations and their relation to Model-Driven Architecture (MDA).

2.1.1. Basic Artefacts of MDSD

The most effective way how to understand complex real-world problems is to build a model. Models are abstractions of the real-world problems or elements. Raising the level of abstraction helps effectively addressing a specific purpose, such as answering a question about the system or influencing its behaviour. We can achieve this by ignoring certain details while focusing on the relevant ones. Models are the central artefact of Model-Driven Software Development (MDSD). MDSD is responsible for defining the models. Moreover, MDSD is bridging the gap between these software models on a high-level of abstraction and program code, which contains implementation details on a very low-level of abstraction. This gap is often very large. MDSD technologies try to automate the process of lowering the abstraction levels. With MDSD, the ultimate aim of software engineers is to build models on a high-level of abstraction and translate them fully automatically into models of lower abstraction level (including program code). A key MDSD artefact to achieve this are model transformations. Models are transformed using model transformations in step-wise fashion, where each step lowers the level of abstraction.

2.1.1.1. Model and Metamodel

In software engineering, models are used in many ways: to predict system qualities, reason about system properties and their changes, and traditionally for communication between different software developers. Models can be developed as a starting point to implement a system, or they can be derived from an existing implementation. Despite the importance of models, there is still no established definition. In the remainder of this thesis, we define model as follows (based on [150, 136]):

Definition 1 Model
"A formal representation of entities and relationships in the real world (abstraction) with a certain correspondence (isomorphism) for a certain purpose (pragmatics)."

Based on this definition, models have three main characteristics: abstraction, isomorphism, and pragmatism. Models can be described as *abstractions* of modelled objects, that allow engineers to reason about the object ignoring some details while focusing on relevant ones. The selection of the modelled details is guided by a purpose. The model represents the real world object with certain level of correspondence, called *isomorphism*. Isomorphism is a projection of considered attributes of real-world object onto the attributes of its model, or in other words, there is certain equivalence between the model and the real world entity. Each model is created for some purpose. This model *pragmatism* determines the level of abstraction and isomorphism. For example, we can create a software model for the purpose of behaviour protocol interoperability checks and another one for the purpose of performance prediction. Both of the models will include entities describing used software components and their interfaces. But, because of the different aim of the model, the behaviour of the components will be modelled with different level of detail. For the interoperability checks we need to know exactly what is the functionality (behaviour protocols) provided by the component. Compared to the performance prediction model, is the first model very detailed model of a component behaviour. For the second purpose, it is enough to abstract the component behaviour to time or resources needed to respond to an user request.

A model is created conforming to one modelling language. A modelling language is defined by its metamodel which specifies the 'grammar' for each model (or the 'word'). A metamodel defines constructs that can be used to build models and contains validity rules associated with this constructs. Models conforming to a metamodel follow the structure defined by the metamodel and do not violate its validity rules. Such models are called instances of metamodel. The modelling community around the website *metamodel.com* [117] defines metamodels as follows:

Definition 2 Metamodel (*metamodel.com*: [117])

"A metamodel is a precise definition of the constructs and rules needed for creating semantic models."

We understand a metamodel as a language that allows the formal representation (model) of entities and relationships in the real world on the certain level of abstraction. In principle, each metamodel is again a model created on a certain level of abstraction using constructs are described by another meta-metamodel. Two metamodels, defining constructs that can be used to describe real world objects from the same domain, can have different expressive power. The metamodel definition limits a level of detail allowed in conform model instances, that is influenced by the level of isomorphism and abstraction of metamodel towards the native language. For example, two metamodels can provide constructs to describe a chair, the first allows to express that the chair has legs, second allows to describe how many round or angled and polished or matt legs the chair has. We can say that metamodel definition influences isomorphism and abstraction level of model instances and therefore we extend the metamodel definition as follows:

Definition 3 Metamodel
"A metamodel is a precise definition of the constructs and rules within a certain domain needed for creating semantic models on certain level of abstraction."

A metamodel is defined by:

- *Abstract syntax*, which defines elements of models and the relations between them. This definition is independent from actual representation of these elements. For example, in programming languages, the abstract syntax is usually represented as an abstract syntax tree.
- *Static semantics*, which describes properties of model elements and relations by which the model can be validated. A common language to express static semantics is OCL [127].
- *Dynamic semantics*, which describes the intention of the model concepts, how to interpret valid model instances and meaning of their elements. In most cases, it is written in prose.
- *Concrete syntax*, which defines the representation of abstract concepts, e.g. an UML notation [124] or Java syntax. While metamodels always have exactly one abstract syntax, multiple concrete syntaxes are possible.

Thus, metamodels define all information necessary to build a model. For example, the UML2 meta-model [124] defines the set of valid UML models. It defines the elements available in an UML model and their connections (syntax). Additionally, it contains the Object Constraint Language (OCL), which allows the definition of semantic constraints. Furthermore, each metamodel describes models from a certain problem domain. The constructs introduced by a metamodel belong to the same domain and all instances of this metamodel describe objects from this domain using the allowed constructs. A metamodel is then understood as a specification language dedicated to a particular domain. We define domain as follows:

Definition 4 Domain
"A domain is a field of study that is defined by common requirements, used modelling constructs and rules."

The Meta Object Facility (MOF) [126] is a meta-meta-model which is self describing and defines the constructs and rules necessary to specify metamodels. Initially, was MOF used to model UML. Therefore, its core concepts are similar to those available in UML class diagrams, although they are on different meta-levels and the described concepts are different. The MOF specification evolved to the "essential" MOF (EMOF). The resulting implementation based on this standard (used in this thesis) is the Eclipse Modelling Framework (EMF) and its meta-meta-model ECORE (see Figure 2.2). Furthermore, the Object Constraint Language (OCL) [127] restricts valid MOF instances and expresses their static semantics.

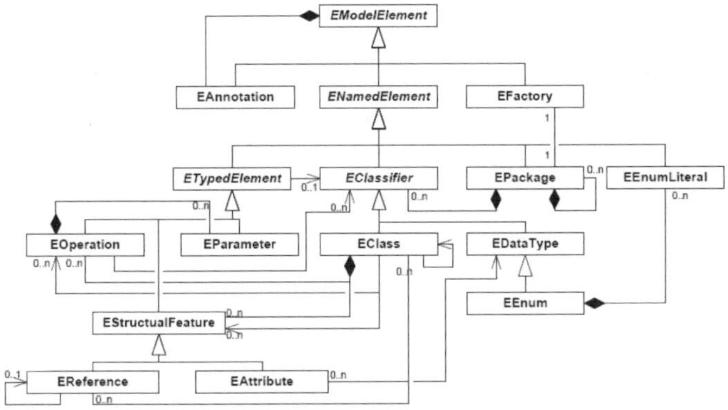

Figure 2.2.: The Ecore metamodel.

2.1.1.2. Transformations

Because many aspects of the modelled object might be of interest, model developers can use various modelling concepts and notations to highlight the relevant details by the means of different views or representations. Developers use transformations to move between different representations, abstraction levels or specialisations of models. Transformations can convert models from one abstraction level to another (usually a less abstract one) by adding more detail to the model. Transformations are the second major concept of MDSD.

Insight into the topic of model transformations, explored techniques, most common languages, and current research papers is collected in a literature study by Biehl [25]. According to his paper, typical usages of model transformations are synthesis, integration (tool integration or model merging), analysis, simulation and optimization. He further proposes a classification scheme for model transformation problems: change of abstraction or not (vertical and horizontal transformation), change of metamodels (endogenous and exogenous transformation), translating between technological spaces (such working contexts could be for example MOF, XML, DBML etc.), number of involved domains (in-place transformation if only one domain is involved), target types used (model or text), preservation of certain model properties (semantics, behaviour or syntax).

The commonly used transformations are classified into two types: *Model-To-Model (M2M)* and *Model-To-Text (M2T)* transformations. Furthermore, transformations that take a number of instances of different metamodels as input are called *Y-transformations*. If one of these inputs configures the transformation itself, we call these Y-transformations *mark transformations* [11]. Another special type of transformations are in-place transformations, which use equal source and target metamodels. Additionally, these transformations operate on one model. Thus, the result of the transformation is directly stored in the model as used as input.

The source and target of a M2M transformation are models. M2M transformations transform an instance of one metamodel into an instance of another metamodel. These metamodels are usually instances of the same meta-metamodel and they can be equal. A transformation is defined by a set of transformation rules on a metamodel elements. Each rule defines its effect using the concepts from source (or input) and target (or output) metamodel. Thus, transformations are specific to the used metamodels. Transformation rules are specified in special languages and are interpreted by a transformation engine for execution. There is a wide range of different transformation engines available, supporting different approaches such as graph-transformations, relational, operational or hybrid transformations.

A special type of M2M transformations are such transformations where the target model of a transformation is an extension of the source model. Such transformations preserve large parts of the source model and adds additional information. They are called refinement transformations [63] and are very similar to completion transformations.

Graph-transformation approaches have the theoretical foundations in graph grammars and as such are applied to models interpreted as graphs of objects. The principle of such transformations is based on mapping between left-hand-side and right-hand-side patterns. When the sub-graph in the input model matches the left-hand-side pattern the sub-graph is replaced in the output model by the right-hand-side pattern. This process is finished when no further left-hand-side pattern can be matched. Similar principle is realised by relational approaches which specify transformation rules in form of formal relations between two domain patterns [45]. The relational transformation engine tests all available relations and updates the output model to fulfil all the relations. The OMG Standard Query/View/Transformation (QVT) [72] specifies a QVT Relational and QVT Core languages, both with relational semantics. In this thesis we use the QVT Relational transformation language to implement our transformations. Furthermore, the QVT standard introduces an operational language (QVT Operational), whose main difference is the explicit definition of execution sequences by a main method from which all mapping operations are called. In contrast, relational transformation languages only describe the relations between input and output of a transformation in a relational (i.e., declarative) manner (non-determinism). Finally, hybrid approaches such as the Atlas Transformation Language (ATL) [90] combine relational and operational approaches.

M2T transformations generate structured text (e.g., executable code) from their input models. These transformations can be visitor- or template-based. Using one of these approaches, M2T transformation engines create for elements of the input model new code snippets.

QVT Relational Transformation Language QVT Relational is part of the QVT standard [72] and describes model transformations in a declarative manner. This means the transformation itself is written as a set of relations that must be satisfied during the transformation process. As QVT Relational is multi-directional, there is no single source and target model but a list of so called candidate models. Each of these candidate models can be chosen as a target of the transformation, identifying the execution direction. When the transformation is invoked in a selected execution direction only the target model is modified so that all relations hold.

```
top relation ClassToTable {
        cn : String;
        prefix : String;
        checkonly domain uml c : SimpleUML::UmlClass {
          umlNamespace = p : SimpleUML::UmlPackage {},
          umlKind = 'Persistent',
          umlName = cn
        };
        enforce domain rdbms t : SimpleRDBMS::RdbmsTable {
          rdbmsSchema = s : SimpleRDBMS::RdbmsSchema { },
          rdbmsName = cn,
          rdbmsColumn = cl : SimpleRDBMS::RdbmsColumn {
               rdbmsName = cn + '_tid',
               rdbmsType = 'NUMBER' },
          rdbmsKey = k : SimpleRDBMS::RdbmsKey {
```

```
            rdbmsColumn = cl : SimpleRDBMS::RdbmsColumn{}}
        };
        when {
        PackageToSchema(p, s);
        }
        where {
          ClassToPkey(c, k);
          prefix = cn;
          AttributeToColumn(c, t, prefix);
        }
    }
```

Listing 2.1: Example of QVT Relational.

QVT Relational is part of the QVT standard [72] and describes model transformations in a declarative manner. This means the transformation itself is written as a set of relations that must be satisfied during the transformation process. As QVT Relational is multi-directional, there is no single source and target model but a list of so called candidate models. Each of these candidate models can be chosen as a target of the transformation, identifying the execution direction. When the transformation is invoked in a selected execution direction only the target model is modified so that all relations hold.

An example QVT-R relation, which matches UML class (`SimpleUML::UmlClass`) to relational database table (`SimpleRDBMS::RdbmsTable`), is given in Listing 2.1. Before we map the class to table, we have to map the UML package to an RDBMS schema. Additionally, after the class is mapped to the table, we have to call the relation `AttributeToColumn`. A relation has two or more domains, that are given as patterns on the candidate models. The pattern usually includes an object graph pattern, properties and associations between objects and defines a variable binding for each pattern match. By using the same variables in different domain patterns, we can define the relation between candidate models. In consequence, the target model is modified for each found pattern binding not being fulfiled to the extent that the relation holds.

Each relation can be marked as *top-level*. This means that the relation has to hold in any case for a successful transformation, while any non-top-level relation only has to be satisfied when directly or transitively referenced from a *where* clause. A top-level relation must hold for every possible combination of elements in the candidate models. The transformation engine starts with the execution of the top-level relations and continues with the relations demanded by the pre- and post conditions of the top-level relations. Thus, non-top-level relations that are never demanded by other relations won't be executed at all. A relation can have *when* and *where* clauses that specify its pre- and post-conditions. A relation only has to be satisfied when all pre-condition relations contained in the *when* clause are satisfied. In a similar manner, each relation contained in the *where* clause has to be fulfiled when the relation containing the clause is fulfiled. Hence, the when and where clauses allow for the introduction of further constraints on the match patterns. Such constraint can be fulfilment of either a query, an OCL-Statement or another relation.

Beyond that, a target domain can be marked as *checkonly*, i.e. the target domain model is only checked for consistency and not modified. Besides this, relations are marked as *enforce* by default, thus insisting on the application of model changes for relations that do not hold.

To visualize QVT transformations the QVT specification defines a graphical representation for a relation. This should make it more intuitive to see and understand a transformation. To make the diagrams more readable, when objects are typed, only the actual name of the type is written. The complete package name would be very long in most cases. In Figure 2.3 one can see the `ClassToTable` relation from the last example in graphical notation.

Transformation diagrams are mainly based on standard UML class diagrams. At some points they extend the class diagrams with new symbols. One new key symbol is the hexagon with the two arrows at the left and at the right. On each limb you can find the name of the models involved in

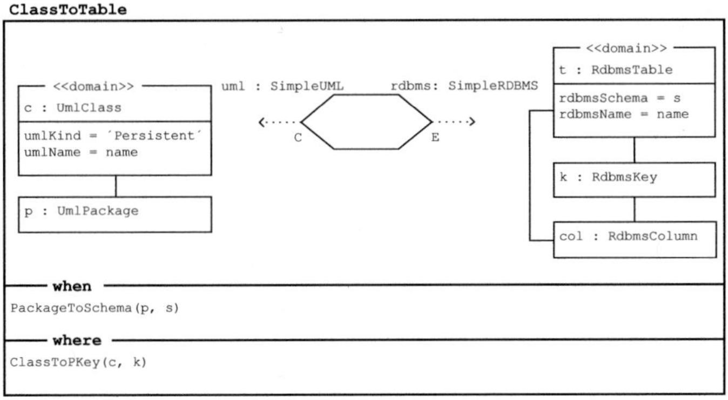

Figure 2.3.: Graphical representation of a QVT relation.

this relation and their corresponding metamodels. Below the arrow a "C" or "E" symbolizes if a model is only checked or if the relation is enforced. Domains or objects are pictured as rectangles, domain are labeled with the keyword domain. This rest of the symbol is the same as in a class diagram. In the upper part of the rectangle there is the name of the object and its type. In the lower part attributes or constraints that the object has to fulfil can be specified. If an object contains other objects they are not written as attributes. They are pictured below in their own rectangle, and are connected to the containing element with a line. At the bottom of a relation optional boxes for the `when` or the `where` clause can be attached.

2.1.2. Evolution of model transformation processes

The crucial role of transformations for the MDSD is visible on the evolution of transformation processes, which shows that only through extended usage of transformations it was possible for model-driven techniques to become an integral part of software development. The evolution of model-driven technologies and architectures can be summarized in three generations.

2.1.2.1. First Generation of MDSD Technologies

This generation is the beginning of modelling, where programming abstractions (e.g., packages, interfaces) are embedded in the code and provided in a form of, for example, programming libraries. A software architecture design exists only in the heads of developers. This situation is, however, inadequate for large, changing teams and for management of software evolution. Therefore, models were used as a mean to communicate ideas about an architecture. In the first generation, models are used in the role of program documentation or code visualization (e.g., UML class diagrams) but are difficult to maintain. However, they helped to increase software quality. These models are essentially diagrams, because of their low-level of abstraction. These diagrams are tightly coupled with code and provide additional means to view and edit at code level. In this generation, MDSD tools were mostly graphical environments helping to draw diagrams. Some of the tools were capable of reverse-engineering code to diagrams, or of creating code skeletons from class diagrams and other implementation-level diagrams (e.g. IBM Rational Software Architect).

2.1.2.2. Second Generation of MDSD Technologies

In the second generation, the automation of forward engineering is the main goal. This generation introduces standard and process guidelines under the name of Model-Driven Architecture (MDA) [125]. MDSD Tools made significant step to generate code comparable to hand-crafted implementation. Models include sufficient detail to enable the generation of an implementation. Most of the model-to-code transformations are template-based, they apply a series of templates on models and map them to code. Many tools also support round-trip engineering and allow synchronising models and implementations during the software evolution. With the second generation of MDSD technologies, the use of models in software development became much wider accepted. Models are an integral part of the software engineering process. This led to the development of libraries of transformations to accomplish several activities automatically, similar to the first generation of documentation [167].

Generative programming The idea of generative techniques has already been applied in compiler construction where programs written in a programming language are transformed by compilers into executable code. The main difference is that compilers usually process a fixed set of programming languages and generate code for fixed amount of processors. Model-driven techniques allow to specify custom metamodels and transformations. Thus, on the model level, it is possible to have any number of metamodels and transformations.

Czarnecki and Eisenecker [46] introduced generator options in their book on Generative Programming which is a predecessor of today's MDA paradigm. They used so called feature diagrams to capture different variants in the possible output of code generators. Feature diagrams model all valid combinations of a set of features called (feature) configuration where a single feature stands for a certain option in the respective input domain. Their work is applied in area of product line engineering [109] especially for domain modelling and domain variance analysis using feature diagrams.

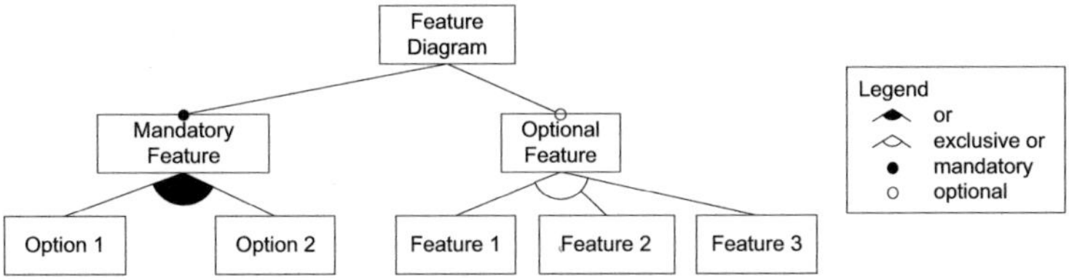

Figure 2.4.: Example of a feature diagram.

Feature diagrams are used to formally capture variabilities of a target domain. Each feature represents an aspect of the target domain. The relationships between features capture additional constraints limiting combinations of features. Some features may require other features as prerequisites or be mutually exclusive with other features. An example of feature diagram is illustrated in Figure 2.4. An instance of feature diagram is called a feature configuration and represents choices of active features. Czarnecki and Eisenecker use feature diagrams to parametrise generators. In this thesis, we use feature diagrams to parametrise model transformations. Simple and intuitive structure of feature diagrams bears the advantage of having a model for the possible transformation parameters which introduces the configuration options in terms easily understandable by software architects and captures the variability in the transformation mapping in a focused way.

Model-Driven Architecture Model-driven software development processes like the OMG's Model-Driven Architecture (MDA) [125] leverage the role of models in software development. In MDA, models serve as input for a series of transformations which at the end generate the system's implementation. Each of these transformations maps models of higher abstraction to models of lower abstraction. The system's implementation represents the lowest level of abstraction.

According to the MDA process, the first model to create is an abstract model of the business domain, the computation independent model (CIM). Based on this model, developers create a model of the system under development without using any details of the technical platform. This model is called platform independent model (PIM) (cf. Figure 2.5). Automatic model-2-model (M2M) transformations refine this model by adding implementation details of particular platforms. The term platform is a broad concept in this context. For example, it can define the type of the realisation (database application, workflow management, etc.) or a specific implementation of a technical concept like different industrial component models (.NET, CORBA, Java EE). Furthermore, a platform can refer to implementation dependent details like different types of configuration files depending on a particular middleware selection. A model which depends on such details is a platform specific model (PSM, cf. Figure 2.5) with respect to a particular platform. The amount of additional platform-dependent information may vary depending on the purpose of transformation step. There are many such transformation steps possible, each adding certain aspects of the target platform.

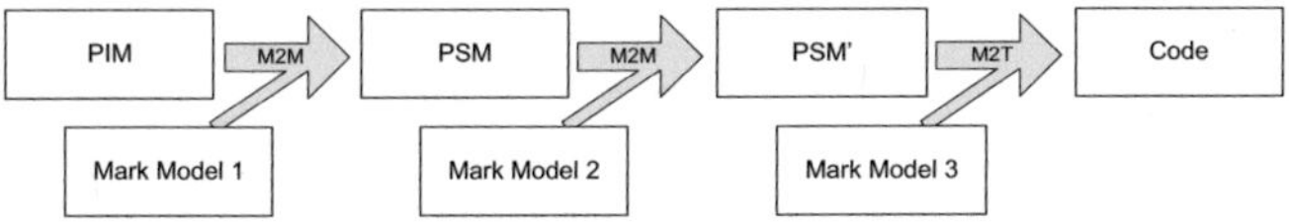

Figure 2.5.: MDA models and transformations.

In Figure 2.5, the refinement process is distributed among a number of transformations forming a transformation chain. Each transformation takes the output of the previous one and adds its own specific details. When refining high-level concepts of transformations into concepts on lower abstraction levels, different alternatives may be available. For example, if different applications communicate via messaging, different patterns for realising the message channels can be used, e.g., with or without guaranteed delivery. If developers want their transformations to be flexible, they can parameterise them allowing transformation users to decide on mapping alternatives themselves. The OMG's MDA standard allows transformation parametrisation by so called *mark model* instances.

In MDA terminology, *mark models* are input models which tell transformations where, and how, platform-specific details should be added to computation-independent models. Mark models are models dedicated to reference entities of input models and to decorate these referenced entities with a *platform description model*, usually specifying configuration options.

Mark models allow users of transformations to decide on mapping variations themselves by choosing from different options. Thus, mark models encapsulate different variants of target models. Depending on the mark model, the transformation generates the result model. For example, a transformation from UML classes to database tables can depend on a configuration of a mark model to generate different types of tables. Using UML stereotypes, we can create marks on the transformed elements. The stereotypes ≪`relational`≫ or ≪`object`≫ will result in different type of tables being generated.

In their book, Völter and Stahl [167] consider MDA application to be impractical, especially because of missing tool support. However, the work of Becker [11] demonstrates that parametrisation of transformations can be applied successfully. The biggest disadvantage of mark models and transformations parametrised by mark models is the maintainability and very hard extendibility of such approach. To provide necessary flexibility the transformation developer has to foresee all possible options in mark model and parametrise the transformation accordingly (implement a structure similar `switch` statement from JAVA). Moreover, when new feature is introduced transformation has to be adapted. We demonstrate in this thesis transformation parametrisation approach which does not require transformation adaptations and we compare our approach to the concept of mark models.

Software Product Lines If there are commonalities between software systems, developers implement the same functionality multiple times in different projects. Software Product Lines (SPLs) [37] standardise such commonalities using domain models to capture the core concepts. SPLs promote planned asset reuse, automation, and composition of large products from smaller parts. The reusable parts are called features in SPL terminology. Each feature represents an increment in functionality. The implementation of a feature extends then the core software system in one or more places.

The development process of an SPL consists of two phases: domain and software engineering. The goal of the domain engineering phase is to describe and develop the common and variable parts. During the software engineering phase, these parts are assembled to build the final product. SPLs can be implemented using a compositional and annotative approach [37]. In the compositional approach, developers implement each feature as independent module. These modules are then composed at compile- or deployment-time. For the annotative approach, they implement features with some form of annotations of the core common part (or source code). Which is very similar to the `#ifdef` and `#endif` statements that surround feature code of C/C++ preprocessors. These two approaches are the basic concepts of SPLs. More advanced approaches using generative, model-driven or aspect-oriented techniques to support SPLs fall in one of these categories. Our approach is compositional (from a transformation generation point of view) and annotative (from a application model point of view).

2.1.2.3. Third Generation of MDSD Technologies

In the third generation of MDSD technologies, transformations are subject of manipulation as well. This is summarized by the statement of Bézivin at al. [23]: "*In MDSD, everything is a model*". Every artefact of the MDSD process can be interpreted (manually or automatically) as a model. Models and transformations are still a central part of the software development process. Furthermore, they start to become an integral part of the developed system as first-class elements of the runtime architecture. As part of the developed system, transformations can be themselves generated and handled by model-driven development, like traditional programs. A wide set of applications for such technologies appeared involving transformations in the roles of both manipulation program and manipulated object. Transformations are taking on different tasks in the development process, besides code generation and documentation. Transformations can, for example, evaluate code quality or generate test cases. A fourth generation of MDSD may involve transformations that take over program logic at runtime.

The concepts introduced in this thesis contribute to the processes of the third MDSD generation. In the following, we discuss the main tool to realize our goal, higher-order model transformations.

Higher-Order Transformations Transformations are very complex as they can form transformation chains, be highly configurable or require additional inputs. A shift of knowledge is observable, as more and more logic is implemented in transformations rather than platform-dependent code. With larger projects, developers not only have to face larger models, but also transformations of higher complexity. Transformations can be represented by a transformation models conforming to a transformation metamodel. However, not all frameworks provide transformation metamodels. In this work, we refer to the Medini QVT framework [88] which contains an implementation of QVT Relational transformation language. While in most languages, Higher-Order Rules are not supported as first class entities (rules cannot be declared through expressions) in some languages, like ATL and QVT, transformations are able to operate on transformations, which are represented as models. As such, transformations can be manipulated equally as any other model. Transformations can be created, modified or analysed by transformations. The ability to treat transformations as subjects of other transformations allows to fully exploit the power of transformation concept, abstraction levels and complex model-driven structures.

Transformations that operate on transformations are called Higher-Order Transformations (HOTs). Tisi et al. [158] understand a HOT as a model transformation such that its input and/or output models are again transformations. In their work, Tisi et al. describe a typical schema of HOTs, which consists of three operations:

1. Transformation injection: The textual representation of the transformation rules is read and translated into a model representation conforming to the transformation metamodel.

2. Higher-order transformation: The transformation model is the input of a model transformation that produces another transformation model. The input, output and HOT transformation models are all instances of the same metamodel.

3. Transformation extraction: The serialization of the output transformation model back to a textual transformation specification is performed.

In our work, the transformation injection (reading of textual syntax or parsing) and extraction (model-to-text transformation or so called *pretty-printer*) are not considered as a part of a HOT. These steps are only explicitly necessary when the framework does not provide support for them. Note, that in our case, the framework provides injection itself. However, since it does not provide extraction, we developed a pretty-printer as a last step before executing a generated transformation. We consider the transformation extraction as technical detail.

2.2. Model-driven Software Performance Engineering

During the last years, many approaches dealing with performance prediction and measurement have been introduced [6, 98]. In the area of Component-Based Software Engineering (CBSE), systems are build out of reusable black-box components (implementing sets of services) interconnected to a component architecture. The modelling of the system is done at a high level of abstraction. One idea behind CBSE is to increase component re-use. Specialised component performance prediction and measurement approaches introduce modelling languages with the aim to understand the performance (i.e. response time, throughput, resource utilisation) of a full architecture based on code-specific performance properties of individual components.

It is generally accepted that performance is a pervasive quality of software systems. Everything affects it, from the software itself to all underlying layers, such as operating system, middleware, hardware, communication networks, etc. [172]. The factors influencing the performance of a software component are difficult to analyse because they depend not only on the component implementation, but also on its usage, deployment and environmental context of the component (see figure 2.6), and occur at different stages of component and system life cycle. A design-time performance prediction requires plenty of details about all influencing factors to be sufficiently accurate [172, 76]. The approach introduced in this thesis is a contribution to ease development of accurate performance models of component-based architectures.

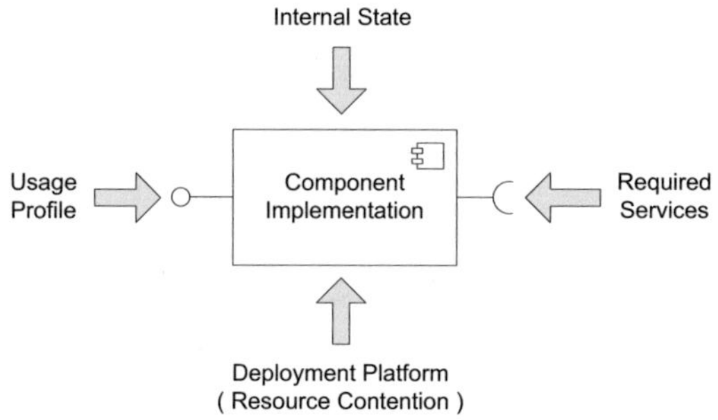

Figure 2.6.: Performance-influencing factors.

In the following sections, we describe the CBSE development process and involved development roles (see Section 2.2.1). We extend this development process in Section 3.3. Section 2.2.2 describes the Palladio Component Model (PCM), which is used in this thesis to express performance models and predict quality properties of component-based architectures (especially performance). The initial approaches for platform completions are summarized in Section 2.2.3. These approaches were inspiration for the first idea of model completions as introduced in this thesis. Finally, Section 2.2.4 presents basics of the Software Performance Cockpit (SoPeCo) used to calibrate PCM models.

2.2.1. CBSE Development Process

In the following, we give some details on CBSE development process and the participating roles [102]. The presented development process is based on the specification by Cheesman and Daniels [31]. They introduced a process consisting of following steps: (1) Requirements analysis, producing a business concept model and use cases; (2) Specification, describing the overall architecture, business interfaces and components with their interfaces; (3) Provisioning, creating component implementations or purchasing components matching specification from third parties; (4) Assembly, creating deployable application by wiring components according to the architecture description; (5) Test, testing application according to use case models; and (6) Deployment, installing application in its target environment.

The division of work targeted by CBSE is enforced by structuring the modelling task to four independent languages reflecting the responsibilities of the four different developer roles (cf. Figure 2.7). We can we distinguish following types of developer roles involved in producing artefacts of a software system:

- *Component developers* are responsible for the specification of components, interfaces, and data types. They implement and describe components and their behaviour in abstract, parametrised way. Components are generally specified via provided (implement services by component) and required (used services by component) interfaces, which describe the contract between a client requiring a service and a server providing the service. Interfaces consist of a list of signatures specifying services, which is very similar to the Corba Interface Definition Language (IDL) [129].

- *Software architects* compose the component specifications into an architectural model. They create assembly connectors, which connect required interfaces of components to compatible provided interfaces of other components. They usually do not deal with component internals, but instead fully rely on the specifications supplied by the component developers. Furthermore, software architects define the system boundaries and expose some of the provided interfaces to be accessible by users.

- *System deployers* model the resource environment (e.g., CPUs, network links) and allocate the components in the architectural model to the resources. Resources have different attributes, such as processing rates or scheduling policies.
- Finally, *domain experts* are familiar with the customers or users of the system. They specify the system-level usage model describing critical usage scenarios as well as typical parameter values.

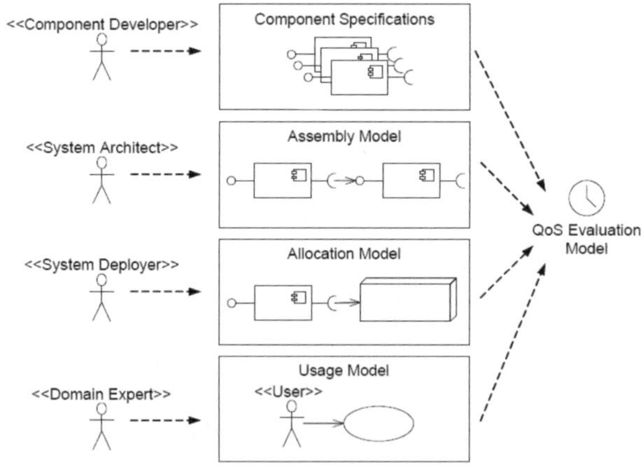

Figure 2.7.: Roles in CBSE development process [19].

The complete system model is then composed from these partial models specified by each developer role. The field of study targeted by this thesis is defined by domain-specific languages for component-based architectures (e.g. Palladio Component Model) that is composed of specific sub-domains mapping described development roles. The specific enhancing attributes of modelled architectures are described by orthogonal technical sub-domains. We are interested in the technical sub-domains of particular quality attributes, especially performance. Therefore, in the following we will describe specifics of PCM with focus on performance.

2.2.2. Palladio Component Model (PCM)

In the following, we introduce the technologies and architectural languages for specifying software architectures and their extra-functional properties. We apply our approach in the domain of performance engineering. For this purpose, we use a performance prediction approach called Palladio Component Model (PCM) [135, 100, 18]. The PCM is a modelling language specifically designed for performance prediction of component-based systems, with an automatic transformation into a discrete-event simulation of generalised queuing networks. Its available tool support (PCM Bench) allows performance engineers to predict various performance metrics, including the response time, throughput and resource utilization. All three properties are reported as random variables with probability distribution over possible values together with their likelihood. The response time is expressed in given time units (e.g., seconds), throughput in number of service calls or data amount per time unit (e.g., kilobytes per second), and resource utilization in the number of jobs currently occupying the resource.

Figure 2.8 illustrates a system model with performance annotations in PCM. It consists of four models created by four developer roles in a parametric way, which allows the models to be updated independently of each other. *Component developers* specify the behaviour and performance properties of components, *software architects* combine components into component assembly with defined system interfaces, *system deployers* define execution environment and allocation of software components to system

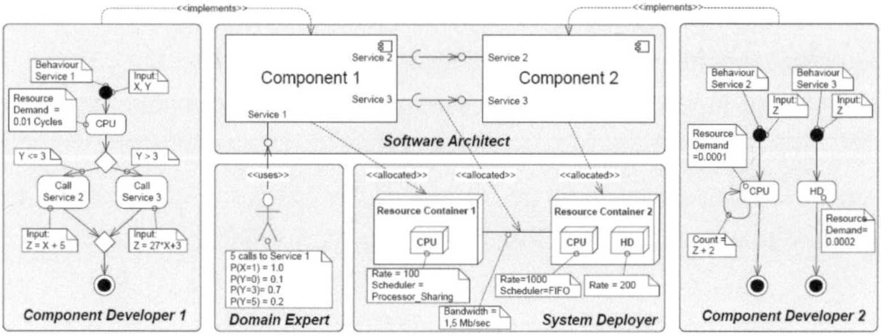

Figure 2.8.: Illustration of a PCM model.

resources, and *domain experts* specify the scenarios of system usage that drives system execution. Thanks to the responsibility separation, roles responsible for the models of the architecture elements can be easily identified in a PCM model.

Software components are the core entities of the PCM. Each component provides and requires services defined by its interfaces. For each provided service, an abstract behavioural specification called Resource Demanding-Service Effect Specification (RD-SEFF) is created. RD-SEFFs model the usage of required services by a component (i.e., external calls), and the consumption of resources during component-internal processing (i.e., internal actions). This description has the form of an annotated control flow graph. Basic components can be composed to composite components, which add hierarchy to the component models. Basic and composite components assembled to form a system by binding required interfaces of one component to the provided interface of another component. These bindings are specified by assembly connectors. Interfaces are first class entities in the PCM, consist of multiple service signatures, and follow the CORBA IDL syntax.

Component specifications in the PCM are parametrised for their later environment. *Component developers* can annotate external calls as well as control flow constructs with parameter dependencies. These dependencies cover influences of required services, different soft- and hardware environments, as well as different input parameters of provided services. This allows the model to be adjusted for different system-level usage profiles. Parameter values can be of different type (e.g., string, int, real, composite) and can be characterised with random values to express the uncertainty.

Similar to UML activities, RD-SEFFs consist of three types of actions: Internal actions, external service calls, and control flow nodes.

Internal actions model resource demands and abstract from computations performed inside a component. For performance prediction, component developers need to specify demands of internal actions to resources, like CPUs or hard disks. Demands can depend on parameters passed to a service or return values of external service calls.

External service calls represent invocations by a component of the services of other components. For each external service call, component developers can specify performance-relevant information about the service's parameters. For example, the size of a collection passed to a service can significantly influences its execution time, while the actual values have only little effect. Modelling only the size of the collection keeps the specification understandable and the model analysable. Apart from input parameters, the PCM also deals with return values of external service calls. Note that external service calls are always synchronous in the PCM, i.e., the execution is blocked until a call returns. This is necessary to consider the effect of return values on performance. A combination of external service calls and fork actions (that allow the parallel execution) can introduce asynchronous communication into the model. However, such models are too complex and require high development effort. In such scenarios model-driven technologies can increase effectiveness of development.

Control flow elements allow component developers to specify branches, loops, and forks of the control flow.

Branches represent "exclusive or" splits of the control flow, where only one of the alternatives can be taken. In the PCM, the choice can either be probabilistic or determined by a guard. In the first case, each alternative has an associated probability giving the likelihood of its execution. In the latter case, boolean expressions on the service's input parameters guard each alternative. With a stochastic specification of the input parameters, the guards are evaluated to probabilities.

Loops model the repetitive execution of a part of the control flow. A probability mass function specifies the number of loop iterations. For example, a loop might execute 5 times with a probability of 0.7 and 10 times with a probability of 0.3. The number of loop iterations can depend on the service's input parameters.

Forks split the control flow into multiple concurrently executing threads. The control flow of each thread is modelled by a so-called forked behaviour. The main control flow only waits for forked behaviours that are marked as synchronised. Its execution continues as soon as all synchronised forked behaviours finished their execution. The asynchronous fork action spawns a new thread and immediately continues the execution of the main control flow. This models an asynchronous service call in the PCM.

In the PCM, *parameter characterisations* [100] abstractly specify input and output parameters of component services with a focus on performance-relevant aspects. For example, the PCM allows to define the `VALUE`, `BYTESIZE`, `NUMBER_OF_ELEMENTS`, or `TYPE` of a parameter. The characterisations can be stochastic, e.g., the byte size of a data container can be specified by a probability mass function:

```
data.BYTESIZE = IntPMF[(1000;0.8) (2000;0.2)]
```

where `IntPMF` is a probability mass function over the domain of integers. The example specifies that `data` has a size of 1000 bytes with probability 0.8 and a size of 2000 with probability 0.2.

Stochastic expressions model data flow based on parameter characterisations. For example, the stochastic expression

```
result.BYTESIZE = data.BYTESIZE * 0.6
```

specifies that a compression algorithm reduces the size of `data` to 60%. Stochastic expressions support arithmetic operations ($*,-,+,/,...$) as well as logical operations for boolean expressions ($==,>,<$,AND,OR,...) on random variables.

Finally, *resource containers* model the hardware environment in the PCM. They represent nodes, e.g., servers or client computers, on which components can be allocated. They provide a set of processing resources, such as CPUs and hard disks, that can be used by the hosted components. Processing resources can employ scheduling disciplines such as processor sharing or first-come-first-served.

Valid PCM models are input, for example, for a model-to-text transformation that maps the architectural model into a discrete-event simulation or other analysis. The PCM could be used to predicts various performance metrics and it supports further analysis of design decisions or trade-off analysis, using automated optimisation approach PerOpteryx [96], which can be used to improve the architecture considering even multiple quality attributes.

2.2.3. Platform Completions

When doing performance predictions in early development stages, the software model has to be kept on a high level of abstraction. Moreover, during early development stages, most implementation details are not yet known. By contrast, detailed information on the system is necessary to determine the performance of the modelled architecture correctly. The complexity and the specific knowledge about the implementation required to create the necessary models would dramatically increase the modelling effort. The complexity of such models reduces the variability of the design models and, thus, increase the effort to evaluate and compare design alternatives. However, detailed information about the system is necessary to determine the performance of the modelled architecture correctly.

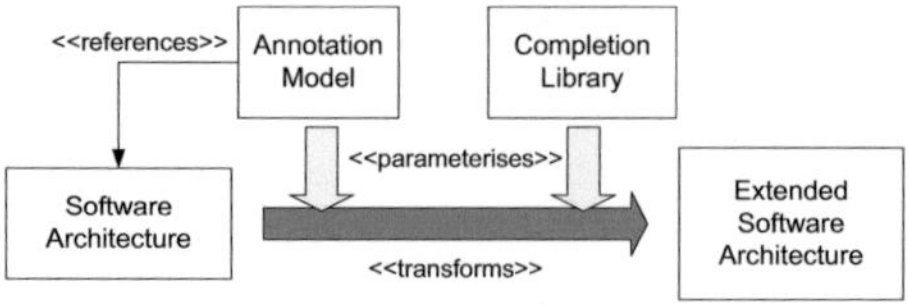

Figure 2.9.: Transformation integrating performance completions.

Performance completions, as envisioned by Woodside [173, 174], are one possibility to close this gap. They are components added to the prediction model that add performance-relevant details to a performance prediction model, but which are not of interest when designing the system's application logic. For example, details about the design patterns or platform are not included within the design model and therefore should be added by completions. These performance completions extend the software model with annotations (or rules) whose extensions (such as additional components, execution environments, or communication design patterns) are added to the original software architecture.

Figure 2.9 shows how performance completions can be realized using the MDA concepts. Elements of a software architecture model, such as components or connectors, are annotated by elements of a mark model using, for example, feature diagrams. Mark models annotate elements in the architecture which are to be completed and provide the necessary configuration options. For example, if a connector is to be replaced by message-passing the mark model can provide information about the type of the messaging channel, e.g., using guaranteed delivery. Model-to-model transformations take the necessary components from the completion library, adjust them to the configuration, and insert them in the software architecture prediction model. The result of the transformation is an architecture model whose annotated elements have been expanded to its detailed performance specifications. This step of model completion has to be automated.

2.2.4. Software Performance Cockpit

The Software Performance Cockpit is an extensible framework to ease, systemize and automate the tasks required to evaluate a software-system's performance. A performance analyst simply specifies the desired measurement scenario and the Software Performance Cockpit then runs these measurements automatically using automated orchestration of analysed software. It enables experts of different aspects of performance evaluation (i.e. setting up the test-environment, measure data, analyse data, and export performance models) to model their requirements at one single point of configuration. When started, the framework executes a series of performance-tests, collects measurement data, analyses the collected data, and exports analysed functional dependencies as performance-models. Expert roles illustrating the Software Performance Cockpit approach, are:

- **Software Experts** provide domain-specific knowledge for the software used in the evaluation-process (based on a GQM plan). For each software, they know its requirements, its functionality and its configurable and measurable parameters. They additionally provide knowledge about how to use the software. They specify how it must be configured and how it can be controlled.
- **System Administrators** set up the test-environment and deploy the software required for the system under test's performance-evaluation.
- **Performance Analysts** are experts in the process of performance-evaluation. They determine strategies to efficiently configure a series of experiments in such a way as to gain meaningful measurement-data within as few experiments as possible. Once the measured data has been analysed, Performance Analysts know how to interpret and present the analysis-results with respect to the tested system's performance.

- **Analysis Experts** provide knowledge in the area of data-analysis. They specify the algorithms to calculate possible dependencies between the system's parameter-configuration and its performance.

In this thesis, we use this approach to calibrate performance models, hence, the performance evaluation requires a large effort to set up systems and knowledge required to conduct performance evaluations is in many cases very system specific. We ease the process of completion development by utilisation of automated performance evaluation methods.

The Goal/Question/Metric Approach: When measurements are to be conducted in order to evaluate the performance of a system, they must follow a certain strategy to minimize the required number of performed experiments and to provide meaningful results. Goal/Question/Metric (GQM) was introduced by Basili et al. [7] as an approach to allow systematic measurements. They emphasise the importance of measurements to be goal-oriented in order to be efficient.

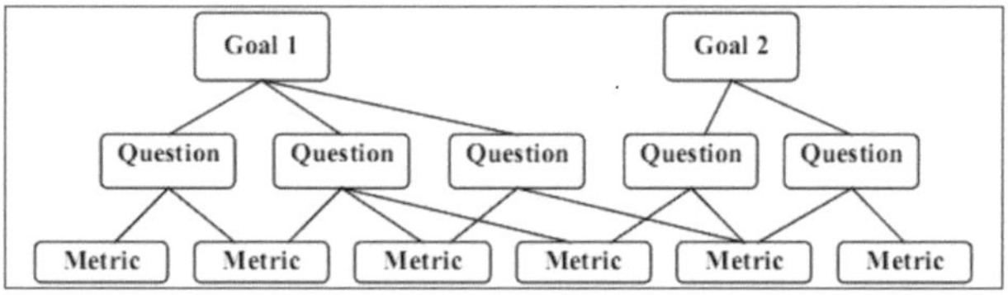

Figure 2.10.: Hierarchy of a GQM-Model [7].

A GQM-instance is a hierarchically structured model consisting of three levels:

- On the - conceptional - first level, a set of *Goals* is defined. Goals are specified in a certain context, which is determined by an issue, a purpose, an object to measure, and the viewpoint from which the goal is defined. The objects of measurement can be products (e.g. documents or programs), processes (i.e. software-related processes like testing or programming), or resources (e.g. hardware-resources or personnel)
- The second level is considered as the operational level. A set of *Questions* is defined to refine the goals and to qualify the objects of measurement with respect to a certain issue of quality.
- On the - qualitative - third level, *Metrics* are specified to allow a quantitative way of answering the questions. Metrics are considered to either be objective or subjective. Objective metrics are independent from the Goals' viewpoint (e.g. LOC of a .class file), where subjective metrics do depend on the goal's viewpoint (e.g. the readability of a text).

The structure of a GQM-plan is shown in Figure 2.10. In order to achieve a Goal, it is associated to a set of Questions. Each Question itself is associated to a set of Metrics. As the graphic shows, a Question does not have to be associated to every specified Metric; however, one Metric can be associated to multiple Questions. The relations between Goals and Questions are analogue. With respect to the approach's goal-orientation, building a GQM-model follows a top-down fashion. The interpretation of measurement-data is done in the opposite direction.

3. Model Completions

In the previous chapter, we summarized the foundations of this work. These foundations are the starting point we build on to support completions of models in the *Model-Driven Software Performance Engineering (MDSPE)*.

The leading challenge this chapter is dealing with is: *How to include purpose-specific aspects to models in an automated but adaptable manner inheriting its standard mechanisms and facilities, including transformations and tools?*

With this objective, we have to consider the well known conflict between automation and adaptability of systems [172]. The systems which are highly automated are difficult to change, and vice versa. We introduce a solution based on an automated and configurable model completions. We embed completions to the classical *Model-Driven Software Development (MDSD)* process and discuss their relationship to the well-known model refinement principle. The following sections describe the particular concepts needed for model completions and apply automated completions to enhance the MDSPE. We illustrate the creation process of completion and its usage on the running example. To automate completions we build on advanced model-driven techniques, such as *Higher-Order Transformations (HOTs)*, which in our approach adapt transformations realising completions. Then we introduce the realisation of completions using HOTs in Chapter 4. Going on with the running example, we incrementally build a first completion, which is also part of a completion library, introduced in Chapter 5.

The remainder of this chapter will be organized as follows. Section 3.1 introduces the main contribution of this chapter: the generalised Model Completion concept covering the integration of purpose-specific aspects as a part of the MDSD processes. As we introduce Model Completion concept, we discuss and complete the view on the MDSD processes and their applications. Moreover, in the section 3.2 we discuss completion-based extension of the MDSPE process for component-based architectures. This section is followed by a description of completion-based development process for component-based models for MDSPE.

3.1. Model Completions and MDSD

In model-driven software development (MDSD), we can distinguish two directions of software development. First - vertical direction, the models of systems are built on different levels of abstraction. *Abstraction* involves the extraction of system properties according to some purpose. Thus, abstraction filters and reduces the initial amount of information that is not needed with respect to the model purpose. *Refinement* is the inverse operation to abstraction ([46], page 734). Refinement adds more details to abstract models, for example towards the implementation.

Second - horizontal direction, which is specializing general models towards a more domain-specific model (e.g., software architecture model for performance prediction) by adding more domain-specific details to the model. A typical example for *specialization* is adding concrete values to parametrized model elements. Every model is created with a specific purpose in mind. Typically, one writes a model to either document an existing system, specify a system to be implemented, analyse quality properties of the system, execute simulations or to provide predictions. The purpose of the model determines the *domain* to specialize for. With the purpose of quality prediction, the domain we have to orient on is a domain of the particular quality attribute (e.g., performance or reliability). Within the process of purpose model specialization, domain specific aspects of the model have to be included.

Because models are often abstract and general at the same time, specialization and refinement might be combined. Typically, specialization and refinement activities are realized by domain experts manually. In this thesis, we use model transformations to refine and specialise models. For each model these transformations could be executed on the way to the purpose-specific model either in horizontal (specialization) or in vertical (refinement) manner (cf. Figure 3.1). A related concept was introduced in [137].

These orthogonal software development activities, as described above, are basic building blocks of MDSD. Both types of activities are in this thesis understood as series of transformations with a goal to automate as much of them as possible. The transformations executed in a direction of more concrete model, so called vertical transformations ([46], page 335), represent software implementation. The transformations executed on the same abstraction level, so called horizontal transformations ([46], page 335), represent *purpose-specific completion* of models. In this thesis, we focus on the horizontal direction. An example of vertical transformation is the model-to-text transformation in the ProtoCom Project, transforming a PCM model to a Java Prototype [15]. An example of horizontal transformation is the model-to-model transformation adding performance annotations to a general model.

Using these basic building blocks, we can build more complex MDSD processes. The vertical direction of development (left hand side of Figure 3.2) is best illustrated by well-known levels of Model-Driven Architecture (MDA), which builds on the chain of refinements starting from requirements on a software product and targeting implementation of a final software product. First, MDA refines the requirements model towards Computation-Independent Model (CIM), then from CIM to a Platform-Independent Model (PIM) and further to a Platform-Specific Model (PSM). These levels define software implementation process. Finally, the last refinement step maps the PSM to an implementation (code), model-driven tests and to a deployment of the final software product [134]. In MDA, the

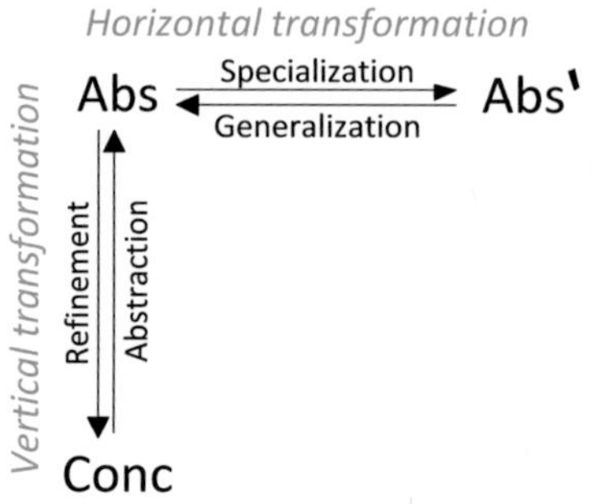

Figure 3.1.: Transformations in the *Model-Driven Software Development (MDSD)*[46].

chain of transformations is executed completely from the top-level (CIM) to the bottom (Code). Whenever the requirements change, only the top-level model is adjusted and all subsequent models and artefacts are newly generated. In the theory (cf. Figure 3.2), we design an abstract model *Abs* that captures requirements on the system and we refine it to a more concrete models until implementation *Conc*. However, there are aspects of the real world activities that conflict with the idea of step-wise model refinement towards implementation.

In the contrary to the theory, model development is an incremental process in practice (right hand side of Figure 3.2). Since requirements on the system are evolving over time or new requirements are introduced, new purpose-specific aspects need to be included in different purpose-specific models. For different purpose different purpose-specific models on the same abstraction level are created. Orthogonally to the refinement, the developers introduce horizontal activities to perform refactorings, to execute migrations, to apply domain-specific optimizations, and to weave new purpose-specific aspects into the model. Today, developers must rely on their instinct and experience to decide how detailed models are needed. They perform manual adjustments of their models to fit required purpose.

This ad-hoc model development may result in models that are either too abstract or too detailed for their purpose. Consequently, the models grow more complex because of the mix of low-level details and high-level abstractions. Often metamodels do not have enough expressive power to allow modelling of required aspects directly and new metamodel elements have to be introduced. When the metamodel changes, the chain of vertical refinements is not reusable or, in contrary, when the metamodel is fixed, the domain-specific development decisions towards model purpose could be limited. In the first case, the vertical transformations realizing the refinement chain need to be adapted after each metamodel change. Furthermore, with growing complexity of metamodels more and more development effort is needed to adapt existing transformations. Therefore, any change of metamodel is expensive and developers try to avoid it through introducing model "hacks" and manual designing of very complex models. The effort to avoid metamodel extension often leads to lost of traceability in design decisions, poorly understandable and maintainable models.

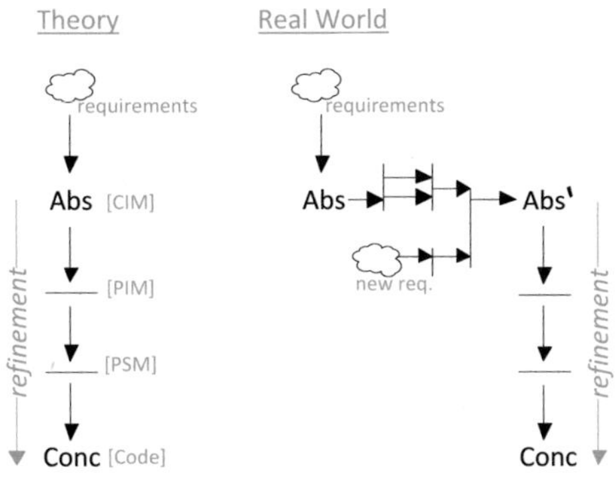

Figure 3.2.: Software development using MDSD.

In any case, it is hard to follow the relationship of created abstract model (*Abs*) to the desired specialised model (*Abs′*, Figure 3.2). Having a detailed look on the (typically manual) activities developers realize towards purpose-specific model (Abs') shows that models specialized for certain purpose are obtained by specializing general abstractions that were designed to be used in more than one domain. For example, a general connector abstraction is specialized as remote procedure call connector, further specialising steps could be adding middleware abstraction and identifying platform dependency (using .Net or J2EE middleware). Such specialized model is needed to solve particular problem, e.g. predicting performance characteristics of a system using modelled connector.

We had a closer look at such processes (right hand side of Figure 3.2) in development of PCM models and we can distinguish independent and focused development activities towards an abstract model (Abs'). The resulting model, Abs', is specified to the necessary detail and specialized for a particular problem domain. Such model is typically created manually. The goal of this thesis is to provide structured and automated approach to support developers to create purpose-specific models. We implement these activities as the vertical transformations resulting in the purpose-specific model. These purpose-specific transformations are called *completion transformations*. Completions increase the specialisation of the model to the required level. Additionally, the completions open a way to decrease development effort through automation and manageability of model complexity. Moreover, development effort is decreased by reusable nature of completions. The complexity of models is encapsulated in and hidden by abstract definition of completions. In the following sections, we discuss purpose-specific completions and related scientific challenges.

3.1.1. Model Completion Concept

We understand purpose-specific model as a model on a such level of specialisation that it includes enough detailed information to serve its purpose. For example, a performance prediction model should include performance-relevant details of a middleware platform to provide accurate predictions.

The goal is to arrive at the sweet-point, where the model is as abstract as possible and as specialized as necessary. We define the suitability of the model to fulfil its purpose by the level of model *completeness*. One model can target more than one purpose. For each model purpose different level of model completeness can be necessary.

Definition 5 Completeness

Model completeness is a quality criterion for models specified by the particular level of detail and correspondence to the modelled entity. Moreover, the level of detail and correspondence are highly dependent on intended purpose of the model.

Initially, it is not possible to quantify model completeness, because it is a purpose-specific quality. The completeness of the model can be evaluated only in the context of the model purpose and its application domain. Considering models for performance prediction, the prediction accuracy can be used as a metric to evaluate model completeness. The model providing more accurate prediction is in MDSPE domain considered as more complete as a model resulting in less accurate predictions. Dependent on the application domain the completeness metric changes. For example, models used as documentation could be evaluated based on their understandability, or models used for code generation could be evaluated based on the additional development effort after code generation needed towards executable code. In this thesis, we discuss the completeness of performance prediction models, therefore, we adapt the definition of completeness for the domain of performance prediction.

Definition 6 Completeness of Performance Prediction Models

Model completeness is a quality criterion for performance prediction models specified by the particular level of implementation detail and correspondence to the real software system. Moreover, the level of detail and correspondence determine the accuracy of the performance prediction.

As mentioned before, the model-driven software development consists of a number of activities, some of vertical (towards implementation), some horizontal (improvement of completeness) nature. For simplicity, let us assume that vertical activities decrease/increase the level of abstraction, but that horizontal maintain the level of abstraction, being concerned mostly with activities such as weaving new purpose-specific aspects into the model. The motivation to maintain the level of abstraction is twofold: (i) separation of concerns: to maintain the models in the responsibility of the same development role on the same abstract level and develop complex domain-specific completions in isolation by a special development role on the level of lower abstraction; and (ii) maintainability: to avoid adaptations of transformations resulting from metamodel extensions to by able to model domain-specific aspects.

We can extract a pattern in these development activities, with implementation activities going vertically and purpose-specific completion going horizontally, as illustrated on Figure 3.3. This incremental pattern is a typical scenario for application of model completions. In this structure the model *Abs''* is considered as the most complete one. Considering this pattern, when the purpose of model creation was, for example, performance prediction the *Abs''* on Figure 3.3 would provide the most accurate predictions and the *Conc''* would be closest to real implementation.

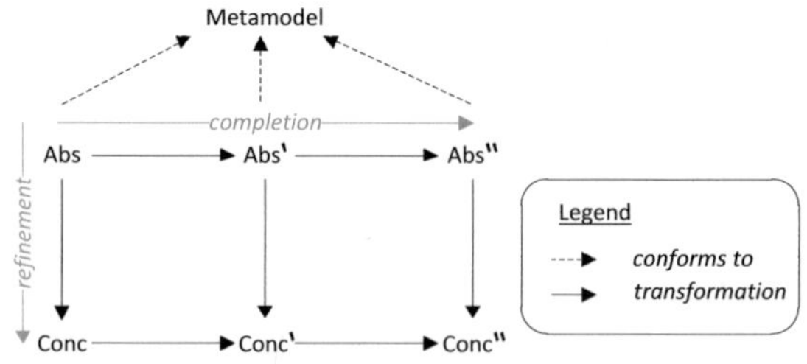

Figure 3.3.: *Model Completion* concept.

In the following, we will focus on the horizontal activities, or so called *completions*, of this concept. As illustrated on the Figure 3.3 these activities have very interesting properties when the input model, Abs or Abs', and output models, Abs' or Abs'', of transformations are conform to the same metamodel. The metamodel is a language that allows a formal representation (model) of entities and relationships in the real world on the certain level of abstraction. Initially, the level of correspondence and abstraction in the description of real-world entities is given by completeness or expressive power of the metamodel specification. The need for adjustment and customization is not only reserved for models. It also arises for metamodels. Metamodels often do not fulfil requirements for special purpose and it is desirable to use a specifically tailored metamodel language. Developers have to extend metamodel by an embedding of required purpose-specific elements. As mentioned before this approach has its disadvantages. The special properties of completions open a way to increase the expressive power of the metamodels indirectly on the model instance level. With the help of completions it is possible to extend the model with purpose-specific aspects, that metamodel does not support directly. Completions add new aspects into the model instance using the language of the meta-(or abstract-)level recursively. Then, we define completions as follows:

Definition 7 Model Completion

A model completion is a configurable purpose-specific transformation increasing model completeness while maintaining the language of the abstract level.

This is an informal definition of completion necessary to discuss the MD-SPE process studied in this chapter. Completions are formally defined and described in more detail later in Section 4.2.4. With this definition of completions it is possible to reuse the existing transformation chain towards implementation even for the purpose-specific completed model as its input. Additionally, completions hide the complexity of the purpose-specific extension, allow configuration of aspect variants and encapsulate domain-specific expert knowledge. As a consequence completion-based evolution of models following the design decisions about implementation on the level of abstract models allows to create purpose-specific models in a traceable way even without the need of domain-specific expert knowledge. Furthermore, the completions that are focusing on their own aspect can be individually maintained, and at the same time interconnected, building an enriched metamodel. In other words, each metamodel could be enriched by a domain-specific language dealing with a particular aspect (or view) of a system. The introduced completions have special properties that are very interesting for our application domain. In Section 3.2, we apply the model completions in the MDSPE domain.

3.1.2. Scientific Challenges in the MDSD context

In this chapter, we summarize scientific challenges related to MDSD, which are as follows:

- **Closing the semantic gap between an abstract model and low-level details:** The conflict between the level of abstraction required from a high-level abstract model and a level of detail required to fit the purpose of the model (e.g., performance prediction) makes it hard for developers to create models they need. Additionally, the required details are often very complex and variable. Inclusion of all required details is in many cases not feasible. The necessary details increase the model complexity in a such way that the model is not usable, understandable, and trustworthy anymore. We deal with this challenge in Section 3.1.1, where we propose the idea of completions on the abstract metamodel level. The realisation of this approach is described in Section 4.7 and formalised in Section 4.2.4.

- **Hiding complexity and reusing expert knowledge:** The completions are used on the abstract level although they encapsulate and hide the complexity of low-level details requiring expert-knowledge. As such they can be used by developers without the required expert knowledge. Therefore, a suitable specification of completions on the abstract level that allows their reuse is very important. Additionally, we have to allow different completions to be used independently, so that the developer or user of one completion does not have to know all other completions that may be used on the models. We discuss this challenge further and create a reusable completion library in Chapter 5.

- **Reusing existing transformation chains:** Automation of model completions allows reusing existing refinement chains in model-driven development process, e.g. generative transformation chains towards implementation (*Conc* in Figure 3.3), at any point of the incremental completion. This requires that all the completions transform their input model towards the input model of the refinement chain without changing or extending modelling language defined by metamodel. The completion concept (Section 3.1.1) addresses this challenge, this pattern uses the same metamodel language for the extensions given by completions as for the input model. Thus, the target model is conform to the same metamodel. By this approach, the metamodel language is maintained unchanged and refinement chain can be reused. The realisation of completions is discussed in Section 4.7.

- **Support of variability:** By their nature completions are very variable and as such a lot of effort is needed to implement and to maintain any automation solution realizing them. The support of variability in the definition of completions and their transformations is crucial for this approach. Because the variability of completions mirrors in the variability of their transformations, this challenge is actually addressing issue of transformation variability. This is the most challenging issue identified in this chapter that the implementation of completions has to deal with. The support for variability in the transformations definition is discussed in a separate Chapter 4.

In the following section, we will introduce MDSPE application domain for completions and summarize challenges related to this domain.

3.2. Model Completions and MDSPE

Model-Driven Software Performance Engineering (MDSPE) supports software developers to identify potential performance problems, such as bottlenecks, in their software systems within the design phase. The concepts of MDSPE (surveyed in [6]) are based on the core idea of Software Performance Engineering (SPE) introduced by Connie Smith [147]. SPE enables the early performance evaluation of software systems. For this purpose, SPE integrates performance predictions directly in the software development process. It bridges the gap between architecture centric models used by developers and formal performance models. In SPE, performance evaluation of software systems is achieved on the basis of simple models [147] that are mapped to well-established performance modelling techniques and thus are made easily accessible for software architects and developers.

In such early stages of the software life-cycle, only little information is available about the system's implementation and execution environment. However, these details are crucial for accurate predictions. Often, detailed information on the execution environment (e.g., design patterns, middleware, database, operating system, processor architecture) is required to get meaningful predictions. The previously introduced completions close the gap between available high-level models and required low-level details. Model-driven technologies can be exploited to add such performance-relevant details to high-level architectural specifications. Using model-driven technologies, completions can include details of the implementation and execution environment into abstract performance prediction models. In the following section, we discuss the integration of completions into the classical MDSPE process.

3.2.1. MDSPE Application Scenario

As mentioned before, the classical MDSPE uses model-driven techniques to close the gap between architecture centric models used by software architects and formal performance models. For this purpose, existing approaches provide transformations from architecture centric models, used by developers, to formal performance models (overview in [20]), such as Layered Queueing Networks (LQN), Stochastic Petri Nets (SPN), or Stochastic Process Algebras (SPA)(c.f. Figure 3.4).

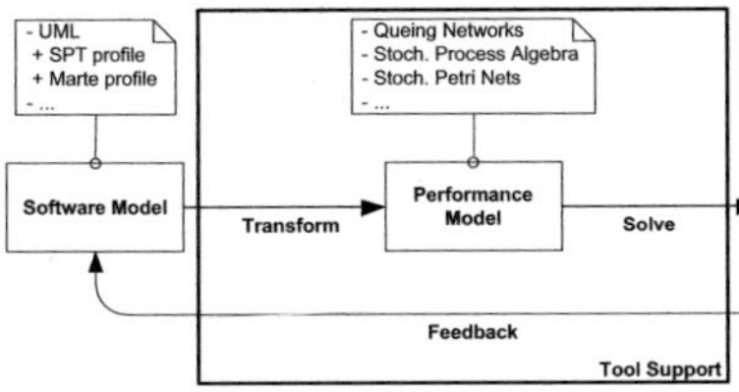

Figure 3.4.: *Model-driven Software Performance Engineering (MDSPE).*

In this thesis, we extend the classical SPE process by introducing completions. Figure 3.5 illustrates the extended process of MDSPE with completions. In this process, software architects describe their system in a language specific to their domain (such as UML [124], UML-SPT profile [124] or MARTE [128]). Alternatively, they can use architecture description languages specialised for performance evaluation, like the Palladio Component Model (PCM) [18].

We extend existing SPE process and provide tool support allowing software architects and developers to annotate their models with completions, more exactly with chosen variant of completion. Thus, in the first step, they annotate software models with configurations of performance-relevant aspects using *completions*. These annotations encapsulate performance-relevant details, which are necessary for the model to provide more accurate performance predictions. They can decide, where to apply certain completion and with which particular configuration.

Because of high-variability of completions and requirement for support for rapid evolution of prediction models, the integration of completions and evolution of models is automated by transformations. The goal is to diminish manual effort, during the development phase, in the highest possible extent; therefore, the transformations integrating completions have to be automatically generated based on the actual configuration. This transformation generation phase is further discussed in Chapter 4. Using resulting transformation is then software model transformed into completed software model. Completions hide the complexity of the full model from software architects when showing only the abstract annotations. They support reusing performance-related expert knowledge. This firts step can be repeated until all required aspects are included.

In the second step, other performance-relevant quantitative information can be included, such as model calibration based on the measurements. This step serves developers to include additional details about implementation or details that should be considered only when other model representation is generated, such us executable code, simulation code or performance models. To derive performance metrics from software models, the software model is transformed into a performance model as shown in Figure 3.5. The annotated software models are transformed to analytical performance models with resource demands based on model calibration and solved parametric resource demands.

Finally, the solution of the performance models by analytical or simulation-based methods yields various performance metrics for the system under study, such as response times, throughput, and resource utilisation. The

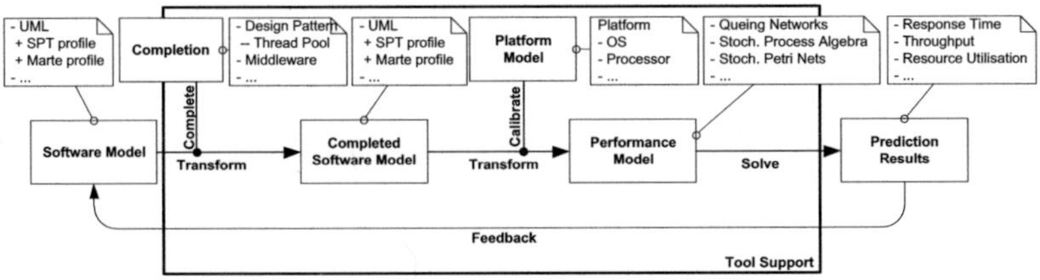

Figure 3.5.: MDSPE with completions.

biggest advantage of completions application in this context is that the specialized models are conform to the same metamodel, or, in the terminology of MDSPE, use the same architecture description language. As such, the transformation to the performance model does not need to know about the changes, or completions, realised on its input model and can be reused completely.

At last, the results are fed back into the initial software model. This enables software architects to reconfigure implementation details and interpret the effect of different design or allocation decisions on the system's performance and to plan capacities of the application's hardware and software environment. In practice, tools encapsulate the transformation and solution of the models and hide their complexity (cf. Figure 3.5).

3.2.2. Performance Completions

In this section, we discuss necessary parts of performance completions. Figure 3.6 sketches the idea of performance completions. The core concept of completions is the separation of structural and quantitative information. The first part is an architecture-specific part that is newly generated for each completion configuration and the second part is an architecture-independent part that models the consumption of resources and is newly measured for each platform. The architecture-specific part consists of components and subsystems. The architecture-independent part are resource demands for specific platform for which the completion was created.

The architecture-specific part is defined in *Completion Structural Skeleton* that reflects, for example the Thread Pool's general (performance-relevant) behaviour. The skeletons are structurally similar for different platforms, but their resource demands may vary. However, the skeleton defines the common structure of the performance completion, it depends on the actual configuration and it has to be newly generated for each configuration. Important part of structural information is the configuration itself. It specifies possible options and their impact on the performance. The completion developer has to identify effect of each configuration on the completions structure and express the model change in a form of structural skeleton.

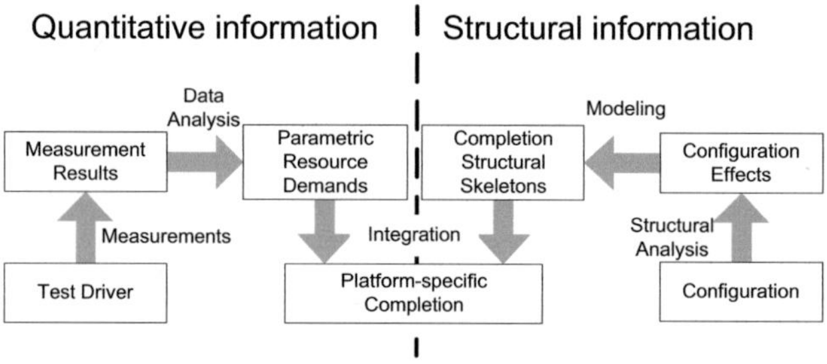

Figure 3.6.: Concept overview of performance completions.

The architecture-independent part is expressed in a form of *Parametric Resource Demands*. Completions are parametric with respect to resource demands of the platform. Therefore, completions are adjusted for each platform. To capture the quantitative information for particular platform, software architects execute *Test Drivers* that take necessary measurements. Based on *Measurement Results*, software architects can determine realistic resource demands for complex platforms, such as Thread Pool implementation in .Net or J2EE application servers on Windows or Linux platform. The software architects then analyse the measurement results and derive platform-specific Parametric Resource Demands. For example, software architects can capture the effect of number of threads on resource demands for a specific Thread Pool implementation. They perform data analyses that result the approximated functional dependency of resource demands on the number of threads.

The integration of the Completion Model Skeletons and Parametric Resource Demands yields the *Platform-specific Completion.* The platform specific resource demands are attached to their corresponding actions of the model skeletons that structurally model the completion's behaviour. The combination of parametric resource demands and model skeletons yields a complete performance model for the specific target platform. Because, extraction of quantitative and structural information for completion is non-trivial task and requires a lot of expert knowledge, the best way is to systematize and to automate the completion design and development process. Ideally, the analyses during this process are performed fully automatically. In the following, we describe the design and development process for performance completions in greater detail.

3.2.3. Scientific Challenges in the MDSPE context

The application of completions, in the domain of MDSPE, bears particular domain specific challenges:

- **Accuracy of performance prediction:** Each completion or combination of completions should increase prediction accuracy, i.e. reduce the deviation of prediction and observation, corresponding better the reality. Therefore, the creation of a completion is challenge itself and requires detailed research of the modelled aspect. The application of completions can increase/decrease resulting performance metrics and influence visible dependencies in resulting performance metrics. The impact of a completion on the performance has to be formalized and clearly stated. We will formalize completions in

Chapter 5 and discuss the performance impact of introduced completions in Chapter 7.

- **Completion calibration:** The automated measurements and analysis that are needed to calibrate the completions is a research field on its own. We do not contribute in this thesis to this research field. Completion approach, however, shows the integration of automated measurements and analysis into the overall MDSPE process. The completion developers use existing measurement frameworks (e.g., the Software Performance Cockpit [169]) to calibrate their models. The resulting challenge is then reduced to the integration of performance results into the completions and architecture-centric models. We discuss integration of automated measurements and parametrisation of performance models in the completion-based development process in Section 3.3.2.

- **Composition of performance abstractions:** The composition of completions is a challenging question, especially because of the application domain, where the performance quality attribute can be influenced by completion composition. We have to analyse if application of completions in different order results in models equal considering their performance. We discuss this topic in Chapter 5.

3.3. Completions in CBSE Development process

In Chapter 2, we discussed the CBSE Development process. Based on this process, we introduce two additional development roles. The role of *completion developer*, who creates the completions and registers them with the library, and the role of *completion user*, who actually uses completions and integrates them into architecture models. Any of the classical CBSE roles can take the position of completion user during the whole CBSE development process.

Generally, the presented completion-based development process is very similar to those with the common goal of reusability and customizability. Our process is focused on reuse of process artefacts, especially those specifying configuration models of completions. The goal of the process is to provide necessary artefacts to automatically generate completion transformations. The overview of this process is illustrated in Figure 3.7 with the most important automated step pointed out by the stripes.

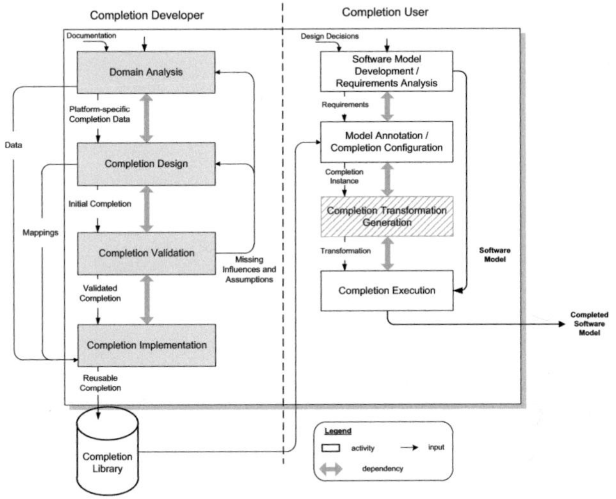

Figure 3.7.: Completion-based development process overview.

We can separate the completion-based process into two phases, first the *domain engineering*, where the tasks of completion developer are located, and second *software engineering*, which is specified by tasks of completion user. In the domain engineering phase the reusable and configurable completions are specified. The initial part is *domain analysis* consisting of the extraction and analysis of possible features and their combinations in the completion. Completions encapsulate possible design decisions that result from requirements on the software. Typically at the beginning of development, there is only an abstract idea about these requirements. Towards later development phases, these incomplete, variable and contradictory requirements could change. The domain analysis task has the main goal to recognize and analyse possible requirements on the software and to define allowed combinations among them. This analysis defines the first step attempting to design a new reconfigurable construct that could be used in software design. This helps to reduce the risk of a complete redesign of software models in the case of major changes in requirements. Once the possible requirements are determined they should by analysed and clearly stated. For this purpose, the configuration model is used, where the possible requirements are specified as configurations of features belonging to a completion.

The next step, the *completion design* defines how configuration options, so called features, and their combinations affect the final software model. Here it is necessary to determine the dependency among different configuration properties, the model structure and the model elements' attribute values. The result of the completion design step is an extension of the predefined configuration model by feature interdependencies and documentation how the features map to the software model changes.

After identifying possible completion features, feature interdependencies and resulting changes of software model based on these features, we validate the initial configuration model by comparison with the real world implementation. This step is called *completion validation* and consists of a set of experiments and measurements on the prediction model and corresponding implementation. When the results of measurements and prediction correspond with required accuracy the implementation of completion can start. In other case, we have to look for and analyse missing assumptions and influences.

Step *completion implementation* represents the activity of developing actual reusable completion. Therefore, it is necessary to formalise the model changes resulting from feature choice and create the final configuration model. Followed by registration into the library and offering it to the actual users.

The phase of the software engineering includes actual *software model development* and *requirements analysis*. The task *model annotation* and *completion configuration* benefits of reusable constructs defined by completion developer. The completion users can annotate their models by completion instances and attach particular configurations to them. The main goal of this step is to make sure that the software model will meet the requirements defined for the product, as well as ensuring that future requirements can be addressed.

The most important step included in the process is the *completion transformation generation*. Here, we apply the approach presented in Chapter 4. The generated transformation is then applied (*completion execution*) to the input software model resulting in the completed software model. In the following, we discuss the completion-based development process in detail and illustrate each step on a running example.

3.3.1. Running Example

This section introduces our running example, that is used throughout this thesis. Moreover, we motivate the choice of the running example.

Today, many applications (e.g., Web servers, Database servers) are designed to process a large number of short tasks that arrive from some remote source (using for example messaging, HTTP, FTP). In the case of server applications, processing of each task is short-lived and the amount of requests is large. The Thread Pool design pattern offers a solution to the thread management and is widely used by many multi-threaded applications. The point of the Thread Pool is to avoid a creation of a lot of threads for short tasks. The Thread Pool pattern reuses each thread for multiple tasks. The main advantages are in allowing of the process to continue while waiting for slow operations such as I/O-intensive tasks, and exploiting the availability of multiple processors. In the running example, we focus on the Thread Pool model since most of server applications are built around processing large number of short requests, which require low-overhead mechanism with resource management and timing predictability. Additionally, the Thread Pool design pattern promises performance increase and realistic optimization of resource usage. Especially, the importance of this pattern for performance prediction motivated our choice to use it as a running example.

In the following, we go through the steps of the completion-based development process and incrementally develop a completion for the Thread Pool design pattern. First, we analyse the structure of the Thread Pool design pattern and discuss performance-related characteristics of this pattern. Second, a brief discussion about the variety of Thread Pool implementations and their characteristics takes place. Afterwards, we discuss the performance measurements of Thread Pool from the literature showing importance of this pattern. Finally, we present the Thread Pool configuration model that will serve further as running example to illustrate the process of automated completion integration. The running example itself results in the definition of a reusable completion for the Thread Pool design pattern. This completion will be included in the completion library and is one of the contributions of this thesis.

3.3.2. Completion-based Domain Engineering

At the beginning of Chapter 3.3, we gave an overview of the completion-based development process. The detailed description of the tasks included in this process is goal of this section (cf., Figure 3.8). We give overview on the usage of model-driven techniques in combination with performance analysis and prediction methods.

3.3.2.1. Domain Analysis

The goal of domain analysis (cf., Figure 3.8a) is to understand the performance of software systems. In the analysis, we focus on a particular implementation detail and its performance properties. The detail that is object of the study in this step is an implementation of particular performance-relevant aspect, such as a design pattern (e.g., Thread Pool) or middleware platform. However, modelling performance-relevant aspects is not always possible when dealing with used third-party- and legacy-software. Such software is used as a black-box component in implementations of complex systems. The necessary amount of time to model this software may outweigh the advantage of performance prediction at design time. Additionally, required information about the system's structure and other properties might not be easily to gather. A way to integrate such kind of software into performance-model is the path of documentation recherché, trying to find out about its properties by testing and analysing its performance in a controlled environment. We systematically evaluate the studied system's performance in relation to its configuration and usage. Such process requires a lot of experience and detailed expertise in the field of benchmarking, data aggregation and analysis methods. In this initial step of completion development, we assume that we have a framework supporting systematic performance evaluation available. In our approach, we use the Software Performance Cockpit [169], that is a framework to systemize and automate the tasks required to evaluate performance of software systems.

First, we *identify* the performance-relevant features of studied aspect, based on documentation and other functional or parameter descriptions. This domain-specific knowledge is used in evaluation process. For each detail, we have to identify its configurable and measurable parameters and their dependencies. Additionally, to start experiments and measurements knowledge about the testing environment is needed. We have to *specify the platform* for the completion. The resulting completions are then platform-dependent and we can provide number of versions of one completion for different platforms.

For chosen system setting, based on the documentation recherché and/or resulting assumptions we create GQM plan for the systematic experiments. At this point, the measurement frameworks, like the Software Performance Cockpit, take over and drive performance evaluation based on the GQM plan. The Software Performance Cockpit provides a language to describe experiment design based on the GQM plan. It is able to determine efficient series of experiments to get the most meaningful measurement-data within as few experiments as possible. The measured data are later used to refine and to focus the *experiment design* on the most promising configurations. The data analysis algorithms are used to calculate possible dependencies between parameter configurations and performance of the system under the test. The Software Performance Cockpit executes following steps: it runs the actual experiment, *collects*) and (*aggregates data*). We described the integration of the Software Performance Cockpit into the completion development process in [77]. During the data collection step, we measure the influence of performance-relevant parameters for the studied system in its target execution environment. The collected data is used to infer (parameters of) a prediction model.

We use statistical inference techniques [79] and genetic optimization, to derive the influence of a studied aspect's usage on its performance. Statistical inference of performance metrics does not require specific knowledge of the internal structure of the system under study. However, statistical inference can require assumptions on the kind of functional dependency of input (independent) and output (dependent) variables. The inference approaches mainly differ in their degree of model assumptions. For example, linear regression makes rather strong assumptions on the model underlying the observations (they are linear) while the nearest neighbour estimator makes no assumptions at all. Most other statistical estimators lie between both extremes. Methods with stronger assumptions, in general, need less data to provide reliable estimates, if the assumptions are correct. Methods with less assumptions are more flexible, but require more data. These analysis methods are supported by the Software Performance Cockpit. The task of completion developer is to extract enough variables and needed assumptions about their dependences (when available) to realise the analysis.

The last step of domain analysis is the *data analysis*. In this step, we formalize the quantitative information needed for completion as described in Figure 3.7. The aspect models inferred in the previous step are later by completion design integrated into software performance models to predict their effect on the overall performance of the system. We use the Palladio Component Model (PCM) in combination with performance completions to evaluate the performance of the system under study. The PCM is well suited for our purposes since it captures the effect of different input parameters on software performance. Stochastic expressions of the PCM can be used to directly include the functions resulting from the statistical analysis into the components of a performance completion. In the data analysis step, we select data necessary for later completion design and express them in the understandable form. In our case, we use the form of stochastic expressions for resource demands in the PCM. The resource demands are platform-specific and have to be determined for each platform and for each execution environment. Determined resource demands are used to parametrise and calibrate the completions in the later steps.

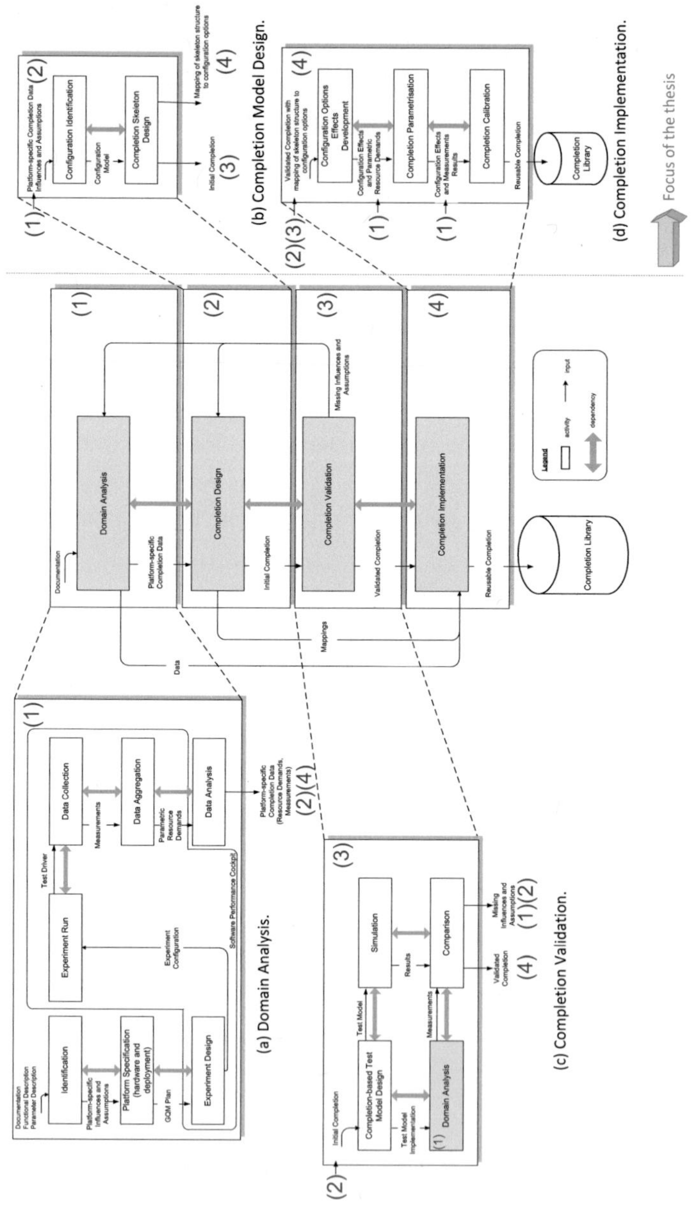

Figure 3.8.: Tasks of the completion developer.

3.3.2.2. Running Example: Thread Pool Domain Analysis

Thread Pool: Structure The Thread Pool design pattern belongs to the group of resource management patterns and is used to increase performance of the application. The implementation of Thread Pool pattern can be illustrated on an example of simple e-Commerce-Application, where customers shop in a product catalogue. The application is implemented with EJB-Technology as client-server application. Clients use Web-Browsers to communicate with Java-Servlet-Engine in parallel. The business logic of the application is implemented in the server component. The server component is connected via Java Database Connection (JDBS) with the database. The product catalogue mirrors current state of the database. The server component connects with the database for each client request and executes necessary SQL request. The results of the SQL request are then propagated to the client's Web-Browser. The Thread Pool is implemented to manage many instances of the same resource, in this case the managed resources are JDBS connections to the database. The pooling concept allows usage (acquire) of the resource instance and their reuse when the instance was set free (release). The Thread Pool creates number of resource instances (threads) in advance and manages a waiting queue for incoming requests that have not assigned free thread yet. A typical usage scenario for Thread Pool is when there are many more tasks than threads and the Thread Pool mostly executes on a single computer. As soon as a thread completes its task (or number of tasks, dependent on Thread Pool capacity) it will accept the next task from the queue of waiting tasks until all tasks have been completed. The thread is then returned to the pool until there are new tasks available. The behaviour of a Thread Pool (with capacity of 3 threads) is illustrated by the Petri net in Figure 3.9.

Thread Pool: Performance-relevant influences and assumptions Within this step we study other research works with focus on

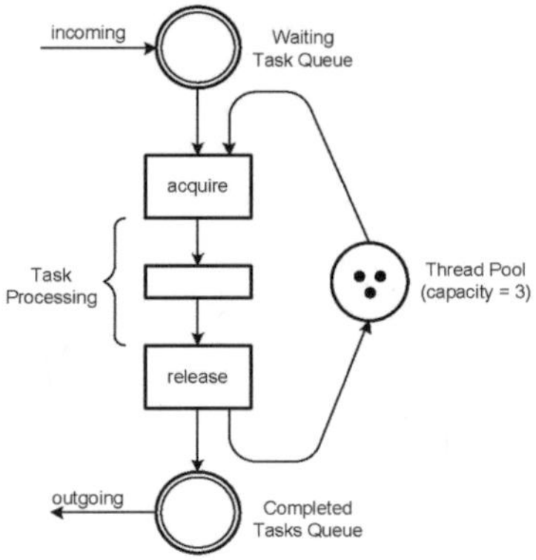

Figure 3.9.: A sample Thread Pool of capacity = 3 with waiting tasks and completed tasks.

Thread Pool performance and analyse implementations of Thread Pool. This recherché provides excessive data, which are basis for the later experiment design. In the following, we provide short exemplary related work analysis.

In the literature, there are works analysing the influence of Thread Pool on performance. Shiping Chen and Ian Gorton [32] have identified Thread Pool size as one of the configurable system parameters that are important for achieving maximal throughput. The implementation of a Thread Pool has a prominent impact on the performance due to its ability to limit the level of concurrency in the system [33]. The most important parameter that can be tuned to provide the best performance is the capacity of the Thread Pool. An excessive number of threads leads to waste of memory and needed context-switching among the threads also decreases performance. Therefore, in some Thread Pool variants the number of threads can be dynamic, based on the number of waiting tasks. Some software providers decided about static size of a Thread Pool in their products, for example in .Net framework by default the Thread Pool has 25 threads per processor. Such a static Thread Pool with fixed pool size, is supported by latest version of

Java JDK 7 [131]. This Thread Pool variant always has a specified number of threads available. Tasks, from an internal queue that holds waiting tasks, are appointed to the threads from the pool, whenever there are more active tasks than active threads.

Thread Pool: GQM plan In order to conduct systematic evaluation of the studied aspect, goals, questions and metrics must be defined to allow a quantification of the system's performance. Using performance metrics (e.g., response time, throughput, utilisation) and configuration parameters (e.g., arrival-rate, number of threads), we can formulate the experiment questions, scenarios and hypotheses. In the following, we give an example of a question in the GQM plan with the observed metrics identification:

QUESTION Q: *Does a greater number of threads in a Thread Pool imply an increased performance?* The focus of question Q lies in the evaluation of a possible correlation between the number of used threads and the Thread Pool's performance.

SCENARIO S: In Scenario S, we use simple Thread Pool variant with variable number of threads in a pool. The total workload is set to reach a Thread Pool utilisation of 80%, which we choose to maximize the representativeness of collected results. The advantage of using Thread Pool could be observed at high loads, when we can study the effects of thread concurrency and scheduling. Therefore, we hold during the experiments a constant utilisation of the Thread Pool at 80% at least.

HYPOTHESIS H: *The Thread Pool performance is expected to grow until the number of threads is higher as number of CPUs in the system.* Hypothesis H1 is based on the assumption that, for a constant workload, an increased number of threads implies increased performance until the increased number of resource-conflicts appears. For example, the resource-conflicts appear in a case of CPU-intensive requests, when the number of threads is higher as number of CPUs. However, this is more complex for I/O-intensive requests, which compete for other resource (HDD) that can be a bottleneck even before a CPU. in this case additional experiment is needed.

METRICS M: *Response time, Throughput*

Thread Pool: Results from measurements and experiments: To illustrate results of the measurement of such experiments, we use the results of a study thesis by Achraf El Ghazi [62]. He analysed and measured the performance of the Thread Pool pattern. His performance experiment evaluated CPU- and I/O intensive requests. His experiments for I/O and CPU intensive requests resulted in a dependency specification of request execution time on different parameters. For example, in the case of CPU-intensive requests, the execution time depends on: thread service time, request arrival rate, the number of requests in system, maximal size of the Thread Pool, and size of time slice in the OS scheduler configuration. To collect the necessary data for calibration of models he measured EJB 3.0 application using GlassFish V2 B41 application server, thus his measurements are specific for this platform. Figure 3.10 represents the measurement results of request execution time relative to the first point in time when the request execution started. The request arrival time in this experiment was 1100 ms and maximal Thread Pool size was 1000 threads. The graph shows a monotone increase of the execution time for the first 36% of the requests. The following requests yield a stable execution time of 30 to 40 seconds.

Thread Pool: Platform-specific Completion Data The results of experiments are then input for specification of platform-specific completion data as used in this thesis. The analysis of the data yields functional dependences between different Thread Pool parameters, workload, and other system settings. In our example, the request execution time depends on the request arrival rate (`Workflow:ArrivalRate.VALUE`), the thread execution time (`ThreadExecutionTime.VALUE`), the maximal Thread Pool size (`PoolSize.VALUE`), the number of requests in the system (defined for a

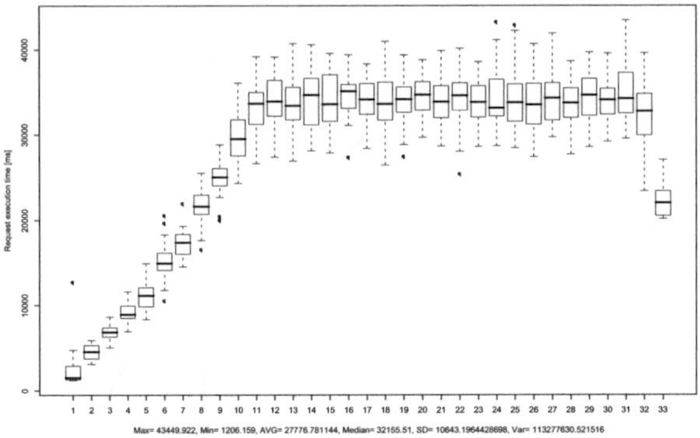

Figure 3.10.: Example of experiment results [62].

closed workflow as `Workflow:PopulationSize.VALUE`) and the configuration of OS scheduler (`TimeSliceSize.VALUE`). Based on this observation, we can define resource demand on CPU as:

$$1/\left[\left(\frac{\texttt{ThreadExecutionTime.VALUE}}{\texttt{TimeSliceSize.VALUE}}\right)\right]$$
$$*min\left(\texttt{Workflow:PopulationSize.VALUE},\texttt{PoolSize.VALUE}+1\right)$$
$$*\texttt{TimeSliceSize.VALUE}$$

Moreover, based on the previous studies we can identify default or even close to optimal Thread Pool configurations, for example:

$$\texttt{PoolSize.Size} = \texttt{ReplicaCount.VALUE} + 1,$$

that defines an optimal number of threads parametrised by number of CPU replicas for CPU-intensive requests.

3.3.2.3. Completion Design

In this section, we introduce details of the completion design (cf., Figure 3.8b). We describe the structural part of completion and its development. The concept of quantitative and structural information separation in the completion design was introduced in Section 3.2.2. Moreover, completion design step integrates the quantitative information needed for completion resulting from previous domain analysis step.

As first to design a completion, we have to create the configuration model and the structural skeleton. For this purpose, we use *feature diagrams* (see Section 4.5.2.1). We extract performance-relevant attributes of the studied aspect as features in a feature diagram.

Configuration Model: Feature diagrams define all valid combinations of application property values, or features. One feature defines a certain option in the considered domain. Actual chosen combinations of features are called configurations (*feature configurations*). Feature diagrams are hierarchical decomposition of features including information if a feature is mandatory, alternative or optional. We use extended feature diagram, that is discussed in detail in Section 4.5.2.1.

Using feature diagrams as configuration models brings the advantage of having a focused and less-complex configuration method understandable by all of the roles in development process. Such feature-based configuration method can be mapped to individual model changes and allows generation of completion transformations. The concept of generation of completion transformations is discussed in Chapter 4. In the following section, we will illustrate the step of feature model specification on the running example.

Completion Structural Skeleton: The separation of concerns in software modelling avoids the construction of large and monolithic models, which could be difficult to handle, maintain and reuse. However, having different models describing different aspects requires their integration into a final model that represents the entire domain. In previous steps, we already identified one part of modelled domain, the quantitative information about the completion. To complete the design of completion we have to specify required information about the structure. The design phase yields completion model skeletons that capture the structure of the completion. The completion model skeleton specifies a set of necessary components, and their behaviour, building the structure of completion. The skeletons only abstractly model the structure and behaviour without any resource demands. All possible variants of completion are captured by its structural skeleton.

We use model weaving to select a subset of the components needed for a particular completion variant based on the current configuration. There is no accepted definition of model weaving, we consider it as the fine-grained relationships between completion configuration and skeleton models. Based on these relationships and correspondences between the considered model parts, we avoid to have large skeleton models for capturing all the variants of the aspect. The completion developer has to have a clear overview about these mappings, that represent model changes required towards completed software model.

3.3.2.4. Running Example: Thread Pool Completion Design

Thread Pool: Configuration Model Based on the previous discussion, we extracted important performance-relevant features of Thread Pool pattern in a form of feature diagram. These features summarize different configuration options of the thread management implementation based on this pattern. The resulting feature diagram is illustrated in Figure 3.11

Java-specific Thread Pool feature diagram: For the purpose of the running example, we simplified the feature model for Thread Pool design pattern. The simplified version is based on the features supported by the last Java JDK (1.6). The Java platform is designed to support concurrent

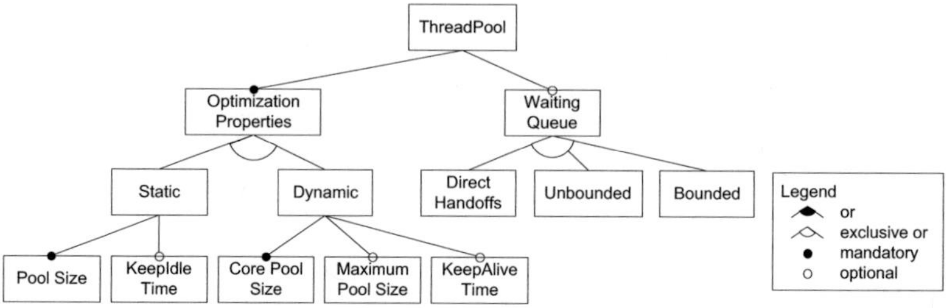

Figure 3.11.: The configuration model of Thread Pool design pattern (used for the running example).

programming and includes high-level concurrency APIs. The concurrency support is implemented in the `java.util.concurrent` packages. The feature model in Figure 3.11, that will be used as a running example, collects Thread Pool implementation options supported by Java platform. To validate this model, we will compare the prediction results with the measured results later in the thesis.

The valid Thread Pool configuration includes the mandatory feature *Optimization Properties*. This feature may define either a static or a dynamic Thread Pool variant. The exclusive selection is indicated by the excludes constraints between both features. Each of these features have to have a number of threads specified. This is either a static pool size or, for the dynamic feature, a core and a maximum number of threads. Additionally, software architect has a possibility to specify the time after which an idle thread in a static pool should be returned to the pool (or "sleep"), avoiding waste of resources by busy waiting. Similarly, for a dynamic Thread Pool he can specify, by *KeepAliveTime*, when an idle thread should be destructed. This provides a means of reducing resource consumption when the pool is not being actively used. If the pool becomes more active later, new threads will be constructed.

Lastly, an important attribute is the queueing strategy in a waiting queue, because use of this queue interacts with pool sizing. There are three different strategies for queueing. *Direct handoffs* is a default choice for a work queue that hands off tasks to threads without otherwise holding them. Here, an attempt to queue a task will fail if no threads are immediately available to run it, so a new thread is required to be constructed. *Unbounded* queue will cause new tasks to wait in the queue when all threads are busy. *Bounded* queue helps prevent resource exhaustion when used with finite maximum pool sizes, but can be more difficult to tune and control. Queue sizes and maximum pool sizes may be traded off for each other: Using large queues and small pools minimizes CPU usage, OS resources, and context-switching overhead, but can lead to artificially low throughput. If tasks frequently block (for example if they are I/O-intensive), a system may be able to schedule time for more threads than you otherwise allow. Use of small queues generally requires larger pool sizes, which keeps CPUs busier, but may encounter unacceptable scheduling overhead, which also decreases throughput.

Thread Pool: Structural Completion Skeleton We designed an abstraction of the Thread Pool pattern (cf., Figure 3.12) for the purpose of performance prediction. The pattern abstraction is a version of a Leader-Follower pattern, where one particular thread takes the role of the leader and waits for the next request. All other threads are either followers (i.e., queued) or leaders (i.e. processing requests). To model this pattern we can easily use one Thread Pool component with a size equal the capacity of the system. The overview about the required changes (e.g., adding/removing components) of the model helps completion developer with later implementation. Therefore, he is required to first model per hand a completion skeleton for each feature and validate them. Based on these analysis he can choose appropriate abstraction and implement the change mappings. In Figure 5.21 the mappings, for one simplified variant, are illustrated by arrows. The semantic of these arrows is addition of the selected components, interfaces, methods or values to the model. To integrate a Thread Pool ab-

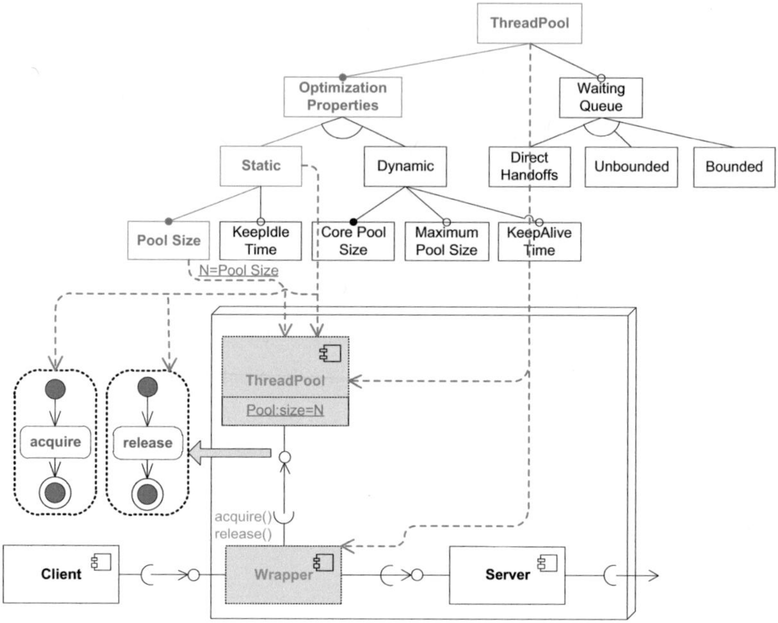

Figure 3.12.: The structural completion skeleton of Thread Pool design pattern.

straction into the model we have to add the `Wrapper` and the `Thread Pool` components to the model. This basic structure of the skeleton is created from the root feature. The child features then add the behaviour specifications (e.g., SEFFs) and parameters to the components (e.g., `PoolSize`).

3.3.2.5. Completion Validation

To validate the initial completion (cf., Figure 3.8d), we create a *test model* and correspondent *implementation* of modelled aspect in a real system. Using the test model we realize a set of *simulations* (e.g., using PCM simulation framework) to predict system's performance. Furthermore, by measuring the implementation we get a real performance data about the system. The *measurements* are again executed automatically taking an advantage of support provided by the Software Performance Cockpit (see the *domain analysis* step). In order to ensure that the completion model captures and correctly models all relevant parameters, developers compare predictions and measurements. Based on the outcome of the *comparison*, it might be necessary to execute further experiments to evaluate observed deviations of predictions and measurements. In such case, the developers extend the domain analysis and the completion design to the required level. When the desired degree of accuracy is reached, developer can start to implement generic and reusable completion.

3.3.2.6. Running Example: Thread Pool Completion Validation

To validate the Thread Pool completion, developers need to compare different predictions and measurements of execution times for different configurations. Additionally, they can compare different Thread Pool variants even when available other thread management strategies, such as Thread Pool versus the Thread-Per-Request model.

In the Thread Pool example, we discussed measurement results for request execution time depending on the start time a request is initially executed. In this experiment the request arrival time was 1100 ms and maximal Thread Pool size was 1000 threads. Using our Thread Pool model, we can execute simulations with the same system settings. The prediction results can be then compared to the measurements as illustrated in Figure 3.13. It is visible from these graphs that the model allows to predict the behaviour of Thread Pool with very good accuracy (see Table 3.1). For the first 49,6% of the requests, before the Thread Pool stabilised, the prediction error is highest. For later requests, the predicted execution time (30,00 s) is very close to the mean value of the measurement results (27,77 s). The mean value of execution time was predicted with the prediction error smaller than 10%. The prediction results promise more accurate predictions when the additional effects on Thread Pool performance are considered (see Section 5.3.5).

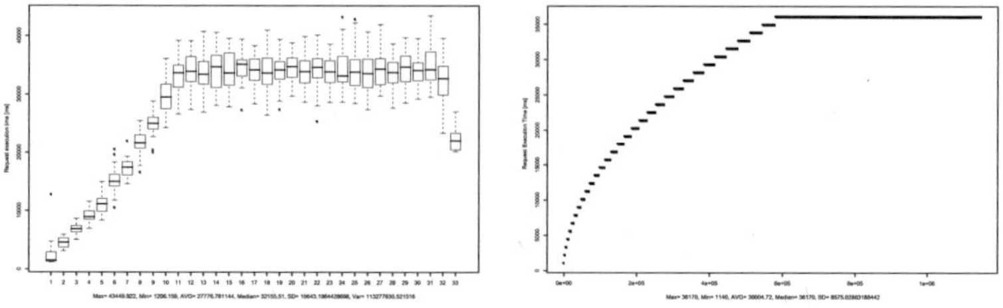

(a) Measurement results (b) Prediction results

Figure 3.13.: Example of Thread Pool model validation [62].

	Mean [ms]	Max [ms]	Min [ms]
Prediction	30004.72	36170.00	1140.00
Measurement	27776.78	43449.92	1206.15
Error [%]	7.42	16.75	5.48

Table 3.1.: Example of the evaluation of prediction accuracy [62].

3.3.2.7. Completion Implementation

The goal of this step (cf., Figure 3.8e) is to implement generic and reusable completion, that can be registered into the completion library and used by the performance analysts. Each of the introduced completion features could have additional information attached as, for example, fragments of code. In the completion design step, we define how features and their combinations affect the software model. We defined mappings specifying the dependences among different feature configurations, the model structure and the elements' attribute values. The result of this step is an extension of the pre-defined feature diagram by dependences and documentation how the features map to the software model changes. We call these extension *feature effects*, they make clear which feature triggers which change.

Definition 8 Feature Effect

Feature effect is a formal representation of a isolated model change resulting from feature selection.

To formalise and implement feature effect, we have to *develop* actual *transformation fragments*, which encode the change to the software model. The result of this activity is a feature model, that is extended by the annotations in a form of model-to-model transformation fragments. In this work, we use to implement transformation fragments the OMG QVT-Relations transformation language.

When the completion is validated and the feature effects are developed, the developers can *parametrise* the performance completion. Therefore, they derive the parametric resource (e.g., dependency of default number of threads on the number of CPUs, etc.) demands for the completion components and adjust the feature effects to integrate into the completed model these demands or static calibrations (e.g., measured platform-specific network overhead) , if necessary. The parametrisations and calibrations are integrated into the model by the feature effects.

3.3.2.8. Running Example: Thread Pool Completion Implementation

As presented in previous section, the nodes of the feature diagram are annotated with feature effects, implemented as transformation fragments. We illustrate the feature effects implementation on the running example (cf., Figure 3.14). The effect of Thread Pool feature is depict by the `relation TP` and creates necessary components (simplified in Figure 3.14). The result of this feature effect is the creation of component `TP`. The effect of Static feature `TP_Static` has a when-dependency to the parent effect `TP`. When the component `TP` exists, the `TP_Static` feature can be used to statically configure the size of the Thread Pool and set the default value. Hence, the transformation fragment belonging to the the feature `Pool size` refers to

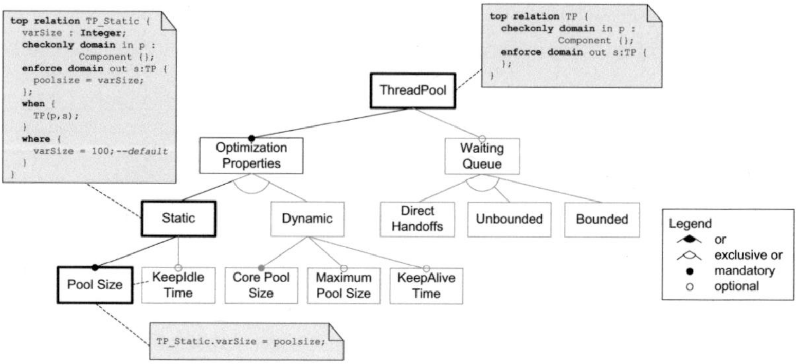

Figure 3.14.: Example of feature effects implemented as fragments of transformations.

the free variable declared in the `TP_Static` fragment of feature Static and overrides the default value. Additionally, transformation fragments can integrate quantitative information into the completion transformation, which addition is straightforward in the fragment implementation. We will discuss the transformation fragments in a more detail in Chapter 4.5.

3.3.3. Completion-based Software Engineering

In this section, we discuss the role of completion user and how he/she can take advantage of the developed completion from completion library. The phases of the software engineering include actual *software model development and requirements analysis*. Starting with the requirements on the software system, the model developers create a software model and meet correspondent design decisions. The task *model annotation* benefits from the reusable completion defined by domain engineering. When model developers find a suitable model completion supporting their design decision, the model can be annotated with the configuration of this completion. Model developers attach required configurations to the model elements where they plan to apply chosen completion. The main goal of this step is to make sure the software application will meet the requirements defined for the product, as well as ensuring that future requirements and design decisions can be addressed.

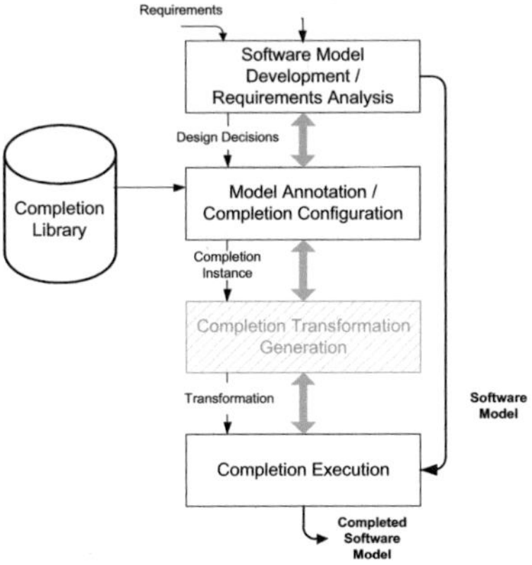

Figure 3.15.: Tasks of the completion user.

The most important step is the *completion transformation generation*. Realisation of this step is a topic of the whole following Chapter 4. The generated transformation is then applied (*completion execution*) to the input software model and results in the completed software model. The completed model is then directly passed to the existing simulation or analysis frameworks and provides more accurate and more complete predictions.

Running Example: Using Thread Pool Completion The software deployer role from the CBSE development process can use the Thread Pool completion as annotation to the resource container. Each user of the completion has to create a correspondent feature configuration. The actual feature configuration based on the Thread Pool feature diagram is illustrated by check(selected feature) and cross(eliminated feature) -marks. For such Figure 3.16 additionally depicts one possible configuration of a Thread Pool. This feature configuration defines a simple *static* implementation of Thread

Pool with the size of 32 threads treating all incoming tasks with the same priority.

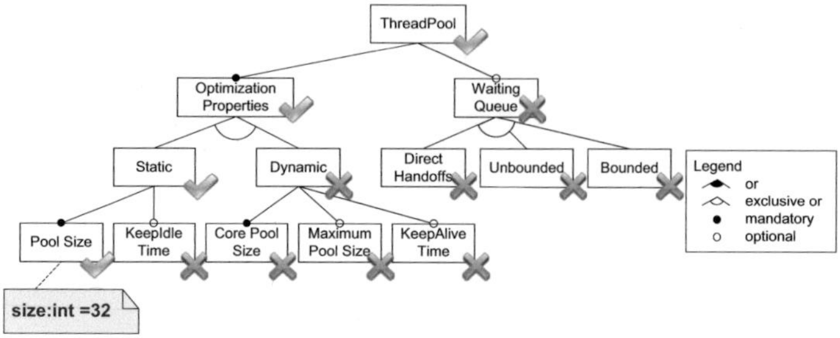

Figure 3.16.: Thread Pool feature configuration.

3.4. Summary

The main contribution of this chapter is the generalisation of the Model Completion concept and its integration into the MDSPE process. In this chapter, we discussed relationship of model completions to MDSD and MDSPE processes. To put model completions into practice, we introduced a general process to design and apply performance completions in the MDSPE. The design of completion-based development process for MDSPE was presented in the invited talk on the EPEW 2010 and published in [93].

The completion developers define completions based on abstract specifications and design patterns and, thus, parametrise over the platform and vendor-specific properties of different platforms. In our development process, we automate the measurement data collection using Software Performance Cockpit. The resulting parametrised completions allow software architects to instantiate the completion for their target platform and annotate their models. The performance completions represent powerful tool to analyse performance of software using complex design patterns and platforms (e.g., application servers). We describe details of the particular steps

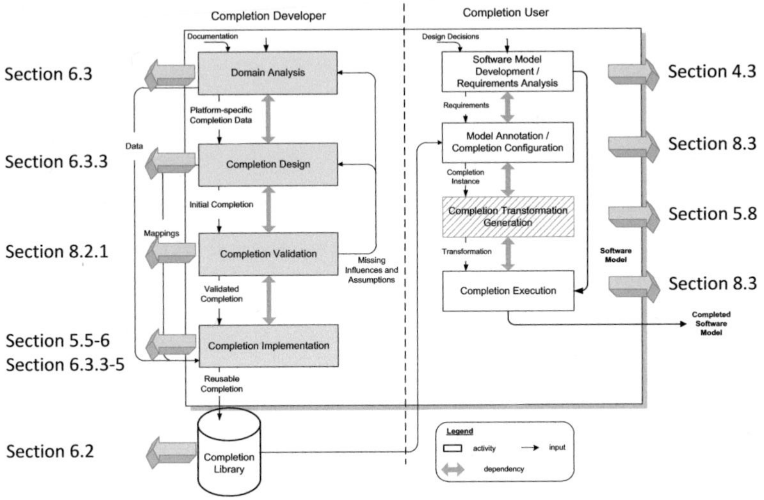

Figure 3.17.: Pointers to the detailed description of particular development steps.

during the completion development process in separate sections later within this thesis.

Figure 3.17 gives an overview about the structure of this thesis and pointers to the chapters where details to the particular steps of the completion-based development process can be found. In the following chapter, we deal with the automated integration of completions and management of their variability using Higher-Order Transformations (HOTs).

4. Variability Management using Higher-Order Transformations

In the previous chapter, we introduced the concept of Model Completions and its application in MDSPE. We discussed the main challenge related to completions in the MDSD context, which is the variability support. The requirement for variability results from the reconfigurability of completions. The model elements to be completed are determined by this configuration. The completions are implemented as model-to-model transformations. Because, it is not feasible to implement a transformation for each combination of configuration options, the variability of completions should be mirrored in the variability of their transformations.

The leading challenge of this chapter is:

How to support configuration-based variability in model transformations?

The remainder of this chapter will be organized as follows. Section 4.1 introduces the problem domain. The main contribution of this chapter, CHILIES approach, is discussed in Section 4.2. Section 4.3 introduces the principle of Higher-Order Transformations (HOTs) and the idea of HOT patterns definition. The patterns used to support completions are described in Sections 4.4, 4.5 and 4.6. The composition of these patterns is discussed in Section 4.7. At last, we summarize the assumptions and limitations in Section 4.8, and conclude this chapter in Section 4.9.

4.1. Problem Domain

In this chapter, we deal with the problem of variability management in transformations given a fixed input model. The variability of transformation results from two sources: First, the requirement to increase expressive power of metamodels through particular model elements originating from domain-specific languages. Second, the requirement to include variable parts into the transformations and adapt their functionality. In the both cases, the changes of requirements on the software product (e.g. changed application domain, or required more detailed model) result in the changes of the transformations. In the following, we discuss both of the cases in more detail.

4.1.1. Increasing Expressive Power of Metamodels

The language features, such as programming language pragmatics [145], have clearly a huge impact on the developers ability to write clear, concise and maintainable code. A typical example of language pragmatics is the `foreach` statement in Java [131]. Analogous aspects apply to modelling languages, especially in the case of very large and complex systems. To increase usability of model-driven techniques we need modelling pragmatics that support efficient model design, too. Often developers claim that the metamodel is not suitable for the purpose of a particular model, that some other metamodel is more powerful. Although, in a sense of expressiveness two metamodel-based languages can be equivalent, both can be used for the same goal, even if it is not straightforward and the models would be too complex, and can be suitable to express anything written in the other. The most important factor contributing to the expressive power of the metamodel are features of abstraction. The modelling pragmatics support the developer to overcome the complexity of the model by abstraction.

As discussed in the previous chapter, in some scenarios, metamodels do not have enough expressive power to allow modelling of all required details.

For this purpose new metamodel elements have to be introduced which requires adapting all transformations based on the metamodel. The required development effort for these adaptations depends on the complexity of the metamodel changes and the transformations. MDSD focuses on the reuse of existing models and supports different transformation chains and tooling working on the same model. Changes of the modelling language with each new purpose of models and related adaptation of their transformations is against this reuse principle. Our goal is to avoid or minimize these adaptations and support extension of metamodels through introduction of modelling pragmatics in a form of completions.

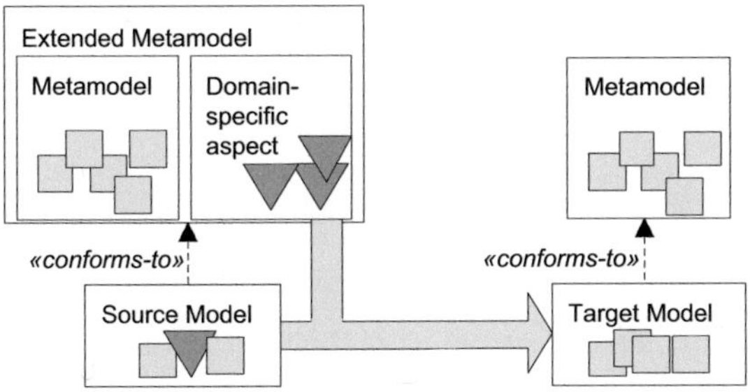

Figure 4.1.: Introduction of new domain-specific aspects to the metamodel by a completion transformation.

Completions increase the expressive power of metamodels indirectly on the model instance level, thus on the metamodel level the same language is maintained (cf., Figure 4.1). They add new domain-specific aspects into the model instance using the same language of the meta-(or abstract-)level, thus they allow an incremental and indirect extension of metamodel through the completion transformations. Such domain-specific aspects can be described by suitable domain-specific languages that introduce new elements into the host language and could be later transformed to subsystems conform to the original host metamodel.

We express these domain-specific languages in a form of a feature diagram. Based on the choice of features from the feature diagram the completion transformation extends the model instance with new aspects from the domain described by the feature diagram. Each completion extends the model by a new concept, that is constructed using existing elements of the host metamodel. This way, we can bridge different domains. Variability, in this case, means that transformation generates different output models, based on the application domain. Because of the aspect's configurability, the transformations realising these extensions should be derived automatically. We call these transformations *completion transformations*. The result is that the applicability of the metamodel increases, using the new metamodel language features supporting abstractions it is easier to create models and the creation of completion transformations is automated.

4.1.2. Supporting Transformation Variability

Classical MDSD approaches face the non-trivial task how to implement transformations creating target models sharing common core, but differentiating by variable parts. Typically, given a fixed source model, there would be one possible target model. In practice, however, different features can be required. For instance, the design decision whether or not to integrate a certain design pattern (e.g., Thread Pool), could change. Variability, in this case, means that transformations generate different output models, based on additional annotation and/or configuration models passed to the transformation. The configuration of the transformation or the transformation itself has to be adapted to integrate different design decisions.

Thus, the main challenge to support model completions in MDSD is their high degree of variability. Each implementation detail can have many configuration options which may change the structure and behaviour of related abstractions. For example, Message-Oriented Middleware (MOM) platforms are highly configurable to meet customer needs. The MOM configuration includes, for instance, durable subscription or guaranteed delivery. These configuration options influence performance and, thus, have to be mirrored by the transformation that realizes the completion.

One solution would be to implement one transformation for each combination of configuration options. Another solution would be to attach one additional input model to the transformation. The most commonly used way to configure model transformations is by means of external annotations to a source model. So called mark models [11] are used to provide configuration details that are specific to the source model. This mark model is considered as an additional input for the transformation on the model level.

However, this way of transformation configuration is not always preferable. Both solutions have to deal with the problem that a high effort is needed to implement and to maintain their transformations. Regarding the first option, it is straightforward that it is not feasible to implement a transformation for each combination of configuration options. Already with 12 binary configuration options, (with only boolean value possible) we would have to implement 4096 (or 2^{12}) transformation variants. However, even the second solution has to deal with many problems. In the case of mark model usage, the transformation is tightly-coupled to the configuration. Thus, when we want to change configuration options, remove them or to introduce a new ones, we have to change the transformation itself. The developer of such a transformation has to consider dependencies between configuration options, which can become very complex.

There are cases where this configuration mostly depends on externally defined properties (i.e., source model independent) and is not specific to special model elements. In this case the configuration happens on a higher level of abstraction. Thus, the decision about used variability is made in later stages (e.g. when transformation is applied) and requires late variability binding, during so called load time of transformation. Moreover, used elements (ie. configuration models, transformations, etc.) should support software developers (i.e., completion users) managing variability. Therefore, it is much more appropriate to decouple the configuration and the actual model. Starting with the same source model, we can get different target models depending on the configuration. Additionally, there is a need to define the configuration model as reusable construct. The configuration model encapsulates domain-specific expert knowledge and as such it would be beneficial to support its reuse in different contexts. For example, the configuration could be read by other development tools and used independently from the original software model. Thus, the configuration model should be specified on a more generic metamodel-independent level.

Additionally, the code of the mark transformation is polluted with code reading and handling the configuration. The configuration management code grows with the complexity of configuration into complex decision trees. Consequently, using mark models the maintainability of the transformations decreases when the configuration model's complexity grows. Transformations with such complex constructs are not only very hard to maintain and to understand, but moreover writing a transformation that considers all possible combinations of selected configuration options or introducing new configuration option, is very tedious and error-prone. Thus, the maintainability of transformations is one more reason to decouple configuration model and transformation. In our application domain, the explicit support of variability in the definition of completions and their transformations is crucial for their application in software performance engineering.

4.2. Introduction of the CHILIES Approach

In this thesis, we focus on variability management in transformations based on configuration models. We use feature diagrams to express configurations. Transformations can then be based on the very same feature diagram to apply the appropriate changes to a model according to currently selected features. For this purpose, specific parts of a transformation are activated depending on the selected features. However, transformations parametrized by configuration require substantial development effort. In our approach, we allow transformation developers to focus on the actual transformation logic. They specify transformation fragments for each feature in the configuration model separately. Thus, the development effort is decreased through separation of concerns. Based on the selected combination of features, a Higher Order Transformation (HOT) generates the specific completion transformation. The direct manipulation of transformations depending on a given configuration makes the relation between configuration and transformation explicit.

In the proposed approach, we lift the configuration model to a higher abstraction level. Therefore, the transformation fragments do not get polluted with code that is only responsible for checking the actual feature configuration. Furthermore, as the binding of fragments and features is more explicit, this alleviates the complexity of transformation evolution as every feature has a clear mapping to the parts of the transformation, which are related to it. We generate an executable completion transformation from a configuration defined by a feature diagram in a number of steps. Each of these pre-processing steps has a specific goal.

CHILIES approach defines the pre-processing steps necessary to generate transformations as general patterns that can be composed together to build an SPL for transformations. These patterns describe the necessary elements, such as models and transformations, to achieve particular goals. Composing these patterns, in this work we focus on the *Routine*, the *Composite* and the *Template* pattern, we can create an SPL with more complex goals. Completion transformations are generated based on these patterns. However, we used the CHILIES approach to systematically support variability of completion transformations, completions are only one application domain and the presented approach could be applied in other contexts as well. The CHILIES approach will be further discussed in the following sections. We start with summarizing the main contributions in more detail.

4.2.1. Scientific Contributions of this Chapter

The main contribution of this chapter is located in the MDSD context and can be summarised as follows:

CHILIES Transformation Variability Management method: SPLs are used to build a family of products, which are subject to variability. Variability should be managed, that is specified, modelled and implemented in a *maintainable* and *effective* way. For model-transformations, variability is defined by a varying set of features integrated in the final transformation. Various approaches [71, 167] show that SPLs can be implemented using MDSD techniques. In this thesis, we created a SPL for model transformations using Higher-Order Transformations (HOTs). Based on the different usage scenarios, where HOTs with different goals could be applied, we identified building blocks, which can be used to build SPLs for transformations. The SPL for transformations works in combination with feature diagram and transformation fragments. The transformation fragments are selected mirroring the corresponding configuration. The specific sub-contributions are:

Higher-order transformation patterns: The used transformation generators are written as HOTs that are building blocks of the SPL for transformations. A HOT compiles the transformation model again into a transformation model. We used these HOTs as pre-processors, at load time of the transformation (e.g. in MDSPE), executed before the actual transformation. In our approach, we use chains of HOTs where each HOT represents a different pre-processing step. We identified a set of higher-order transformation patterns formalizing different goals for the application of HOTs. Based on these patterns, software engineers can build pre-processor chains to generate transformations on demand and integrate them into the existing model-driven process. By formalising these patterns, we build a framework allowing the *reuse* of HOT specifications. The main objective of our solution is to manage variability efficiently. Composing the HOT patterns, we developed an advanced MDSD infrastructure. Our approach can also be applied to other MDSD infrastructures with a need to manage variability. We defined a set of usage guidelines and Higher-Order Transformation patterns, that are recipes and building blocks for using and building a similar infrastructure. Further, we present three patterns as an example illustrating our approach. The whole set of HOT patterns is described in Appendix B. In this chapter, we introduce only the HOT patterns used to support completions in more detail:

1. *Routine* pattern: Our experience with development of complex transformations shows that a lot of routine work is needed to specify usable transformations. To decrease development effort, we propose a generative method to take the routine work from developers. We automate generation of routine activities as copying, multiplying elements or flattening of the models. Using Routine pattern we can generate a frame, which in the most cases, only copies model elements. The frame can be then a basis for integrating customisations and creating transformation variants.

2. *Composite* pattern: Today's transformation languages do not support the *composition* and reuse of transformations sufficiently. To create a transformation from fragments we have to compose the relevant fragments and resolve their dependencies. In this thesis, we introduce an approach for transformation composition using additional information provided by feature diagrams. This approach defines and

implements a set of constraints to compose transformation fragments based on their position in a tree structure of feature diagrams.

3. *Template* pattern: Transformations often have a similar structure differing only in parameter values and application context. To achieve this, our solution supports modularity by using modular constructs (e.g. templates) as much as possible. Furthermore, modularity can improve reusability of transformations. In this thesis, we introduce a method for the automated instantiation of transformation templates. Additionally, we provide an initial set of transformation templates for common transformation parts in the domain of CBSE.

4.2.2. Software Product Lines for Transformations

A Software Product Line (SPL) is a set of systems with well-defined commonalities and variabilities [37]. The most important aspect of an SPL is the management of variability. Using the concepts of SPLs, software developers and architects can build a family of products which are subject to variability. In this thesis, we apply SPLs for transformations to completions in the domain of component-based software software engineering. Although the injection of completions into the model is straightforward, the development of the completion transformation is an non-trivial task. The transformations depend on the configurations and, therefore, are subject to the variability themselves.

To provide variability support in transformation definitions, we studied the design of SPLs. In our approach, we introduce a variability modelling concept for model transformations. We create an SPL for transformations that generates variants of model transformations, for example, completion transformations as illustrated in Figure 4.2. The SPL for transformations is used to generate completion transformations executed in the horizontal direction of the Model Completion concept. The goal is to fully automate the transformation generation. The SPL reads configurations $(Config_1, ..., Config_N)$ and generates the required transformations. The configuration of the variable parts determines the transformation to be generated and, thus, the product. The illustrated approach provides methodologies to capture and reuse the common parts of transformations and also provide techniques to manage the variable parts of a transformation.

The process of building an SPL consists of two phases: *domain engineering* and *software engineering* [37]. These phases can be mapped to the tasks of the roles Completion Developer and Completion User introduced in Chapter 3.3. In the domain engineering phase, all the common parts of a transformation are identified and implemented. Additionally, models that describe the variable parts (in our approach feature models and feature effects) and their relations are created. These models represent the variable parts of a (completion) transformation. The development of transformations has to be done systematically, with the focus on their reusability. In the case of completion transformations encapsulate domain knowledge that can be (re)used in different contexts. This means that the developed transformations have to be generic and independent from an input model. In the software engineering phase, the transformations (which have been created during the domain engineering phase) are selected, configured and applied to a software system.

The CHILIES approach realises an SPL for model transformations using MDSD technologies. MDSD is one approach to cope with the challenges of product line engineering [123]. We propose HOTs as generally applicable variability modelling concept for transformations. The combined concepts of SPL and MDSD enable the automated generation of customizable transformations. Our SPL built with MDSD technologies is a sequence of HOTs each of which addresses a different part of the transformation generation process (e.g., generating a copy transformation that is extended by other

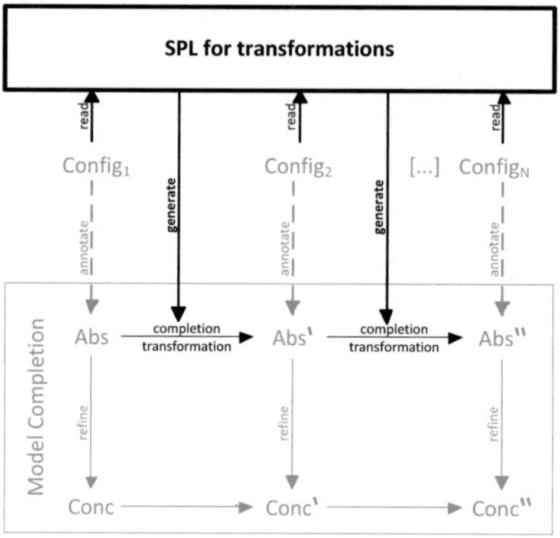

Figure 4.2.: SPL for model transformations generating completion transformations.

HOTs). The transformation sequence, and its elements (ie. models and meta models) can be regarded as a software platform. A family of products can be automatically generated using different customizations. In this scenario, the product of our SPL is again a transformation. The Higher-Order Transformation Patterns (described in Section 4.3) give further insights into the implementation of our SPL for transformation development.

4.2.3. Transformation Variability

Variability is one of the core aspects of Software Product Lines. In the context of SPLs for transformations, we can distinguish different types of variability. In this section, we discuss the relevant variability types and their manifestation in transformations.

Specifying variability Transformations of one family of products usually have many common parts, although they can carry significant differences. Typically, these differences define the variation points. We understand variant and variation point as follows:

Definition 9 Variant and Variation Point
One variation choice, defined by one configuration instance, is called *variant*. A group of all possible product variants defines a *variation point.*

In the running example described in Section 3.3.1, one variant is a static Thread pool with a pool size of 32 threads, defined by the feature configuration shown in Figure 3.16. We use the concept and notation of feature diagrams to model variation points and corresponding feature configurations to specify variants. The resulting model can include more than one variant that origin from the same (in different location in model) or different variation points. The syntax and semantics of the used feature diagrams is specified by a metamodel that is introduced in Section 4.5.2.1.

Feature diagrams allow an independent definition of variability. In large development projects, the complexity of variability can easily overwhelm developers. The benefit of using a separate definition of variability is clearly visible in such projects. A feature diagram-based definition of variability in a form of a tree allows to, when necessary, hide a variation point or dive in a variation point and implement it in separation. Thus, developers can work on the system using different views on the system with the required level of detail. The implementation of the selected feature configurations is then realized automatically as a transformation or generator that expands all the required details and their configurations in the target model.

Moreover, by using feature diagrams we allow easy configuration of variants, by choosing from several configuration alternatives. Constraints between the alternatives limit the choices to valid combinations. Such variability specification is simple and easy to use. Transformation developers do not need to learn complex formalisms, they simply select a set of options.

Characteristics of Variability The type of variability considered in this thesis is source model independent and source metamodel dependent. Source model independent means that the feature effects are only defining mapping between the feature and the realisation of this feature by elements conform to the source metamodel. Thus, there is no mapping needed between the feature effect and the source model. The realisation of feature effects is source model independent. However, feature effects are applied to and transform elements of the source metamodel. As such, feature effects depend on the source metamodel.

Variability of Completions In the previous chapter, we discussed performance completions. The variability of completion manifests as follows (cf., Figure 4.3): (i) in completions many configuration options have parameters ($P1, P2$) that can be varied. Precisely, the parameters are stored in feature effects of the feature diagram. One part variability implementation is resolving these parametrisations. A variant is constructed by providing values ($V1$) to these parameters (e.g., `Pool:size=32`). This variability is limited only on the locations where the parameters are defined.

In the next step (ii) the annotated (or other relevant) model element (called pivot element) from the source model is removed and on its place is the required detailed model subsystem (e.g., completion instance) injected. The completion instance is composed from resolved feature effects (black triangles in Figure 4.3), corresponding the feature configuration. The feature effects are illustrated in Figure 4.3 by triangles with parameters ($P1, P2$) and as composed triangles with resolved parameters ($V1$) in the target model.

The feature effects correspond to the elements (e.g. component, connectors), that are defined by the used metamodel and could be instantiated into a model. The implementation of the model-to-model transformation realizing this correspondence is implemented in declarative transformation language QVT-Relations. A feature model defines the variation point. A

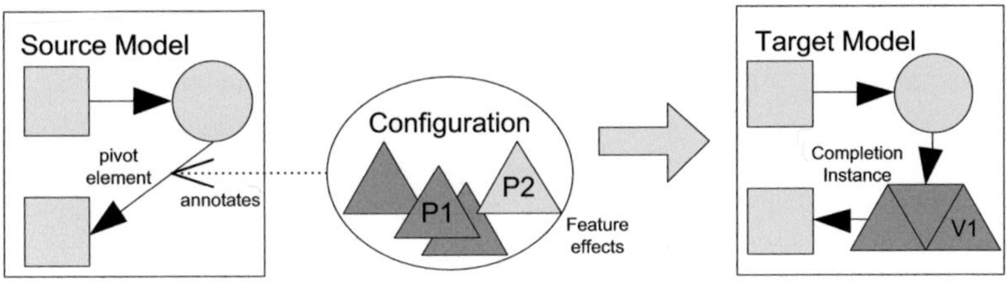

Figure 4.3.: Variability implementation with configuration.

feature configuration is a driver of the transformation and defines one variant.

4.2.4. Formalisation

This section captures the idea of variable transformations for model completions formally. We formalize the essential terms of the completion concept beginning with definition of models, transformations and transformation chains. Based on these initial definitions, we introduce a formalisation of model completions and completion transformations.

4.2.4.1. Basic Terms

Models and Metamodels: Let MM be a metamodel, expressed as an instance of some meta-metamodel MMM. For example, the PCM metamodel is an EMOF instance. An instance of the metamodel is a model defined as M. Then the set of all valid model instances that are *conform* to this metamodel MM is defined as follows:

$$conf(MM) = \{M | M \text{ is conform to } MM\}$$

Applied to the PCM, this definition allows to specify a valid model conform to the PCM metamodel as $M \in conf(PCM)$, where $PCM \in conf(EMOF)$.

Model Transformations: Let t be a function, which maps an instance of a source metamodel MM_S to an instance of the target metamodel MM_T:

$$t : conf(MM_S) \rightarrow conf(MM_T), \text{ where } \forall M_T \in conf(MM_T)$$

$$\Rightarrow \exists M_S \in conf(MM_S)$$

$$t(M_S) = M_T$$

For example, consider a transformation:

$$t_{PCM2SOFA} : \ conf(PCM) \rightarrow conf(SOFA)$$

$t_{PCM2SOFA}$ maps instances of the PCM to instances of SOFA metamodel.

Model Completion: Let c be a function, which is a left-total relation, thus every source model is associated with one or more target models. Thus, c maps instances of a source metamodel $M_S \in conf(MM_S)$ to a set of target models (P), which are instances of the target metamodel $M_T \in conf(MM_T)$:

$$c : conf(MM_S) \rightarrow P(conf(MM_T))$$

In the following, we specify the applied completion by the description c above the transition arrow ($\xrightarrow{c}$).

The exact target domain of the completion is defined by its purpose. In the following, we understand source model M_S as a set of model elements (i.e., links between elements and attributes are transformed implicitly). The definition of completion does not force c to map every element of M_S to an element (or number of elements) of M_T. Therefore, we can define a source model M_S' as a subset of M_S that is mapped to M_T.

Functions mapping only a subset of the source model are called partial functions, which allow to specify relations between two domains. Moreover, starting with the same source model and using two different completions (or only two different configurations of one completion) the transformation can result in two different targets. However, such completion definition is not enough to support the implementation of our completion-based processes. To support such processes, we it has to be possible to map every model M_T to at most one model M_S. Thus, we need additional variability specification. Therefore in the following, we define a suitable variation specification allowing unambiguous definition of completions.

Completion Specifics: In case of completions, the source model M_S and the target model M_T are instances of the same metamodel ($MM_S = MM_T$):

$$M_S \in conf(MM) \wedge M_T \in conf(MM)$$

Thus, the relation between source and target model is (i) reflexive ($M_S \stackrel{c}{\rightarrow} M_S$), when for c was any pivot element identified; (ii) asymmetric ($M_S \stackrel{c}{\rightarrow} M_T \not\Rightarrow M_T \stackrel{c}{\rightarrow} M_S$), for each c; and (iii) transitive ($M_S \stackrel{c_i}{\rightarrow} M_{T_1} \wedge M_{T_1} \stackrel{c_j}{\rightarrow} M_{T_2} \Rightarrow M_S \stackrel{c_{ij}}{\rightarrow} M_{T_2}$), for $c_i \neq c_j \wedge c_{ij} = c_i \circ c_j$ (where '$\circ$' defines a composition of transformation in a sequence). Such a relation is called partial order and formalizes the intuitive concept of ordering, sequencing, and arrangement of the elements in a set of completions. We discuss sequences of completions in Chapter 5.

Further, we focus on the definition of the completions and the variability in the completion transformation ("c"). The goal is to define completion transformations that associate one, and only one, target to any particular input.

4.2.4.2. Variability Management

Variation Points and Variations: In this thesis, we deal with variability where, for a given fixed source model M_S and a transformation t, a finite set of possible variants v should be derivable. A set of all possible variants $P(V)$ of one variation point V is defined as:

$$V = \{v | v \in conf(MM_T)\}$$

In the completion approach, one completion c defines at least one *variation point* (a completion can define multiple variation points in one software architecture). All possible variation points are members of $C = \{c_i | i \in I\}$. The set C denotes a finite set of available completions, called completion library. Furthermore, the set V_i with $i \in I$:

$$V_i \subseteq \{v_i^j | j \in J\}$$

denotes a countable set of possible variants for one completion c_i.
To continue with our example, the variation point defined by completion $c_{ThreadManagement}$ is

$$V_{ThreadManagement} = \{v_{ThreadManagement}^{TP_{static}}, v_{ThreadManagement}^{TP_{dynamic}}, v_{ThreadManagement}^{ThreadPerRequest}, v_{ThreadManagement}^{SingleBackgroundThread}\}$$

Variant Composition: In the following, we use an operator $\triangleleft$ to specify the variant composition. The $\triangleleft$ operator introduces variants into any source model and weaves model elements defined by the completion variant into the source model. The semantics of the $\triangleleft$ operator are represented by the relationship that exists between the variant model and the source model. More formally the semantics of $\triangleleft$ operator is defined as follows:

$$\triangleleft : conf(MM_S) \times P(V) \Rightarrow M_T, where M_T \subseteq conf(MM_T).$$

Variation Implementation: Each v_i^j can be implemented as a transformation that realises the variant composition and constructs one variant of $M_S \in conf(MM_S)$ by weaving an instance (v_i^j) of variation point c_i:

$$t : conf(MM_S) \xrightarrow{c_i} conf(MM_T) : conf(MM_S) \triangleleft v_i^j$$

Applying one variation of a completion, e.g. $c_{ThreadManagement}$, results in a composition of the source model and the configured variant, e.g. $v^{TP_{static}}_{c_{ThreadManagement}}$.

Each variant of a completion could be applied to a number of elements in the source model. The pivot element defines a type of model element the completion can be applied to. Applied to the PCM, this definition allows to specify, for example, completions applicable to connectors, components or resource containers (also called infrastructure).

Model Elements: As the application domain of our approach is CBSE, we identified possible pivot elements. Let $E = E_{comp} \cup E_{conn} \cup E_{infra}$ be the set of model elements (identified in the source model) of three types: *components*, *connectors* and *infrastructures*, respectively. Each of the sets is finite (possibly empty). Each c_i can be applied to a model element $e \in E_s$, where $s = comp, conn, infra$, and realise necessary model changes until variant v_i^j reached. If v_i^j is again a set of valid model elements (which does not need to be the case), e is removed and replaced with v_i^j in E.

Since t is a function, which has at most one corresponding result in the target domain per element in the source domain, more parameters are needed to be able unambiguous generation of the result. This yields an idea to extend the function t so that it would accept an additional input of ,i.e., the configuration model. We use feature diagrams as configuration model. Thus, the additional input is $fd \in FD$, where FD is a set of feature diagrams. Each completion is then defined as a tuple of the metamodel element type e (so called *pivot element*), and a feature diagram fd:

$$c_i = (e, fd_i)$$

A feature diagram defines a configuration metamodel, for example, $fd_{ThreadManagement}$ is a metamodel for the domain of $c_{ThreadManagement}$, its instance is a specific configuration $fc \in conf(fd_{ThreadManagement})$ (e.g., which defines one variant $v_{TP_{static}}$). The $fd_{ThreadManagement}$ itself is an instance of a metamodel for feature diagrams MM_{FD}, $fd_{ThreadManagement} \in conf(MM_{FD})$.

Variability management with a Mark Transformation: One option to support variability, transformations can be parametrised by a configuration model. Such transformations are called mark transformations as explained in Chapter 2. We formalise mark transformations as follows. Let t^M be a transformation, which maps an instance of a source metamodel MM_S and an instance of a configuration metamodel MM_{Cfg} (e.g. metamodel of feature diagrams) to an instance of the target metamodel MM_T:

$$t^M : conf(MM_S) \times conf(MM_{Cfg}) \rightarrow conf(MM_T)$$

Thus, for one source model $M_S \in conf(MM_S)$ and one configuration instance $M_{Cfg} \in conf(MM_{Cfg})$ the transformation t^M derives one target model $M_T \in conf(MM_T)$.

For example, consider a transformation:

$$t^M_{PCM \triangleleft ThreadMng} : conf(PCM) \times conf(fd_{ThreadManagement}) \rightarrow conf(PCM)$$

mapping instances of the PCM and a Thread Pool configuration to new instances of the PCM. The transformation takes $ThreadManagement$-specific aspects as configuration.

Because the mark transformations depend on the mark model and the source model, the transformations have to implement a mapping for each possible configuration. To reduce the complexity of mark transformations we use higher-order transformations introduced in the following.

Higher-Order Transformation A higher-order transformation t^{HOT} is a transformation whose target and/or source model are again transformations. Thus, in general t^{HOT} maps an instance of a transformation metamodel MM_{Transf} to an instance of the transformation metamodel MM_{Transf}:

$$t^{HOT}_{General} : conf(MM_{Transf}) \rightarrow conf(MM_{Transf})$$

This type of transformations is especially useful for transformation manipulations, such as modification, insertion or merges. In the case of completions, we generate the completion transformation from the configuration model. Thus, t^{HOT} maps an instance of a configuration metamodel MM_{Cfg} to an instance of the transformation metamodel MM_{Transf}:

$$t^{HOT} : conf(MM_{Cfg}) \rightarrow conf(MM_{Transf})$$

Variability management with a Completion Transformation: Let t^C be a completion transformation, which maps an instance of a source metamodel MM_S and applies completion c to it. The target model is an instance of the target metamodel MM_T. The t^C transformation is created by a higher-order transformation t^{HOT}. The transformation t^{HOT} maps an instance of a configuration metamodel MM_{Cfg} to an instance of the target metamodel, in this case it is a transformation metamodel MM_{Transf} and generates required completion transformation t^C:

$$t^{HOT} : conf(MM_{Cfg}) \rightarrow t^C, \text{ where } t^C \in conf(MM_{Transf})$$

$$t^C : conf(MM_S) \stackrel{c}{\rightarrow} conf(MM_T)$$

Thus, for one configuration model MM_{Cfg} the higher-order transformation t^{HOT} derives one transformation variant t^C.

For example, consider a transformation:

$$t^{HOT} : fd_{ThreadManagement} \rightarrow t^{c_{PCM \triangleleft ThreadManagement}}$$

$$t^{c_{PCM \triangleleft ThreadManagement}} : conf(PCM) \stackrel{c_{PCM \triangleleft ThreadManagement}}{\rightarrow} conf(PCM)$$

mapping instances of the PCM to instances of PCM metamodel. The transformation $t^{c_{PCM \triangleleft ThreadManagement}}$ is generated already considering the $fd_{ThreadManagement}$ and its configuration. The transformation implements only chosen the $ThreadManagement$-specific aspects and description how to instantiate these aspects in resulting PCM models. The configuration instance of $fd_{ThreadManagement}$ is used to generate $t^{C}_{ThreadManagement}$.

Now, we can define a completion transformation as follows. Each variant $v_i^j \in V_i$ (defined by an instance of a configuration metamodel MM_{Cfg}) can be implemented by a completion transformation:

$$t^{c_i}_{v_i^j} : conf(MM_S) \xrightarrow{v_i^j} conf(MM_S)$$

constructing a one variant of M_S ($M_S \triangleleft v_i^j$) using variation point c_i.

4.2.4.3. Transformation Chains

In this section, we discuss sequences of transformations, that represent an ordered chain of model-to-model transformations. We focus on sequences of higher-order transformations that build a software product line for transformations. Sequences of completion transformations are discussed in Chapter 5.

Chains of Transformations: Are ordered set of transformations t_i. The t_i transformations are executed sequentially with t_1 being the first and t_n being the last transformation. The source model of transformation t_i is $M_S = M_i \in conf(MM_i)$ and the target model is $M_T = M_{i+1} \in conf(MM_{i+1})$:

$$t_i : \; conf(MM_i) \rightarrow conf(MM_{i+1})$$

The chain of transformations t^* is then executed as follows:

$$t^* : \; conf(MM_i) \xrightarrow{t_i} conf(MM_{i+1}) \xrightarrow{t_{i+1}} \cdots \xrightarrow{t_n} conf(MM_{n+1})$$

Chains of Higher-Order Transformations (HOTs) An example of a classical chain of transformations is a chain of higher-order transformations t^*_{HOT}. Let T_{HOT} be an ordered set of HOTs. Similarly as chains of classical model transformations, the members of the HOT chain generate a model, which is then input to the next HOT transformation. In the case of completions, we express t^*_{HOT} as follows:

$$t^*_{HOT} : conf(MM_{Transf_i}) \rightarrow conf(MM_{Transf_{i+1}}) \cdots \rightarrow conf(MM_{Transf_{n+1}}),$$

In the completion approach HOTs take as an input model a configuration model $conf(MM_{Cfg})$ or a transformation $conf(MM_{Transf})$, or even a metamodel $MM \in conf(MMM)$ could be an input for a HOT. These HOTs are then executed sequentially to derive the required completion transformation. We introduce the HOT chain in the following sections.

4.3. CHILIES: Higher-Order Transformation Patterns

With the growing trust in MDSD, projects of greater complexity and size are developed based on the model-driven paradigm. Since the technology for executing transformations, especially written in high-level, declarative transformation languages, is of very recent date, there is very little knowledge available on how to write such transformations (see Chapter 8).

As mentioned above the goal of this chapter is to provide software developers with an automated method to manage variability in transformations. We assume that developers have identified possible variation points relevant for their goal (e.g. performance prediction). Starting with these variation points, we aim to generate the corresponding transformation variants realising the related design decisions. For this purpose, we build an SPL for transformations from building blocks called HOT patterns. These patterns are reusable in different contexts and for different MDSD projects. The HOT patterns define a body of knowledge on transformation engineering and they introduce a number of useful guidelines for generation of complex transformations.

4.3.1. Motivation

Principles for the development of model transformations are crucial for the success of MDSD. The importance of model transformations is comparable to the importance of compilers for high-level programming languages. The development of transformations currently takes place on a low-level of abstraction, lacking appropriate reuse mechanisms. The support of large transformation scenarios is still missing [171, 153], since the methods, patterns, and building blocks for their development are not available.

The young field of transformation engineering needs principles for reuse and modularity similar as for classical programming languages. *Structured Programming* was introduced as a means to facilitate reuse, maintainability, and to ease understanding. Similarly, most transformation languages provide language constructs to define modules, many of them even support rule inheritance. *Meta-programming* is a programming paradigm with the intend to write highly complex programs concisely by implementing software on a higher level of abstraction. Model-driven engineering is strongly related to meta-programming [9]. Meta-programming is about writing programs operating on programs as first-class entities, and model-driven engineering is about modelling transformations which operate on models as first-class entities. The same fact accounts to *Generative Programming*, where configurable generators are build capable of creating programs within one specific domain. Today's MDSD paradigm embodies many ideas of Generative Programming. *Domain Engineering*, or *Product Line Engineering* is a process to systematically reuse domain knowledge, with the objective of factoring out shared assets of a family of systems.

In more complex scenarios transformations can be specialized more than once, for instance as more purpose-specific information becomes available. This specialization can happen at different stages through the lifetime of a transformation. Subsequently, the transformation should create a substantial part of the final software product. Often the parts of the software are expressed in a domain-specific language (DSL) that is better suited to the problem at hand than a general purpose programming language. The usage of DSL's promises a shorter time-to-market, higher quality, reusability, maintainability, portability, and interoperability. The reason is especially the encapsulation of domain knowledge and improved communication with domain experts through DSLs. A shift of knowledge is observable, as more and more logic is implemented in transformations (Chapter 8). With larger projects, developers not only have to face larger models, but also transformations of higher complexity.

One way to cope with the aforementioned challenges is to apply the ideas of model-driven engineering to its own artefacts again. This immediately leads us to raising the abstraction level even further with Higher-Order-Transformations (HOTs), i.e. transformations which operate on transformation(-model)s. The required transformations are generated and manipulated by a HOT. This generation results in a more efficient transformation code and generation overhead is minimal. Generated code can be involved in further transformation generation and can itself generate transformations, providing full multi stage capabilities.

4.3.2. Higher-Order Transformations

Transformations are an integral part of the developed system as first-class elements of the model-driven architecture. As such, they can be themselves generated and handled by MDSD, exactly like traditional programs. This allows reusing MDSD tools and methods to generate new one (since transformations of transformations can be transformed themselves). A wide set of applications for such technologies appeared involving transformations in the roles of both manipulating program and manipulated object. Such transformations are called Higher-Order Transformations (HOTs). We define HOTs as follows:

Definition 10 Higher-Order Transformations

A Higher-Order Transformation is a model transformation manipulating or generating transformation models. The input and/or output models of such transformation are again transformations models.

In the recent past, a number of approaches appeared where HOTs are incorporated as a means to solve various problems in the model-driven domain [161, 158, 68]. Many application scenarios for HOTs explained in these papers are based on similar patterns. Classifying all these scenarios in a precise manner can, first of all, help to find new patterns, for example by improving, synthesising, abstracting or refining existing ones. Furthermore, it can also help to detect shortcomings of transformation languages. Last but not least, a set of scenarios can help designers incorporating HOT techniques in future MDE architectures. Initial contributions [158] in this area classify HOTs according to different categories such as synthesis, analysis, etc. However, these patterns build only very low-level primitives and a deeper insight into the area of application as well as practical experiences with complex generator structures are not gathered, yet. Examples of such applications are synthesis of transformations from a source other as transformation, as applied in [68]. Other applications are analyses of transformations, as well as modification and composition of transformation from a number of input transformations.

In this section, we present a set of Higher-Order Transformation Patterns (*HOT patterns*) for transformation generation that allow manipulating and generating transformations on lower levels of abstraction. These patterns realise more complex goals and are solutions to reoccurring problems in transformation engineering. In our implementation, the transformation manipulation primitives are provided through a library of patterns rather than as a language extension, allowing a more robust and maintainable approach than language extensions. The HOT patterns foster reuse and abstraction allowing for larger transformation scenarios and better overview over complex model-driven systems. Moreover, we provide an implementation of these patterns to realise Model Completions, which serve as an application scenario for the HOT patterns. We realize the Model Completion approach composing together three of the HOT patterns. Additional HOT patterns identified during our work can be found in Appendix B. These patterns encapsulate our experience with the application of HOTs.

4.3.3. Notation

In [158], Tisi et al. give a valuable overview on application scenarios for HOTs. Their paper proposes a coarse classification of HOTs into what they call base patterns. Base patterns make applications of HOTs distinguishable by the types and characteristics of their input and output models. The four base patterns are *synthesis*, *analysis*, *composition*, and *modification*. At least one input model or one output model needs to be a transformation model, otherwise we are dealing with ordinary transformations. We consider these patterns as basic primitives and we classify our scenarios representing more complex patterns according to these primitives.

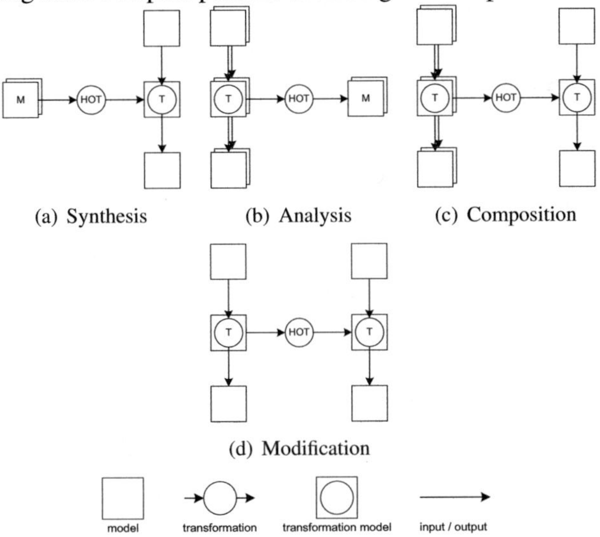

Figure 4.4.: Patterns of higher-order transformations (according to [158]).

Figure 4.4 illustrates all four patterns following Yourdon & Coad's notation [38] of data flow diagrams (DFDs), displaying models as external entities (rectangles) and transformations as processes (circles). We use the same notation to illustrate HOT patterns. Thus, a transformation model, being a model (rectangle) and a transformation/process (circle) at the same time, is depicted as a circle surrounded by a rectangle.

To document the HOT patterns, we use a fixed notation inspired by Gamma et al. [59], consisting of the following elements: the *name* of the pattern, *motivation* for the pattern including the class of problems that the pattern solves, specification of the solution using the QVT Relations language including *implementation* details and discussion of *benefits and drawbacks* regarding the pattern's applicability.

4.4. *Routine* HOT Pattern

Transformation developers often have to implement repeatedly functionality, such as copy routines, multiplying, referencing, mappings, markings or flattening of models. However, many transformation languages (e.g., QVT-R, ATL) lack support for such default rules. Thus, transformation developers need to define these rules explicitly. It is a significant amount of work particularly for completion transformations which, for example, copy large parts of a model. We propose a generator pattern to derive generic rules for given metamodels.

4.4.1. Definition

Name: Routine HOT pattern

Motivation: Writing a model-to-model transformation can be a tedious task. Our experience with development of complex transformations shows that a lot of routine work is needed to specify usable transformations. Most transformations contain certain routine principles that frequently occur.

Only after implementing these routine parts, it is possible to realise the initial goal of the transformation. More specifically, to implement model customisation, we first have to copy the necessary model elements before integrating customisations. Although in-place transformations are useful to describe this type of model changes, there are several reasons to prefer the creation of a new models. First, in some scenarios, the source model needs to be preserved. For example, in MDSPE developers typically use the source model for a wide range of purposes, this source model offers a highly-abstract view on the system, which is crucial to allow experts from different domains to work with this model. Moreover, the customisations of this model need to be propagated to the different purpose-specific models. Thus, starting with the same source model we have to create different purpose-specific and customised target models. As consequence, the traces between source model and target model become more explicit. Finally, we are not restricted to endogenous transformations (i.e., transformations with the source and target model in the same language), as in-place transformation are. In such scenarios, we can not avoid routine copies (or mappings) of model elements. To alleviate from this issue, the *Routine* pattern takes advantage of the fact that the metamodel is also a model at the same time. Thus, from the metamodel as input the HOT generates a transformation that creates a required model, for example an exact copy of a given instance of that metamodel.

To decrease development effort, we propose a generative method to take away the routine work from developers. We automate the generation of routine activities such as copying, multiplying elements or flattening of models. Using the Routine pattern we can generate a frame, which in most cases only copies model elements. This frame can then be used as a basis to integrate customisations and create transformation variants.

Specification of the Routine pattern was motivated by the need to implement a set of frequently occurring patterns in transformations. The basic transformation patterns (*Mapping*, *Refinement*, *Abstraction*, *Duality* and

Flattening) that frequently occur in model-to-model transformations were introduced by Iacob, Steen and Heerink in [87]. The patterns *Mapping*, *Abstraction*, *Flattening* are typical applications for the HOT Routine pattern. Model transformations realising these patterns do not introduce new semantic or duality to the model instances and, therefore, they can be synthesised for any metamodel language without any additional expert knowledge. Patterns such as *Refinement* or *Duality* require additional information about the semantic of the target model and as such they can not be generated simply from the metamodel. The additional patterns (identified by us), which suit as very fortunate application scenarios, are *Copying* or *Marking*. For the creation of the transformation frame, that is basis for the customisation of transformations, the last two patterns are especially important, therefore we focus on these patterns in a more detail (see Section 4.4.2).

MAPPING: The goal of this pattern is to establish a one-to-one relations between elements from the source model and elements from the target model. Mapping is used when the source and target models are conform to different metamodels. This pattern is the only one assuming that the source and target metamodel are not equal. As such this pattern as only one requires additional mapping model that specifies the mapping between two metamodel languages. Because of the intuitive importance of this base pattern it is the most implemented pattern in existing MDSD tools. Most of the tools, for example [111, 90], require to specify the mapping model using a graphical user interface. Based on the resulting mapping model a transformation is generated. This transformation then maps any instance of the source metamodel to a corresponding instance of the target metamodel. The generated mapping rules are specified as follows:

```
top relation XYMapping {
nm: String;
enforce domain source x: X {context = c1: XContext {}, name = nm};
enforce domain target y: Y {context = c2: YContext {}, name = nm};
when {ContextMapping(c1,c2);}
}
```

Listing 4.1: Mapping transformation rule (based on [87]).

This bidirectional mapping specifies that some element `x` of type `X` is related to some element `y` of type `Y`, when their parent contexts are related as defined by another mapping relation `ContextMapping` and their names are equal. For example, using this pattern we can map a `BasicComponent` defined in the PCM metamodel to a `Component` defined in the SOFA metamodel using this base pattern. Thus, we can translate any model in one syntax (e.g., PCM) into another syntax (e.g., SOFA) using mapping transformations.

In the following, it is assumed that the source and target model are conform to the same metamodel, i.e. we implement endogenous transformations. Thus, the generated transformations would be a modifier of the model instances to fulfil a particular goal.

ABSTRACTION: This pattern abstracts from model elements in the source model while keeping the incidence relations of its model elements [87] and, thus, from specific information in the models. The abstraction pattern can, for example, be used to remove subtypes that carry additional information from a model. In a meta-model for component-based software architecture, we can, for example, remove the distinction between basic components and composite components which both are specialisations of components. The generalised abstraction rule, where `X` is a subtype of abstract type `ModelElement`, is specified as follows:

```
top relation XAbstraction {
checkonly domain source x: X {
    inIncidence = in : Incidence { name = nm_in: String, source = ss1:ModelElement{}},
    outIncidence = out : Incidence { name = nm_out: String, target = tt1:ModelElement{}}};
enforce domain target e: ModelElement {
    name = nm_in + nm_out, source = ss2:ModelElement{}, target = tt2:ModelElement{}};
when {Mapping(ss1,ss2);Mapping(tt1,tt2)}
}
```

Listing 4.2: Abstraction transformation rule (based on [87]).

FLATTENING: This pattern removes the hierarchy from the source model. The reason to create hierarchical models is usually the understandability of the models, however, in order to generate code based on such models or formally analyse them it may be necessary to flatten the model. For example, in component-based models `ComposedComponents` contain a set of `BasicComponents`. All the components are either `BasicComponents` or `ComposedComponents`. The goal of the flattening pattern is to create models only containing `BasicComponents`, removing the model's hierarchy. The generalised flattening rule is specified as follows:

```
top relation XFlattening{
checkonly domain source c_x: Composite_X {context = c: Composite_Context {}};
enforce domain target x: X {};
when {XMapping(c,x) or XFlattening(c,x);}
}

top relation XMapping{
nm:String;
checkonly domain source x1: X {name = nm, context = c1: Context {}};
enforce domain target x2: X {name = nm, context = c2: Context {}};
when {XMapping(c1,c2) or XFlattening(c1,c2);}
}
```

Listing 4.3: Flattening transformation rule (based on [87]).

The transformation strategy is to map all the `Composite_X` elements to the simple `X` elements in the target model. The relation is created by `XMapping` or `XFlattening` when the context was composite itself.

COPYING AND MARKING: The *Model Copier* pattern introduces means to overcome the lacking support for in-place transformation and a copy operator in QVT Relations (QVT-R). Such transformations keep most model elements as they are while adding, removing or modifying only specific entities. QVT-R does not support a way to easily create such transformations as there is no in-place transformation or copy operator available.

QVT-R does not support default copies. In contrast to QVT-R, QVT Operational Mappings (QVT-O) provides a deep copy operation that can be used within imperative mapping rules. The Atlas Transformation Language (ATL) even supports a special mode that allows the transformation programmer to specify that a transformation should be run as a refinement transformation. This means that all elements are copied by default while those elements that are matched by transformation rules within the actual transformation are not. Triple Graph Grammars (TGG) [144] naturally support in-place transformations. To be able to implement refinement scenarios with QVT-R more efficiently we introduced the automated creation of a default copy transformation using the Routine pattern. The generated copy and marker rules are specified as follows:

```
top relation XCopy{
checkonly domain source x: X {name = nm, context = c: Context {}};
enforce domain target copied_x: X {name = nm, context = copied_c: Context {}};
where {XMark(x,copied_x);
            ContextMark(c,copied_c);}
}

relation XMark{
checkonly domain source x: X {};
checkonly domain target copied_x: X {};
}
```

Listing 4.4: Copy and Marker transformation rules (based on [68]).

The first relation in the Listing 4.4 is a copy relation, which simply matches an instance of required type in the source model and enforces (i.e., creates) a corresponding instance of this type in the target model. It is a top relation and as such is applied to every instance of this type in the source model. In the `where` clause of this relation, a so-called the marker relation is called. A marker relation is a non-top relation that can only be called from the `where` clause of a copy rule after the particular element was copied. By this principle, marker relations indicates which elements have already been copied.

Implementation: The base patterns introduced above can be used to specify a routine transformation for an arbitrary metamodel. The patterns are generic with respect to the metamodel and therefore they can be directly generated from a given metamodel. In this section, we investigate the structure of the model-driven generator and its used elements (models, metamodels and transformations). Figure 4.5 illustrates the implementation of the generator. Figure 4.5(a) shows the case where the source and the target metamodel are not equal. In this case, we may need an additional mapping model *Map* to implement the mapping pattern. Figure 4.5(b) shows the setting when the source and target metamodel are equal. In this case, the only input for the HOT is the metamodel. Based on the metamodel, we can generate a copy transformation that serves as a frame for later, more complex transformations..

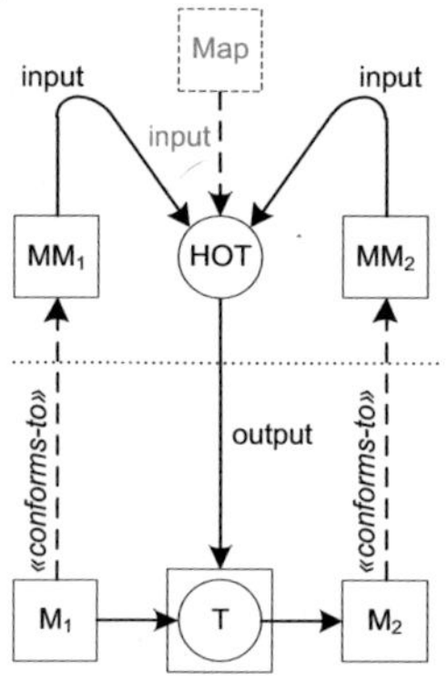

(a) Routine with non-equal source and target metamodel

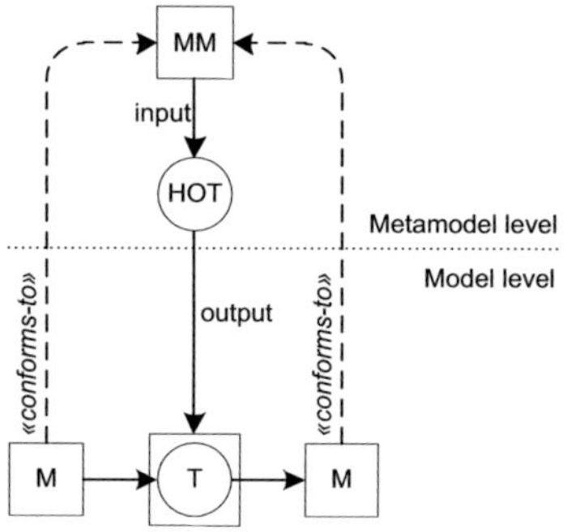

(b) Routine with equal source and target metamodel

Figure 4.5.: Routine HOT pattern.

To implement the copy and mark pattern, the HOT generates a *copy transformation* from a metamodel as follows (cf. Figure 4.5): First, the HOT creates one rule for each metaclass which copies the respective instance model element and another helper rule marking it as copied. Copy rules use marker rules [88] to ensuring exactly one copy. Accordingly, the HOT creates similar rules for attributes and relations.

Once the copy transformation exists, we need a mechanism to override rules for elements which should be left out (i.e. deleted), added, or modified for the implementation of a transformation. Transformation engineers can declare such rules separately or weave them into the transformation defining the copy rules using another HOT. Alternatively, it is possible to use QVT-R's native rule overriding mechanism.

Benefits and Drawbacks: The routine pattern takes the development effort from developers and automates the generation of frequently used transformation frames. By implementing the abstraction or flattening patterns, we can provide model versions with different levels of abstraction. Developers can use these transformations to prepare their models for analysis or code generation.

The most significant benefit is the *incrementability*. As the metamodel evolves and new entities are introduced HOTs can incrementally add routine rules and, thus, keep transformations up to date. If necessary, transformation engineers can adapt the generated transformation in an iterative way. *Traceability*, originally provided by the underlying language framework, can be utilised in a beneficial way to support any subsequent customisation process: the trace model of the HOT is able to indicate those parts that did change since the last run.

Although, throughout this thesis, we use routine pattern only to generate copy rules, this pattern is applicable to derive other rule types too.

4.4.2. Completions Support: Generation of a Routine Transformation Frame

The completion transformations copy large parts of a source model, this is a tremendous task. Since QVT Relations does not support default copies, a completion definition needs to specify copies explicitly. In this section, we investigate copies in QVT Relations. First, we use the generic patterns for copy rules. Second, we provide a way to generate the definition of a copy transformation for a given metamodel. The generation is specified as a higher-order transformation. Finally, we explore several ways to derive a completion from a generated copy transformation.

```
transformation Ecore2copyQVT (mm: ecore, oclstdlib: ecore, qvt: QVTRelation) {
top relation Package2Transformation {
n:String;
checkonly domain mm ePackage: ecore::EPackage {
            name = n
            };

enforce domain qvt t: QVTRelation::RelationalTransformation {
            name = 'Copy' + n,
            modelParameter = sourceMM: QVTBase::TypedModel {
                  name = 'source',
                  usedPackage = uPackage: ecore::EPackage{}
            },
            modelParameter = targetMM: QVTBase::TypedModel {
                  name = 'target',
                  usedPackage = uPackage: ecore::EPackage{}
            }
       };
when {
              ePackage.eContainer().oclIsUndefined();
            }
where {
              uPackage = ePackage;
              MarkTypedModel(sourceMM, targetMM);
              MarkTransformation(t);
            }
}

relation MarkTypedModel { ... }
relation MarkTransformation { ... }

top relation Class2CopyRelation { ...}
top relation SubClass2MarkerCallInWhen { ... }

top relation Class2MarkerRelation { ... }
top relation Attribute2Relation { ... }
top relation Reference2Relation { ... }
top relation ExternalReference2Relation { ... }
```

```
top relation MarkBooleanType { ... }

relation Class2Domain { ... }
relation Attribute2Template { ... }
relation Reference2Template { ... }
relation Class2MarkerCall { ... }
relation Class2MarkerCallInPattern { ... }
```

Listing 4.5: Overall structure of the Routine HOT (based on [68]).

In the completion approach we embed a special DSL for completions into host language. We exploit the fact that a large part of the completions could be expressed relying on the facilities of the host language. In our scenario the host language is defined by the PCM metamodel. Macros were often used for this purpose. Embedding a DSL into an existing host language allows inheriting its standard mechanisms and facilities, including transformations and tools. Each DSL is specified as an individual feature model.

To integrate model instances conform to the DSL defined for the particular completion, we have to implement completion transformation. Using HOT patterns and chains built by these patterns we generate completion transformations. The first step of this generation is creation of a routine transformation frame providing a copier functionality.

The generator for a copier transformation was introduced in [68]. We discuss the implementation for the purpose of completion transformations. The Routine HOT is written in QVT Relational and captures the patterns discussed in the previous section. The source model of the Routine HOT can be any Ecore metamodel and the output model is a QVT Relational transformation. For this purpose, the Routine HOT requires the Ecore meta-metamodel, the OCL standard library, and the QVT Relational metamodel. After executing the Routine HOT the model of the routine transformation is created. In our case, it is the copy transformation, implementing the Copying and Marking pattern. The resulting transformation model is expressed in its abstract syntax (of the QVT-R metamodel) and can be used directly

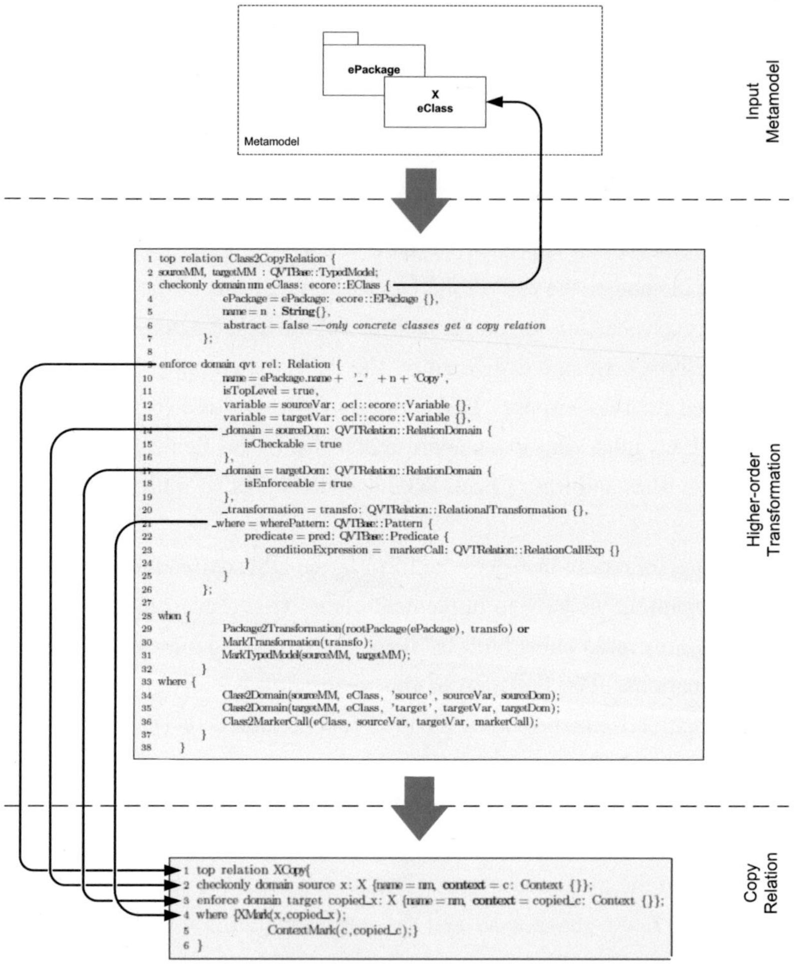

Figure 4.6.: Generating a copy relation (based on [68]).

in this form for further manipulation. However, for the execution we use a simple pretty printer to generate its textual syntax.

The overall Routine HOT works basically analogously to the patterns shown in the previous section. The overview through the basic generator structure is shown in Listing 4.5. As shown there, a copy transformation is generated (c.f. `Package2Transformation`) for each package in the metamodel. The remaining relations of the Routine HOT generate relations of the copy transformation.

In the following, we discuss the most important parts of the Routine HOT implementation. The relation `Class2CopyRelation` generates a copy relation for each non-abstract metaclass. For each subclass the relation `SubClass2MarkerCallInWhen` adds a negated call to the corresponding marker relation to the `when` clause of the created copy relation. Then, the marker relation for each metaclass is generated by the relation `Class2MarkerRelation`. Additionally, we have to create a copy relation for each attribute and reference as well. This is done by the relations `Attribute2Relation` and `Reference2Relation`. The details of this generation are discussed in [68]. In the following, we focus on the implementation of the relations `Class2CopyRelation` and `Class2MarkerRelation` and their mapping to the base patterns from Section 4.4.1.

Figure 4.6 illustrates the generation of copy relations from metaclasses within one metamodel package. For each relation, a `where` clause is created and the corresponding marker relation is called. Furthermore, the necessary domain patterns to match the source and target constructs are created by the `Class2Domain` relation.

Figure 4.7 shows relation generating the marker pattern that is created for all metaclasses including abstract ones. That results in a call from the `where` clause to mark relation of the superclass. Similarly, we can generate routine transformations based on the other patterns introduced in the previous section. Figure 4.8 illustrates the generation of the abstraction rules

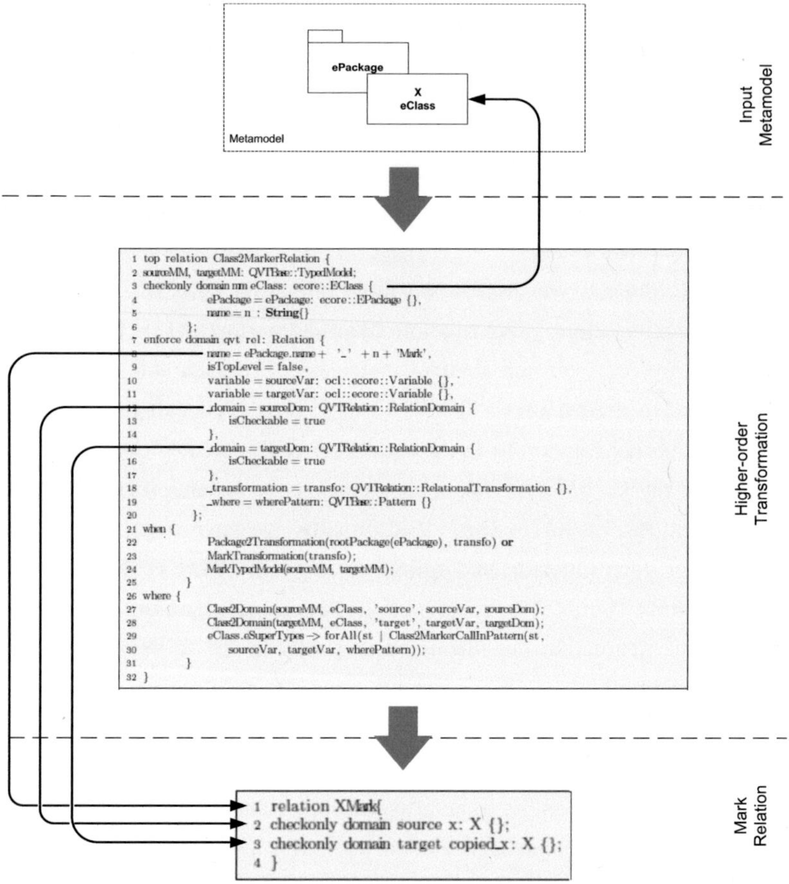

Figure 4.7.: Generating a marker relation (based on [68]).

for all classes in the metamodel. All subclasses will be replaced by their corresponding superclass after executing generated relation.

4.4.3. Summary

Using the HOT Routine pattern, we can generate transformation frames necessary for the integration of the customisations. In our case, the resulting transformation frame for a completion is generated from the PCM metamodel. Listing 4.6 shows a fragment from this transformation frame.

```
transformation CopyPCM_Frame(source: pcm, target: pcm) {
relation MarkBasicComponent {
        checkonly domain source sourceBasicComponent:pcm::repository::BasicComponent{};
        checkonly domain target targetBasicComponent:pcm::repository::BasicComponent{};
        where {
            MarkImplementationComponentType(sourceBasicComponent, targetBasicComponent);
        }
    }

    top relation CopyBasicComponent {
        checkonly domain source sourceBasicComponent:pcm::repository::BasicComponent{};
        enforce domain target targetBasicComponent:pcm::repository::BasicComponent{};
        where {
            MarkBasicComponent(sourceBasicComponent, targetBasicComponent);
        }
    }
...
...
...
}
```

Listing 4.6: The transformation frame for copying of PCM models

To generate more complex transformations, the next HOT in a chain can inject customisation (i.e., transformation fragments) in a transformation frame. The injection is controlled by a configuration model that specifies the activated features as well as necessary input parameters. Additionally, we have to define exception rules for the model elements that must not be copied. For example, as explained above, the completions annotate so called pivot elements. These elements are replaced by the customisations

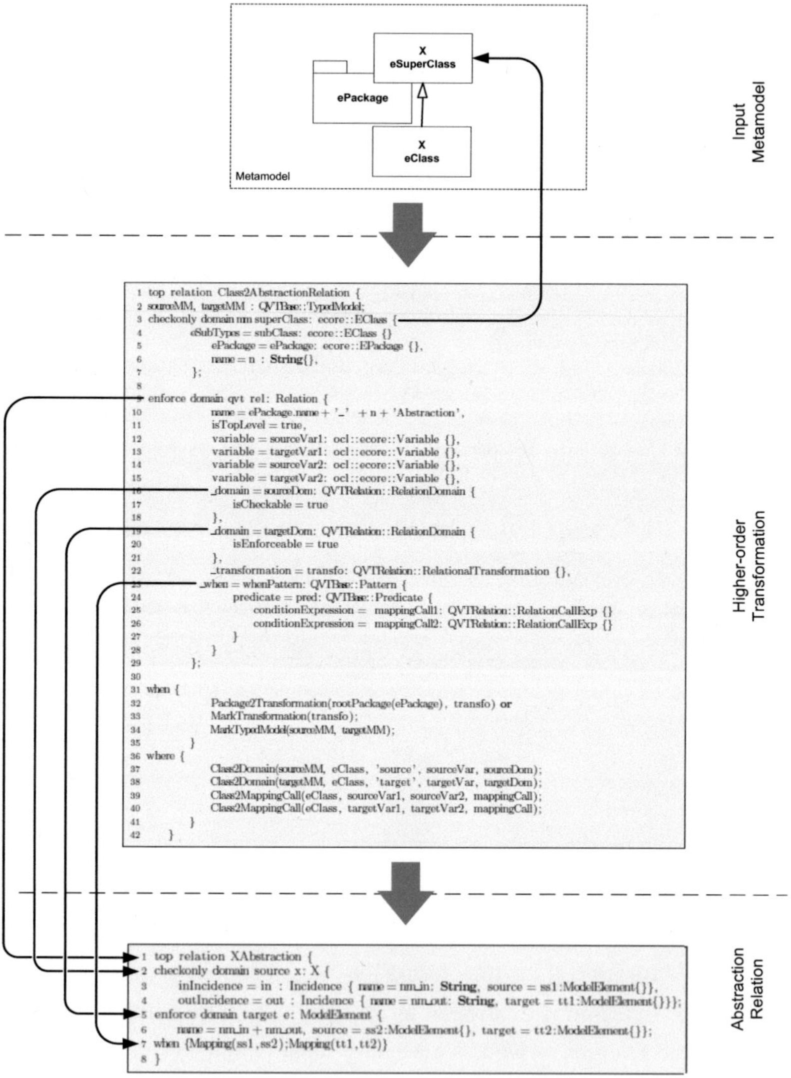

Figure 4.8.: Generating an abstraction relation.

and on their place we integrate more detailed subsystems. Thus, the next HOT could modify the generate frame itself. For this purpose, the most natural possibility to introduce exception rules is to manually introduce rules that are called instead of the overwritten ones. Another, option is to create a set of exception rules and use a simple HOT to integrate these in the generated frame.

In case of completions these exceptions are rather simple. The pivot elements that can be annotated by completion are only of three types. Applied to the PCM, completions are applicable to connectors, components or resource containers (also called infrastructure). Thus, we have only three types of simple exception rules. For example, an exception rule for a basic component would be an top-level relation that overrides the generated `CopyBasicComponent` rule and marks the component with a tag `isAnnotated = true` as already copied. After this step, would the exception rule calls the original `CopyBasicComponent` rule to copy all other components.

The Routine pattern is used to generate completion transformation as a first pre-processing step. Into the resulting transformation frame we integrate feature effects defined by the completion configuration. The next pattern called Composite HOT is dealing with the issue of customisation of transformations and follows the Routine HOT in the chain of preprocessors.

4.5. *Composite* HOT Pattern

Model-driven application engineering builds on the concept of model transformations that have to be customised for different purposes. With existing MDSD tools, application developers need to define customisation transformations manually, including all possible configuration combinations. Due to the high number of possible initial requirements, such a development method is costly and means significant effort. Currently, there is a lack of automated support for integrating these configuration decisions into the development process of transformations.

To address these issues, we introduce the Composite pattern that weaves additional customisations into transformations. In many cases, these customisation are highly variable and configurable.

In Chapter 3 we discussed the *Model Completion* concept. In the following, we introduce a novel approach for automated feature-model-based generation of completion transformations. For this purpose, we introduce the Composite HOT pattern that can be used to build generators composing transformation fragments depending on configuration.

4.5.1. Definition

Name: Composite HOT pattern In many domains, requirements regarding the final software product are constantly evolving. Customisations that are based on these requirements are a foundation for the creation of product variations and have to be integrated in transformations. Requirement of customisation introduces demands for highly efficient and low-complexity reconfiguration methods.

In our application scenario, we use feature diagrams to express configurations. The completion transformation is based on this feature diagram. Using the completion configuration on the abstract level we can generate transformations to complete the models with completions on the lower level of abstraction. Thus, we customise our models for the performance prediction.

Although our proposed approach has a wide range of application domains, we further investigate opportunities in the component-based applications domain (see Section 4.5.2). To illustrate the application of the presented pattern, we use the Thread Pool running example introduced in Chapter 3.3.1.

Motivation: Required completions could occur in different configuration variants (e.g., middleware configuration). The most frequent way to configure model transformations is by means of external annotations to a source model, i.e., mark models. Mark models are used to provide configuration details that are specific to the source model. However, this way of transformation configuration is not preferable in our scenario. The details of the *Model Completion* concept and its motivation are further discussed in Chapter 3.

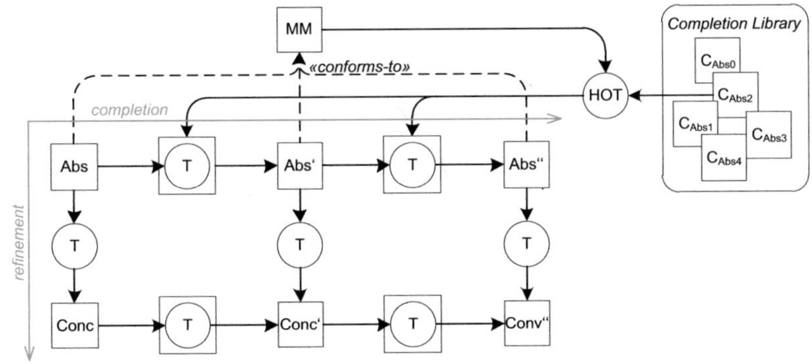

Figure 4.9.: Overview of Model Completion concept.

In our scenario, configuration happens on a higher level of abstraction. In this case, configuration itself is a definition (or model) of the transformation on the lower level of abstraction. The Composite pattern decouples the source model and the configuration. The configuration is then source metamodel-independent and can be reused in different contexts. Such configuration allows to define independent completion transformations that are building blocks used to realise the same completion activities in different contexts as illustrated in Figure 4.9.

Implementation: The implementation of the Composite pattern consists of two steps: (i) first, we have to implement a reusable and configurable construct encapsulating a required variation point, which can be, for example, a completion registered in a completion library; (ii) second, we need a HOT able to compose necessary transformation fragments (defined for the variation point) and integrate them into one transformation (cf. Figure 4.9).

Figure 4.10 shows the structure of this pattern in more detail. On the metamodel level, we define variation points VP in the form of configuration models (in our case, feature diagrams) conform to the configuration metamodel MM_{VP} (feature diagram metamodel). Each configuration model encapsulates a set of transformation fragments TF mapping the configuration options (features). These transformation fragments are transformations themselves, as such they are conform to the transformation metamodel MM_T and require references to the source and target domain. The source and target domain are defined by the source MM_1 and target metamodel MM_2. Similarly as the Routine pattern, the Composite pattern has a variant with an equal source and target metamodel. In this case, the source and target domain are defined by the same metamodel. On the model level of this pattern, we can instantiate variants *Var* conform to the variation point metamodel VP. Starting with a variant *Var* a HOT generates a completion transformation T. This HOT merges transformation fragments to the resulting transformation.

Benefits and Drawbacks: Performing the model transformation configuration automatically based on external configurations instead of models separates the development of variable construct from the actual model. This separation of concerns can achieve high variability and flexibility in the development of software applications. The required transformation fragments do not get polluted with code that is only responsible for checking the actual feature configuration. Furthermore, as the binding of fragments and features is more explicit this alleviates the complexity of transformation evolution.

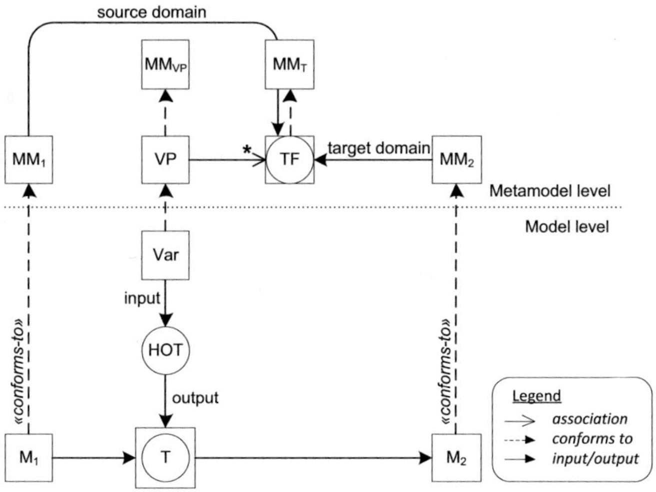

Figure 4.10.: Composite HOT pattern with non-equal source and target metamodel.

The main advantage of using HOTs in this scenario is that developers can focus on the impact of one selected feature on the model at a time and develop transformation rules for this feature only, they are not concerned with all the feature combinations and their dependencies. Using conventional transformation development, the developer has to consider all the possible configuration combinations and check the state of features (selected or eliminated) by accessing the configuration model from the respective transformation rules. Even later in development, the dependencies (*where*- and *when*-clause) between the relations need to be resolved manually. Our approach solves these dependencies by the transformation generation based on defined relations and constraints in the feature model. Additionally, the generated transformations are more structured and therefore better understandable.

Despite the advantages in simplifying the configuration of transformations with our feature model based approach there are also some drawbacks that need to be discussed. One problem arises when the feature configuration is changed and the target model needs to be updated according to the newly woven transformation. The transformation traces that were stored during the last transformation execution will potentially become invalid as the structure of the transformation may have changed significantly. Incremental updates (which are mostly based on the transformation's trace links) then are impossible. However, this problem only occurs if the transformation engine uses typed traces that are specific to the transformation that created them. Generic trace links pose less problems to the approach.

Another drawback of applying HOTs in this scenario is the debuggability of the transformation. The debugger of the transformation engine will execute and observe only the generated and woven transformation. Hence, a transformation developer will need to understand the generated transformation in order to be able to debug it. A specialised debugger would be needed if debugging should be possible on the configuration level.

4.5.2. Completions Support: Generation of a Completion Transformation

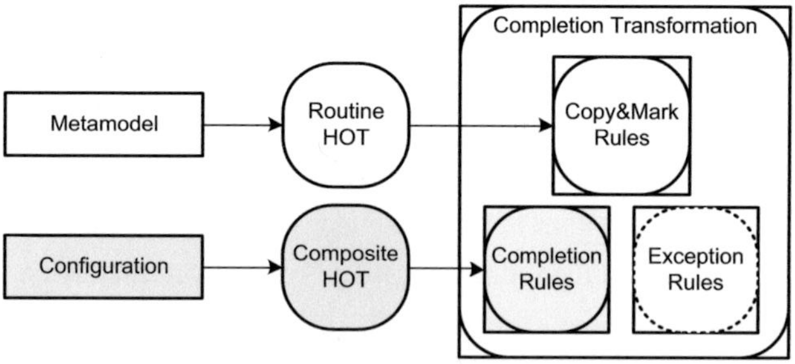

Figure 4.11.: Building elements of completion transformation using Routine and Composite pattern.

The basis for a completion transformation is a copy transformation generated by the Model Copier pattern. The parts of the model that are completed by the configured transformation will then replace the standard copy rules for the corresponding metamodel element. The composition process of the transformation fragments based on a feature selection that follows here is realised using a HOT (cf. Figure 4.9). The integration of completion transformation and the optional exception rules into the frame of copy transformation is illustrated in Figure 4.11.

In the following, we discuss the used configuration model and its metamodel. Further, we introduce the fragment composition principle and its implementation as a higher-order transformation.

4.5.2.1. Metamodel of the Extended Feature Model

Feature models are hierarchical decomposition of features including information whether a feature is mandatory, alternative or optional. The features could be user-visible characteristics of the application, for example evolution of application variants in product lines or more specific optimisations for better performance.

The metamodel of the used feature diagrams is illustrated in Figure 7.1. To be able to use feature diagrams to configure transformations, we extended the feature diagrams introduced in [46].

The extensions to the feature model metamodel make it possible to add transformation rules as annotations to the features. These extensions to the used metamodel are depicted in Figure 7.1. The most important, even quite non-intrusive extension, was the addition of a reference from the `Feature` to the `Relation` class the QVT Relational metamodel. This allows to annotate transformation fragments to features. As we also want to allow the specification of variable values through feature configurations we additionally added a reference to the `OperationCallExp` from the OCL metamodel. This allows features to refer to the '='-operation from the OCL Standard Library and thus assigning values to variables that are e.g., present in parent features. The third extension was the addition of so called 'DisambiguationRules' which are explained in Section 4.5.2.2.

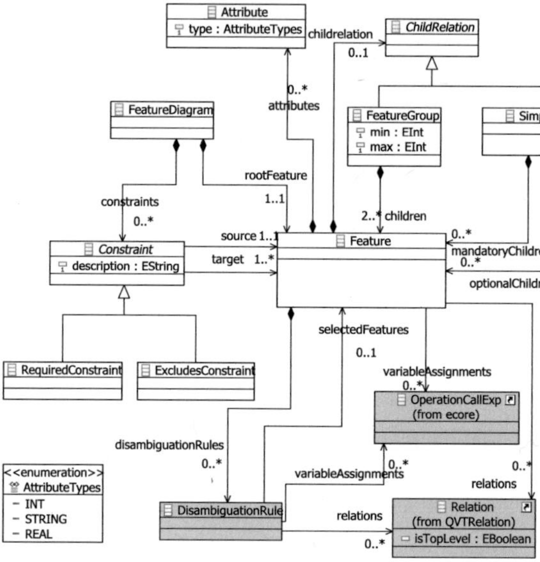

Figure 4.12.: Extensions to the Feature Model Metamodel.

Furthermore, the feature model could include feature composition constraints, that indicate which feature combinations are valid and which are not. These constraints can either be hard (depends or excludes constraints) or weak (default values or allowed override). We will refer to this constraints further in Section 4.5.2.2.

4.5.2.2. Feature-based Composition of Transformation Fragments

Transformation Fragments in the Feature Model Tree: The divide-and-conquer paradigm is an essential strategy for the development of transformations with variability and in fact for the resolution of variability problems in general. Dividing the variability domain in partial tasks focusing on an one aspect of the model at a time decreases the complexity. As presented in Section 4.5.2.1, the nodes of the feature diagram are annotated with transformation fragments. The transformation fragments implement always only one aspect of the variability. The ability of the compositional approach to produce complex transformations from smaller units allows to compose these variability aspects and create different transformation variants.

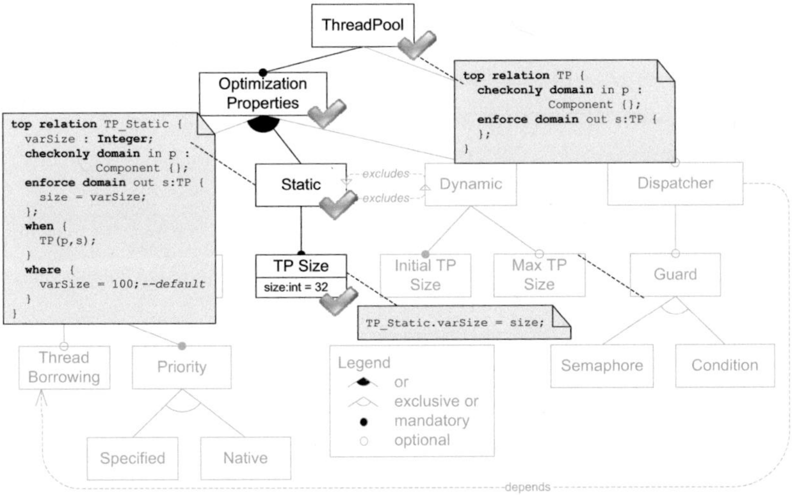

Figure 4.13.: Simplified transformation fragments for the running example.

There are two ways how to implement the transformation fragments. The language standards for model transformations offers two dialects: relational language and operational language. Each one of these dialects can be used in isolation. Combining of these approaches results in a hybrid transformation approach. We can implement transformation fragments in a strictly declarative or in a hybrid manner. The hybrid transformation fragments can call black-box operations implemented in an operational language between the rules in relations. This can be used, for example, to manipulate used variables more directly, or to trace the execution flow in the relations. Thus, hybrid implementations are defined externally as relational and internally use operational constructs.

For simplicity, we will consider only transformation fragments implemented in strictly declarative manner. The important advantage of using these declarative features over operational, is that they allow a high degree of decoupling between the different aspects of variability. In a strictly declarative rule-based approach to model-transformation, the transformation is defined by a predicate, relating the models before and after the transformation. For the composition paradigm, it is required to define the transformation fragments TF as follows:

Definition 11 Relational Transformation Fragments

A transformation fragment TF is a non-empty set of relational rules *RR* that are defined as tuple:

$$RR = (Var, Map, Pre, Post),$$

where *Var* is a set of local variables, Map a set of mappings, *Pre* a set of necessary preconditions and *Post* postconditions. The preconditions and postconditions are rule references and can refer to the rules that are defined in other fragments, this property distinguishes a fragment from a transformation.

Furthermore, as we create a transformation by composing transformation fragments, for such transformation should hold that all the references in preconditions and postconditions of a relation are resolved. Let *res* denote a function that resolves a reference in a precondition or postcondition, i.e. that return the referenced model element for a given precondition or postcondition ($res(x) = RR \in T : x$ points to RR). Then, we define such transformation as follows:

Definition 12 Fragment-based Transformation

A fragment-based transformation T is a non-empty set of transformation fragments TF, for which holds:

$$\forall RR_i \in T\ \forall pre \in RR.Pre\ \exists RR_j \in T : res(pre) = RR_j \wedge$$

$$\forall RR_i \in T\ \forall post \in RR.Post\ \exists RR_j \in T : res(post) = RR_j$$

Although the transformation fragments are implemented using declarative transformation language, we support software engineers with a view on the transformation, its variants, and its execution order at a highly abstract manner. The used feature diagrams allow to control execution order through the structure of the feature tree. The tree structure is used to compose fragments and resolve their dependencies, thus it defines the execution order. At this abstract level software engineers can influence the transformation execution, without fighting with maintainability overhead resulting from a verbose declarative transformation definition. The declarative structure of the targeted QVT Relations transformation engine makes the composition possible without having to deal with issues regarding the operational ordering of the rules. Moreover, studies in the area of program comprehension [43] show that visualising the program structure in form of a tree helps the understandability and developers can better focus on the development of isolated features.

We distinguish two types of transformation composition. External composition deals with chaining separate model transformations together by passing models from one transformation to another; we discuss this type of composition more in Chapter 5. Internal composition composes two model transformation definitions into one new model transformation, which typically requires knowledge of the transformation language. The latter method requires the model transformations that will be composed to be expressed in the same language. The Composite pattern focuses on internal composition of transformation fragments into an one rule-based model transformation.

The composition of transformation fragments based on the feature diagram is language-independent and can be used for any relational transformation specification (such as QVT Relational or ATL). The feature trees capture the essence of a transformation's modular structure. By its hierarchy, the feature model represents a general structure of the transformation abstracting from language-specific details. For example, the hybrid implementation of a transformation fragment using operational constructs internally would not have influence on the composition. This composition technique can be used for other languages than QVT, as long as the transformation language has the concepts of rules and modules that contain those rules. QVT Relations is such a transformation language, therefore we use this language to implement Composite pattern.

Since it has to be possible to compose those fragments together to a single transformation, there are several constraints on the way the transformation fragments are specified. Those constraints result mainly from the structure of the feature model and the patterns, which can occur in such a structure. As the composition of transformation fragments follows the structure of the feature tree, the HOT weaves the transformation fragments into the final transformation based on the set of composition constraints considering position and type (e.g., optional or mandatory) of the related feature in a tree. We discuss necessary constraints in the following section.

Constraints for the Transformation Composition: According to the different kinds of relations that can occur between features in a feature model (cf., Figure 4.13, adapted and with feature `Dispatcher` added for the purposes of constraints explanation), different constraints apply for the transformation fragments that are annotated to the features. These constraints are guidelines for the composition. Constraints C_i (C_1 to C_5) describe the rules that have to be obeyed when annotating transformation fragments to a specific feature. Furthermore, these constraints serve as basis for the generation of the resulting transformation. We use the running example to explain the different constraints. Figure 4.13 illustrates the annotated feature diagram for Thread Pool.

Constraint C_1: The basic shape of a feature model is that of a tree. Features can have sub-features forming a parent-child relationship. A child-feature can only be activated, if its parent feature is activated. For the scope of the transformation fragments that are attached to the child node this means that the children's rules may reference those of the parent within it's `when`- and `where`-clauses.

Definition 13 Ancestor Function

An ancestor function f_A of transformation fragment TF is defined as follows:

$$f(n) = \begin{cases} TF, & \text{if } TF \text{ belongs to the root feature,} \\ TF \cup f_A(TF_P), & \text{otherwise, where } TF_P \text{ is parent of TF.} \end{cases}$$

A parent TF_P is a transformation fragment belonging to the parent feature F_P of the feature F holding TF ($F \in F_P.children$).

Definition 14 C_1: Relation access for child features

For each relation $RR \in TF$ holds:

$$res(RR.Pre) \subseteq f_A(TF) \wedge res(RR.Post) \subseteq f_A(TF)$$

EXAMPLE: In the running example this pattern is depicted in Figure 4.13 this pattern occurs between the *ThreadPool* and the *Static* feature. The transformation fragment of the *Static* feature `TP_Static` has a `when`-dependency to the transformation fragment `TP` of its transitive parent *ThreadPool*. Listings 4.7 and 4.8 show how the child feature can call the relation defined by a transformation fragment of the parent feature (see relation `CreateThreadPoolComponent`).

```
transformation ThreadPoolRoot (source: pcm, target: pcm) {

    top relation CreateThreadPoolComponent {

        checkonly domain source sourceRepository:pcm::repository::Repository{
        };

        enforce domain target targetBasicComponent:pcm::repository::BasicComponent{
            entityName = 'ThreadPool',
            ...
        };
        when {
            CreateIThreadPoolInterface(sourceRepository, threadPoolInterface);
        }
        where {

        }
    }

    top relation CreateIThreadPoolInterface {
        ...
    }
```

Listing 4.7: Transformation fragment for the feature `ThreadPool`

```
transformation ThreadPoolRoot (source: pcm, target: pcm) {

    top relation CreateThreadPoolComponent_Static {

        checkonly domain source sourceBasicComponent:pcm::repository::BasicComponent{
            entityName = 'ThreadPool'
        };

        enforce domain target targetBasicComponent:pcm::repository::BasicComponent{
            entityName = 'ThreadPool',
            providedRoles_InterfaceProvidingEntity = providedRole : pcm::repository:
            :ProvidedRole {
                ... },
          serviceEffectSpecifications__BasicComponent = acquire : pcm::seff:
           :ResourceDemandingSEFF {
                ... },
            serviceEffectSpecifications__BasicComponent = release : pcm::seff:
             :ResourceDemandingSEFF {
```

```
            ... },
        passiveResource_BasicComponent = threadPoolResource : pcm::repository:
         :PassiveResource {
            entityName = 'ThreadPool',
            capacity_PassiveResource = ThreadPoolSize : pcm::core::PCMRandomVariable {
                specification = '100'
            }
        }
    };
    when {
        CreateThreadPoolComponent(sourceBasicComponent, targetBasicComponent);
        CreateIThreadPoolInterfaceAcquire(sourceRepository,
         threadPoolInterfaceAcquire);
        CreateIThreadPoolInterfaceRelease(sourceRepository,
         threadPoolInterfaceRelease);
    }
    where {

    }
}

relation CreateIThreadPoolInterfaceAcquire {
    ...
}
relation CreateIThreadPoolInterfaceRelease {
...
}
```

Listing 4.8: Transformation fragment for the feature `ThreadPool.Static`

Constraint C_2: Additionally to the access to `when`- and `where`-clauses it is possible for transformation fragments of child rules to control the assignment of free variables of their parents.

Definition 15 C_2: Variable assignment for child features

For each relation $RR \in TF$ holds:

$$RR.Var \subseteq f_A(TF)$$

EXAMPLE: See figure 4.13 and listing 4.9 for an application of C_1 and C_2. Feature *TP Size* can be used to statically configure the size of the thread pool. Hence, the transformation fragment refers to the free variable declared in the `TP_Static` fragment of feature *Static* (for the sake of simplicity a simple path notation with the fragment's name as prefix is used to denote the referred relation). This way the value specified in the feature configuration ($size = 32$) ends up in the assignment within the `where`-clause of the resulting generated transformation. Listing 4.10 shows abnother value assignment for the variable `ThreadPoolSize`.

```
—Resulting composed transformation
top relation TP_Static {
    varSize : Integer;
    checkonly domain in p : Component {};
    enforce domain out s : TP {
        size = varSize; };
    when{ TP(p, s) }; — Application of C1
    where { s = 32; } — Application of C2
}
```

Listing 4.9: Example transformation fragments (C_1,C_2)

```
transformation ThreadPoolRoot (source: pcm, target: pcm) {

top relation CreateThreadPoolComponent_Static_PoolSize {

        checkonly domain source sourceBasicComponent:pcm::repository::BasicComponent{
            entityName = 'ThreadPool'
        };

        enforce domain target targetPassiveResource:pcm::repository::PassiveResource{
            capacity_PassiveResource = ThreadPoolSize : pcm::core::PCMRandomVariable {
                    specification = '32'
            }
        };

}
```

Listing 4.10: Transformation fragment for the feature `ThreadPool.Static.PoolSize`

Constraint C_3: Feature models distinguish between mandatory and optional features. As mandatory features are always activated it is possible to reference rules of mandatory features of (transitive) parents within child rules. This means that even siblings can use each other's rules within their `when`- and `where`-clauses if both of them are mandatory within their parent feature.

Definition 16 C_3: Inheritance of mandatory features

For each relation $RR \in TF \cup TF_S$, where TF_S is a fragment belonging to the sibling feature, holds:

$$RR.Var \subseteq f_A(TF) \cup f_A(TF_S)$$

$$res(RR.Pre) \subseteq f_A(TF) \cup f_A(TF_S) \wedge res(RR.Post) \subseteq f_A(TF) \cup f_A(TF_S),$$

if both of the features F and F_S are mandatory.

EXAMPLE: The fragments of the *Dispatcher* feature presented in Thread Pool feature model can reference fragments of the *Optimization Properties* feature.

Constraint C_4: In addition to the parent-child relationship, a feature can depend on other features within the feature tree. Such dependencies are modelled as *depends*-relationships. For the scope of the transformation rules of the dependent feature this results in an import of the rules of the required feature and its scope (that is computed using C_1 to C_3). All imported rules may then again be used in `when`- and `where`-clauses of the current transformation rules.

As counterpart to *depends*, *excludes* inhibits a concurrent activation of two features. As both features can then never be activated at the same time an interference of their transformation fragments is also impossible.

Definition 17 C_4: Referencing through constraints - DEPENDS

For each relation $RR \in TF$ and a fragment TF_D related to the TF by *depends*-relationship, holds:

$$RR.Var \subseteq f_A(TF) \cup f_A(TF_D)$$

$$res(RR.Pre) \subseteq f_A(TF) \cup f_A(TF_D) \wedge res(RR.Post) \subseteq f_A(TF) \cup f_A(TF_D)$$

Definition 18 C_4: Referencing through constraints - EXCLUDES

For each relation $RR \in TF$ and a fragment TF_E related to TF by *excludes*-relationship, holds:

$$\text{if } TF \in T \text{ then } TF_E \notin T$$

EXAMPLE: In the thread pool example (Figure 4.13) this pattern would apply for fragments of the *Dispatcher* feature referencing relations from the *Thread Borrowing* feature.

Constraint C_5: An *exclusive-or* between sub-features poses no problem, as they may never occur at the same time and thus their transformation rules can never interfere which each other. A more challenging construct is the *inclusive-or* relationship. Features connected within such a relationship may occur in an arbitrary combination.

To be able to specify this disambiguation, special disambiguation rules were introduced into the feature metamodel (cf. Figure 7.1). The disambiguation is configured by defining one `DisambiguationRule` for each combination of features that should be treated exceptionally. Within the `DisambiguationRule` the combination is specified by assigning the features for which the rule applies to the `selectedFeatures` reference. In theory it would be possible to make a transitive selection of inclusive-or-ed children. However, in the current version of the approach this is not supported. Therefore, a constraint (see listing 4.11) applies to the selection of features, restricting the possible selection to direct children of the current feature.

```
self.selectedFeatures->forAll(f |
    if self.disambiguatedFeature.childRelation.
          oclIsTypeOf(featuremodel::FeatureGroup) then
       self.childRelation.oclAsType(featureModel::FeatureGroup).
          children->includes(f)
    else --then its a Simple relation
       self.childRelation.oclAsType(featureModel::Simple).
          optionalChildren->includes(f)
    endif
)
```

Listing 4.11: Constraint on DisambiguationRule

Definition 19 C_5: Disambiguation of inclusive-or

For each set of transformation fragments $S_{TF} = TF_1, TF_2, \ldots, TF_N$, where fragments are in *inclusive-or* relationship, holds:

$$S_D \subseteq S_{TF} \wedge S_D \in T,$$

where S_D is a disambiguation set specified by a disambiguation rule $R_D \in F_P$. Feature F_P is shared parent of $TF_1 \wedge TF_2 \wedge \cdots \wedge TF_N$

EXAMPLE: In the thread pool example such different combination possibilities could occur with the *Optimization Properties* feature: Either *Thread-Pool Policy*, *Static* or *Dynamic*, a combination of them (excluding *Static* or *Dynamic* selected at the same time, due to the *excludes* relationship between them) or none of them could be selected. Each possibility results in a different transformation rule in the generated transformation.

4.5.2.3. Implementation of HOT for Composition of Transformation Fragments

The first input for this HOT is a feature diagram with mapped transformation fragments, these fragments are used by for the actual transformation generation. The second input is the actual feature configuration, which defines the selected features and values of attributes. For composition of completion transformation T, is responsible HOT that merges fragments so that composition holds previously introduced constraints on transformation fragments.

```
transformation Ecore2copyQVT (feat: featureconfig, qvt: QVTRelation, pcm: ecore) {

top relation Config2Transformation {...}
relation MarkTypedModel {...}
relation MarkTransformation {...}

/*
 * C1:
 * Copy the relations from each selected feature
 */
top relation SelectedFeatureRelation2Relation {
    n : String;
    checkonly domain feat selectedFeature: featureconfig::ConfigNode {
        configState = featureconfig::ConfigState::SELECTED,
        origin = originFeature : featuremodel::Feature {
            name = n,
            relations = featureRel : QVTRelation::Relation {} }
    };
    enforce domain qvt targetRel: Relation {
        _transformation=transfo:QVTRelation::RelationalTransformation {}
    };
    when { MarkTransformation(transfo); }
    where { MarkFeatureRelation(originFeature, targetRel);
            CopyRelation(featureRel, targetRel); }
}

/*
 * C2:
 * Copy the assignments from each selected feature
 */
top relation SelectedFeatureVariableAssignment2VariableAssignment {
    n : String;
```

```
    checkonly domain feat selectedFeature: featureconfig::ConfigNode {
        configState = featureconfig::ConfigState::SELECTED,
        origin = originFeature : featuremodel::Feature {
            name = n,
            variableAssignments = assignment : OperationCallExp {},
            parentRelation = parentRel : featuremodel::ChildRelation {
                parent = parentFeature : featuremodel::Feature {} }
        }
    };
    enforce domain qvt targetRel: Relation {
        _transformation=transfo:QVTRelation::RelationalTransformation {},
        _where = whereClause : QVTBase::Pattern {
            predicate = pred : QVTBase::Predicate {
                conditionExpression =
                    copiedAssignment : ocl::ecore::OperationCallExp {}
            }
        }
    };
    when { MarkTransformation(transfo);
           MarkFeatureRelation(parentFeature, targetRel); }
    where { CopyAssignment(assignment, copiedAssignment); }
}
relation CopyRelation {...}
relation CopyAssignment {...}
relation MarkFeatureRelation {...}
```

Listing 4.12: HOT for transformation fragments composition (C_1 and C_2).

The HOT for composition of transformation fragments that follow constraints C_1 and C_2 is shown in listing 4.12. It weaves the transformation fragments of the selected features into the final transformation. The transformation is based on a generated copy transformation for QVT Relational itself (see Routine pattern in Section 4.4). The copy rules (such as `CopyAssignment` or `CopyRelation`) are used to copy the rules that are specified by the transformation fragments on the selected features. Relation `SelectedFeatureRelation2Relation` is responsible for matching features that are optional from the feature model and copying the annotated transformation relations to the final transformation. A corresponding relation `MandatoryFeatureRelation2Relation` is provided to match all mandatory features which do not need to be selected explicitly. Similar HOTs are provided for the weaving process of constraints C_3 to C_5.

4.5.3. Summary

Using the introduced transformation generation technique based on the Composite HOT pattern, we can generate a transformation variants that include selected customisations into the transformations. The Composite pattern allows to generate completion transformations and decrease the development effort resulting as a consequence of the variability. To fully automate generation of completion transformations we have to combine both of the introduced patterns HOT Routine and HOT Composite. Moreover, we can automate the development of the transformation fragments using the Template pattern introduced in the following section.

Despite the advantages in simplifying the configuration of transformations with our approach based on feature model, there are also some drawbacks that need to be discussed. One problem arises when the feature configuration is changed and the target model needs to be updated according to the newly woven transformation. The transformation traces that were stored during the last transformation execution will potentially become invalid as the structure of the transformation may have changed significantly. Incremental updates (which are mostly based on the transformation's trace links) are then impossible. However, this problem only occurs if the transformation engine uses typed traces that are specific to the transformation that created them. Generic trace links pose no problem to the approach.

4.6. *Template* HOT Pattern

Model transformations are a major instrument of model-driven software development used in various contexts. Especially in relational transformation approaches, the structuring of transformations depends to a large extent on the structure of the source models and the generated artefacts. In many cases, similar code is written for transformations that deal with the same source or target metamodel. Writing such transformations can be simplified significantly if re-occurring parts within the transformation rules can be specified in a reusable way.

Current approaches to transformation development include means for transformation reuse as well as inheritance. However, modularisation along the boundaries of different parts of domain metamodels is still lacking. Furthermore, the possibilities to reuse transformation fragments that re-occur in multiple transformations is limited. We introduce a Template HOT pattern to support usage of domain-specific templates for transformations with well-defined instantiation points, so called *hooks*. Transformation templates enable a modular specification of transformations and thus yield a simpler definition of transformations that can be grasped more easily and developed more efficiently.

In addition, we present a set of transformation templates in the context of the MDSPE for component-based software architectures. The specified templates give insight into the application of the presented pattern for different domains.

4.6.1. Definition

Name: Template HOT pattern

Motivation: Transformations are mainly determined by the source- and target-domains on which they operate. The structure of a transformation depends to a large extent on the structure of its source and target models. Furthermore, domain-specific patterns for the creation of a target model may occur multiple times in a transformation leading to large parts of duplicated transformation code. In many cases, transformations require annotations [63, 120] which software engineers attach to individual elements of a model. Annotations specify which elements are to be refined by subsequent transformations. Such annotations and the underlying model are then transformed into a target model [63]. Writing such transformations can be simplified significantly if re-occurring parts within the transformation rules can be reused.

However, there is little experience available about how to design and implement transformations using modern relational transformation languages. One reason for this is the fact that model transformations are written in languages of very recent date (e.g. QVT Version 1.0 was published in 2008) [72, 90]. Therefore, a basis of formalised knowledge and experience with model transformation development is not yet available at a broad basis. First initiatives for transformation design template specification focused on generic patterns [87] for model transformations. Although these patterns define a ground to build on, they do not exploit domain-specific knowledge of the transformation's source and target models. For example, they do not make use of design patterns that are often part of software models.

The Template pattern is based on our experience with the implementation of transformations used for customizing software architectures. We observed that configurable model transformations follow certain patterns defined by the domain of their metamodels. The approach introduced in this thesis allows reusing and customizing transformation parts. Transformation templates are based on known design patterns and enable a modular specification of completion transformations. They yield simpler definitions of transformations that can be grasped more easily and developed more efficiently. Thus, the Template pattern can increase reuseability and modularization of transformations.

The Template pattern is an analogy to templates in established programming languages, such as C++. For example, developers can can write metaprograms using C++ templates that are executed during compilation. This technique can be used to perform code selection and code generation at compile time. In the following, we describe the pattern in more detail.

Implementation: The Template pattern takes advantage of the possibility to reuse transformation parts to further automate transformation development. Transformation templates are parametrised and contain well-defined instantiation points. They are instantiated during load-time of a transformation.

Figure 4.14 shows the structure of the pattern. Transformation templates (Tmp) are stored in a template library. New customisation rules can be specified instantiating ($TInst$) and composing the existing templates. Furthermore, templates are configurable by a set of parameter values of their instantiation points. The template instantiation process presented is realised using a HOT (cf. Figure 4.14). It creates template instances, merges the transformation using the instances and creates a transformation based on the actual configuration given by the template configuration model. Further parts of the HOT are responsible for binding the instantiation points of the templates to the elements from the actual template configuration. The implementation of Template pattern is discussed in Section 4.6.2.4 in more detail.

Benefits and Drawbacks: This scenario allows to specify reusable transformation templates that occur in transformation development for specific metamodels. Based on these templates, model transformations can then be generated using HOTs. This results in a creation of a SPL for transformations. Therefore, we also exploit the advantages of SPLs, i.e., improved reusability and easier creation of new members of a SPL. Similarly as in the previous pattern, one particular drawback of our approach is the debuggability of the transformation.

4.6.2. Completions Support: Generation of Transformation Fragments using Templates

In this section, we describe the realisation of the Template pattern to support completions, furthermore, this solution was published in the MDI Models

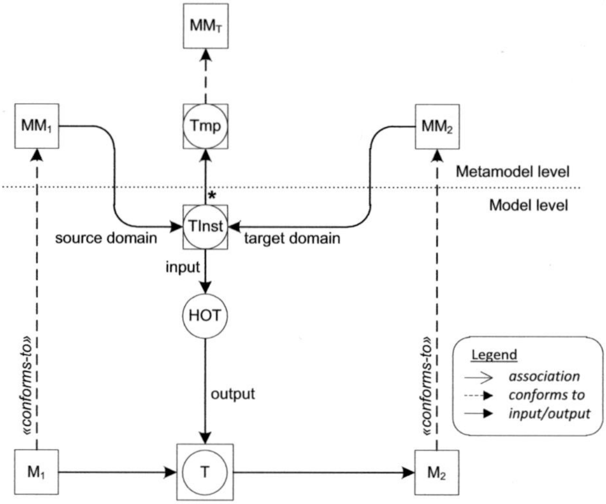

Figure 4.14.: Template HOT pattern.

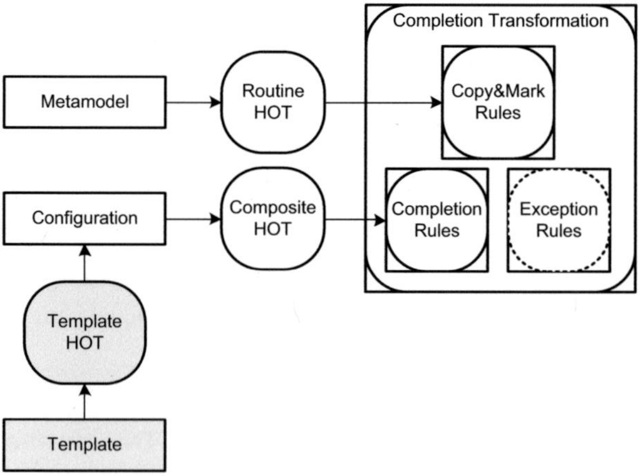

Figure 4.15.: Building elements of completion transformation using Routine, Composite and Template HOT pattern.

2010 proceedings [92]. To support transformation developers, we provide a set of templates for reoccurring transformation patterns. The instantiation of the templates is realised using a HOT (cf. Figure 4.15). In the following, we discuss the implementation of this pattern for the purpose of completions.

4.6.2.1. Configuration-aware Transformation Templates

The automated generation of completion transformations presented by the Composite pattern significantly reduces the effort needed to specify such transformations. However, the customisation rules implemented as transformation fragments still tend to contain a large set of similar elements, especially for architectural models. Therefore, we propose transformation templates as an additional mean to ease the specification of completion transformations.

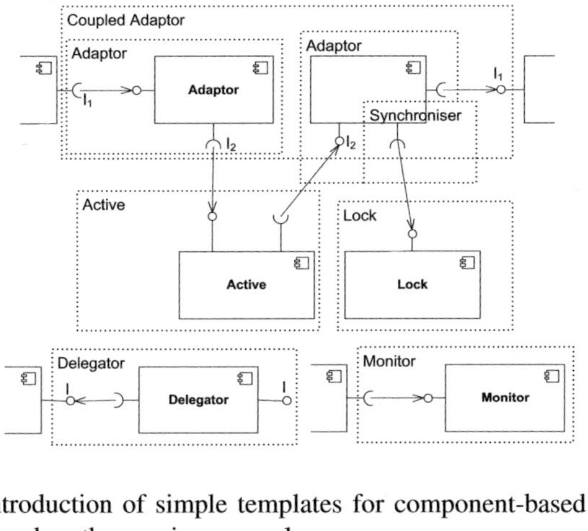

Figure 4.16.: Introduction of simple templates for component-based architectures based on the running example.

Figure 4.16 illustrates the set of templates we have identified so far for the running example. A *Coupled Adaptor* allows sender and receiver to adapt their interfaces to the same standard and, for example, use the same middleware. This template can be used in the case of completion by coupled actions, such as encryption and decryption, or composition and decomposition. The *Synchroniser* is used when a component has to acquire a lock before accessing a certain service and release a lock when finished. Same synchronisation pattern could be observed in the case of dependent actions. In the example, this template is used for the wrapper component to acquire locks through the thread pool interface. An *Active Component* template is used to model a component with a complex internal behaviour. This template refines the model with an element introducing independent behaviour branch. An additional wrapper is provided for the functionality defined as an internal action of the component behaviour. To provide, for example, a queue for competing consumers the *Lock* template is used. This template possesses a semaphore element and can be used when introducing a state holding element to the model. The *Monitor* template is applied to the component to provide a wrapper for simple monitor functionality, such as a timer. The last template introduces new functionality into the model and could be independently required by already existing model elements.

In following section, we describe the adaptor template, as a representative, in more detail. To document the transformation templates, we use a standard description schema for templates defined in [59] and [87]. This includes the following information: the *name* of the template, the *goal* of the template, the *motivation* for the template, the *specification* of the template using the QVT-Relations language, *applicability* defines constraints for the usage of a template and an *example* in which the template is applied.

4.6.2.2. The Adaptor template

In this section, we illustrate the concepts introduced above with the example of the adaptor pattern [59]. For the application within a completion transformation, further details concerning the specific metamodel are necessary.

NAME: *Adaptor*

GOAL: Change the provided or required service interface.

MOTIVATION: When new functionality is needed in an architecture (for example message filtering), its implementation could result in a change of a service's signature (or input or return parameters). The adaptation of the interface is considered as a configurable change and allows developers to define changed attributes without the need to reimplement the whole transformation for the integration.

SPECIFICATION: The adaptor template is specified by a relation that creates an *Adaptor* component which requires the interface provided by the adapted component and provides the interface required by the calling component. Additionally, based on a designer defined method mapping, it requires or provides a modified interface to another component in the system. As illustrated in Listing 4.13, an `adaptorComponent` is created with the modified interface `targetInterface` in the target domain .

```
transformation CBSE_Adaptor (source: CBSE, target: CBSE) {
    top relation Adaptor_template_CreateAdaptor {
        checkonly domain source sourceInterface:{ —adapted interface
            <fromInterface:TemplateInstantiationPoint>
        };
        checkonly domain source targetInterface:{
            <toInterface:TemplateInstantiationPoint>
        };
        enforce domain target adaptorComponent:{
            name = <adaptorName:LiteralExpInstantiationPoint> —name
            requiredRoles = reqRole:RequiredRole{
                requiredInterface = sourceInterface }
            providedRoles = provRole:ProvidedRole{  —modified interface
                providedInterface = targetInterface }
            serviceEffectSpecifications =          —behavior specification
                seff:ServiceEffectSpecification{ ... }
        }
    };
}
```

Listing 4.13: Template Specification of the Adaptor template.

Applicability: The applicability of templates defines constraints for the usage of a template. For the *Adaptor* template such a constraint is defined by the requirement that a instantiation point should be of type *interface*.

Example: An example of an *Adaptor* is shown in Figure 4.16. This *Adaptor* provides an interface to the receiver and adapts its required interface to communicate with used middleware (*Active Component*) and require a lock for each request. This lock models the thread pool size used for the communication.

Template	Goal	Instantiation Point (Hook)
Delegator	Provides a wrapper for a required or provided interface and delegates additional information without adjusting the signature.	Interface
Coupled Adaptor/Delegator	Adapts two interfaces allowing their communication. Or in a case of delegation to allow them to use communication connection together without changing their signatures.	Interface
Synchroniser	Provides an interface requiring a software resource (thread pool, queue or semaphore).	Interface
Lock	Models a component providing a passive software resource (thread pool, queue, semaphore).	Passive Resource
Active	Provides a component with its own, independent control flow thread.	Component
Monitor	Adds a controller or monitor (e.g., mutex to all method calls allowing only a single thread to access the component at one time.)	Internal action

Table 4.1.: CBSE Transformation Templates.

Additional examples illustrating the instantiation point approach for model transformation templates are given in Table 4.1. The instantiation point types map known element types for specification of component-based architectures (e.g. components, interfaces, signatures, resources, etc.). A detailed description of these templates is provided in Section 4.6.2.5.

4.6.2.3. Metamodel for the Templates Definition

To define a framework supporting the definition and configuration of transformation templates, we need to describe them and their instantiation in a general way. This description is provided by means of a metamodel introduced in this section and illustrated by Figure 4.17.

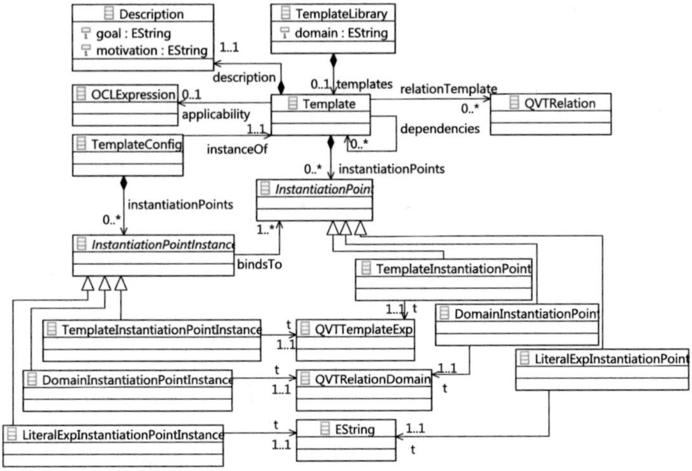

Figure 4.17.: The metamodel for the transformation templates.

As a main element of the transformation templates metamodel, we introduce the `Template` element. This element represents the concept of a transformation template in our terminology and defines a reconfigurable and reusable transformation fragment for the model transformation generation. The `Description` of a template contains a definition of the `Goal` of the template as well as a textual `Motivation` for the `Template` definition. Each `Template` defines the applicability, or usage scenarios, by specifying an OCL `Constraint`. To be able to apply a template in a certain context, this constraint needs to evaluate to `true`. The `Template` element refers to a set of `Relations` from the QVT Relational metamodel. These relations form the basis of the template as they will be parametrised by `InstantiationPoints` as defined below. Furthermore, the `Template` definition contains a set of `InstantiationPoints`. These instantiation points define possibilities for variations within the basic relations. A `InstantiationPoint` is defined by a reference to either a template expression (`TemplateExp`) or relation domain (`RelationDomain`).

These points are defined by subclasses of `InstantiationPoint` named `TemplateInstantiationPoint`, `DomainInstantiationPoint`, and `Literal-InstantiationPoint` (for the specification of variable literals within a template).

The association `dependencies` of the `Template` class expresses dependencies between transformation templates. Defined transformation templates depend on each other and therefore these constructs need access to results of required transformation templates.

In complex cases, the dependencies on a design template definition or its instance could mix. However this type of variations defines very complex transformation templates relations. The fine granular model provided by the introduced metamodel allows a low-effort definition of such dependencies. This is possible by the fine granular `InstantiationPoint` definitions and their sharing.

The binding of a template to an actual transformation fragment is done as soon as the template is referenced within an actual transformation fragment that is defined for a concrete feature model. The actual application of the transformation template is defined by the `TemplateConfig`. For each defined `InstantiationPoint` the template configuration includes *InstantiationPointInstances* which bind the *InstantiationPoint* to actual templates or relation domains specifications. *InstantiationPointInstances* can be assigned to multiple *InstantiationPoints* stemming from different transformation templates. This yields the possibility to combine transformation templates to build more complex model variations.

4.6.2.4. Implementation of HOT for Model Template Instantiation

The instantiation process presented in Listing 4.15 is realized using a HOT. It merges the transformation using the templates and creates a transformation based on the actual configuration given by the template configuration model.

```
transformation templateInstantiation(source:templateDefinition,
            config:templateDefinition, target: QVTRelation)
            extends CopyQVTRelation {
top relation Library2Transformation {
        n:String;
        checkonly domain source templateLib: templateLibrary {
            _domain = n };
        enforce domain target t: QVTRelation::RelationalTransformation {
          name = n + '_templateInstantiation' };
        where { MarkTargetTransformation(t); }
    }

relation MarkTargetTransformation {
        checkonly domain target t:QVTRelation::RelationalTransformation{};
    }

top relation AddTypedModels {
        checkonly domain source templateRep: templateRepository {
            modelParameter = mm: QVTBase::TypedModel {  }  };
        enforce domain target t: QVTRelation::RelationalTransformation {
            modelParameter = mmCopy: QVTBase::TypedModel { } };
        when {  Repository2Transformation(templateRep, t);
            Mark_QVTBase_TypedModel(mm, mmCopy); }
    }

top relation IntegrateRelations {
        n:EString;
        checkonly domain source templateConfig:
                            templateDefinition::templateConfig {
            instanceOf = template : templateDefinition::template {
                name = n,
                templateRelations = templateRel : QVTRelation::Relation {}
            }
        };
        enforce domain target targetRelation: QVTRelation::Relation {
          name = n + '_template_' + templateRel.name ,
          _transformation = t : QVTBase::Transformation {}
        };
        when { MarkTargetTransformation(t);
            Mark_QVTRelation_Relation(templateRel, targetRelation); }
    }
    ...
}
```

Listing 4.14: Higher-order transformation for instantiating templates.

The first step of the Template Instantiation is the creation of a copy of the relations that were specified within the template. Therefore, we use a generated copy transformation for the QVT-Relations metamodel. The `Mark-QVTRelationRelation` relation that is used here is a part of this generated transformation. Using this, it is possible to retrieve the copied instance of a given original relation. For each class in the corresponding metamodel such a relation exists. The template instantiation transformation extends this copy transformation. `Repository2Transformation` creates a new transformation that will then contain the configured templates. Furthermore, `AddTypedModels` adds the model parameter of the transformation to the transformation as they were specified in the template repository. Each used and configured template is then added to the newly generated transformation by the `IntegrateRelations` relation. All other template relations that were copied from the template repository by the copy transformation will be ignored.

Further parts of the HOT are responsible for binding the instantiation points of the templates to the elements from the actual template configuration. Listing 4.15 shows the necessary relations for binding a `Template-InstantiationPoint`.

```
top relation BindTemplateInstantiationPoint {
    n:EString;
    instantiationPointBindings:OrderedSet(InstantiationPoint);
    checkonly domain source instantiationPoint :
                              templateDefinition::TemplateInstantiationPoint{
        name = n,
        relationTemplate = relationTemplate : QVTRelation::Relation {},
        template = instantiationTemplate : QVTTemplate::TemplateExp {}
    };
    checkonly domain config instantiationPointInstance :
                    templateDefinition::TemplateInstantiationPointInstance{
        bindsTo = instantiationPointBindings,
        template = instanceTemplate : QVTTemplate::TemplateExp {}
    };
    enforce domain target targetTemplate: QVTTemplate::TemplateExp {     };
    when { Mark_QVTTemplate_TemplateExp(instanceTemplate, targetTemplate);
           instantiationPointBindings->includes(instantiationPoint); }
```

```
    where {
        Mark_QVTTemplate_TemplateExp(instantiationTemplate, targetTemplate); }
}
    ...
```

Listing 4.15: Binding of template variation points.

An extension to the generated QVT-R copy transformation is made by overriding the generated copy relations for those elements that may be instantiation points in the templates. In the example above this would be all copy relations that inherit from `TemplateExp`. Listing 4.16 shows how this is done for the `ObjectTemplateExp`. This extension will cause the copy transformation to omit all `TemplateExp` that are instantiation points during the copy process. For each binding that is configured in the template configuration the `BindTemplateVariationPoint` relation in Listing 4.15 will call the `Mark_QVTTemplate_TemplateExp` relation. Due to the functionality of the copy transformation this will cause the copy relations to treat the substituted template as the copy of the original and will assign it to all points in the template's copy where the original template was used. The copy transformations are created applying the Routine pattern.

```
—Override the Generated Copy Rule:
top relation Copy_QVTTemplate_ObjectTemplateExp
    overrides Copy_QVTTemplate_ObjectTemplateExp{
    checkonly domain source instantiationPoint:
                    templateDefinition::TemplateInstantiationPoint{
        template = instantiationTemplate : QVTTemplate::TemplateExp {} };
    checkonly domain source sourceObjectTemplateExp:
                            QVTTemplate::ObjectTemplateExp{ };
    enforce domain target targetObjectTemplateExp:
                            QVTTemplate::ObjectTemplateExp{ };
    when { not (sourceObjectTemplateExp = instantiationTemplate); }
    where {
        Mark_QVTTemplate_ObjectTemplateExp(
                sourceObjectTemplateExp, targetObjectTemplateExp); }
}
    [...]
```

Listing 4.16: Overriding Copy Rules.

4.6.2.5. Further Transformation Templates

The Delegator Template GOAL: Provide a wrapper for a required or provided interface and delegate its functionality based on the unchanged signature.

MOTIVATION: A delegator can be used for example, when for each request a semaphore lock should be asked to allow access the semaphore provider service before allowing the request to reach the interface.

SPECIFICATION: This template is specified by a relation that creates a delegator component that requires or provides delegated interface to other components in the system. Additionally a delegator could request services from other components. This template could be used to generated the initial structures for this.

```
transformation CBSE_Delegator (source: CBSE, target: CBSE) {

top relation Delegator_template_CreateDelegator {
        checkonly domain source delegatedInterface:{
        };
        enforce domain target delegatorComponent:{
            name = <delegatorName:LiteralExpVariationPoint>
            requiredRoles = reqRole:RequiredRole{
                requiredInterface = delegatedInterface }
            providedRoles = provRole:ProvidedRole{
                providedInterface = delegatedInterface }
            serviceEffectSpecifications =
                seff:ServiceEffectSpecification{...}
        }
    };
}
```

Listing 4.17: Template Specification of the Delegator template.

APPLICABILITY: For the *Delegator* template it is required that a instantiation point is not of type *interface*.

EXAMPLE: The example of a *Delegator* is shown in Figure 4.16 as an additional template. This *Delegator* provides interfaces to the request receiver with the same interface.

The Coupled Adaptor/Delegator template **GOAL:** To adapt two interfaces and to allow their communication. Or, in a case of delegation, to allow them to use communication connection together without changing their provided functionality.

MOTIVATION: When it is needed to build a connector between two communicating components or to build a chain of delegators to access certain external functionality in a certain state of message delivery.

SPECIFICATION: This template is specified by a relation that creates two *Delegator* or *Adaptor* components that mirror their adapted or delegated interface.

APPLICABILITY: For the *Adaptor/Delegator* template is required that instantiation point should/shouldn't be of type *interface*.

EXAMPLE: The example of a *Coupled Adaptor* is shown in Figure 4.16. This construct allows sender and receiver to use the same active component.

The Synchroniser template **GOAL:** To provide an interface requiring a software resource (thread pool, queue or semaphore).

MOTIVATION: When component has to acquire a lock before accessing a certain service and release a lock when finished.

SPECIFICATION: This template is specified by a relation that extends in a model already existing component with an interface requiring an external service providing acquire() and release() on a lock resource holded be called component. This specification implies an existence of an *Lock* manager in a system.

```
transformation CBSE_Synchroniser(source: CBSE, target: CBSE) {

top relation Synchroniser_template_CreateSynchroniser {
        checkonly domain source synchronizedInterface:{
```

```
        };
        enforce domain target synchroniserComponent:{
            name = <synchroniserName:LiteralExpInstantiationPoint>
            requiredRoles = reqRole:RequiredRole{
                requiredInterface = synchronizedInterface,
                requiredInterface = <lockName:TemplateInstantiationPoint> }
            providedRoles = provRole:ProvidedRole{
                providedInterface = synchronizedInterface }
            serviceEffectSpecifications =
                seff:ServiceEffectSpecification{ ... }
        }
    };
}
```

Listing 4.18: Template Specification of Synchroniser template.

APPLICABILITY: For the *Synchroniser* template is required that instantiation point should be of type `LockManagerReference`.

EXAMPLE: The example of a *Synchroniser* is shown in Figure 4.16 and illustrated by extention to receiver adaptor component with an additional synchronisation interface.

The Active component template **GOAL:** To provide a wrapper for a functionality defined as internal action of a component behaviour.

MOTIVATION: When it is needed to model a component with a complex internal behaviour.

SPECIFICATION: This template is specified by a relation that creates an *Active* component that requires or provides a delegated interface to the another components, depending on a developer specification. In case of this template is the template only a frame for implementation, it is the most complex template with no restrictions on instantiation points.

APPLICABILITY: There are no restrictions for this template. Consequently this template requires higher user interaction to implement.

EXAMPLE: The example of a *Active* component is shown in Figure 4.16 and illustrated by a shared component, providing a common functionality (e.g. middleware).

The Lock manager template **GOAL:** To model a component providing a passive software resource (thread pool, queue, semaphore).

MOTIVATION: When a synchronization mechanism based on a lock strategy is used in a system.

SPECIFICATION: This template is specified by a relation that creates *Lock* component that provides an interface with two signatures *acquire()* and *release()* on its internal passive resource.

```
transformation CBSE_LockManager (source: CBSE, target: CBSE) {

top relation LockManager_template_CreateLock {
        checkonly domain source appRepository:{
        };
        enforce domain target lockComponent:{
            name = <lockName:LiteralExpInstantiationPoint>
            requiredRoles = reqRole:RequiredRole{}
            providedRoles = provRole:ProvidedRole{
                providedInterface = lockInterface }
            serviceEffectSpecifications = acquireLock
                seff:ServiceEffectSpecification{ ... }
            serviceEffectSpecifications = releaseLock
                seff:ServiceEffectSpecification{ ... }
            passiveResource = lock{
                <lock:TemplateInstantiationPoint> }
    };
}
```

Listing 4.19: Template Specification of Lock manager template.

APPLICABILITY: For the *Lock* manager template is required that the instantiation point is of type *passiveResource*.

EXAMPLE: The example of a *Lock* is shown in Figure 4.16. This lock manager provides, for example, a queue for competing consumers.

The Monitor template **GOAL:** To provide a wrapper for simple monitor functionality.

MOTIVATION: When it is needed to model a component that only gains and stores data, or provides some timing control. For example a clock component required by a connector or accessing middleware, providing a control interface externally to set a clock and providing an interface internally for other components in assembly to ask a clock.

SPECIFICATION: This template is specified by a relation that creates a *Monitor* component that requires or provides a delegated interface to the another component. This component has only a simple internal action defined and is creating processing delay through computation.

APPLICABILITY: For the *Monitor* template is required that variation point should be of type *internal action*.

EXAMPLE: The example of a *Monitor* is shown in Figure 4.16 as an additional template. This monitor provides, for example, a clock for a connector.

4.6.3. Summary

The introduced HOT Template Instantiation pattern allows to build a classical SPL for transformations using template-based approach. The Template Instantiation pattern allows to automate development and supports reuse of transformation fragments in completion-based approaches. In the following section, we will shortly discuss other HOT patterns and later using here introduced patterns we will build a chain of HOT patterns to fully support model completions.

4.7. CHILIES: Chains of HOT patterns

In some complex scenarios, it is useful to compose multiple HOT patterns in a chain. Figure 4.18 shows an example of such a composition where a transformation is generated using all three introduced patterns: (i) HOT_1 Routine generates a frame (copy rules), (ii) HOT_2 Composite overrides some of the copy rules and adds custom rules dependent on configuration, (iii) HOT_3 Template overrides some of the rules and adds template instances.

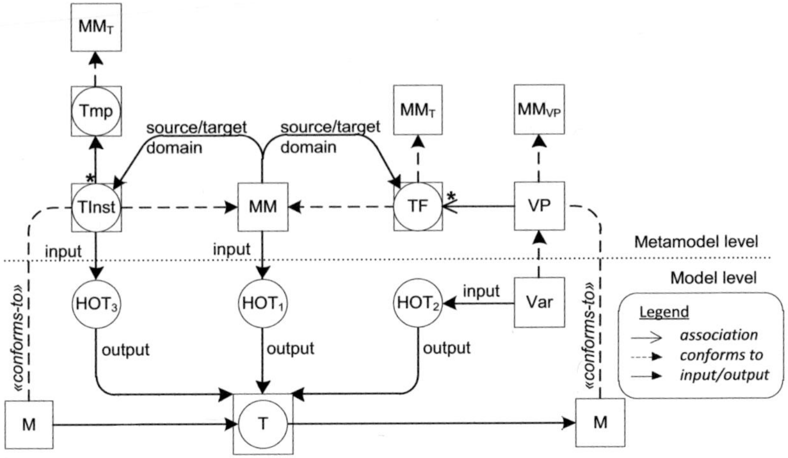

Figure 4.18.: Chain of HOT patterns: HOT_1 - Routine, HOT_2- Composite, HOT_3-Template

Similarly, a deeper view on the process of completion generation (c.f. Figure 4.19) shows the dependencies and connections between the concepts introduced above. The process depends on the specification of several inputs for HOTs, which build the HOT Chain.

The transformation fragment composition is realized using a Model Completion HOT, illustrated on a Figure 4.19. The first input is a *Feature Model* with attached *Transformation Fragments* (*Custom Rules*). These fragments are used by a Composite HOT for the actual transformation generation. It merges the transformation fragments that are annotated to the feature model nodes together creating the final completion transformation. The second input is the actual *Feature Configuration*, which defines which features are selected as well as the values of feature attributes. In contrast to an in-place transformation, a completion transformation may also be specified to create a new model where the completions are applied. In this case, the completion transformation extends a copy transformation (*Frame*) generated by the Routine HOT. As we rely on QVT Relations for the implementation of our transformations which does not provide native support for copy transformations, we use the Routine HOT to automatically create a copy transformation from the metamodel of the application model. The Composite HOT includes the *Transformation Fragments* into the generated copy transformation. Custom rules will then replace the standard copy rules for the corresponding metamodel element.

The goal of the templates is to ease the custom rules development. This is achieved through instantiation of *Transformation Templates* from *Template Library* on a place of transformation fragments in the feature model. Transformation templates are stored in a *Template Library* (cf. Figure 4.19). New *Custom Rules* can be specified instantiating and composing the existing *Templates*. Furthermore, templates are configurable by a set of parameter values. Based on the template and its configuration, the Template HOT creates *Template Instances* and adds the necessary rules to the completion transformation.

The result of the HOT Chain is a *Completion Transformation* that when applied to an *Architectural Model* generates the corresponding *Completed Architectural Model*. The line *Meta-Level Boundary* separates the generation of the transformation (domain engineering phase) and its application (software engineering phase).

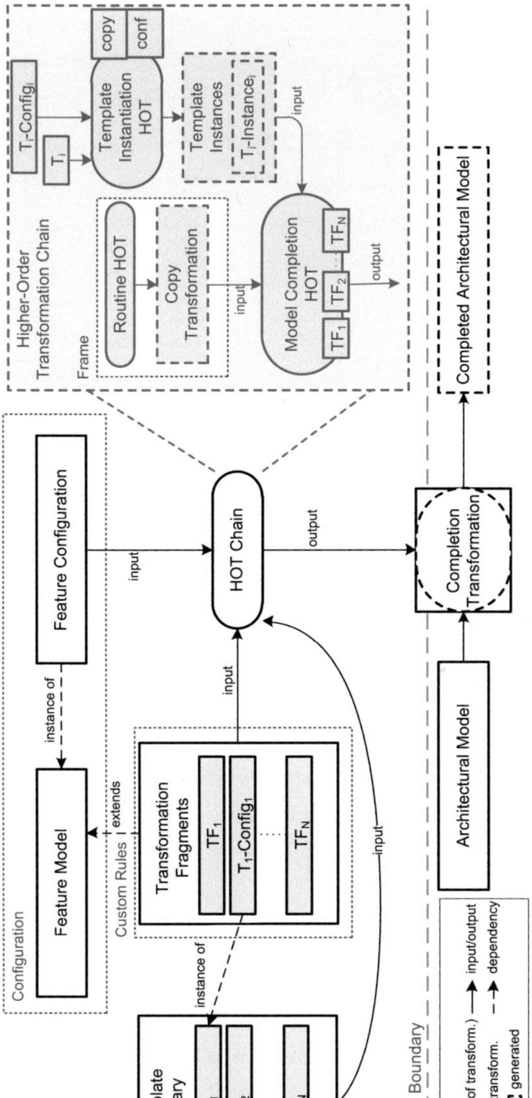

Figure 4.19.: HOT Chain to support Model Completions in MDSPE Application Scenario

4.8. Discussion

In the following, we discuss the assumptions and limitations of the contributions presented in this chapter. The experience in the area of HOT applications is still missing since transformations on higher abstraction levels are not extensively used so far. Despite the advantages in simplifying the development of variable transformations with HOT patterns, there are also some limitations that need to be discussed.

Complexity of HOTs Creating a HOT is not an easy task. Especially as the HOT engineer has to think on two different levels using probably the same language constructs. Developers need to get accustomed to thinking on a meta-level, and write/modify abstract syntax. HOTs naturally have a higher complexity coming along with power of abstraction. Therefore, development of HOTs can be error prone and should only be conducted by experienced transformation engineers.

Debuggability This issue is not a new one, as it occurs whenever software language artefacts are subject to automated modification. In these cases, debugging can be a problem. Developers work and develop on a certain development version of an artefact (either also a transformation or some other artefact, for example configuration, from which a transformation will be derived). However, the debugger of the transformation engine will execute and observe only the generated and woven transformation. Hence, a transformation developer will need to understand the generated transformation in order to be able to debug it. This can lead to confusion and additional effort for understanding these modifications when the developer needs to debug the transformation. To alleviate this issue, a debugger that is capable of mapping the debug information to the higher level artefact is required. A specialised debugger would be needed if debugging should be possible on the meta level.

Routine HOT pattern This pattern is currently only implemented for the Ecore metamodels. The Routine HOT requires an Ecore metamodel on input and generates a QVT-R transformation on output. However, the extension of this HOT for other relational transformation languages is only a question of implementation.

Composite HOT pattern The assumption, we took by this HOT pattern is that all transformation fragments are composable. Although, the composability of relational transformations is straight-forward in comparison to the operation languages, we require a valid design of feature model on input. The valid design of feature model is described in the following section.

Valid design of feature model The constraints for composition of transformation fragments in the Composite HOT pattern require a valid feature model to function correctly. A valid feature model does not include:

- Nested inclusive-OR structures – such structures increase the complexity of disambiguation rules exponentially, because the related fragments have to consider all possible combinations of all nested features in the inclusive-OR sub-tree. Our assumption is that such structures result from invalid identification of relations between features by domain analyst during modelling of the domain.
- Cyclic/Negated dependencies – the usage of the constraints in the feature model is limited and does not allow to create cyclic or negated dependencies between two features, thus, two DEPENDS-constraints in opposite direction or two constraints, one EXCLUDE and one DEPENDS, between two features are not allowed.
- Incomplete relations in feature effects – the relations in feature effects are required to be complete, thus, include everything (e.g., all opening and closing brackets) needed for their valid execution

in a transformation engine, only missing parts could be pre/post-conditions or variables, which are parametrised and do not danger the relations validity.

Usage of declarative transformations The declarative transformation definition is easily extendible with additional features, therefore, we limit our approach to this family of languages. This is achieved by separation of concerns and usage of declarative code as much as possible (minimizing usage of imperative code). Declarative code is very suitable for generative approaches. In our approach, we follow the philosophy of modular and declarative transformation rules with implicit execution order.

Template HOT pattern The Template pattern builds on the existence of templates for certain domain, in our case CBSE domain. The templates we introduced help to create parts of the models, but some of them have to be completed manually, for example the internal behaviour of the Adaptor template. We do not consider the templates applicable in general, they are dependent on a domain and a purpose of the model. The generality of the templates is out of scope for this thesis.

Composability of HOTs The usage of QVT-R to implement HOTs and completion transformations is motivated by the special properties of relational languages, especially composability. There are various approaches to support model transformation composability, either they are based on internal or external composition of transformations. An transformation implemented in relational transformation language consists of a number of mapping rules. These mappings may be combined by calling, or other facilities, such as inheritance, merge and disjunction. These strategies are used for internal composition of transformations. The composition of transformations as black-box artefacts is called external composition. We limit our approach to the external composition of HOTs to form a transformation chain. The internal or rule-based composition was not considered in this work. In the case of transformation chain, the composition is straightforward with assumption that the interfaces fit. We assume that the HOTs are implemented in a such way that they can be composed together (i.e., output of previous HOT is of the same type as input of the next one). In addition, it would be suitable to have possibility to to pass parameters to the transformations and the possibility to retrieve the output of a transformation and to pass as input to the consequent transformation.

4.9. Summary

In this chapter, we introduced a set of HOT patterns to solve different goals as a part of complex model-driven processes. Despite their complexity, HOTs have the potential of solving problems in an efficient way. Especially when a lot of variability needs to be managed within a transformation project, lifting this variability to a higher level can ease the development of otherwise complex transformations (see patterns 4.5 and 4.6). HOTs enable a better separation of concerns and therefore better maintainability of the employed transformations. In scenarios where a large amount of manual effort for a relatively simple task can be avoided, HOTs also unfold their potential (see Section 4.4). Here, otherwise tedious and error prone tasks can be easily automated using a HOT-based approach.

Furthermore, we described the automated support of completion transformation development using the presented HOT patterns. Using this approach the transformation generation phase in the Completion-based Software Engineering (see Chapter 3) is fully *automated*. In the next chapter, we focus on the realisation of the completion library. Additionally, we discuss the execution of completions in sequences.

5. Completions for Software Performance Engineering

In the previous two chapters, we discussed the Model Completion Concept and its realisation through composing HOT patterns for different goals. In this chapter, we discuss integration of completions in the *Completion Library*. The structure and usage of this library is the main topic of this chapter. The structure of the Completion Library supports reduction of application conflicts in the sequence of completions. Moreover, we introduce a set of completions for MDSPE. This initial set of completions is focused on the concurrency design patterns and targeted to support developers to create complex models of concurrent systems.

The leading challenge of this chapter is:

How to structure the Completion Library to reduce possible conflicts in an application of multiple completions?

The remainder of this chapter will be organized as follows. Section 5.1 introduces the application context and motivates the structuring of the Completion Library. In Section 5.2.3 we describe the method for the reduction and resolution of conflicts in application of multiple completions. In addition, Section 5.3 presents an initial set of completions for concurrency design patterns. We discuss limitation of presented approach in Section 5.4 and, finally, we summarize the contributions in Section 5.5.

5.1. Motivation

Completions transparently integrate low-level details that affect a system's quality (e.g. performance impact of *compression* or *encryption* configuration) into component-based architectural models, using model-to-model transformations. When multiple completions are to be applied, the necessary completion transformations are executed in a chain. In such scenarios, application conflicts (i.e., *compression* before *encryption* influences resulting data volume, and the other way around) between different completions are likely. The dependencies among completions define where and when certain completions can be woven into the model. The execution order of the completions may affect the target model in a way that the following completions are not applicable any more or that the analysis results are altered. Therefore, the application order of completions must be determined unambiguously in order to reduce such conflicts. Problems of conflicting transformations and their application order have already been addressed in the area of model-driven development [82]. However, in the domain of software performance engineering, quality attributes captured by the architectural models have to be considered as an additional dimension of conflict. The execution order of a set of completions can affect the quality predictions for the resulting architectural models. Thus, the knowledge about the quality impact of a particular order of completions can be used to resolve conflicts and to identify the suitable order in which completions have to be applied to achieve the best overall quality of the system.

One approach to handle conflicts is that software architects decide on the suitable transformation order manually. However, this approach is time-consuming, can be error-prone, and is likely to result in suboptimal designs. Especially, with growing number of completions the complexity of this decision grows. Therefore, a semi-automated and structured solution supporting software architects should reduce these conflicts in completion order and help with their resolution.

We define a systematic approach to identify, reduce or avoid conflicts between completions that are applied to the same model. The technique reduces conflicts, based on the development role separation and locally optimises the order of completions in a sequence. For this purpose, we clarify the roles in the development process responsible for specific completions, when additional information to reduce conflicts is necessary. The principle of development role separation is mirrored in the structure of the completion library. Furthermore, in Section 7 we validate this approach by applying it to an architecture model of a component-based business information system and analyse the impact of different sequences of completions.

The main scientific contribution of this chapter is located in the MDSPE context and can be summarised as follows:

Structured Completion Library for Software Performance Engineering

- **Reusing expert knowledge:** The decisions about the required steps going from an abstract model *Abs* (cf., Figure 3.2), based on a set of initial requirements, to an abstract model *Abs′*, suitable for required purpose (e.g. performance prediction), requires a lot of domain-specific expert knowledge (e.g. for performance prediction it is knowledge about performance-relevant implementation details). Additionally, the same activities are often repeated, e.g. usage of the same design pattern or integration of the same middleware platform. Standardization of possible design decisions in a form of reusable constructs (e.g., completions) allows reusing and tracing design decisions. This allows to build a 'Performance Knowledge Base' as envisioned by Woodside et al. [172]. Design decision are explicitly modelled as a part of a development already on the abstract level, and mapped to the requirements. Models with trace to design decisions considering even implementation details not only provide better predictions, but can help to document managerial decisions (e.g. which middleware will be used) on the abstract level. Therefore, we provide a support for completion library where completion encapsulating expert-knowledge can be registered. In addition, we provide a initial set of completions, which allow to reuse expert knowledge about modelling of the concurrency design patterns.

- **Completion conflict reduction:** Because multiple application of completions on the same model could can lead to conflicts in their application, we developed a completion reduction method. Completions are realised as model transformations. Completion transformations executed in a sequence may not permit or require certain changes specified by a following transformation, in other words, the following transformation would not be applicable. We call such conflict a *validity conflict*. In addition in the SPE domain, the order of completions in a sequence can influence the results of predictions, thus, two permutations in a sequence can provide different results. We call this kind of conflict a *quality conflict*. Therefore, we designed a structured library of completions that supports reduction and resolution of these conflicts. Our method for conflict reduction builds on the relation between the transformations and the metamodel. The quality conflicts are resolved with the help of quality heuristics.

5.2. Structured Completion Library for Conflict Reduction

Model Completions are implemented as model-to-model transformations and as such they inherit all their properties. One specific property of model transformations is their connection to the metamodel they are developed for, the, so called, metamodel coverage (see Section 6). By studying the metamodel coverage of transformations it is possible to identify which model elements are modified by the transformations.

Our observation is that metamodels are often structured. It is a good practice to structure metamodels into packages grouping together semantically-related elements. This package structure often follows the separation of concerns principle, for example, the structure of packages in the PCM metamodel follows the domains of the CBSE development roles introduced in Section 2.2.1, where each development role has a separate package set. When it is possible to identify such separation in a structure of metamodel, then it is possible to identify transformations covering only these separate domains. For example, a completion applied by a system architect can modify only instances of model elements belonging to the domain of system architect and therefore such completion is not in conflict with completion applied by a component developer. This simple idea could be applied to manage any transformations developed for a structured metamodel. We apply this idea to reduce conflicts of completions for performance engineering and we use the PCM metamodel for this goal.

The introduced approach for reducing and resolving conflicts between executed performance completions builds on a few systematic steps. First, we identify responsibility domains for the CBSE development roles in PCM. Second, we minimize the conflicting set and, third, we resolve remaining conflicts using quality-based heuristics. These heuristics give an indication of most advantageous sequence, however, because we analyse the sequences only locally and not in a context of whole system, the final resolution step requires an interaction from user, who has to deal only with small reduced set of conflicting completions. In the following, we describe the problem of conflicts between executed performance completions on the model level formally.

5.2.1. Formalisation

In the previous chapter, we discussed formalisation of model completions, related transformations and their variants. In this part of formalisation, we summarize necessary definitions and focus on the chains of completions.

Before completing a model element, the completion is instantiated according to a selected variant. Possible variants of a $c_{ThreadManagement}$ com-

pletion can be for instance $v^{TP_{static}}_{c_{ThreadManagement}}$. The instantiation results into a completion transformation
$t^{c_{PCM \lhd ThreadManagement}}$, which can finally be applied to a pivot element. After application of a completion transformation we create a valid model element (or subsystem). Thus, the next completion can be applied and multiple applications of different completions in a *completion chain* is possible.

Let now $C = \{c_i | i \in I\}$ be a finite set of available completions, that we call a *completion library*. Then, V_i is a countable set of possible variants v_i^j for one completion c_i (Section 4.2.4). For example, the $V_{locking}$ of a completion $c_{locking}$ (enhancing a component A with a critical section locking strategy) is $V_{locking} = \{v^{scoped}_{locking}, v^{double-checked}_{locking}, \ldots, v^{strategized}_{locking}\}$. Each variant is realised as a completion transformation t^C that integrates chosen v_i^j into the source model. The transformation is generated based on a configuration and completion definition including specification of pivot element and feature diagram ($c_i = (e, fd_i)$, see Section 4.2.4).

This section discusses a sequences of transformations, that represent an ordered chain of completion transformations, as presented for model-to-model transformations in Section 4.2.4. As mentioned above, each model element $e \in E$ (for the definition of E see Section 4.2.4) can be enhanced by multiple applications of (different) completions, i.e. a chain of completion transformations.

Consistent Set of Completions: For the purpose of completion chain definition, we define a set of possible completion variations (or completion instances) in a chain as

$$CI = \{v_i^j \mid i \in I, v_i^j \in V_i\},$$

and limit that a *completion set* $CS \subseteq CI$ is *consistent* only if each completion in CS occurs in at most one variation, thus

$$\forall v_i^j, v_k^l \in CS : i \neq k \Rightarrow v_i^j \neq v_k^l$$

Chains of Completion Transformations: Thus, given a consistent completion set $CS \subseteq CI$, a *completion chain cc over CS* is defined as

$$cc = c_{i_1} \circ c_{i_2} \circ ... \circ c_{i_n}, c_{i_j} \in CS,$$

where '$\circ$' defines an external composition of transformations in form of a chain of transformations. The chain of transformations t^*_{cc} is then executed as follows:

$$t^*_{cc} : conf(MM) \overset{t^C_{i_1}}{\rightarrow} conf(MM) \overset{t^C_{i_2}}{\rightarrow} \cdots \overset{t^C_{i_n}}{\rightarrow} conf(MM),$$

$$where\ t^C_{i_j} \text{ instantiates } c_{i_j} \in CS$$

Note that not all sequences of execution of a completion set CS on a given element e need to be valid for the system model. Some of the completion chains cc over CS may result in an invalid set of model elements $cc(e)$, not satisfying a given set of validity constraints. Such constraints can be specified in terms of rules or grammars, and can be verified on both the resulting elements $cc(e)$ and the completion order $cc = c_{i_1} \circ c_{i_2} \circ ... \circ c_{i_n}, c_{i_j} \in CS$, since some of the orders can be a priori forbidden. In our formalization, we use $CC(CS,e)$ to denote the set of all *valid* completion chains over CS for element e.

For example, the set CI for the completion $c_{locking}$ is defined as $CI = \{v^{scoped}_{locking}, v^{double-checked}_{locking}, v^{strategized}_{locking}\}$, and a consistent completion set can be $CS = \emptyset$, $CS = \{v^{scoped}_{locking}\}$, or others. When we assume CS includes an additional completion configuration of the completion $c_{messaging}$, e.g. $CS = \{v^{scoped}_{locking}, v^{conn\_1:N}_{messaging}\}$, we would identify two possible completion chains $cc_1 = v^{conn\_1:N}_{messaging} \circ v^{scoped}_{locking}$ and $cc_2 = v^{scoped}_{locking} \circ v^{conn\_1:N}_{messaging}$.

Completion Conflicts: Based on previous definitions, a *completion chain* cc_i is an ordered set of completion transformations $< t^C_1, t^C_2, ..., t^C_N >$ $, i \in I$. The *completion chain* cc_i is in *conflict* with $cc_j; i, j \in I$, when an order of completion execution in $cc_i \neq cc_j$ and the validity of the model structure (*validity conflict*) or the result of analysis (*quality conflict*) is different for each of the chain definitions.

Finally, we say that a set of all completion chains over CC is *conflicting on the element* $e \in E$, if there are two completion chains $cc_i, cc_j \in CC$ such that

$$Q(cc_i(e)) \neq Q(cc_j(e)),$$

where Q is a quality function, e a pivot element, and $cc(e)$ an element e completed by a completion chain cc applied to the model. Here, Q specifies the quality semantics of the set of model elements $cc_i(e)$, resp. $cc_j(e)$, which result from e after applying all the completion configurations in cc_i (resp. cc_j) to it, in the left-to-right order. Note that, we are interested to apply the definition only to the sets of valid completion chains $CC(CS,e)$ over a consistent completion set CS and model element $e \in E$, but for the reason of generality, we define it for a wider domain (any set of completion chains).

5.2.2. Method for Reduction of Completion Validity Conflicts

This section introduces the method to minimize the conflicting set in a sequence of completions. To reduce possible conflict between completions, we have to investigate, for each new completion, its dependencies to other completions already registered in the library. We reflect the need for identification and reduction of conflicts by introducing three levels of *conflict* reduction:

1. **Roles and Responsibilities Separation**: The first resolution question is *"Who is able to provide all necessary information to use and configure the completion?"*. The selected role in the development process has to have all necessary input data to specify the completion's configuration during software design. Furthermore, he/she has to profit from completion usage. Ideally, the assignment of completions to roles will lead to identification of disjointed sets of com-

pletions. Each role is only responsible for the completions in one disjointed set.

Each time a new completion is introduced, we analyse its dependencies to other already known completions. Therefore, we focus on a related group of completions where conflicts are more likely. This way, possible conflicts are limited to the completions in responsibility of one role. Additionally, separation of concerns based on the roles in the development process creates a hierarchy (identifying domains of concern) in the metamodel of used architecture description language.

To focus our reasoning, we categorise completions based on the metamodel elements they could be assigned to. This way we reduce possible conflicts on a metamodel level. The proposed categorisation maps the roles in the CBSE development process [102] to groups of completions. It is best practice in metamodel design to structure the metamodel considering the development process the metamodel will used in and the different subdomains or technology domains. This allows to identify independent parts of the metamodel in competence of one development role. The metamodel part that belongs to one development role is called *cluster*. This is illustrated by a hierarchy of `packages` in the PCM metamodel in Figure 5.1.

The goal of this step is to identify sets of completions where conflicts are possible. Based on the metamodel structure, we can identify completion transformations their input and output model are created from instances of metamodel elements belonging to two different clusters. Therefore, two such transformations could not result in a validity conflict. In Figure 5.1 the transformations T_3 and T_4 are in conflict, because they modify model elements from the same cluster. The transformation T_2 is an example of a limitation of the introduced resolution approach, we do not allow completions to change a model in a responsibility of other role. This way, we define disjunct sets of completions C_i. For each two completions $c_k \in C_i$ and $c_l \in C_j; C_i \neq C_j$ conflicts are not possible. Only in a case of completions located in the same metamodel cluster, conflicts are possible. In this case, we have to proceed to the next level and further specify affected elements.

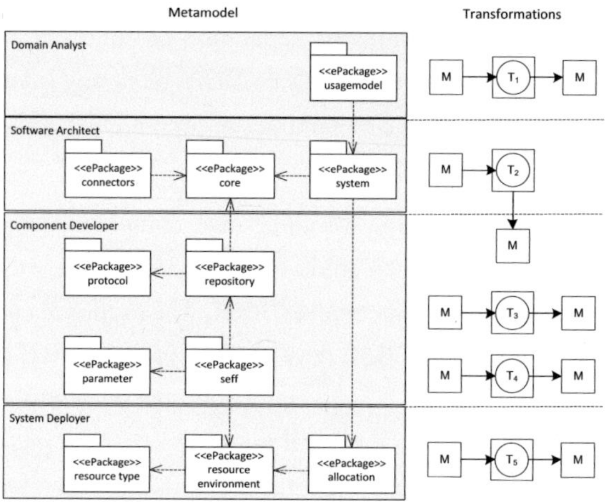

Figure 5.1.: A role hierarchy in the PCM metamodel.

2. **Conflicting Model Elements Identification**: If conflicts can occur, we further analyse the question *"Which model elements are affected?"*. For this purpose we have to know how the completions are modelled and at which places of the architecture they can be applied. We can identify affected elements as a difference between source and target model. Identified elements specify more exact locations where conflicts may occur.

   The evaluation of completion chain *cc* for *conflict-potential* is a function

$$\phi : T \to S,$$

where domain S is the set of possible conflicting instances of meta-model elements. For example, when evaluating order in a sequence of completions for locking and stateful wrapper (both of them should be applied to the same component) we identify on the model level the possible conflict set that includes all elements needed in component and its behavior definition. This results in further separation of conflict domains and decreasing the number of completions that could introduce conflict on a model level. We define sets of potentially conflicting completions (*conflict space*):

$$ConflictSpace := \{t_i, t_i\}$$

where $i \neq j$ and t_i potentially conflicts with t_j on a model element $e \in S$, where S is a set of conflicting elements orthogonal to the hierarchy from the previous level.

Since we apply completions to component-based software systems, we identify the model elements of component-based architectures that can be refined, and discuss the completions applied to them. We assume three types of model elements (the main architectural elements of CBSE) that can be completed: *components*, *connectors*, and the *infrastructure*. Thus, for our domain we can define $S = \{$component, connector, infrastructure$\}$.

While there may be many component and connector elements in the model, there is always at most one infrastructure element to consider from a completions point of view. All these model elements are assumed to be *independent* for the completions, i.e. the order of completing two different elements within the model does not influence the result. In the following, we describe the model settings, to which we frame our problem.

Components are black-box (or sometimes grey-box) entities characterized by the services they provide to others and the services they require from third parties. In our approach, we can deal with components in two ways. In the first case, we assume that components are entirely black-box. Thus, completion-based model refinements are not allowed to change the internals of the components (or its services). Instead, completions attach wrappers to the components that delegate the same interfaces (require and provide the same services as the original component) and include additional quality-relevant details to the service specification. In the second case, we assume that components are grey-box and their behaviour is captured on an abstract level by a behaviour specification. Completions must not change a component's behaviour with respect to its functionality. However, they may extend the behaviour specification so that only its non-functional properties are affected. For example, a completion can add a particular locking strategy to a critical section around a component's behavioural specification.

Connectors define communication links among components and model interaction of components along these links. Additionally, the communication between remote components can be configured through connector properties. A connector can have a complex internal structure and implement non-trivial interaction logic. Therefore, the connector layer can be viewed as a net of independent connector subsystems connecting the components. The connector completions integrate independent connector subsystems into the architecture. These connector subsystems do not change the connector model from the view of interacting components. As such connector subsystem could be considered as independent.

The hardware environment forms the system's *infrastructure* and is typically understood as a separate layer of a component-based architecture, underlying the component assembly. Thanks to this, infrastructure completions integrate usage of services provided by lower-layers of software stack, and hence allow to adjust the environment independently.

After this resolution step is the resulting set of completions is minimized on completions applied by the same role to the same model element. Thus, we proceed to the last level of conflict resolution.

3. **Completion Dependencies Identification**: At the end, we need to answer the question *"What are the dependencies to other completions from the same conflict space?"*. From the previous levels, that already identified the roles and model element types the completions enhance, we get a reduced set of completions. Further, we need to identify their intersections (affected model elements) on instance level. At this point a interaction with user is required, hence, the application of completion is system specific from this point on. Users can generalise dependencies between completions by definition of mutual exclusion or require relationships in a completion specification in the time of completion registration. Our assumption at this point is that remaining set of completions applied by the same role to the same instance of model element is so small that it is possible to resolve the validity conflicts manually.

The presented approach allows to reduce and avoid model completions conflicts on a model-level (*Conflicting Model Elements Identification*) or meta-model level (*Roles and Responsibilities Separation*). Thus, the complexity of conflicts is decreased (avoiding non-determinism of conflicts similar as in graph grammars). The effort for manual conflict resolution is minimised on a small set of model elements and the number of cases when the resolution of validity conflict cannot be automated.

5.2.3. Method for Resolution of Completion Quality Conflicts

To allow the reasoning about completion order, we need to decide on the abstraction filter that allows us to identify the preferred completion order, based on the evaluation of the architectures resulting from the application of the completions. In our case, we employ a *performance-driven view* on the system model.

Performance is a pervasive quality of software systems, everything affects it [173], from the software itself to all underlying layers, such as operating system, middleware, hardware, communication networks, etc. Within the domain of performance engineering, we focus on the *response time*, *throughput* and *resource utilization* as the main quality properties. These properties can be related to the identified architectural elements as follows. *Components* are characterized by the response time and throughput of the services they provide, and partially by the resource utilization during their execution. *Connectors* are characterized by the response time of the communication over the connectors, and the throughput and utilization of the link they employ. The *infrastructure* is characterized by the utilization of the resources that form the infrastructure. The contribution of this section is then the examination of the order of *completions* in a *completion chain*, which could be optimised and used to improve the design of future system or for fine-tuning quality attributes of the system during development.

For the domain of component-based performance models, this section defines the quality function Q employed by the heuristics for the resolution of completion conflict, and justifies the locally-oriented definition of a completion conflict. The justification is based on the understanding of performance interdependence of completed model elements. Finally, the observations are compiled into a method of completion order definition and conflict resolution within this context.

5.2.3.1. Quality Heuristics

In the following, we study the performance semantics of completions based on the quality heuristics for the completed elements. The performance semantics of a completion is defined as the completion's impact on the completed element's performance (observation of a decrease in response time or utilisation, and an increase in throughput has a positive impact on a performance). To this end, we define quality functions used to evaluate different completions. We specify three quality functions for the three model elements that can be annotated with completions in component-based architectures. These quality functions specify heuristics for identification of a completion's performance impact, based on local evaluation. The exact performance evaluation with a global quality function would in large-scale systems be hardly feasible. For our problem, the locally defined functions (dependent on a single element) provide already enough information to decide about the performance semantic of the completion even for large-scale systems. The completions are locally applied (to specific model element) therefore this assumption holds. However, the optimisation of system-specific changes is the focus of multi-variant optimisation, such as [113]. In this work, we do not consider such change scenarios.

As defined in Section 5.2.3, the quality function $Q : E \rightarrow \mathbb{R}$ quantifies the quality of system *components*, *connectors* and the *infrastructure*, based on their performance impact, which is under our performance abstraction the primary metric for our architecture. Note that, the conflict definition relies on two simplifications, which are worth to be discussed. First, it relies on purely quantitative characterization of system model, not taking the resulting model structure into account. The reason for this lies in the employed abstraction of viewing the system model through its performance properties. Our experience shows that if the structural changes introduced to the model are significant, then they either result in an invalid set of model elements (and hence are detected during constraint checking), or influence the performance properties of the model, and hence are detected with Q anyway. Second, it localizes the conflicts only among completion chains executed on the same model element $e \in E$, disregarding from the dependencies on other elements in E. Thus, it provides only an indication (the accuracy of the values is not guaranteed) of the most suitable chain based on the direction of the heuristic. However, because of the locality principle our method provides a user with a short localised tests, which do not require to run overall system analysis.

Let $E = E_{comp} \cup E_{conn} \cup E_{infra}$ be the set of model elements representing *components*, *connectors* and *infrastructures* identified in system model. Then, the quality function $Q : E \rightarrow \mathbb{R}$ is based on the type of its argument. The positive semantic of this function is in the direction of smaller values and is defined as follows.

Component Quality Function:

$$\forall e \in E_{comp} : Q(e) = \sum_{s_i \in S} \frac{rt(s_i)}{thp(s_i)},$$

where S is the set of services provided by component e, $rt(s_i)$ is the mean response time of service s_i, and $thp(s_i)$ is the mean throughput of service s_i. We do not include service utilisation of underlying system resources in the component quality function, because it is highly dependent on the infrastructure level. This way we hold the quality function independent of the remaining elements, while still characterizing component quality from the user point of view.

Connector Quality Function:

$$\forall e \in E_{conn} : Q(e) = \frac{rt(e)}{thp(link)},$$

where $link$ is a communication resource (network) used by connector e, $thp(link)$ is the mean throughput of the link, and $rt(link)$ is the mean response time of the communication over the connector (round-trip), dependent on the communicating components. Note that, this definition is independent of the usage of the connector by the connected components. The connector usage is defined by the communicating components. Therefore their quality function has to be defined before.

Infrastructure Quality Function:

$$\forall e \in E_{infra} : Q(e) = \sum_{r_i \in R} ut(r_i),$$

where R is the set of available infrastructure resources, and $ut(r_i)$ the mean utilisation of a given resource.

5.2.3.2. Interdependence of Model Elements

The three types of model elements are in component-based performance models understood as layers, with the infrastructure on the bottom, connectors in the middle, and components on the top. Based on this layering, the accuracy of performance prediction is determined by the depth of information inclusion, starting from the component layer, possibly including the connector layer, and sometimes even the infrastructure layer. This implies the interdependence among the layers, which is with respect to performance completion only bottom-up. In particular, the components are completed independently of the connectors and the infrastructure, connectors completions may be dependent on components, and the infrastructure completions can be dependent on both the connectors and components.

Thanks to the nature of completions applied to the different types of model elements (components, connectors and infrastructure), which concern only the internals of the elements, we can claim the completion independence between elements of different types. In other words, having two elements of different types, e.g. a component e_{comp} and a connector e_{conn}, we can decide independently of the most suitable completion chain for e_{comp} and for e_{conn}. The order of choosing the completion chains for the two elements does not matter. Within each layer, we can see relative independence of the elements (of the same type). Having two components e_{comp1} and e_{comp2}, where e_{comp1} requires a service provided by e_{comp2}, we may first need to resolve completion conflicts in e_{comp2} to have enough information to decide on the optimal completion order for e_{comp1}. This is implied by the quality quantification $Q(e_{comp1}) = \sum_{s_i \in S} \frac{rt(s_i)}{thp(s_i)}$ defined over the performance qualities of component's provided services $s_i \in S$, i.e. $rt(s_i)$ and $thp(s_i)$, which are in PCM defined in a parametric way based on the resource demands of the services.

At the connector layer, the connector usage is defined by the communicating components. Therefore, completions of connectors could influence the decision on the component layer. However, it only changes the ratio not the performance semantic of the completion. The completion independence of connectors (occupying the connector layer) is guaranteed simply from the non-existence of direct connections between connectors, and thanks to the nature of connector completions, which touch only the internals of the connectors. The same argument holds for the infrastructure layer that consists of a set of resource containers or nodes. Completions applied to one resource container cannot affect completions applied to another resource container.

This is however the issue only for component elements, which are interconnected via their interfaces. Having the idea of component reusability in mind, we consider components as black-box elements. Throughout the completion process we can take advantage of these component-based properties. Additionally, the components use the services (e.g., communication link) provided to them by connector. As such we first optimise the components and only later connectors completion chain. Connector elements are independent due to their nature of not relying on the rest of the architecture, and there is always only one infrastructure element, hence having nothing to be in conflict with.

Based on the above, we adopt the following order of completing the elements in a system model:

1. Component layer: Components are independent of all elements in the remaining two layers of the system model (connectors and the infrastructure), but are dependent on the components required by their provided services. To evaluate the quality of the services, we first need to know the quality of required services that hence need to be completed and evaluated first. For this reason, we first connect the components into a call tree (starting in the user interface), and then complete the components in a bottom-up fashion, starting from leafs and finishing in the root. If the call graph contains cycles, then the completion orders for the individual components can be detected in an iterative way, starting with a seed of random (but valid) completion chain for each component, and iteratively optimising the dependent components, propagating the already computed performance values from the previous iteration.

2. Connector layer: Connectors can be completed independently of each other. They may however be influenced by the component elements whose communication they mediate. Therefore, the completions of connectors should follow after the completions of components.

3. Infrastructure layer: Last, the infrastructure completes the target model. The infrastructure provides physical services for connectors and components (such as middleware). So it represents the lowest-level details that should be added to the model last. Therefore, we apply infrastructure completions in the order from the highest to the lowest layer of software stack.

5.2.3.3. Conflict Resolution for an Individual Element

In the ideal case, the completion set CS intended to be applied on a model element $e \in E$ is not conflicting. Then, we can choose any valid completion chain (permutation order) over CS, and apply the completions according to that order. If it is not the case, the idea behind the method of conflict resolution (chain selection) is the following.

If a completion set CS is conflicting, then we select the completion chain cc over CS with the *minimal* value of $Q(cc(e))$ (with the best performance) and return it as the result to the software architect. This is a suggestion to the software architect. He/She can choose between proposed completions chains with defined performance semantics (increasing/decreasing performance), however, possibility to change the completion order depends on the chains supported by the used platform. The completion-chain selection problem can be understood as a single-criteria optimization of completion-configuration order with constraints. The constraints define the architectural validity of the configuration order (completion chain) for the given model element, and the objective function is given by our quality function Q that is minimized. Existing algorithms can be employed to solve this problem, including popular heuristic-search techniques, which traverse the space of all candidates (permutations of the given completion set) taking the constraints into account (excluding invalid completion chains), and search for a (near-)optimal candidate to minimize the quality-function value.

Pivot Element of a Transformation If v_i^j yields not only a single model element but a set of model elements, we identify the element that resembles the starting point of the next transformation, i.e., the *pivot element* of a transformation. We assume that, for each completion that is to be applied in a chain, its pivot element has been defined explicitly. In the following, we describe the rule of thumb how the pivot element of a transformation can be identified for component, connector, and infrastructure completions.

- Component Completions build a hierarchy of wrapped components. Thus, the next completion is to be applied to the highest wrapper in this hierarchy. The pivot element of a component completion is the outer wrapper introduced by the completion.
- Connector Completions always consist of an operation and its inversion (e.g., marshaling and demarshaling). Both operations are (or can be) represented by separate components linked by a newly introduced connector. This connector is the pivot element of the connector completion.

- Infrastructure Completions affect multiple connectors or components in one container. The container itself is never changed and thus remains a constant pivot element.

5.3. Completion Library: Concurrency design patterns

Predicting the performance of software systems is especially challenging if software components communicate based on a complex interaction pattern. Such interaction is defined by concurrency, message-based communication, and synchronisation patterns. In the following, we investigate some of these patterns. We discuss the integration of performance abstractions in a form of completions on the place of connectors or to enhance components or connectors. First, we discuss the group of concurency design patterns in general. Second, we give examples of completions in each sub-group of patterns. We motivate each of the introduced examples and further discuss its feature diagram and sketch the skeleton design of the completion.

5.3.1. Motivation

Parallel programs are generally complex, hard to understand and rise implementation and modelling effort. Lee [107] discussed the problems and complexity of parallel programs. Despite all the difficulties, the deployment of concurrency concepts in software systems is the most important possibility to increase performance. To simplify implementation and modelling of parallel software is one of the most important questions of software engineering.

Today, in the world of multicore processors, the development of parallel software is more and more important. The threads and processes could be divided between available cores and allow efficient usage of the underlying hardware [155]. Software developers and software users get double (at least in theory) computation power by adding a second core. Similarly, the performance should rise by processors with four or eight cores. However, this promised performance increase it is not for free. Programs running on multicore processors have to be specifically structured to use the promised advantages. The whole architecture should allow for the computation or whole parts of architecture to run in parallel on the available cores. So the software architectures should be designed using parallel structures. Although, introduction of parallel execution promises increase in performance, the development effort for this increase is high. Additionally, in some cases the performance increase is not so big as expected. Therefore, it is important to test influence of concurrency on performance in advance. Design-time prediction of performance with concurrency allows software architects to make good decisions and identify where introduction of concurrency is necessary to increase performance and where the increase of performance would be too small in comparison to required development effort.

In the area of performance prediction the models of parallel software are very complex as well. For accurate prediction detailed models are necessary. Such models include already expert knowledge and low-level implementation details. Often creation of such models in early design time is impossible or only realisable with a lot of effort. The main idea to solve this problems is to simplify and refine performance predictions with help of model-driven performance completions. Sutter and Larus [155] already identified the need for higher abstractions for concurrency and in this way to simplify the development of parallel programs. This could be done with a help of model constructs, such as completions, that encapsulate the knowledge about behaviour and performance parameters of concurrency design patterns. The design patterns for concurrency reduce the complexity, make the systems more understandable and modelling simpler. Hence, design patterns describe generic solutions for known software design problems. This way they help developers to design more effective and robust software.

Even though it might be known that a certain pattern influences the quality of a system [143, 51], the extend of the effect in a certain scenario is unknown. Furthermore, a design pattern may affect several quality attributes. For example, replication increases the availability of a service, but does not impact its performance directly. If multiple patterns are combined to enhance quality, synchronise components, or ensure data consistency, their overall effect cannot be assessed manually. Schmidt et al. [143] described the most important design patterns for parallel software. They identified service configuration, service call, event-management, concurrency and synchronisation as most important tasks for design and implementation of parallel and distributed systems.

In this chapter we analyse concurrency design patterns based on their applicability in component-based architectures. Furthermore, for some of them completion construct are introduced and integrated in PCM. We use model-driven performance prediction techniques to evaluate the influence of concurrency patterns on the quality of a software architecture. Additionally, in the following section, we apply our approach for completion conflict reduction to concurrency design patterns.

5.3.2. Categorisation of concurrency design patterns

In our approach, we simplify the design and the development of concurrent software architectures by completions for concurrency design patterns. We provide predefined parametrized performance completions based on a knowledge about concurrency design patterns and their implementation details. In general, design patterns provide enough information to allow accurate performance predictions. Patterns for concurrent and distributed systems address multiple aspects, such as synchronisation, communication, and Quality of Service (QoS). For example, the patterns MonitorObject [143], Thread-Safe Interface [143], Guarded Call [51], and Rendezvous [51] provide different means for synchronisation and communication. Patterns like Half-Sync/Half-Async, Leader Followers, Reactor, and Proactor as described Schmidt et. al. [143] are used in servers to efficiently dispatch and process concurrent requests. Furthermore, Replication and Load Balancing are employed to enhance different QoS attributes in distributed systems.

We apply the conflict reduction method to this group of design patterns. For this purpose, we categorise the design patterns in the conflict groups using the levels of conflict reduction introduced in Section 5.2.3. The categorisation of design patterns based on a development roles and their responsibilities separation builds the basis for reduction and avoidance of conflicts. Additionally, based on this categorisation software developers can select suitable patterns for certain problem domain without detailed knowledge about their structure. DWe categorised concurrency design patterns according to the development roles, that most likely will use them (see Table 5.1).

	Event-based communication	**Synchronisation**	**Concurrency**	**Message-oriented communication**
Component Developer		Scoped Locking Strategized Locking Thread-safe Interface Double-checked Locking Optimisation Rendezvous/Barrier	Thread-specific Storage Monitor Object Replication	Messaging Endpoints
Software Architect	Asynchronous Completion Token		Pipeline	Message Channel Message Routing Message Endpoints
System Deployer	Reactor Proactor Acceptor-Connector		Active Object Half-Sync/Half-Async Leaders Followers Thread Pool	Message Bus

Table 5.1.: Roles and Responsibilities Separation: Mapping design patterns to development roles.

Component Completions: The category *Component Developer* includes patterns used for a definition of basic thread-safe components. These patterns solve the issues related to parallel usage of the component provided service, for example, data inconsistency. Here, the patterns supporting data concurrency so that task could be executed in parallel on all elements of the same data structure. This type of concurrency is called *data concurrency* and especially patterns for synchronisation deal with this type of concurrency.

Connector Completions: The category *Software Architect* consists of patterns for specification of component interactions, such as coordination and optimisation of communication between components. It is so called *pipeline concurrency*, when data should be handled one after other by a number of tasks, where parts of the data could be handled by different tasks at the same time. We can distinguish linear (Pipe and Filter), non-linear (Pipe and Filter Pattern with Distributors and Aggregators) or special (Producer/Consumer Pattern with synchronisation) types of pipeline.

Infrastructure Completions: The category *System Deployer* subsumes patterns that are used to build middleware platforms for concurrent software systems. For example, the concurrent processing of requests by an application server can be realised by a Leader/Follower pattern. So called *task concurrency* patterns in this category are allowing that some task could be executed in parallel, that mean the task will be executed in a number of threads.

There exist many different parallel patterns, in this work, representants of these patterns were chosen and completions were specified for them.

5.3.3. Component Completions

The first group of the completions is defined based on design patterns that affect model elements describing component behaviour. These patterns complete behaviour by integrating new actions (e.g. external call, acquire or release) into the component's control flow, or they create wrappers around the completed component and delegate its interfaces so that the change of the component is externally invisible (e.g. Replication pattern or State Manager). For example, all design patterns for synchronisation and thread-safety belong to this group, e.g., Locks, Monitors, State Managers or the Barrier pattern. In the following, we evaluate the Replication pattern and introduce completion for this pattern.

5.3.3.1. Replication Completion

We analysed replication completion in [34], where we created a model of this completion and provided simulation experiments using different configuration options of replication. This section is based on results of these experiments.

Motivation There are two purposes for replication, thus having multiple component instances of one component: improving a software system's performance and reliability. The goal of replication is, first, improving response times for incoming requests, as these can be assigned to different replicas, in effect handling several requests in parallel, and second, improving reliability, by assigning the tasks of failed replica to one of its identical copies.

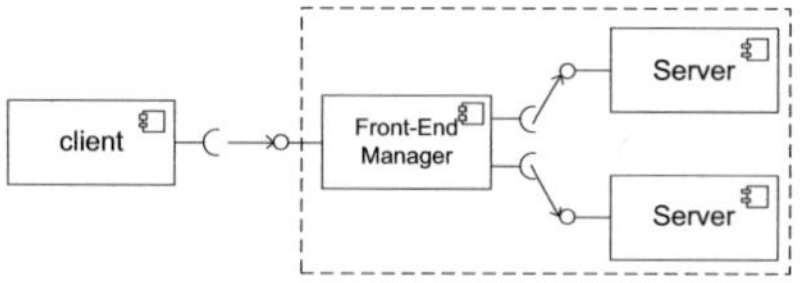

Figure 5.2.: Replication Pattern.

In Replication pattern (cf., Figure 5.2), the clients send their requests to, and also get their responses returned from, the Front-End Manager only. How their requests are handled by the Front-End Manager and the replicas is transparent to the clients. A Front-End Manager can provide shorter response times for its clients by distributing the incoming requests among the available replicas. When the Front-End Manager receives a request from a client, it multicasts this request to all replicas. The replicas process the request, and send a reply back to the Front-End Manager, which in turn gathers the replies and selects a final response for the client.

There are two basic modes of request handling: active replication and passive replication. When all redundant replicas process each request, we call it active replication, or the requests are directed only to a single replica, and the other servers act as backup, then we call it passive replication. The second mode is sometimes called primary-backup replication [147]. In contrast to active replication, there is only one primary replica. It is the only replica that gets the request from the Front-End Manager, and also the only replica that sends a reply. This reply is sent back to the Front-End Manager and additionally to the other replicas. The other replicas just update their state to keep the entire system consistent. Replicas may be stateful or stateless. If stateful, after a change in one replica has been detected, all other replicas must be updated to ensure consistency.

Replication Completion: Feature Diagram Further, we studied quality effects of replication with the goal to extract feature diagram, which builds a basis to implement replication completion. Replication intuitively improves reliability. Additionally, load-balancing can improve performance between number of replicas.

However, because of a huge amount of routine work (e.g., copying) when modelling replication the cost of the model may increase and maintainability may be decreased due to higher complexity of the model. Therefore, is especially important to automate replication mechanism. However, while we identified that replication configuration (except replica count) has very minimal impact on performance, there is still a lot of effort needed to create models of replication, especially because of changes of topology and needed copies of a large number of elements. Therefore, we created a completion that automates this effort. Impact on performance of this completion is evaluated in following.

Based on the domain analysis, we identified features influencing performance and created feature diagram for replication completion. The feature diagram (cf., Figure 5.4) contains all configuration options, which we assume to have an influence on the quality properties of a system.

In replication feature diagram the *Replica Count* property defines how many identical copies of the component, which is to be replicated, should be created. The results of the simulations reflect the benefit of balancing system load among replicas in real-world systems. The system is able to generate answers faster, the more replicas are available, which is shown by the averages and medians of the response times, as seen in Figure 5.3 (i.e., voting 1 to 5 active replicas).

The more stress the usage scenario puts the system under, the more clearly you can see how the system scales. Considering the minimal usage scenario, the addition of a replica to the system makes not much difference. For the balanced usage scenario, the advantage of additional replicas begins to show. Compared to a system using a single replica, one with five replicas can generate a reply in less than half the time. Eventually, the system response time is noticeably reduced for the demanding usage scenario, demonstrated by the system becoming almost 4 times as fast the more replicas it has available.

From the identified options, *Load Balancing* and *Replica Count* are straightforward additions. Which replica is chosen to process a request can be decided for every single request, or for all requests per client. We model the per-request choice only. Different strategies for the load balancing decision are available, namely "Random", "Round Robin" and "First Available". A Front-End Manager using the "Random" strategy chooses one replica randomly for each received request, which will then process it. While not optimal, this strategy offers a significant increase in performance.

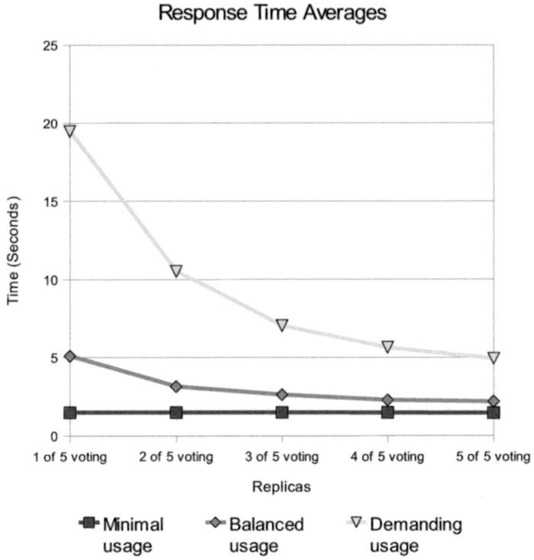

Figure 5.3.: Random Load Balancing: Graphical comparison of the response time averages for three differently demanding usage scenarios.

With the "Round Robin" strategy, the Front-End Manager defines an order on its available replicas. Following this order, every request is forwarded to the currently selected replica, and the next replica is selected, one after another. With the "First Available" load balancing strategy, a Front-End Manager assigns each client to a randomly chosen replica. All requests received from an assigned client are then always processed by the same replica. In the case of the last two strategies, the Front-End Manager needs to keep track of the current state of its replicas.

In the distributed variant of replication, a new resource container is created for every replica of the component. These resource containers get the same processing resource specifications as the resource container that contains the original component. We replicate homogeneously (i.e., together with all components on it, leading to identical server replicas) to make the system more manageable and the overview easier. On the other hand, if local replication is chosen, the already existing processing resources are

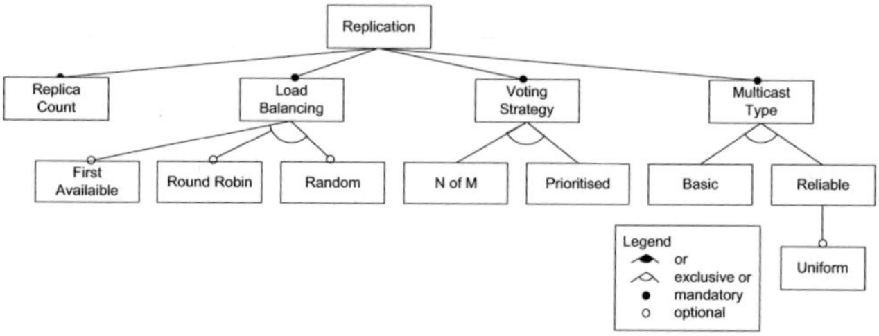

Figure 5.4.: Feature diagram for the replication design pattern.

multiplicated inside the original resource container. This is done as many times as the replica count option specifies, so that every local replica has its own exclusive set of resources.

We also added the *Voting Strategy* to our feature diagram. We think the voting strategy is a major factor for reliability. This becomes important for safety-critical systems, which we also want to allow to be simulated. A common application of the "N of M" voting strategy is absolute majority voting. Taking a system with five replicas as example, an absolute majority is achieved when three identical responses are returned, and the Front-End Manager may already send the response to the client without waiting for the remaining two replicas. However, we can support an arbitrary number of required answers without additional effort. This may be of use for a system architect who needs less certainty than a total majority, or who needs an even higher certainty of the correctness of the gathered answers. The basic idea behind the rules for N of M voting is using a counting semaphore, stopping the main execution thread until enough replicas have finished and replied. Additionally, we need to insert a mutex, so that each thread can use the semaphore exclusively, undisturbed from other threads. Otherwise, it would be possible that race conditions occur. When evaluating the N of M voting strategy, we determined that the number of required answers influenced performance. Factoring the influence of the replica count into the voting strategy, both N and M are important options.

The choice of the multicast type concerns data consistency among replicas. When basic multicast is chosen, nothing needs to be changed in the models. In this mode, requests are forwarded from the Front-End Manager to all replicas without taking any steps to ensure data consistency.

Reliable multicast, however, is implemented using acknowledgements in actual systems. A replica sends an acknowledgement back to the Front-End Manager when it received a request. The Front-End Manager can thereby verify that all replicas received the request successfully. Therefore, acknowledgements improve the reliability of the communication between the Front-End Manager and its replicas, at the expense of increased network traffic. We can model this by adding the usage of a network resource, while changes to other models are not necessary.

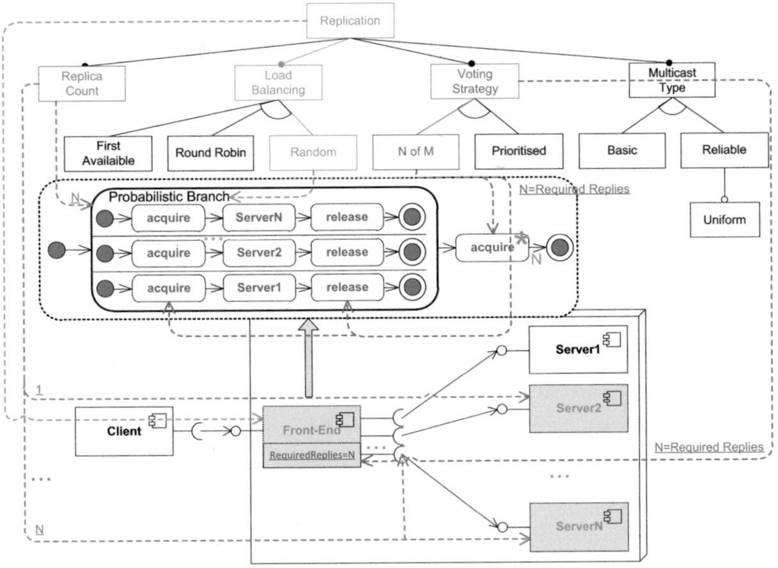

Figure 5.5.: Replication Completion Skeleton.

Replication Completion: Completion Design In PCM a component instance can be replicated in two ways: first, on the assembly layer, i.e. a component instance in two different contexts is composed to build the system; second, on the deployment layer, i.e. a component instance is mapped to several deployment contexts. The replication on the deployment layer is invisible in the systems structure. Therefore, software (e.g., parallelizable software) that could gain advantage from the replication can not be tested for it properly. Another point about deployment layer replication is that all the replicas are actually copies, concerning the functionality, quality properties and deployment environment. The replication on the assembly layer does not implicitly mean this level of equality between replicas. In some scenarios where, for example, the most performant replica has highest priority, it is appreciated when this information propagates to the system architect as well. Therefore, we implemented only the replication on assembly level, anyhow, it is conceptually very similar to realise replication on the deployment level.

When a component should be replicated, first, a Front-End Manager component is inserted into the system (cf. Figure 5.5). Second, the replicated component is copied a number of times, as defined by the value of the replica count. Front-End Manager shall manage the requests that formerly were sent to the replicated component directly, therefore, it provides the same interface as the replicated component. Furthermore, the Front-End Manager requires the same interface a number of times, determined by the value of the replica count, so that it can forward the requests to the replicas.

In the system diagram, the replica count determines how many replicated components and connectors to them are created. Furthermore, the replicated components can require services from other components. We can deal with these required components twofold: first, all the required components as replicated too; second, only the selected component is replicated. In our solution, all components that provide a service used by the replicated components are replicated as well, such could become a bottleneck for the system, if they resided on the original, local resource container. Without replicating these components as well, each would be accessed by all replicas concurrently, provoking system overload. However, we assume that there is small number of these required components (not more as two) and we replicate only components originally located in the same resource container. This approach, however, should be further evaluated, which is out of scope of this work.

Another important point is that we can replicate these additional components without additional changes, because all components are originally stateless in the PCM. Would they be stateful, we would have to ensure synchronisation and data consistency via additional constructs. The stateful extension of this completion is required at this point, similarly as it was done of the MOM completion in Section 7.2.1, this is part of the planned future work.

Based on the option distributed or local for the replica location, a new resource container is created for every replica of the component or the already existing processing resources are multiplicated inside the original resource container. This is done as many times as the replica count option specifies, so that every local replica has its own exclusive set of resources. The created resource containers get the same processing resource specifications as the resource container that contains the original component.

The voting strategy is simulated with the passive resource of capacity equal to the required number of replies from replicas. Each replica releases the passive resource when finished. The Front-End has to acquire the whole capacity of this resource before sending reply to the client. Thus, the waiting for the replicas to finish is simulated.

The load balancing strategy is simulated by a probabilistic branch where number of branches is determined by the value of the replica count. In each branch one replica is called. The model of "Random" strategy is straightforward, for example, when we have 2 replicas each of the branches gets the probability of 50%. The model of "First available" and "Round robin" requires stateful extention. However, because experiments [55] showed a little difference between these strategies we model these strategies with similar model as for the "Random" strategy. For exact model of these strategies we plan the stateful extention in the future.

Replication Completion: Summary We identified the features of replication that are included in the feature model and modelled with the means the PCM provides. These features were evaluated on a relevant impact on performance of a simulated architecture. Additionally, we implemented a completion in a form of feature model with related transformation fragments.

The future work for the replication completion includes to evaluate the other alternatives to active replication, such as passive replication with a primary replica or stateful replicas. Another area for future work is modelling and evaluating local replication. This should become possible once the implementation of multicore support in the PCM is completed, that means utilising multiple processing resource definitions of the same type in one resource container.

5.3.3.2. State Manager

We analysed the stateful components and implemented stateful extension to the MOM completion, which is further explained and validated in Section 7.2.1. This completion was then implemented using the technique introduced in Section 7.2.1 and resulting transformation is evaluated in Section 7.2.3. In this section, we introduce necessary changes and extensions to the PCM allowing modelling of stateful components. In Appendix A, we further discuss stateful performance engineering and related concepts. Because this completion is not an explicit construct available to the users, a State Manager is in current PCM used only as extension of existing completion, we do not introduce a feature diagram. The reason for this decision (in

PCM) is the possible complexity of stateful models that would be allowed, if the stateful concepts were available explicitly.

Motivation In the following, we give an example for the influence of state on software performance which is taken from the area of message based systems. In particular, we are interested in the delivery time (time from sending a message until it is received) of messages send within a transaction. Messaging systems, which implement the Java Message Service standard [74], explicitly support transactions for messages. The transactions guarantee that all messages are delivered to all receivers in the order they have been send. To achieve such a behaviour, Sun's JMS implementation MessageQueue 4.1 [1] waits for all incoming messages of a transaction and, then, delivers them sequentially. Figure 5.6 shows the measured

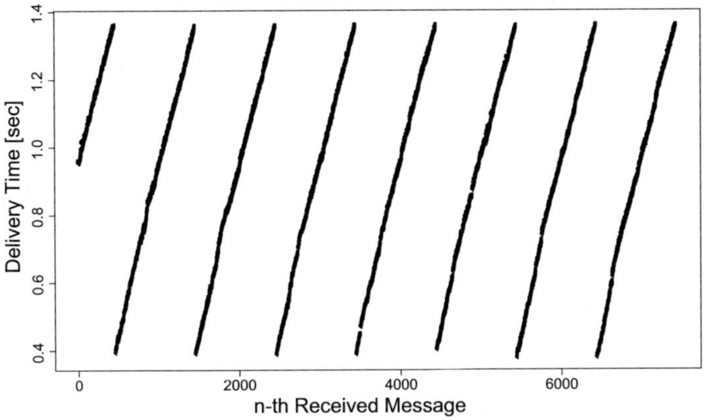

Figure 5.6.: Time series of a transaction with 1000 messages per transaction set.

delivery times for a series of transactions with 1000 messages each (the sender initiates a new transaction (as part of a session), passes 1000 messages to the MOM, and finally, commits the transaction). All messages arrive within the first 0.4 seconds and are delivered sequentially within the next second. This behaviour leads to delivery times of 0.4 seconds at minimum. The delivery times grow linearly until the transaction is completed. In this example, the position of a message in the transaction set determines its delivery time. Thus, the measured delivery times are *not* independent and identically distributed but strongly depend on the number (and size) of messages that have already been sent. As a consequence, to predict performance accuratelly we need to keep track of the messages that are part of a transaction. Additionally, the periodical utilisation of resources (e.g., CPU) influences performance. To model such a behaviour, we need a notion of state as part of our performance model.

State Manager: Completion Design In the MOM Completion introduced in [76] the transactional delivery is not supported, because of requirement on the PCM that prohibits to use stateful components because of complexity issues. We decided to extend MOM Completion so that the usage of stateful components will be hidden. The Statefull Manager will be inserted by the transformation into the target model as an wrapper around previously stateless component. This wrapper will then manage calls to the methods of the component based on the state value.

We extended the component behaviour model of the PCM (the SEFF) to allow the modelling of component internal state. With this extension, also system specific global state (cf. Appendix A) can be modelled by adding a blackboard component that makes its internal state available to other components in the system. Only two additions to the PCM metamodel are required to model component internal state and global system state. First, we declare a set of state variables for a component. Only a declared state variables can be used within a SEFF. Second, we add a `SetStateAction` to the SEFF, which allows to set the state variable to a given expression. Input data of the SEFF, other state variable values and the previous state variable value can be used in the expression. Now, the state variable can be

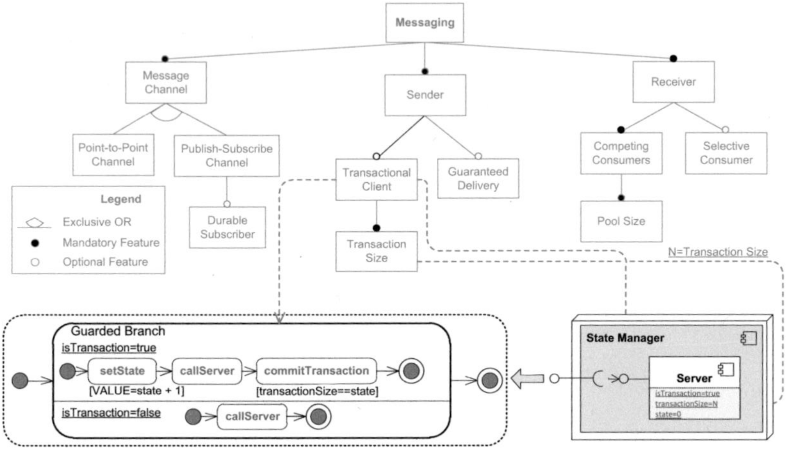

Figure 5.7.: MOM Completion Skeleton for transactional delivery.

used in branch conditions or resource demands as a parameter. The use of *PCM Stateful* extension is illustrated in section 7.2.1.

Figure 5.8 illustrates the PCM extension. Assume a Component A processing data. It performs clean-up task after each Megabyte of processed data. Thus, it keeps track of the amount of data processed. In the model, we store the limit of 1 MB in a component parameter named `dataLimitInMB.VALUE`, defining component configuration state. We declare a state variable `processData.VALUE` and initialise it with the value 0, defining component internal state. The SEFF of the component is shown in a state-chart-like notation in the figure. First, we modelled a `SetStateAction` to add the currently processed amount of data (available as `inputData.BYTESIZE`) to the `processData.VALUE` variable. Then, the data is processed in the `InternalAction` process. We omitted the resource demands for brevity. After processing the data, we check whether a clean-up is required in the `BranchAction`. If `processData.VALUE >= dataLimitInMB.VALUE`, we do the clean-up of 1 MB and set back the state

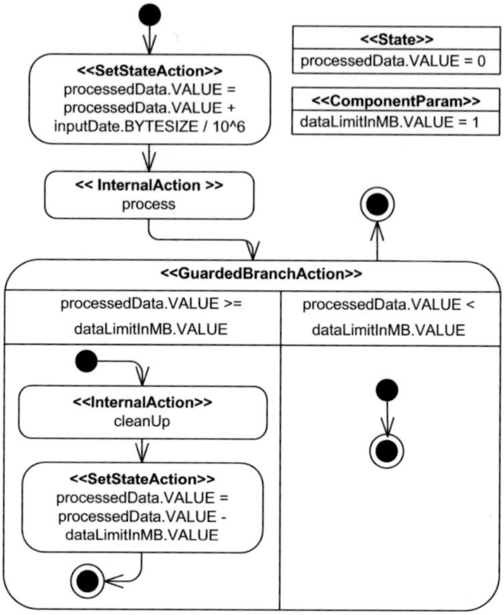

Figure 5.8.: Example stateful SEFF.

to `processData.VALUE` - `dataLimitInMB.VALUE`. The second branch is empty.

State Manager: Summary An extended PCM model can be analysed with the extended version of the *SimuCom* simulation presented in [18] to obtain the performance metrics. At simulation runtime, each component is instantiated and holds its state variables. When a `SetStateAction` is evaluated, its expression is evaluated and stored in the state variable. If `BranchActions` and `InternalActions` access state variables, the value is retrieved. The extension increases the expression power of SEFFs and allows programming, although the language does not become Turing complete (all loops are bounded). As multiple requests to the system are analysed concurrently, we can encounter race conditions and resulting unexpected behaviour. In our example above, race conditions are excluded because the branch condition and `SetStateAction` are evaluated in the same simulation event (no time passes in simulation). However, in general, if a resource demand is executed between reading the state in a `BranchAction` and setting the state in one of the branches, both actions are executed in separate simulation events. Here, a second request to the component could read or change the state in between, leading to race conditions.

With the extended state modelling, steady-state behaviour is not guaranteed any more. While this limits analysability, it also can help to detect problems in a software design. For example, assume a system service that becomes the more expensive the more requests have been served. Then, the response time of the system will ever increase ('The Ramp' antipattern [147]) and no steady state can be reached. With the extended state modelling, this performance antipatterns can be detected in the simulation results.

5.3.4. Connector Completions

Assembly connectors [165, 12] are the most complex type of model elements that can be enhanced by completions. For connectors, several performance completions can be applied on one connector instance so that their order has to be determined.

The first kind of completion provides details about the type of the connector, i.e, whether it is 1:1, 1:n, or n:1. Connectors of type 1:1 are typical message passing or RPC style connectors which connect a single client component instance to a single server component instance. In case of 1:n connectors, a single client component sends requests to a set of server components which is semantically the case for server replication scenarios or voting based server queries. Finally, n:1 connectors are the usual case of n clients instances talking to a thread-safe server instance.

Orthogonal to the type of the connector, connector performance completions also include details about the processing of the communication

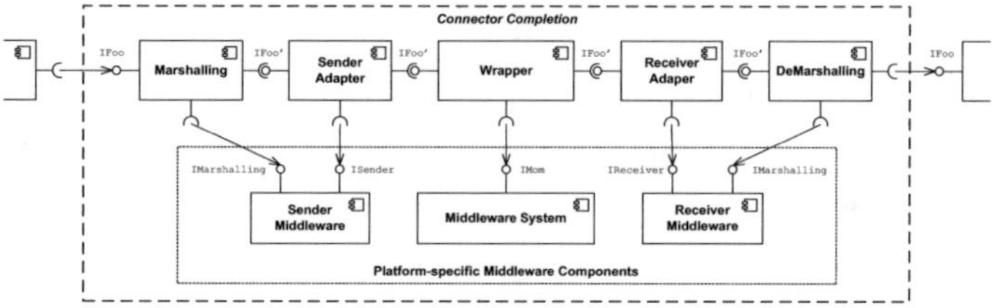

Figure 5.9.: Connector Middleware Completion [76].

(synchronous or asynchronous) in the participating middleware layers as illustrated in Figure 5.9 [76]. Here we find services for message marshaling, message encryption, call authentication, message compression, etc. For these types of message processing steps, existing performance completions insert a completion component for each processing step. However, the order of these services is important because of the differences in the data flow involved. For example, the size of the message to be sent over the network is different if the message's body is first encrypted and then compressed versus an initial compression followed by a subsequent encryption step. Hence, for the processing steps the order of application of a set of performance completions does matter and needs clarification. We analyse this issue further in Section 7.2.2.

Connector completions rely on introduced components which reflect the performance related behaviour of the used middleware. As a consequence, these middleware components implement both, the resource demand caused by the middleware's processing but also the data transformations they perform on the message to be sent over the network. Note, that in some usecases the size of the message is not of major interest for the overall performance of the network link. In such cases, the data transformations become neglectable and consequently also the order of applying the corresponding performance completions does not matter any more.

As a result of the discussion of connector completions, we can conclude that we need at least two types of annotations. The first annotation class determines the connector kind and defines the exact implementation semantics of 1:1, 1:n, and n:1 connectors, e.g., whether voting or replication is used for a 1:n connector. The second class of annotations defines the pre- and post-processing details of the messages used by the connector for remote communication. Here, the annotation gives details about marshaling, encryption, compression, etc. A clear definition of the order in which such completions are added to the performance model is necessary to get accurate performance predictions from the refined performance model. This section gives details on how to build more complex connectors, based on an abstraction inspired by Pipe&Filter pattern.

5.3.4.1. Pipe&Filter Connector

In this section, we present the architecture of performance abstractions for connectors, the feature diagrams we developed and finally the architecture we implemented in transformations for the PCM. This section is based on our work presented in [119].

Motivation Because, we aim to model only performance abstractions of connectors we can abstract from the functional details and concentrate on the performance-relevant dependencies. In general, from a performance point of view connector is a chain of components producing a load dependent on the size of data to send. The exact functionality of connectors is not of the interest for the performance prediction. Therefore, it is possible to model connector as a chain of activities whose performance determines the performance of the whole connector. The performance of the connector then depends only on the properties of transferred data (such as data byte-size). In such highly abstract connector model we can simplify connector on two types of activities: buffering of transferred data and computation or I/O activities with the data. Which is very similar to the *Pipes & Filters* pattern, which is an architecture pattern for data stream processing systems. The connectors's task is then divided into several independent incremental processing steps (filters) connected by pipes, altogether forming a pipeline.

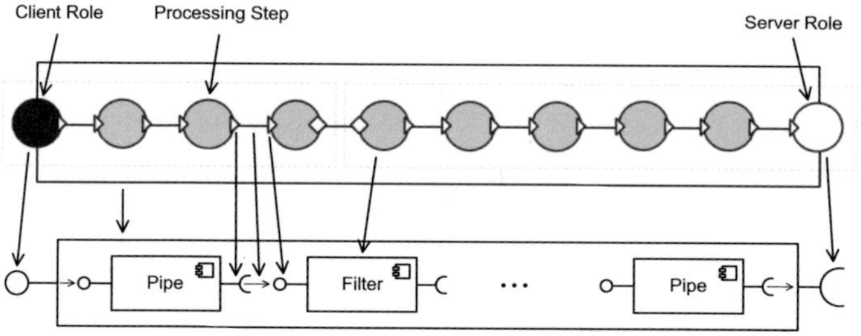

Figure 5.10.: Mapping the connectors on the abstractions in the performance model.

In our case the scope will be connectors and their tasks. We will use pipes and filters to model connectors which in turn are assembled using basic constructs provided by PCM. The main advantage would be high level of abstraction and low-complexity of the composition of independent tasks in connector. We build all the connector variants from the basic constructs, e.g. pipes and (active/passive) filters. The connectors will be variable considering non-functional properties and other aspects of communication. The advantage of our approach is that we need to compose multiple instances of two simple building blocks (pipe and filters) and calibrate them with performance data. In addition, our approach to build performance abstractions of connectors simplifies the generation technique because it is enough to have a few of reusable fragments of transformations (in our case three: pipe, active and passive filter) that could be composed to generate the connector (cf., Figure 5.10). The connectors we modelled within the PCM are based on [30].

The settings in which a particular connector can be used are determined by its topology. Four different topology types can be distinguished [30] as shown in Figure 5.11.

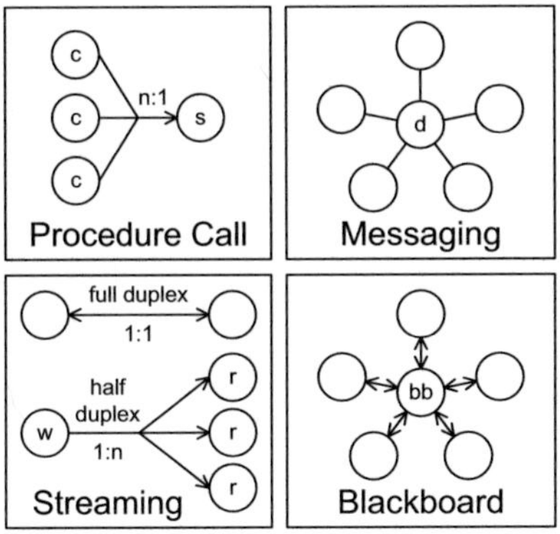

Figure 5.11.: Connector Layout.

The *Procedure Call Connector* features unidirectional communication from multiple client components (c) to one server component (s). It operates in both a synchronous and an asynchronous call mode. However, its influence on the performance is significant, the communication of multiple client components with a single server component (n:1 relationship) can be modelled.

The *Messaging Connector* has a typical star layout. In the middle there is the distributor unit (d). A component can be connected as sender, receiver or both. It operates only in an asynchronous mode.

The *Streaming Connector* comes in two variants. The *Full Duplex* implementation features bidirectional point to point communication for two coequal components. The *Half Duplex* variant limits communication to one direction with one writer component (w) whilst enabling multiple receivers/readers (r). As is the nature of streaming transactions they are processed in an asynchronous mode.

The *Blackboard Connector* has a star shaped layout similar to the messaging connector. In the middle there is the *black board storage* (bb). Every component is attached to the connector by a provided and a required interface. Through the required interface it can send write and read requests to the storage. Write requests are processed asynchronously while read requests operate synchronously.Through the provided interface the components can be notified about changes to the blackboard.

Pipe&Filter Connector: Procedure Call Feature Diagram In the following, we introduce in more detail the structure of Procedure Call Connector. The architecture of this connector is shown in Figure 5.12. The connector is divided in two deployment units, one for the client and one for the server side. They are allocated to the resource containers of their respective component. The simplest form is the point to point connection from one client to one server, thus also featuring only one client and one server deployment unit. In general, multiple clients are possible.

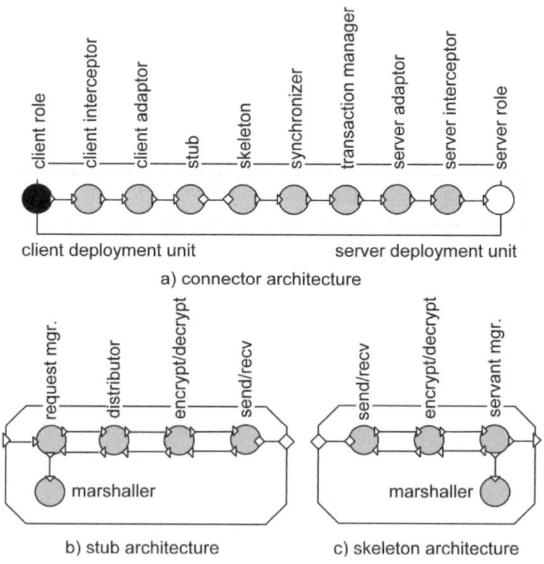

Figure 5.12.: Procedure Call connector architecture [30].

When considering the individual elements from which the connector (cf., Figure 5.12) is composed, many of them can be mapped directly to the abstractions based using simple pipes and filter components.

The *client adaptor* maps to a single filter in our model. Its resource demands are configurable over a feature diagram. The *Stub*, the next element of the connector, is a composed element consisting of smaller tasks, from them the distributor and encryptor/decryptor are of interest to us. In our model the *encryptor/decryptor* is also realized by a filter. The *distributor* is resembled by a filter with multiple required interfaces. Its SEFF does not contain resource demands, but chooses which required interface or interfaces the outgoing call shall invoke. The first element in the server deployment unit is the *skeleton*, which is again a composed element and the counterpart to the stub. From its subelements the *encryptor/decryptor* define a coupled pair of filters in our model. The *synchronizer* is used to establish the beginning of a critical section. Usually it is used to guard code which is not thread safe. In these cases the capacity for the critical section will be set to one. It is also possible to choose another value if the resource, the critical section guards, has a higher capacity. The next element manages transactions. This functionality is already covered by the Middleware completion. In our model there is a placeholder which is referenced by the transaction feature in the feature diagram. The server adapter and interceptor are analogous to their client counterparts. The *Interceptor* implements the *Monitoring* feature, which allows to interrupt passing calls. In our model it resembles a special filter component with an additional required interface through which it sends the call before passing it along down the connector. Intended for profiling (creation of statistics) the interceptor can be used very flexibly, making it an all-purpose processing step.

Our feature model is shown in Figure 5.13. The node labelled *target connections* resembles a list of all assembly connectors which are to be merged into this connector. As it can be annotated with multiple values, it

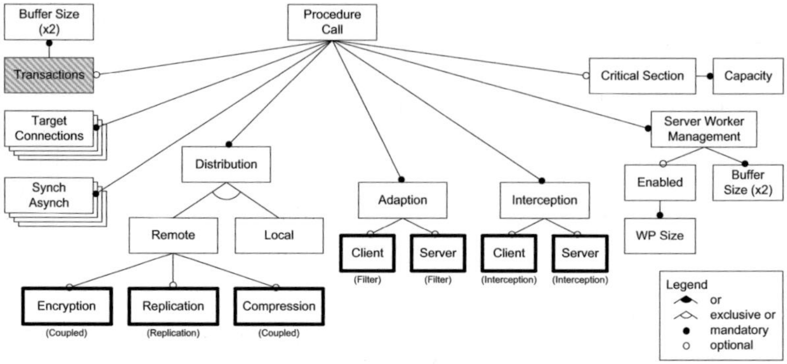

Figure 5.13.: Procedure Call Feature Diagram.

is illustrated as multi node. Only assembly connectors of the same interface are allowed. The other multi node labelled *synch/asynch* configures if calls should be performed in the synchronous or asynchronous mode. It does that for each method signature within the used interface. It does only make sense to activate the asynchronous mode for a method with no return value or if the return value is not used by the callee. As soon as there is at least one method, operating in the synchronous mode, some subtrees have to be duplicated. This is because the synchronous calls travel through the connector twice. By duplicating the trees resource demands, worker pools, data size changes and buffering capacity can be configured two times. Whenever a node and all of its child nodes have to be duplicated it is indicated by a (x2).

The *server worker management* subtree configures the buffering capacity of the last pipe and if the server should be connected to the connectors worker management. By enabling it, a `BoundedSinkAdapter` is used instead of the normal `SinkAdapter`. When it is disabled, the buffer capacity has no effect on calls travelling to the sink, because it accepts all calls instantly. However the second buffering capacity very well has effect on returning calls. This is not reflected in the feature diagram, because it would have made the diagram even more confusing. The *critical section* feature adds the synchronizer component to the connector. When selecting it, the number of calls which are allowed to enter the section has to be chosen. The *transaction* feature is set in grey because it refers to another completion as mentioned before.

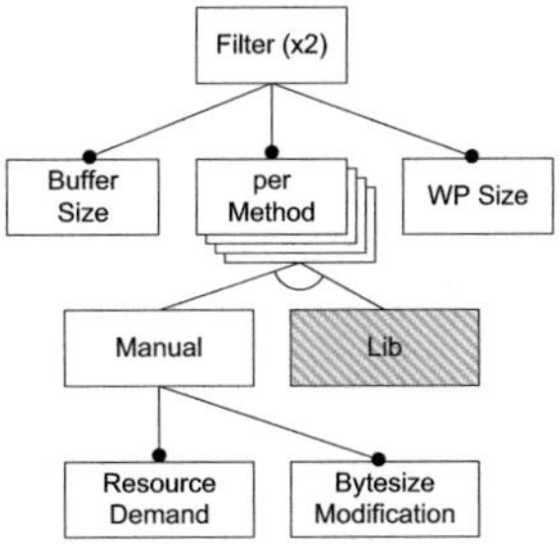

Figure 5.14.: Filter Subtree.

The *adaption* feature can be enabled for either the client, server or both. Deploying both adapters may be necessary due to communication methods or the use of middleware. Because the adapters are implemented by simple filters, the filter subtree (cf. Figure 5.14) is referenced for both adapters. The fact that a node represents a subtree is illustrated through a thicker frame. Per filter the worker pool size and the buffer sizes of the pipe in front of the adapter have to be set. Also per filter the resource demand and byte size change has to be configured for every method. It is possible to choose these from a library with predefined formulas. However the library is not supported by our work, but can be retrieved from the work of Becker et al. [10, 14].

Compression is a feature a coupled feature in the feature diagram (cf., Figure 5.13). The feature node references the subtree for coupled activities which can be found in Figure 5.15. It merges two filter subtrees into one, because some values appear twice. For example if the connector operates in

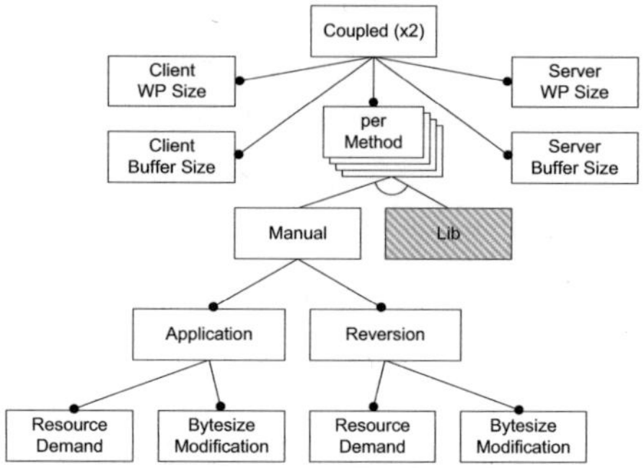

Figure 5.15.: Coupled Activity Subtree.

synchronous mode, the values (resource demands and data size change) for the compression would be configured once for the first filter and again for the second filter (for returning calls). The feature is implemented by simple filters and is intended to reduce the size of the calls data before sending it over the network. When it is enabled, it adds one filter to the client and one to the server deployment unit of the connector. The worker pool size of these filters and the capacity of their pipes can be configured separately, as shown in the coupled activities subtree. The compression method can be either set manually or retrieved out of a predefined library. It can be configured individually for each method which the connector supports. However we cannot support such a library in the scope of this work, so the node is set in gray. Note that it is possible to add special parameters to the call (e.g. entropy). These can be used in the compression formulas to achieve a more accurate prediction than solely though data size consideration. Middleware completions may contain compression completions. This has to be considered by the connector completion developer, so that no conflicts between these completions arise. The *encryption* feature is also realized as a coupled activity. The configuration is analogous to that of the compression feature.

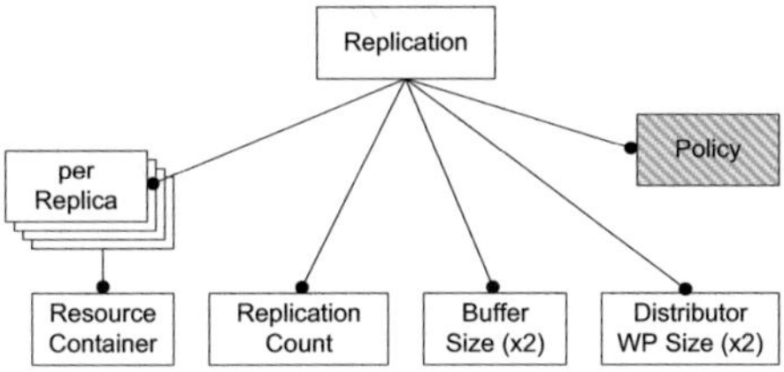

Figure 5.16.: Replication Subtree.

The *replication* subtree references the replication completion, which was already introduced in Section 5.3.3. The replication and connector completions should be linked in the Completion Library, so that they can be applied together and do not conflict. Compression, encryption and replication only make sense, if the connector is not located within one resource container, because this means that calls have to travel over a network connection. The connection quality feature is not included in our feature model. This is because the architecture of the connector does not influence the connection quality. In the PCM the connection quality is defined by the resource environment.

Pipe&Filter Connector: Procedure Call Completion Design In the following, we discuss the structural elements creating completion skeleton. These structures map the features introduced by the feature diagram. The architecture of the full featured client deployment unit is shown in Figure 5.18. For the sake of clarity we did not include the worker management. Each pipe is configured over the feature of the filter to its right. The client unit fans out at the *distributor*. Exemplarily it is illustrated with three outgoing interfaces. It is only contained, if replication is enabled; i.e. there is more than one server.

A more detailed view of how the distributor is connected to the worker management of all adjacent pipes can be found in Figure 5.17. We called

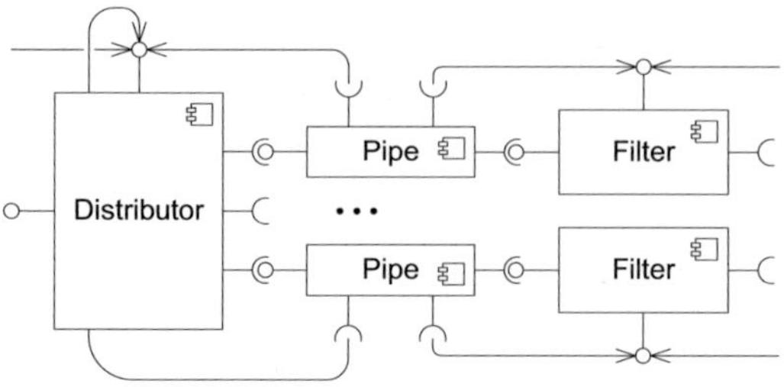

Figure 5.17.: Distributor Worker Management.

the filter which handles encryption and decryption *cryptor*. It is possible for the client unit to be completely empty, if none of its features are selected.

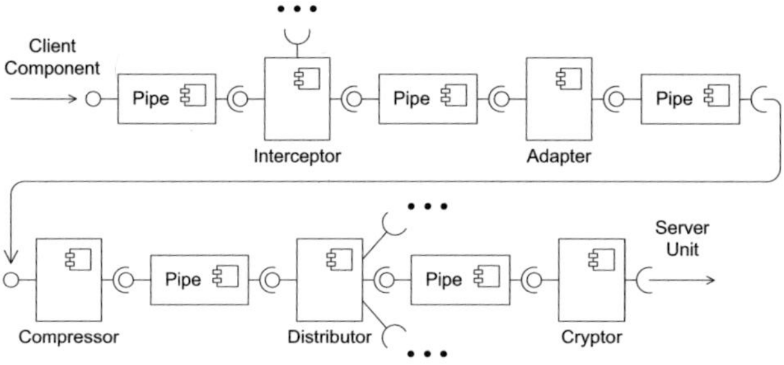

Figure 5.18.: Procedure Call Connector Client Unit.

Figure 5.19 shows a fully featured server deployment unit. Each connected client unit gets its own pipe. This has to be considered because the first processing step can vary, dependent on the selected features. The *syncher* marks the beginning of the critical section. It takes the place of a pipe and its buffering capacity is determined by the feature configuration of the following processing step. When operating in the asynchronous mode, the SEFFs of the pipes which follow the syncher must not fork the call. However it may be possible to shift the syncher in the direction of the sink as long as the single processing steps are thread safe. The minimal server unit consists only out of the sink and its pipe.

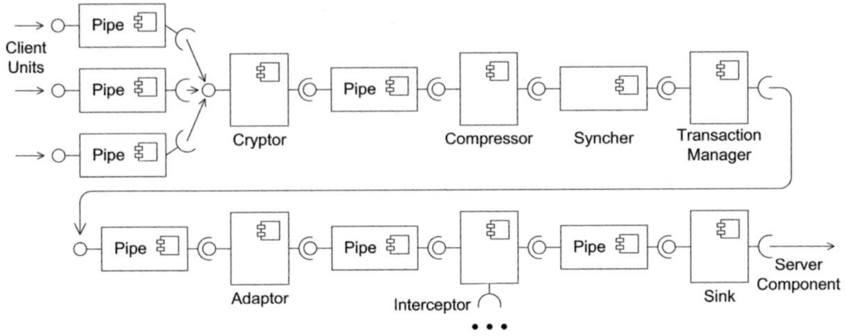

Figure 5.19.: Procedure Call Connector Server Unit.

Pipe&Filter Connector: Summary In this section a connector completion (Procedure Call Connector), its feature diagram and architecture design, was discussed. The concept of Pipe&Filter abstractions for connectors simplifies the design of models. It provides an overall concept for composition of connectors from simple building blocks suitable for performance prediction. The resulting connectors model very accurately blocking effects (limitation of concurrency) in connectors, simple asynchronous communication and when they are calibrated the predictions using these models are very accurate (cf., Section 7.2.2). In addition, the transformations integrating these connectors could easily reuse transformations fragments (cf., Appendix C).

5.3.5. Infrastructure Completions

Today, many applications (e.g., Web servers, Database servers) are designed to process a large number of short tasks that arrive from some remote source (using for example messaging, HTTP, FTP). In the case of server applications, processing of each task is short-lived and the amount of requests is large. The infrastructure completions introduce possibilities how to manage incoming tasks based on different threading models. We discuss the performance of these models.

Thread-Per-Request model A simple model to deal with incoming tasks would be to create a new thread each time a request arrives and process the request in this thread. The Thread-Per-Request model has a significant disadvantage in producing overhead when creating a new thread for each request. A server will spend more time and consume more system resources creating and destroying threads than it would processing actual requests. As a consequence the cost of creation could significantly hamper performance. Additionally, each active thread consumes resources (CPU, Memory). Too many active threads (in one JVM or Application Server) could result in excessive memory consumption and the system could run out of memory. To prevent such problems, applications need some means to limit number of requests processed at the same time. The Thread-Per-Request model is suitable when the frequency of task creation is low and the mean task execution time is high. However, there are other ways how to support use of multiple threads within a server application, as described in the following.

Single-Background-Thread model Another common threading model introduces a single background thread and request queue for tasks of a certain type, which is not suitable for long-running tasks or for high-priority tasks where predictability is important. With the Single-Background-Thread model executing of asynchronous I/O-intensive operations is difficult. Additionally, this model is not optimal on multi-core systems because of its limited parallelizability.

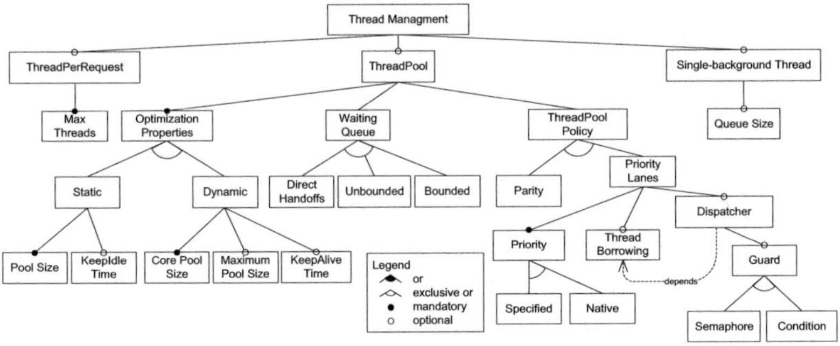

Figure 5.20.: The generic configuration model of thread management strategies.

Thread Pool model The Thread Pool design pattern offers a solution to the problem of thread creation, management and destruction overhead, and the problem of excessive resource usage. The point of the Thread Pool is to avoid creating lots of threads for short tasks. The Thread Pool pattern reuses each thread for multiple tasks. This way the overhead needed for thread creation is spread over many tasks. Additionally, because thread already exists when a request arrives, the delay introduced by thread creation is eliminated and request is serviced immediately. Thread Pools are widely used by many multi-threaded applications. The main advantages are allowing processing to continue while waiting for slow operations such as I/O-intensive tasks, and exploiting the availability of multiple processors. However, usage of Thread Pool deals with certain risks.

Thread Management: Feature Diagram Based on the previous discussion, we extracted important performance-relevant features of thread management in a form of feature diagram. These features summarize different configuration options of the thread management implementation. The resulting feature diagram is illustrated in Figure 5.20

The software architect has a possibility to decide between *Thread-Per-Request*, *Single-Background-Thread* or *Thread Pool* model. The features in the *Thread Pool* subtree are described already in Section 3.3.2.4. For the *Single-Background-Thread* model is an important configuration attribute the size of the request queue. These patterns have a prominent impact on the performance due to its ability to limit the level of concurrency in the system. The *Thread-Per-Request* model separates the processing of incoming and outgoing requests and for each direction we can define a maximal capacity of the system. This completion belongs to the infrastructure completions, for which we allow only one of these completions per resource container, consequently, no conflicts are possible.

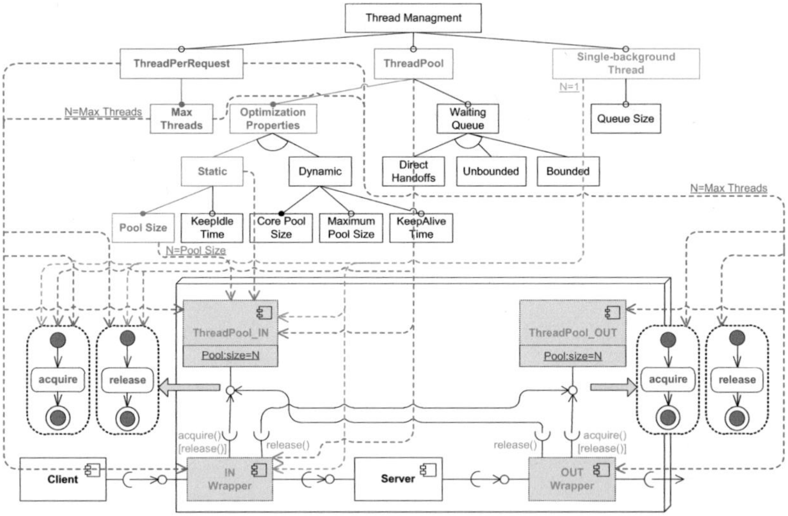

Figure 5.21.: The structural completion skeleton of Thread Management.

Thread Management: Design Dispatching and the management of threads are addressed by a set of patterns dealing with thread management and the infrastructure's support for concurrency. Therefore, completions for dispatching annotate resource containers to which necessary components can be allocated. From the perspective of performance prediction, these patterns can be abstracted as variations of the Thread Pool pattern. We designed performance component-based abstractions for thread management patterns: (cf., Figure 5.21) i.) *Single-Background-Thread*: The abstraction realises synchronous communication. This pattern could be abstracted as Thread Pool with a size of one thread for a client; ii.) *Thread-Per-Request*: The pattern separates the processing of incoming and outgoing requests. For each type there is a distinct pool of worker threads. Therefore, we can abstract the pattern as incoming and outgoing Thread Pool couple with a size equal the capacity of the system; and iii.) *Thread Pool*: The pattern abstraction is a version of a Leader-Follower pattern where one particular thread takes the role of the leader and waits for the next request. All other threads are either queued (i.e., followers) or processing requests (i.e. workers). To model this pattern we can easily use one Thread Pool component with a size equal the capacity of the system. The overview about the required changes (e.g., adding/removing components) of the model helps completion developer with later implementation. Therefore, he is required to first model per hand a completion skeleton for each feature and validate them. Based on these analysis he can choose appropriate abstraction and implement the change mappings. In Figure 5.21 the mappings are illustrated by arrows. The semantic of these arrows is addition of the selected components, interfaces, methods or values to the model.

Thread Management: Summary In this thesis, we focused on the Thread Pool completion, which is used as a running example. The validation of Thread Pool completion is provided in Section 7.2.1. In addition, different implementation of the transformations integrating Thread Pool completion are discussed in Section 7.2.3.

5.4. Discussion

In the following, we discuss the assumptions and limitations of the contributions presented in this chapter.

Structured Metamodel The strongest assumption of the introduced approach is that we expect the metamodel to be designed with a certain structure in mind. However, the current state-of-art in MDSD does not provide a standard set of best practices for metamodel design. Metamodels are mostly designed on demand, without clear guidelines for design and in ad-hoc manner. We showed that structured design of metamodel can support other engineering processes using this metamodel language. Thus, we see here a great potential for future research.

Size of the conflicting set We assume that the conflicting set after the conflict reduction is so small that it is possible to resolve remaining conflicts manually. As the principle of separation of concerns already divides different completions in a responsibility of different roles, thus, completions in one group are semantically very similar, we do not expect a huge number of choices from a number of completions for one role and one element. For example, it is not reasonable to deploy one component using two different messaging middleware completions. Thus, it is very likely that the remaining group of completions would be rather small.

Independence of model elements We assume that independent enhancement of three element types (i.e., components, connectors, infrastructure) in CBSE is possible. In particular, the components are refinable independently of the connectors and the infrastructure, connectors refinement may be dependent on components, and the infrastructure refinement can be dependent on both the connectors and components. This assumption has to be further investigated. Consequently, we have to investigate the sequences of the connectors and components, and cyclic component interdependencies, which make the problem even more challenging.

The applicability of quality heuristics The introduced heuristics quantify the quality of system components, connectors and the infrastructure, based on their performance impact, which is under our performance abstraction the primary metric for our architecture. These heuristics give indications of resulting performance increase or decrease in dependency on some attributes (e.g., bytesize). The indications are results of local analysis of completion subsystems using standard tests. Thus, the exact values would change for a different system or a different usage profile. However, we assume that the performance semantic of the completion remains unchanged and the local heuristics can provide enough information to build learned knowledge about completions and support software developer's decision about the order in completion sequence. To automate this decision further we need to employ automated optimisation techniques, such as the PerOpteryx approach [113].

5.5. Summary

In this chapter, we introduced a method to handle conflicts in a sequence of completions and help software architects to decide on a suitable transformation order. The core of this method is the structure of the completion library, where completion encapsulating expert-knowledge can be registered. The completion library allows archivation and reuse of expert-knowledge. In addition, the initial completions for concurrency design patterns build guidelines that help software architects to create models of parallel architectures. These design patterns are already important and very complex part of parallel programming techniques and as such they are suitable as application domain for completion approach.

In the next chapter, we discuss the quality properties of model transformations integrating introduced model abstractions.

6. Model Transformation Analysis: Evaluating Maintainability

In the previous chapter, we introduced the CHILIES approach based on HOTs. We used a chain of HOTs to process and generate completion transformations. For the success of this approach is critical that the elements (i.e. models, metamodels and transformations) have certain quality characteristics. The main artefacts of MDSD are domain-specific languages (e.g. specified by metamodels) allowing modelling on a higher-level of abstraction and transformations supporting automated generation of different target models. The prominent role of model transformations in MDSD requires that they are treated as traditional software artefacts. The maintainability and ease-of-use of transformations is influenced by various characteristics – as with every programming language artefact. Code metrics are often used to estimate code maintainability, because, transformations, similarly as traditional software artefacts, should be used by different development roles and reused in different contexts, the understandability of transformations is of our concern. In this chapter, we focus on the maintainability and understandability of M2M transformations. We published the work about code metrics for M2M transformations and their evaluation in the proceedings of QoSA 2010 Conference: Research into Practice - Reality and Gaps [91]. This chapter discusses these metrics in the context of this thesis.

The leading challenge of this chapter is:

How to analyse maintainability of relational transformations?

Most of the established metrics do not apply to relational transformation languages (such as QVT Relational) since they focus on imperative (e.g.

object-oriented) coding styles. In this chapter, we define quality metrics for relational transformations, which can be used to analyse the structure of HOTs and completion transformations. Furthermore, we discuss the connection between the transformation and the metamodel. The connection between the transformation and the metamodel is called *metamodel coverage* and is specific for transformations only, no similar property for traditional software artefacts exists.

The remainder of this chapter is organized as follows. Section 6.1 motivates our work and introduces the context of metrics application. Section 6.2 discusses the problem and general observations about the maintainability of transformations. Section 6.3 introduces the maintainability metrics for M2M transformations and specifies the metrics using QVT relational metamodel. Our approach uses the Analysis HOT pattern (see Appendix B) to automatically compute the metrics for M2M transformations implemented in QVT Relational. The automated metrics collection is described in Section 6.4. Finally, Sections 6.5 and 6.6 discuss limitations and summarize the contributions of this chapter.

6.1. Motivation

Model transformations are often used to transform software architectures into code or analysis models. Ideally, these transformations are written in special transformation languages like QVT [72]. With an observable increase in the application of Model-Driven Software Development (MDSD) in industry and research, more and more transformations are written by transformation engineers. Thus, an increasing set of transformation scripts have to be maintained in the near future, i.e., they demand to be understood by other developers, bugs need to be tracked down and removed, and enhancements need to be implemented because of evolving source or target metamodels.

Today there are two main streams of model-to-model transformation languages: operational (i.e. imperative) and relational (i.e. declarative) languages. For operational languages like *QVT Operational*, we can reuse existing literature about software code metrics for imperative, e.g. object-oriented, languages. However, for relational model-transformation languages like *QVT Relational* there is not even a comparable amount of literature.

In traditional object-oriented software development, *software metrics* are used as a mean to estimate the maintainability of code [17]. The estimated maintainability then indicates when the code base becomes too hard to maintain. Software developers take corrective actions like refactorings [58] or code reviews to keep the code in a maintainable state. However, these metrics do not yet exist for relational model transformation languages. Nevertheless, some initial research targets metrics for functional programming languages in general like Lisp or Haskell. Being part of the same language family, some metrics for functional programming languages can serve as a starting point for the definition of metrics for relational model-transformation languages. In this work we draw upon their ideas in defining our own set of metrics for model-transformation languages.

As an initial step towards estimating the maintainability of relational model transformation languages, we present a set of metrics usable to get insight into the maintainability of QVT Relations transformations. For this, we analysed existing metrics for functional programming languages and combined them with general code metrics (e.g. Lines of Code (LOC)) and complemented them with our own experiences from applying QVT Relations. This set of developed metrics shall finally serve as a basis to judge internal transformation quality and to guide the development of transformation refactorings or review checklists (i.e., a list of bad smells to look for). The metrics are described in detail and their ranges of 'bad' values are characterized including a rationale explaining which type of maintainability problem the metric detects.

In CHILIES approach, we used QVT Relational to implement HOTs and completion transformation (i.e., feature effects). Hence, we studied the metrics' applicability and evaluated QVT Relational transformations implementing model completions. This study shows that understanding of relational transformations quickly turns out to be a difficult task. The difficulties increase faster than linearly when transformation sizes increase and single relations become more complex. As an reference example, we evaluated our metrics on the standard model transformation example given by the QVT standard specification [72]: the transformation from UML models to entity-relationship models to show that the metrics (a) are computable and (b) give insight into the transformation's internal quality. The evaluation of the completions transformations and HOTs is described in more detail in Section 7.2.3.

6.2. Problem Domain

The goal of our work is to quantify the maintainability of model transformations. Therefore, we start by defining suitable metrics in this context. We identified a lack of quality metric definitions for relational transformation languages in the literature. Hence, we focus on model transformations created using QVT Relational (QVT-R), but we assume that our metrics can be applied to model transformations created using other relational transformation languages as well. The main observed difference between relational and operational languages is the fact, that operational transformation languages describe a sequence of statements to create certain output. In contrast, relational transformation languages only describe the relations between input and output of a transformation in a declarative manner, not the way how it is computed (non-determinism). This results in special characteristics of relational transformation languages which have to be reflected by the metrics to be defined.

General Observations on Maintainability of QVT-R Transformations: QVT-R can be for example applied in e.g. transformations between languages, code generation and incremental or completion transformations. One main advantage of QVT-R is its brevity and conciseness. In the QVT-R language, the structure of transformations is mainly characterised by the interdependencies of its relations. On the other hand, relations can be defined in a way so that they match overlapping sets of elements. Consequently, this increases complexity in cases when a new relation is introduced and it is influenced by other relations. For example, let transformation T be defined as a set of relations R, $R = \{a,b,c,d\}$. Suppose we want to extend T with a relation e, but e depends on a result of a and a depends on a result of both b and c, while c depends on d. Thus, we first need to understand how relations a,b,c and d are related in order to correctly include e into the transformation. In the case of more complex transformations, it is very hard to have all dependencies in mind. Because of this net of dependencies, it is hard to say if a new introduced relation conflicts with other relations or influences them in an undesired way. One possible design of relational transformation could be clustering of relations that match or create the same element (clustering of top-level relations). Furthermore, the identification of possible execution paths, how long they usually are and what they depend on, is a very complex task.

In following section, we discuss a collection of metrics for relational transformations. These metrics give a quick insight in transformation quality. Additionally, because of the declarative nature of the family of relational transformations we can define metrics to study structure and dependencies between the fragments of the transformations. This technique can be easily built on the system of preconditions and postconditions defined for each relation. The dependency data have various useful applications in the development and maintenance of transformations. By identifying of dependencies between relations and avoiding cyclic dependencies, the understandability of transformations may increase. Also, undesired calls to relations or relations that are never called can be easily recognised.

6.3. Metrics Definition

This section introduces metrics for measuring the quality of model transformations created using relational transformation language, such as QVT-R. For each metric, we give a *description*, including a brief *motivation*. We also include the *rationale* behind the metric giving insights in why we believe the metric indicates the maintainability of a transformation. Additionally, we include a way for the *computation* (if possible using QVT-R and OCL) of the introduced metrics.

6.3.1. Automated Metrics

In this section, we discuss the metrics derived for QVT-R that can be automatically computed. We identified four categories: Transformation *Size* metrics, *Relational* metrics, *Consistency* metrics and *Inheritance* metrics. In the following sections, we give the names, descriptions and rationales of the automated metrics. Table 6.1 then gives the computation directions using OCL for the presented automated metrics.

6.3.1.1. Transformation Size Metrics

The size of the transformation has an impact on the understandability of a transformation. This metric for a whole transformation can be measured in several ways. The number of *lines of code*, for instance, is a simple metric measuring the pure code size of a transformation. This is comparable to measuring lines of code in programming languages. Comments and blank lines are also included in this metric. The number of code, comment and blank lines can also be viewed separately. Used in conjunction with other metrics we can derive valuable measures of a transformation, e.g. when compared to the number of top level relations.

The *number of relations* is a metric that can be used to derive the degree of fragmentation and modularisation of a transformation. Higher number of relations can be considered better, as it is an indicator for a high degree of modularisation. A high degree of modularisation can support the maintainability of a transformation and also the reuse of a transformation or parts of it. The *number of top level relations* gives a picture about the independent parts of a transformation. A top level relation is a starting point for a transformation and can trigger the execution of other relations. An execution of a transformation requires all top level relations to hold. The ratio of top level relations to non-top level relations shows the rate between independent and dependent parts of a transformation. An interesting metric is *number of starts* defined by the number of top relations without when-clause. A higher number of starts increases the number of possible execution paths and therefore makes the transformation less maintainable. The metric *number of domains* expresses the complexity of a transformation dependent on the number of match patterns. The *number of domains predicates* additionally gives information about the complexity of these patterns. The *number of when-predicates* and the *number of where-predicates* defines how complex the dependency graph between relations is.

The *number of metamodels* in a transformation has an impact on the complexity of the transformation itself and its match patterns. The *size of the metamodel* (defined by a number of classes) on which the relations match elements might also have a great impact on the structure and therefore on the understandability and modifiability of the transformation. The larger the metamodel the larger the set of possible instances of this metamodel. Therefore, more combinations may have to be considered in the match patterns of the relations.

6.3.1.2. Relational Metrics

The size of a transformation relation can be measured in different ways. The OMG specification of QVT states that a relation has one or more domains and that every domain has a domain pattern that consists of a tree of template expressions. The size of a relation can be expressed in terms of its number of domains or the depth of the domain patterns. Additionally, relations can define when- and where- predicates giving pre- and postconditions. This leads to three different metrics for measuring the size of a relation: *Number of domains* , *Number of when/where predicates, Size of domain pattern per domain.* Another derived metric, the *ratio between the size of the relations and the number of relations* might also give hints about the maintainability of the transformation itself and shows the linear dependency of effort needed to modify the transformation on the number of relations. However, the direction of the metric (e.g., for better maintainability) remains to be evaluated. For example, having many but small relations helps to understand the transformation punctually, for specific relations. However, grasping the interconnections of many small relations is also a tedious and error-prone task, thus leading to the conclusion that having larger but fewer relations may be also good for maintainability. Still, defining a functional dependency between size and number of relations in a transformation might give hints on the maintainability of the transformation.

The metric *average number of local variables per relation* additionally gives indications on the dependencies within a relation that a developer needs to grasp when trying to understand and modify the relation. A measurement for the complexity of the interconnections between relations is the average number of arguments in the form of its domains and the number of variables that are bound by calls to other relations in when- or where- predicates. These metrics are denoted *val-in* and *val-out*. Note that in QVT-R *val-in* is always the same as *number of domains*. A high number of *val-*

out means that a relation is strongly dependent on the context, which might decrease the reusability of a relation.

Relations generally depend on other relations to perform their task. The dependency of a relation *R* on other relations can be measured by counting the number of times relation *R* uses other relations or queries. These dependency metrics are denoted *fan-in* and *fan-out*, where *fan-in* is the number of calls to *R* and *fan-out* is the number of relations that are called by *R*. A high value of *fan-in* indicates that the relation is reused quite often and therefore is highly reused or somehow more central to the overall transformation. A high value of *fan-out* means that a relation uses a lot of other relations or functions (maybe delegates functionality to library queries), again making the relation more central. The metric *number of enforce/checkonly domains* expresses a rate of change between the domains of the relation (e.g., source and target domain). The metric expresses the number of possible match patterns by the number of checkonly domains and the level of change provided by a relation (a number of diverse change patterns) by the number of enforce domains. The complexity of a transformation may furthermore be affected by the *number of OCL helpers* and *number of lines/restricted elements per OCL query*, which encapsulate more complex behaviour.

6.3.1.3. Consistency Metrics

A high degree of inconsistency in the transformation is a reason for confusion during development and may lead to reusability and transformation completeness problems. To detect an inconsistency in a transformation we introduce a number of consistency metrics. An example of inconsistency could be a relation that was not completed during development. Such a relation could be identified as a relation without domains, with only one domain or with domains without predicates. Therefore, we defined the metrics *number of relations without domains*, *number of relations with singular domains* and *number of domains without predicates*. An additional metric for the detection of incomplete relations is the *number of unused variables*. Unused variables pollute the code and complicate navigation within the transformation.

The already introduced consistency metrics are easy to automate. Another quite generic but still interesting metric is *number of clones*. However, the automation of this metric is a research field by itself. This metric identifies code duplicates, which are, as in other fields of code maintainability, candidates that impact maintainability of the code.

6.3.1.4. Inheritance Metrics

QVT-R transformations can extend each other and override relations from parents. Inheritance metrics measure the level of inheritance of the transformation and its complexity.

<table>
<tr><td>Name</td><td>OCL expression</td></tr>
<tr><td colspan="2">Transformation t</td></tr>
<tr><td>Number of relations</td><td>t.rule → size()</td></tr>
<tr><td>Number of top level relations</td><td>t.rule → select(oclAsType(QVTRelation::Relation).isTopLevel) → size()</td></tr>
<tr><td>Number of starts</td><td>t.rule → select(oclAsType(QVTRelation::Relation).isTopLevel
and oclAsType(qvtrelation::Relation).when → isEmpty()) → size()</td></tr>
<tr><td>Number of when</td><td>t.rule → iterate(r:qvtbase::Rule;sum:Integer = 0|
sum + r.oclAsType(qvtrelation::Relation).when → size())</td></tr>
<tr><td>Number of where</td><td>t.rule → iterate(r:qvtbase::Rule;sum:Integer = 0|
sum + r.oclAsType(qvtrelation::Relation).where → size())</td></tr>
<tr><td>Number of metamodels</td><td>t.modelParameter → size()</td></tr>
<tr><td>Number of OCL queries</td><td>t.ownedOperation → size()</td></tr>
<tr><td colspan="2">Relation r</td></tr>
<tr><td>Number of domains</td><td>r.domain → size()</td></tr>
<tr><td>Number of enforced domains</td><td>r.domain → select(isEnforcable) → size()</td></tr>
<tr><td>Number of checkonly domains</td><td>r.domain → select(isCheckable) → size()</td></tr>
<tr><td>Number of when-predicates</td><td>r.when.predicate → size()</td></tr>
<tr><td>Number of where-predicates</td><td>r.where.predicate → size()</td></tr>
<tr><td>Number of local variables</td><td>r.variable → reject(v | TemplateExp.allInstances().bindsTo.includes(v))
→ size()</td></tr>
<tr><td>Val-In</td><td>see number of domains</td></tr>
<tr><td>Val-Out</td><td>Set{r.when} → including(r.where).predicate → collect(p |
collectVariableArguments OfRelationCallExps(p)).variable → asSet() →
size()</td></tr>
<tr><td>Fan-In</td><td>RelationCallExp.allInstances().referredRelation = r</td></tr>
<tr><td>Fan-Out</td><td>Set{r.when} → including(r.where).predicate → collect(p |
collectRelationCallExps(p))
.referredRelation → asSet() → size()</td></tr>
</table>

Table 6.1.: Automated metrics.

The *balance* metric shows size and distribution of transformation functionality between children. This metric is calculated as the ratio between a number of relations, domains and equations per child transformation in comparison to the average.

In a similar way as in object-oriented programming the dependency of children on their parents can be measured by counting the *number of transitive parents per child* and *number of direct/transitive children per parent.* Based on these metrics and the fan-in and fan-out metrics we can get a view of the dependencies between relations in the different transformations (create a dependency graph). The metric *number of overrides* gives information on how many relations from a parent transformation were overridden by a child relations. The larger this value gets, the more effort has to be invested into understanding which parts of the transformation hierarchy are actually used (combination of non-overridden (inherited), overridden and additional non-inherited parts).

6.3.2. Manually Gathered Metrics

In the following, we describe metrics that are not gathered fully automated, but require manual or semi-automated analysis to determine the actual value of a metric.

6.3.2.1. Similarity of Relations (frequent patterns)

The *Similarity of relations (frequent patterns)* indicates how many similar patterns can be found in a transformation. A large part of the complexity of a transformation and of an abstract model of the transformation comes through the need to understand patterns that occur within these models. The more complex a transformation is, the harder it is to maintain it. Thus, to be able to grasp the complexity of transformations, we propose to emulate human information processing through pattern mining on models. Human analysis of software products is conducted either top-down or bottom-up according to [116]. Using a top-down approach, the analyst tries to apply his/her knowledge about design and domain to classify the software product under analysis. In order to do this he/she tries to gain an overview of the whole application. Developers can then successively pick selected software segments and determine their relevance for his current mental model of the software. Using a bottom-up approach, the analyst will start reading comments of source code or other software artifacts. The control flow of certain sections will then be inspected sequentially and arbitrary selected variables will be traced throughout the flow. Especially in declarative transformation languages, this is a difficult task as there is no explicit control flow. The information gained will be integrated to a mental software model which is the opposite to the top-down approach.

Masak [116] notes that top-down analysis is being conducted more often by experts whereas bottom-up analysis is being used more often by novice analysts. These findings give strong indication that experts may have abstract mental patterns at hand which are being used for analysing the software product whereas novices must resort to documentation. If analysability is measured in terms of time to analyse parts of a software product, the required time will be low if the analysed parts dominantly adhere to the expert's patterns. On the other hand the time will be very high, if the expert can apply only a few of his/her patterns or the software heavily differs from patterns known to him/her. These general observations were also stated for visual patterns in [148] which is why we propose to incorporate them into an analysability metric.

This metric can be computed by using the frequent pattern mining algorithm presented in [105] to identify possible frequent patterns. From these candidates the relevant patterns can be selected and their similarity can be estimated. However, the result of these pattern mining is mostly a superset of frequent patterns as they would be found by a human. Thus, manual selection needs to be performed to see whether each of the most frequent patterns is really a pattern that occurs as repeating structure in the transformation or if it is just the result of constraints on e.g., the transformation metamodel. For example, in QVT Relational a frequent pattern that is the result of the language concept would be that each relation domain has a root variable which refers to a meta-class that is contained in the package referred to by the domains typed model (see [72] for the QVT-R metamodel). However, this construct in inherent to QVT relations and is not a frequent pattern that would be relevant for the analysability of a transformation. Thus, this metric cannot be computed fully automatically but needs an additional manual filter action. For example, a result of this metric could be that 30% of all relations of a transformation employ a pattern involving the matching or creation of a certain tree structure consisting of specific types of model elements within the source or target model. As humans are pretty good in pattern matching, a developer would then be able to recognise this combination over and over again thus helping him/her to more easily understand these 30% of relations.

6.3.2.2. Number of Relations that Follow a Design Pattern

The *Number of relations that follow a design pattern* may be another important indicator for transformation maintainability. The determination of this metric is a tedious manual task as a design pattern is an abstract concept. It may occur in a form that can only vaguely be identified.

The number of design patterns employed in the transformation may be a strong indicator on how good a transformation can be understood by external readers. However, as the area of transformation development is still quite immature, only few design patterns have been identified yet. To determine this metric, we need to count the number of design patterns and their occurrences within the transformation. For example, if a transformation uses the *Flattening Pattern* from Section 4.4 throughout its whole implementation and a developer knows what that pattern is used for he or she can grasp the meaning of the transformation more easily.

6.3.2.3. Type Cut Through Source/Target Metamodel

As mentioned at the beginning of this chapter, the metamodel coverage is specific for model transformations. The relation between the transformation and the metamodel is analysed through studying metamodel coverage. Each model transformation transforms source model which conform to a source metamodel to a target model which conform to a target metamodel. Some transformations transform all elements defined by the metamodel (e.g., translation). Other transformations transform only a subset of the metamodel elements (e.g., refinement or completion). We already used this analysis in Chapter 5 to minimize conflicts between transformation in a sequence of completions.

To acquire insight about the parts of metamodel covered by a transformation we propose to study a *Type Cut Through Source/Target Metamodel*. The metric *Type Cut Through Source/Target Metamodel* represents the rate of overlapping rules with respect to the transformation's metamodels. The type cut concerning a metamodel is the set of patterns that match instances of the same parts of a metamodel. In the UML to RDBMS example from the QVT standard (from which an excerpt is shown in Listing 2.1) the type cut concerning the meta-class `UmlClass` would be all those relations that contain a pattern that matches any `UMLClass`. The greater this overlap is, the more attention has to be paid when patterns of relations are modified in order to not lose coverage of possible instances of the metamodel.

To compute this metric we need to count the number of relations that overlap over the same part of a metamodel. For example, Relations *a*, *b* and *c* can all match instances of the same meta-class *m*. Thus the overlap rate concerning class *m* would be 3. Finding type cuts that only refer to a certain element of the metamodel, such as one meta-class *m* can be done straightforward. However, it might be more interesting for more fine-grained patterns that are matched using several different relations. How such a detailed type cut can be identified remains subject of future research.

6.4. Computation of Metrics

We implemented a tool set to analyse the metrics presented in Section 6.3 automatically. In the first step (cf. Figure 6.1), the transformation code (*QVT*) is parsed which results in a transformation model (*QVTModel*). This model can be then analysed using our maintainability metrics. The description of metrics is given by the metrics model (*MetricsQVT*) on the higher-level of abstraction. A HOT then generates transformations for actual analysis based on this metrics description. Here, we implement the Analysis HOT pattern introduced in Appendix B. The resulting metrics model gives information about the quality properties of the analysed transformations. Using a pretty-printer, we can extract an input to other analysis tools from the metrics model. Note that for some metrics an additional input could be required, such as metamodels for *Type Cut Through Source/Target Metamodel* or models of transformation design patterns for *Number of relations that follow a design pattern.*

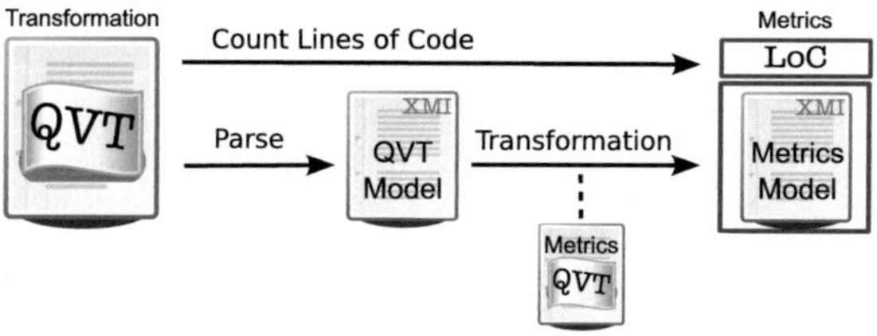

Figure 6.1.: Workflow for omputation of metrics.

The automated metrics described in section 6.3.1 can mostly be expressed as OCL expressions on the QVT-R meta-model. These OCL expressions can be used to count the number of elements of a specific type, for instance the number of relations a transformation has. The expressions have to be evaluated in the context of a transformation or a relation depending on whether a transformation local or relation-local metric is calculated. Table 6.1 shows the OCL expressions used for calculating the metrics. To bring these metrics together, relation local metrics can be aggregated by calculating an average.

```
query countSubExps(templ:QVTRelation::TemplateExp) : Integer
{
    if (templ.oclIsTypeOf (QVTTemplate::ObjectTemplateExp))
    then templ.oclAsType(QVTTemplate::ObjectTemplateExp).part->iterate(p:QVTRelation:
                                            :PropertyTemplateItem; acc:Integer = 1|
                                            acc + countSubExps(p.value.
                                            oclAsType(QVTRelation::TemplateExp)))
    else
     if (templ.oclIsTypeOf (QVTTemplate::CollectionTemplateExp))
     then countSubExps(templ.oclIsTypeOf (QVTTemplate::CollectionTemplateExp).
                                   member.oclAsType(QVTRelation::TemplateExp)))
     else
     1
     endif
    endif
}
```

Listing 6.1: Query function for calculating the domain predicate count.

For more complex metrics like the domain pattern tree depth it was necessary to write more complex OCL query functions. Listing 6.1 shows an OCL query function for recursively counting the nodes of a domain pattern tree. To easily apply all metric expressions and query functions, we developed a QVT-R transformation that transforms a QVT transformation to a special metrics model. The metrics metamodel allows for compact storage of metrics for every relation in a transformation and for the transformation itself. Moreover, it is possible to store the aggregated values that are also calculated by our metrics transformation. Furthermore, for measuring the lines of code, we utilised common methods used for programming languages. We distinguished whitespace, pure comment and code lines. Figure 6.1 shows the workflow for retrieving the metrics.

6.5. Discussion

The definition of metrics with the goal to estimate quality attributes, such as maintainability, always comes with the wish to indicate whether a lower or a higher value of a metric is better or worse. However, this decision cannot be made without a sound validation of the 'meaning' of a metric. For example, having a low number of relations, at first glance, seems to be good for maintainability whereas a high number seems to be bad. On the other hand, if these few relations are very long they may be harder to maintain that more but smaller relations. Thus, in this chapter we only identified what could be possible indicators that may resemble maintainability of transformations. We intentionally did not decide, for most of our metrics, which 'direction' of a metric is good or bad concerning maintainability. We leave it to future work to determine and evaluate this meaning. Through empirical evaluations need to be performed in order identify how meaningful each metric is.

Furthermore, the implementation of the metrics extracting limits our approach to the transformations implemented in QVT-R. Despite, this limitation is motivated by the application of these metrics to evaluate completion transformations which are implemented in QVT-R, it is obvious that for their application in other contexts we have to generalise these metrics further. We expect that presented metrics can be applied to other model transformation language, however it has to by further investigated.

6.6. Summary

In this chapter, we presented an initial set of quality metrics to evaluate the maintainability of QVT Relational transformations. However, such metrics could be applied to different relational transformations, they play important role when considering completion transformations. We apply proposed metrics in Chapter 7 to compare different implementations of the completion transformations. Moreover, we demonstrate the use of these metrics on a reference transformation and HOTs implementations to show their application in real world settings.

The presented metrics help software architects to judge the maintainability of their model transformations. Based on these judgements, software architects can take corrective actions (like refactorings or code-reviews) whenever they identify a decay in maintainability of their transformations. This results in higher agility when changing metamodels of software architectures or their platforms, which together with metamodel build basis for transformation definition.

7. Validation

This chapter presents the validation of the contributions presented in this thesis. We identified two main goals for the validation: (i) to asses the validity of the model completion as an artefact in the MDSPE process and (ii) to evaluate the quality properties of used MDSD artefacts. We structure the validation based on these goals.

Our hypotheses are evaluated based on different levels of validation for prediction models as introduced by [27]. For the first goal, we validate several aspects: we evaluate the accuracy of model-driven quality prediction using performance completions introduced in Section 5.3. Furthermore, we evaluate the compositionality and the ordering in a sequence of completions. For the second goal, we evaluate the understandability and maintainability of the completion transformations quantitatively. In particular, we study the maintainability of the completions and necessary HOT transformations. For this purpose, we use the approach and metrics for evaluating maintainability of model-to-model transformations presented in Chapter 6. Moreover, we sketch further validation studies for empirical evaluation.

This chapter is structured as follows. In Section 7.1, we discuss the validation goals. In Section 7.2.1, we study the validity of model completions presented in Section 5.3. Furthermore, Section 7.2.2 discusses the composition of completions. In Section 7.2.3, we evaluate the maintainability of used transformations. Section 7.3 summarizes and discusses the validation goals.

7.1. Validation Goals

Within the validation of our approach, we study the validity of model completions and the quality properties of used MDSD artefacts. The validation goals and derived validation questions for these two aspects are presented below in Section 7.1.1 and Section 7.1.2 respectively. As introduced by [27], we can validate model-driven prediction approaches on several levels. We discuss these validation levels in the following and apply them to validate our goals.

Levels of validating model-based prediction approaches In the work of Böhme and Reussner [27], several levels for validating model-based prediction approaches are introduced. These levels characterise validations of model-based prediction approaches. The automated completion-based enhancements of MDSPE introduce variability and incremental completion concepts to the models. Thus, we extend the description of validation levels below to explicitly cover the model completion step as well.

7.1.1. Validation Type I: Accuracy Validation

The first level of validation (metric validation [27]) compares the prediction results (e.g., response time) of the model-driven prediction approach to the measured properties of the real-world subject (e.g., measured response time of an implementation). The studied property of the prediction approach is the accuracy of the prediction.

In the case of completion support, additional aspects are important. The prediction approach is required to: (i) deliver more accurate predictions using models with completions as without and it should deliver accurate predictions for each variant of a completion that is derived based on a feature model. Moreover, when multiple completions are used, (ii) their valid compositions should provide accurate predictions, as well.

TYPE I: PREDICTION ACCURACY The accuracy of performance prediction approaches has been studied in several case studies, c.f. [98]. In this work, we focus on performance and assume that the quality prediction approaches used are valid. Thus, the goal of the validation is to evaluate individual completions, assuming a perfect underlying prediction model. The completion developer is responsible for the validation task during the completion development process. Each completion has to be validated before it is registered in the completion library. We give an example how this completion validation task can be realised and validate the completions introduced in this thesis. The first question we need to answer for this purpose is:

Q1: Can completed model provide more accurate performance predictions?

To validate the accuracy of the completion in this study, we compare the results of performance prediction based on the completed model and the performance measurements on the real implementation. Additionally, we study real-system properties (such as state dependency) which can be modelled in PCM using completions. We validate three completions in this work: (i) Statefull 'Message Oriented Middleware' (MOM), (ii) 'Thread Pool', and (iii) 'Procedure Call Connector'.

The detailed description and results of the validation can be found in Section 7.2. We validate platform-specific completions for particular software platforms (using particular version of middleware). In our studies, we can demonstrate that it is possible to create meaningful completions that yield accurate predictions. However, we do not claim that our observations are transferable to all other platforms and software systems, due to further developments of platforms and related complex effects on performance. Certainly, this validation can be repeated for new platforms and completions can be recalibrated.

TYPE I: COMPLETION COMPOSITION AND ORDERING In this validation step, we evaluate the compositionality and the ordering in a sequence of completions and their accuracy in composition. We pose the second evaluation question:

Q2: Can models be automatically completed using a multiple completions to provide more accurate performance predictions?

For this goal, we validate the composition and ordering of three completions in the Procedure Call Connector, i.e. its abstraction using Pipe&Filter pattern. The detailed description and results of the validation can be found in Section 7.2.

7.1.2. Validation Type II: Applicability Validation

The second level of validation addresses the applicability of model-driven prediction approaches. The validation of applicability assesses the information that has to be obtained to apply the approach, the creation of prediction models, the execution of the prediction or analysis, and the interpretation of the results.

The completion-based approach inherits the applicability properties from the used prediction methods, or the MDSPE process integrating the completion step. Therefore, the applicability regarding required information, model creation and results interpretation is mainly a property of the used prediction model. However, we study the applicability of completion-related method enhancements. We can distinguish two different levels at which the applicability of completions has to be discussed.

Completion users have to understand the feature models to be able to apply them to the CBA model. The questioned is, if is the specification of configuration models using feature diagrams is appropriate. The instantiation of completions happens automatically and as such is not in concern of completion user. The completions and their feature models are created once by experts for a specific prediction metamodel (i.e., PCM in this thesis).

Feature models are a well known and intuitive method to illustrate decision trees. Their applicability properties are inherited from the definition of feature model metamodel and its syntax and semantics.Feature diagram have been used in the domain of generative programming and SPLs for more than a decade. They have been introduced by Czarnecki et al. in [46] in 2000. The completion-related extensions of the feature model are not visible to the completion user and are necessary only for the implementation of automated transformation generation. As such, the feature models are considered as well-known and applicable for a completion-based approach.

The completion developer, however, has more complex task to create a completion and register it with the completion library. Here, we build on the very important prerequisite that the task of domain engineering is supported by automated benchmarking approaches, such as Software Performance Cockpit [169]. Having this prerequisite in mind, the collection and analysis of measurement data is of no major concern for completion developer. Using such automated measurement approaches, it is possible to validate all configuration combinations, which would be a huge effort to do manually. Since the actual domain engineering step and the completion validation is automated, it requires no additional manual effort and inherits its applicability properties from the measurement approach.

Instead of validating the applicability of our method in isolation, it seems more promising and to result in more insight to conduct an empirical study of model-based prediction method with completions and comparing it to model-based prediction method without completion mechanism as a whole. However, such empirical study is out of scope for this thesis and brings no added value at this point, therefore we use established evaluation techniques using code metrics indicating the applicability of our approach. We focus in this evaluation on the complexity of the completion implementation. Especially, the complexity of completion transformations gives indicators on applicability of CHILIES for completion development.

Thus, the remaining applicability aspect for the completion developer is the ability to identify necessary model changes and implement transformation fragments. The identification of model changes is dependent on the developer's domain specific knowledge and as such is hard to measure or quantify. In this validation, we focus on the understandability and complexity of transformations and transformation fragments. The development effort necessary to implement required transformations and transformation fragments is discussed in the second goal of this validation. The complexity and maintainability of transformations is evaluated using the metrics introduced in Chapter 6. We present the validation plan and the results for this goal in Section 7.2.

TYPE II: COMPLEXITY COMPARISON This part of the validation discusses maintainability and applicability properties of completions, related models and transformations. Based on code metrics and their results collected for the evaluated transformations, we discuss and assess the development effort necessary to create and maintain completions. In the following, we pose the third evaluation question:

Q3: What are the quality, especially maintainability, properties of used transformations?

Furthermore, we have to discuss the fragmentation of transformations and its complexity. Therefore, we pose a forth evaluation question:

Q4: Is the complexity of transformations decreased by separation of concerns in feature-related transformation fragments?

We use the maintainability metrics for transformations introduced in Section 6 to evaluate these goals.

TYPE II: EMPIRICAL STUDY As mentioned before, an empirical study of model-based prediction method with completions as a whole is out of scope for this thesis. We inherit the applicability properties of the used PCM approach. A initial validation of the understandability and applicability of the PCM approach was conducted in two empirical studies [140, 112]. The additional validation of the remaining aspects related to completions applicability can be derived from these studies. In both studies, participants, with background software engineering knowledge, were trained in making quality prediction with PCM. The participants were asked to create models, execute the prediction method and analyse results of the prediction. Using PCM tools, they had to create performance abstractions, now encapsulated in completions, by hand without any automated support. Thus, these case studies indicate that abstractions encapsulated in completions can be understood and parametrised, reusable models can be created by a trained user. The most significant advantage of completions is separation of concerns, reuse and automation. Completions decrease manual development effort previously need to create the performance abstractions of performance-related aspects. However, to quantify the decrease of development effort using completions we have to conduct more focused studies comparing groups of trained users building their models with and without completions. More details on the conducted studies can be found in [140, 112], including the posed questions, a detailed discussion of the results, and the threats to validity. Further validation studies for applicability evaluation are part of the future work.

7.1.3. Validation Type III: Cost/Benefit Validation

The third level is called "benefit validation" and is concerned with the cost/benefit evaluation of a prediction method. In this type of validation, the costs, resulting from usage of the method, are compared to the expected benefit, which can be an improvement of the modelled subject, an evaluation of planned alternatives, and the recognition of not favourable design decisions. The common benefit of all prediction approaches is the reduction of effort in later development phases of the software life-cycle, such as correction of wrong design decisions or performance problems.

To validate approaches on this level, a controlled experiment is needed during which whole software projects have to be executed with and without using the presented approach. After the development projects finish, we can evaluate benefits resulting from completion usage. Such validation is the most expensive level of validation (with respect to time and effort) and, thus, is rarely executed in practice. Due to the high effort, we cannot conduct this type of validation in the scope of this thesis.

7.2. Improving Prediction Accuracy using Performance Completions

We claim that our approach supports developers in improving the accuracy of quality predictions using the completed models. In this step, we assume that developers have a software architecture model with quality annotations (e.g., PCM) and an automated measurement framework (e.g., Software Performance Cockpit) available. In this section, we present the validation settings and results for the validation goals specified in the previous section.

7.2.1. Type I: Prediction Accuracy

First, we address question $Q1$ regarding the prediction accuracy:

Q1: Can completed model provide more accurate performance predictions?

As the prediction accuracy using completions depends on the accuracy of underlying performance prediction method, we reviewed previous work discussing the accuracy of PCM prediction method. In the context of the PCM, numerous case studies demonstrate that accurate prediction models can be created [101, 103, 75, 100, 15, 18, 76, 80, 106, 86, 104]. In this work, we do not focus on the accuracy of PCM models, but on the prediction accuracy of specific completions.

Additionally, some of the mentioned studies [101, 75, 80, 86] use PCM models that have been created and calibrated using measurements of the studied system. Such models are validated by the comparison between the predicted performance properties and measurements of the system. The studies mentioned above assessed the accuracy of PCM models at hand. They do not make a statement about the prediction accuracy of model variations without recalibration . Some of the case studies [103, 15, 18, 104, 76, 77] also discussed the issues of model variants, changed parametrisation, and calibration. Two studies [103, 15] demonstrated that it is possible to vary parts of a model in isolation. In the case studies, a component was added to the architecture of the initial system. The component was measured, modelled and calibrated in isolation. The predictions for the resulting system were successfully compared to measurements of an analogously changed implementation.

Other two studies [18, 76] evaluated the accuracy of systems using initial MOM completion across different platforms. The effects of the messaging configurations such as message size, messaging protocol, and use of encryption and authentication were studied. The encryption and authentication were measured in isolation. The performance abstractions were weaved into the initial models, exchanged or refined model elements and changed the systems topology. The predictions using resulting models were successfully compared to the with measurements of real systems. These studies demonstrate that completions can be parametrised, can be calibrated using measurements, and are reusable in different execution contexts.

In the following sections, we discuss two completions: (i) the stateful enhancements to the 'Message Oriented Middleware' and (ii) the infrastructure completion 'Thread Pool'. For each completion we discuss the goal of the measurement, used metrics and assumptions, created models and corresponding implementation, and the results of the comparison between measurements and prediction results.

7.2.1.1. Validation: Connector Completion 'Statefull Message Oriented Connector'

To provide accurate predictions, performance models have to include many low-level details. Reusable performance completions ease development of such models and are built using the MDSPE process introduced in Section 3. In this section, we validate enhancements to the 'Message Oriented Middleware' (MOM) first introduced as manually (i.e., implemented in JAVA) created completion by Happe et al. in [76]. In their work, the MOM Completion was validated in the context of real system, such validation here, therefore brings no added value, instead we focus on the specific aspects of this completion. We introduced enhancements to MOM Completion allowing its automation in [93, 92]. Additionally, we introduced a State Manager (see Section 5.3.3.2) to the internal 'message transfer' component of the completion skeleton. Our extensions of MOM completion allow to model transactional communication between components. From the performance prediction point of view, we discuss especially the stateful properties of this completion. The validation of these aspects is based on our work in [94]. The foundations of the stateful performance engineering concept is discussed as additional contribution of this thesis in Appendix A. Furthermore, we implemented this completion in three ways (i) manually in JAVA, (ii) partially automated using mark model and (iii) fully automated using transformation fragments. We discuss the advantages and complexity of such implementations in Section 7.2.3.

SETTING: QUESTION, METRICS, ASSUMPTIONS The key challenge of performance completion design is to find the right performance abstraction for the system under study. To identify the performance-relevant behaviour and factors, we employ a combination of goal-driven measurements and existing knowledge about the functional system behaviour. The process to build feature diagram, identify and implement feature effects is described in Section 3.3. In this validation case study, we start with the basic structure of the completion for message-based systems which was introduced in [76]. In Figure 7.1, a feature model describes the possible configurations of the MOM Completion.

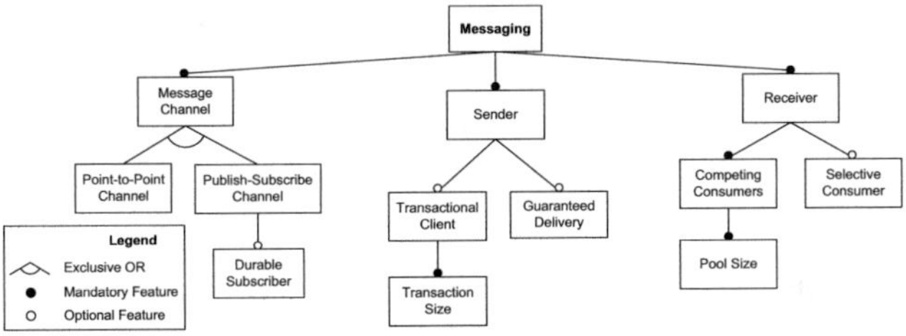

Figure 7.1.: Feature Model for the MOM Completion [76].

The feature model captures possible configurations for a messaging system. The configuration includes the type of *Messaging Channel* as well as characteristics of the *Sender* and *Receiver*. For example, a Messaging Channel can be configured as a *Point-to-Point Channel* if only a single Receiver is needed. The *Message Size* is a property of the Sender and expresses the amount of data transferred. Furthermore, the number of *Competing Consumers* at the Receiver's side can be specified. The choice of either of these features results in a change of the architectural model. The complexity of these changes varies from setting a parameter, through structural changes, to globally changing the deployment of a whole system.

In our case study, we consider a feature configuration with the selected features: *Point-to-Point Channel*, *Competing Consumers*, *Pool Size* of 4, *Transactional Client*, *TransactionSize* of 1000 messages, and *Message Size* of 1 kilobyte.

The configuration of a message-oriented middleware (e.g., a size of a transaction) can affect the delivery time of messages [94] as illustrated in Figure 7.2. Unfortunately, software architects cannot include these details into their architectural models. The middleware's complexity and the specific knowledge on the implementation (that is required to create the necessary models) would increase the modelling effort dramatically. While most of the implementation details are not known in advance, a rough knowledge about the design patterns that are to be used might be already available. This knowledge can be exploited for further analysis, such as performance and reliability prediction, and for code generation.

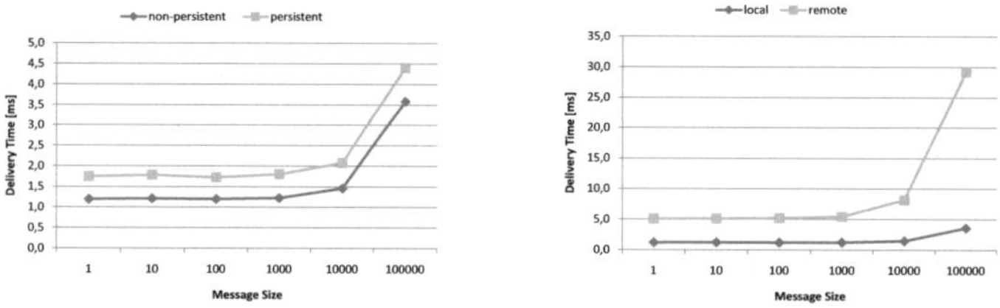

(a) Persistent vs. non-persistent message transfer.

(b) Local vs. remote message transfer.

Figure 7.2.: The influence of message size on the delivery time [93, 76].

We extended the MOM Completion to include the state-dependent effects to the PCM models and allow to study their properties too. In the following, we give an example for the influence of state on software performance which is taken from the area of message based systems. In particular, we are interested in the delivery time (time from sending a message until it is received) of messages send within a transaction. Messaging systems, which implement the Java Message Service standard [74], explicitly support transactions for messages. The transactions guarantee that all messages are delivered to all receivers in the order they have been send. To achieve such a behaviour, Sun's JMS implementation MessageQueue 4.1 [1] waits for all incoming messages of a transaction and, then, delivers them sequentially.

Figure 7.3 shows the measured delivery times for a series of transactions with 1000 messages each (the sender initiates a new transaction (as

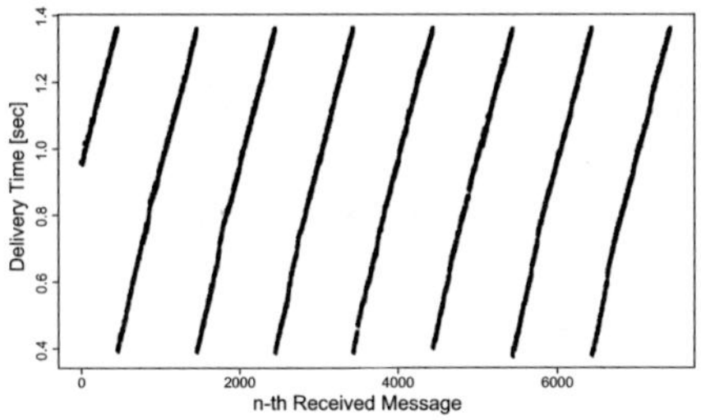

Figure 7.3.: Time series of a transaction with 1000 messages per transaction set.

part of a session), passes 1000 messages to the MOM, and finally, commits the transaction). All messages arrive within the first 0.4 seconds and are delivered sequentially within the next second. This behaviour leads to delivery times of 0.4 seconds at minimum. The delivery times grow linearly until the transaction is completed. In this example, the position of a message in the transaction set determines its delivery time. Thus, the measured delivery times are *not* independent and identically distributed but strongly depend on the number (and size) of messages that have already been sent. As a consequence, we need to keep track of the messages that are part of a transaction. Additionally, the periodical utilisation of resources (e.g., CPU) influences performance. To model such a behaviour, we need to extend our model and introduce a notion of state as part of our model.

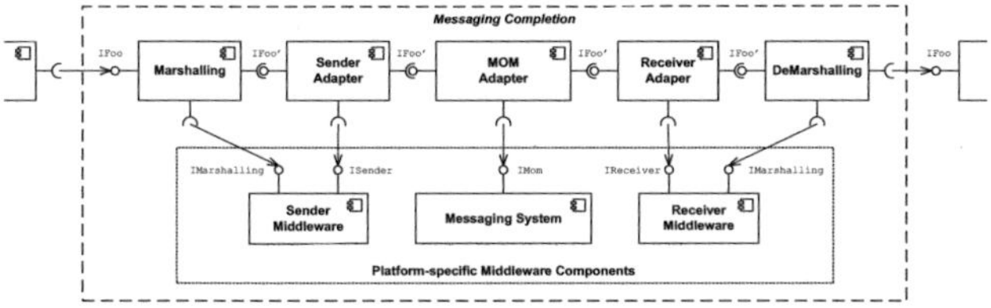

Figure 7.4.: Components of the MOM Completion [based on [77]].

IMPLEMENTATION Transactional messages are common in today's enterprise applications, such as implemented by *SPECjms2007 Benchmark* [152]. However, the transactions used in the supply chain management supermarket of the benchmark are limited to small, predefined transaction sizes. To provide a better evaluation, we implemented an application that allows to configure the number of messages send in one transaction following the philosophy of SPECjms2007. We excluded external disturbances (such as database accesses) and focussed on the evaluation of the messaging system.

For performance prediction, we extended our performance completion for message-oriented middleware called messaging completion in the following [76]. The messaging completion subsumes several components that reflect the influence of different middleware configurations such as guaranteed delivery, competing consumers, or selective consumers. In [76], it was already demonstrated that the messaging completion can predict the performance of a SPECjms2007 scenario with an accuracy of 5% to 10%. In the subsequent paragraphs, we present an extension of our messaging completion that enables the prediction of influences of transactions on the delivery time of a message.

Completion for Message-oriented Middleware: Figure 7.4 shows the components and connections that are generated by the messaging completion (see [76] for details). The completion consists of *adapter components* and *middleware components*. The first forwards requests and calls the middleware components that issue platform-specific resource demands. The `Marshalling` component computes the message size based on the method's signature. The message size is passed to subsequent adapters as an additional parameter, so that the original interface (`IFoo`) needs to be extended (`IFoo'`). The `Sender Adapter` calls the `Sender Middleware` which loads the resources of the sender's node and forks the call to the `MOM Adapter` to reflect the asynchronous behaviour of the messaging system. The `MOM Adapter` realises the transactional behaviour of the messaging system. The `Receiver Adapter` calls the `Receiver Middleware` and,

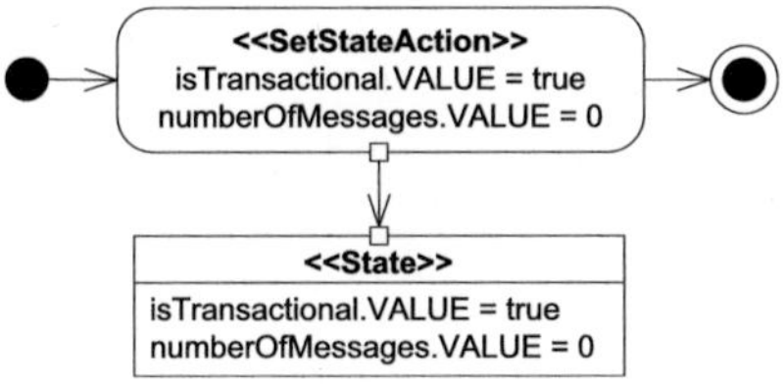

Figure 7.5.: Starting a new transaction.

thus, loads the resources of the receiver's node. It forwards the requests to `Demarshalling` which maps the extended interface (`IFoo'`) back to the original interface (`IFoo`).

Modelling transactional behaviour of the `MOM Adapter`: In order to start a transaction, the sender has to explicitly call method `startTransaction`. Its behaviour (see figure 7.5) consists of a single `SetStateAction`, which resets the number of messages to zero (`numberOfMessages.VALUE = 0`) and enables the transactional message transfer (`isTransactional.VALUE = true`). When `startTransaction` has been called, all messages send in the following will be part of the transaction until `commitTransaction` is executed. The behaviour of the `MOM Adapter` varies for transactional and non-transactional messages (see figure 7.6). The `MOM Adapter` behaviour is extended as it is illustrated by Figure 5.7.

If the message is not part of a transaction, the adapter simply calls the `Messaging System`, which loads its local resources with the service demands necessary for transferring the message, and forwards the messages. Otherwise, if the message is part of a transaction, then the `MOM Adapter` increases the current number of messages of the transaction (numberOfMessages.VALUE = numberOfMessage.VALUE + 1) and queues the message. The queueing is modelled by two actions. The first external call action (`IMOM.queueMessage`) loads the resources of the `Messaging System`. The second action acquires the passive resource transactionQueue, which blocks the message transfer until the transactionQueue is released.

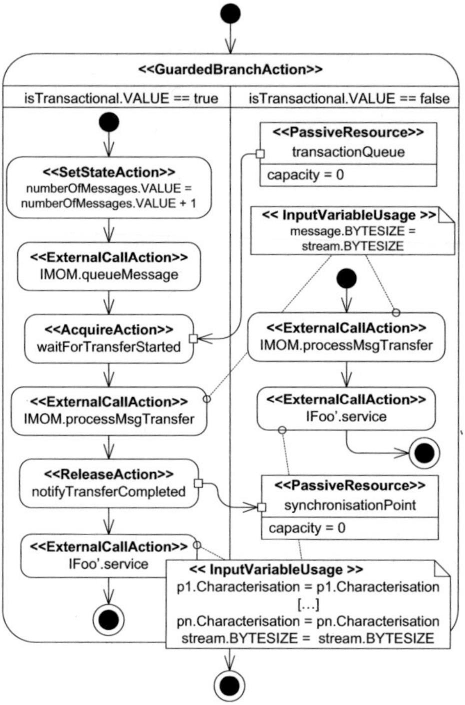

Figure 7.6.: MOM Adapter: Message Transfer.

When the transaction is committed and the messages blocked at the transactionQueue are released, the MOM Adapter processes the message transfer (IMOM.processMessageTransfer). Furthermore, it notifies the behaviour of commitTransaction that the message has been transfered (transferCompleted is released). Finally, the MOM Adapter forwards the message to the Receiver Adapter. This behaviour ensures that all messages are delivered in the same order as they have been send. Figure 7.7 shows the behaviour executed to commit a transaction. The RD-

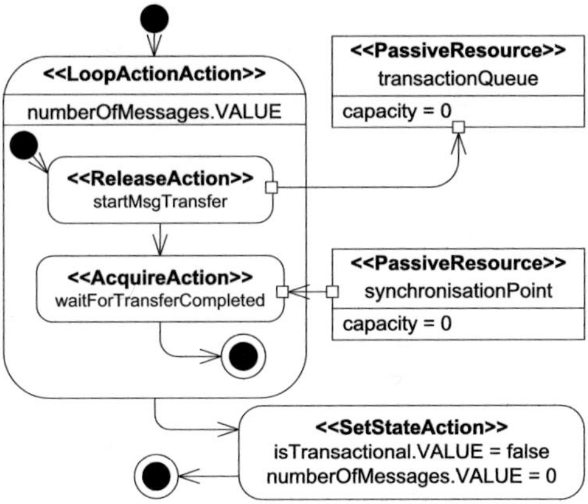

Figure 7.7.: MOM Adapter: Commit Transaction.

SEFF reflects the successful execution of a transaction and neglects possible rollbacks and re-executions. To commit a transaction and deliver all messages to the receivers, a loop action iterates over all messages blocked during the transaction (`numberOfMessages.VALUE`). For each message, it unblocks its transfer (releases passive resource `transactionQueue`. To ensure the sequential delivery of messages, it waits for the successful transfer of the message (aquires passive resource `synchronisationPoint`) before it continues. Finally, the transaction is terminated (`isTransactional.VALUE = false`) and the number of queued messages is reset (`numberOfMessages.VALUE = 0`).

RESULTS We used the PCM's simulation environment SimuCom [18] to predict the performance for three different configuration variants of message-oriented middleware. Basically, SimuCom interprets PCM instances as a queuing network model with multiple G/G/1 queues. To instantiate the parametric performance completions, we applied model-driven transformations mirroring chosen configuration for each of the alternatives.

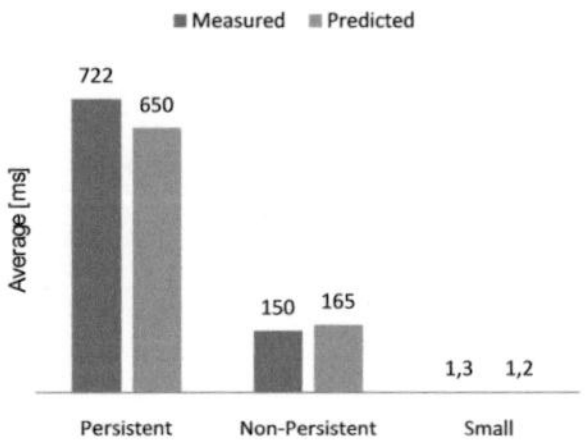

(a) Average of the delivery time.

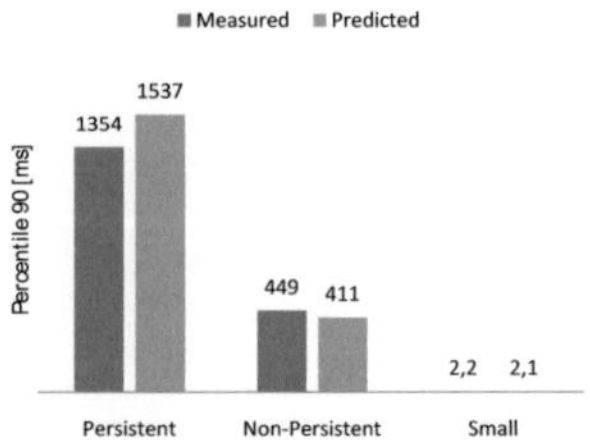

(b) 90% percentile of the delivery time.

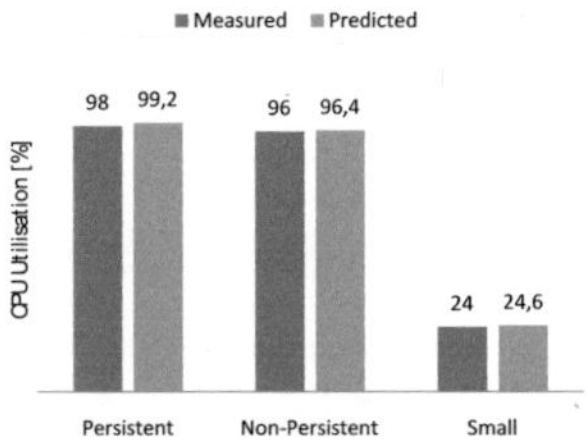

(c) CPU utilisation.

Figure 7.8.: Predictions and measurements of the three design alternatives [93, 77].

Figure 7.8 summarises the predictions and measurements for the three design alternatives. These results were analysed by Happe et al. in [77]. In the following we summarize them, as a proof that we started with accurate calibration of initial MOM completion. The results show the average and 90% percentile of the delivery time as well as the CPU's utilisation. Measured values are printed in dark grey, predicted values in light grey. The prediction error for the average delivery time and the 90% percentile is below 15% in all cases. The CPU utilisation with an error below 3%. Among the considered alternatives the third one, called 'small' (with reduced data size), shows the best performance. The considered scenario in this thesis is the usage of not-persistent message transfer, where the measured and predicted average times for one message are 1,50 ms and 1,65 ms. The stateless model predicted that 90% of all messages in transaction are delivered in less than 411 ms.

Figure 7.9 shows the prediction results for transactional messages with stateful model. The corresponding real measurement is shown in figure 7.3. The predictions correctly reflect the dependency of a message's delivery time on its position in the transaction. This behaviour was not visible in the prediction results using the stateless variant of MOM completion. Furthermore, the predicted delivery times range from 400 ms to 1400 ms which corresponds to the observed delivery times for the transaction size of 1000 messages. Moreover, Figure 7.10 illustrates the prediction results for the CPU utilisation using stateful model. The prediction results illustrate delay

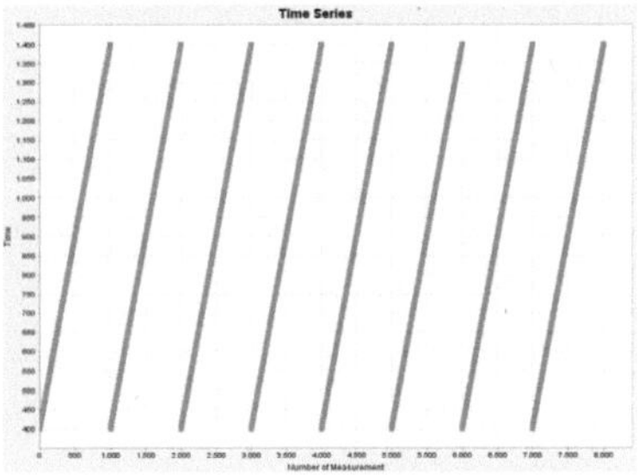

Figure 7.9.: Predicted delivery times for messages.

in transfer of messages in transaction, the first message in transaction is the fastest one and the last one is the slowest one. Thus, with the position of the message in the transaction increases the time spent in the message channel too. In Figure 7.9 is the delay in message transfer, the start and commit of one transaction clearly visible. In stateless model, the distribution of the time for message transfer shows highest probability between 1,6ms and 1,75ms (cf, Figure 7.11). However, the mean value for the transfer of whole transaction shows very small difference (for correct mean value it is enough to multiply transfer time of one message by the number of messages in transaction), the error in median increases significantly with the size of the transaction. Additionally, stateful model shows that the transfer time for one message is highly dependent on the position in the transaction.

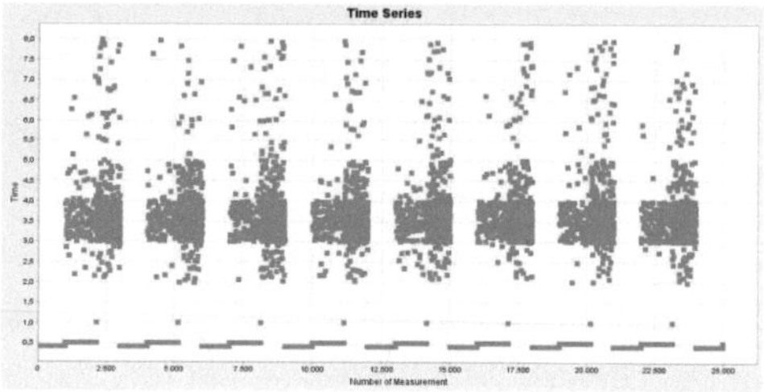

Figure 7.10.: Periodical CPU utilisation in stateful model.

Table 7.1 lists the predicted and measured median values for different transaction sizes. Due to the high variance of the delivery times, the median serves as a representative value for a specific transaction size. However, the median can only be considered as an indicator for the prediction accuracy, it is very good indicator for the variance. In table 7.1, predictions and measurements deviate less than 4%. These results indicate, that the extension of our messaging completion can accurately predict the influence of (successfully completed) transactions on the delivery time of a message.

DISCUSSION We discuss stateful performance engineering in more detail in Appendix B. Based on the presented case study we can, however, already here make these conclusions. The increased expressiveness of stateful models comes at a cost. Stateful models may have much higher complexity and size, which may complicate their analysis. Even if the models are not analysed fully, and are examined with simulation methods (like in the case of PCM), model complexity may have an impact on the time needed for sufficiently accurate performance prediction (duration of a simulation run). The time necessary to execute a simulation run is further influenced by the variability of simulation results. The state-dependent system

Transaction Size	Measurement (Median)	Prediction (Median)
1	1,665 917ms	-
2	2,506 566ms	2,609 999ms
4	4,157 104ms	4,619 999ms
10	9,145 595ms	9,050 000ms
20	17,012 373ms	17,079 999ms
100	82,752 583ms	85,440 000ms
400	356,843 626ms	360,980 000ms
1000	943,539 863ms	943,370 000ms

Table 7.1.: Measurement/Prediction Comparison.

variability mirrors in the variance of the results and consequently influences the number of measurements necessary to achieve results with a high confidence. The cost of a single simulation measurement depends on the length of the simulated trace. Explicitly modelled states have only little effect on the length of simulation traces, which mainly depend on the modelled software architecture (e.g., loops dependent on a state value).

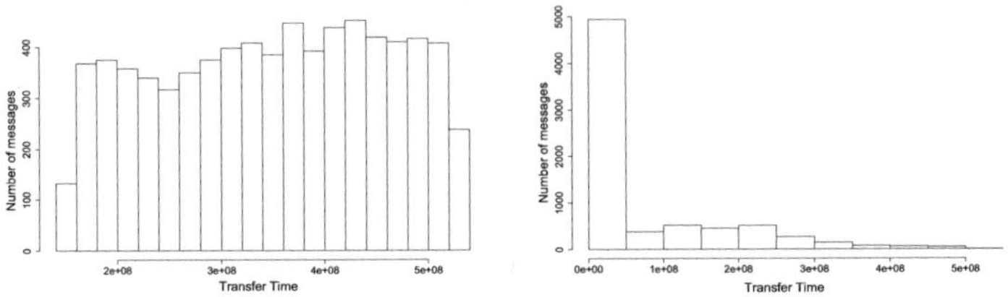

(a) Transaction (size=400).

(b) No transaction.

Figure 7.11.: Message transfer time.

On the other hand, one should to keep in mind that the confidence about the correctness of predicted values will be higher if a low-coverage simulation is run on a more accurate (stateful) model, than if a high-coverage simulation is run on an unrealistic (stateless) model. Moreover, as the stateful dependency was in our case encapsulated in completion (invisible to the completion user) we can conclude that the complexity of the model from the user point of view has not increased.

Modelling transactional messages probabilistically results in a comparable distribution of response times. However, the model does not reflect the stochastic dependency of sequentially arriving messages. Furthermore, it provides less flexibility since delays caused by transactional behaviour have to be known in advance. In most cases, such information is not available or the delays are changing constantly. In these cases, an explicit state model eases the design of performance models and allows accurate predictions with the necessary flexibility. Additionally, approximating state by a probabilistic abstraction results in decreased possibility of reuse of the component because the probabilities are specific for a one system, a one allocation and one usage profile. More detailed discussion on this topic can be found in Appendix B.

7.2.1.2. Validation: Infrastructure Completion 'Thread Pool'

SETTING: QUESTION, METRICS, ASSUMPTIONS Thread pools allow the asynchronous processing of jobs. They support the creation and pooling of a number of threads to process these jobs. In Section 5.3.5, we presented an analysis of thread management strategies and possible variations of them. In the domain analysis, we identified that the most important parameter, that can be tuned to provide the best performance is the capacity of the Thread Pool. Figure 3.11 shows the feature diagram for Thread Pool design pattern based on the configuration options provided in `java.util.concurrent` packages by the Java JDK (1.6). The two most important parameters influencing the choice of optimal pool size are the number of processors available for the application and the nature of the incoming tjobs.

In the following, we describe the most important metrics we used to evaluate performance-influences of different Thread Pool variants, as well as the parameters we used to configure the experiments.

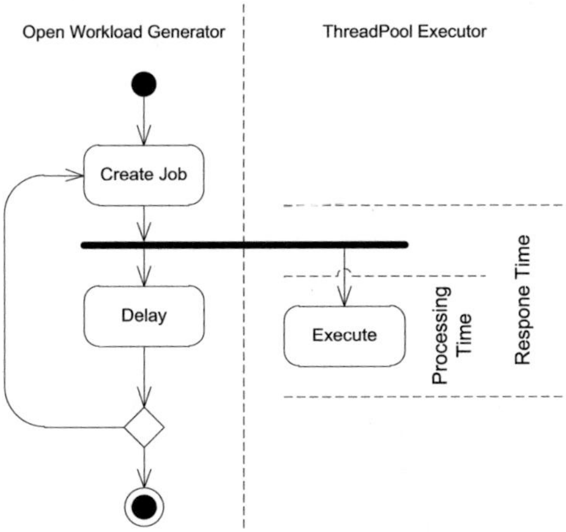

Figure 7.12.: The experiment setup.

Figure 7.12 illustrates the experiment setup. A workload generator creates new jobs and inserts them in the queue of the `ThreadPoolExecutor`. The job itself consists of a single processing job that consumes the specified CPU processing time. We use the `de.uka.ipd.sdq.resourcestrategies` from PCM to generate the corresponding CPU demand.

Let t_c be the time a job is created and put into the `ThreadPoolExecutor`'s queue, t_s the time the a job is assigned to a thread (its processing starts), and t_f the time the job is finised, then we can observe the following metrics for each job:

- Response Time t_r: The time passed from the moment a new job is put in the `ThreadPoolExecutor`'s queue (t_c until it processing is finished (t_r): $t_r = t_f - t_c$.
- Processing Time t_p: The processing time is the time a request is being processed by a thread, i.e. the time passed between the moment the job is assigned to a thread (t_s) until it is finished (t_f): $t_p = t_f - t_s$.
- Waiting Time t_w: The waiting time is the time the request resides in the `ThreadPoolExecutor`'s queue. It is the time passed for a job's creation (t_c) until its processing starts (t_s): $t_w = t_c - t_s$.

Based on the definition of the timing metrics we see that: $t_r = t_w + t_p$.

Configuration Parameters: In the experiment, we vary following parameters:

- Arrival-Rate: The arrival-rate λ_i for a waiting jobs queue q_i is defined as average number of requests sent to the Thread Pool to be processed per second. For the total number of requests A_i and a measurement-time T. The arrival-rate can be calculated as:

$$\lambda_i = \frac{A_i}{T}$$

  . The time between two requests is called *inter-arrival time*.
- Number of Core Threads: The number of threads in the pool that are always kept.
- Maximal Number of Threads: The maximal number of threads in the pool.
- Request Size: The size of a request is defined by the average (i.e. specified) processing time for this request.
- Queueing Strategy: Strategy to be used to queue jobs if more jobs arrive then can be processed. Valid queueing strategies are `unbounded`

(an unlimited queue), `bounded` (a limited queue with a size defined by configuration parameter *queue length*), and `direct-handoff` (no queue all jobs are processed immediately or rejected).

- Queue Length: In case of a `bounded` queue this parameter determines the number of jobs that can be kept in the queue.

Observed Metrics: Furthermore, we observe the following metrics of the Thread Pool itself:

- Rejection Rate: Percentage of jobs that is rejected by the `ThreadPoolExecutor` in case of bounded queues or direct hand-offs.
- Number of Active Threads: Observed average number of threads that have been active during an experiments.
- Number of Threads in Core Pool: Observed average number of threads in the core pool during an experiment.
- Observed Queue Length: Observed average number of jobs in the queue during an experiment.
- CPU-Utilisation: The Thread Pool average CPU-utilisation U_{CPU} is the quotient of the total time the CPU is busy (B_{CPU}) and the total measurement-time T:
$$U_{CPU} = \frac{B_{CPU}}{T}$$
.

Using predefined metrics and configuration parameters, we can formulate the experiment questions, scenarios and hypotheses (see Section 5.3.5). Moreover, based on the domain analysis results we could identify default (close to optimal) Thread Pool configurations:

Optimal number of threads parametrised by number of CPU replicas (n) for CPU-intensive requests:

$$PoolSize = n + 1$$

In our experiment, we use CPU-intensive requests, thus, we await results showing increase of Thread Pool performance (decrease of contention) until the moment when the size of Thread Pool is close to the $n+1$ value. After this value we await that no increase of performance would be observed.

MEASUREMENTS The implementation of the prediction model is based on the design of the Thread Pool completion presented in Section 5.3.5. The completed model is illustrated in Figure 7.13. We calibrated the completion skeleton using measured data illustrated in Figure 7.14. These data are results of measurement experiments with the Thread Pool design pattern implementation.

For the performance measurements, we used a computer with following settings: Windows 7 Enterprise (64Bit), Intel Core2 Duo T7300@2GHz, RAM 4GB, and CPU set to the maximum performance. Each experiment used a workload generator for open workload with an exponentially distributed inter-arrival time. The duration of measurement was 100 seconds for each experiment (i.e. parameter combination) and we computed the average for the measured values.

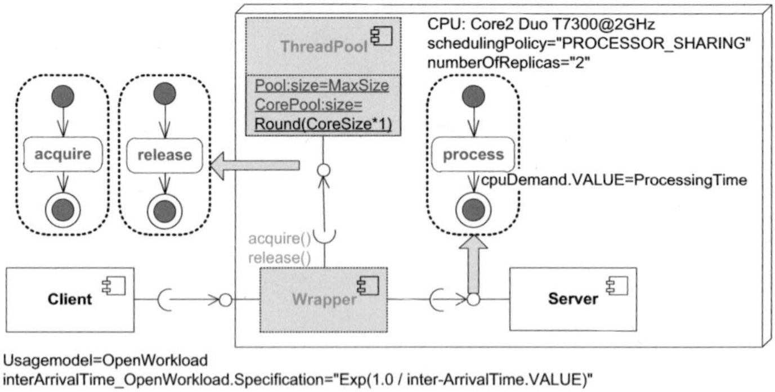

Figure 7.13.: Completed Thread Pool Model in PCM.

In Figures 7.14(a)(b) we can observe that with the length of the queue the processing time increases. This is explained by the decrease in the number of active threads in the second graph. In Figure 7.14(a), processing time first increases then decreases slightly. This behaviour is also reflected in the number of active threads (Figure 7.14(b)) Figure 7.14(c) gives an explanation for this behaviour. It illustrate that the increased rejection rate because of queue contention. For short queues, a larger number of jobs (more than 20%) is rejected by the threadpool. In total, less jobs have to be processed by the pool resulting in less parallelization and shorter processing times. For longer queus, more jobs are accepted, so that the total workload of the pool increases. This behaviour also affects the average response time (Figure 7.14(d)) for each job.

In Figures 7.14(e)(f) the observed queue length and the waiting time explodes for processing times larger than 250 ms. This is caused by an over-utilisation of the CPU – not all incoming jobs can be processed. As a result, the queue length and response times increase as jobs pile up at the pool. We used the knowledge from the measurement experiments to build the Thread Pool completion.

Experiment	**Processing Time**	**Core Pool Size**
Core Pool Size	4	0 to 10 in steps of 1
Maximum Pool Size	4	10
Pre-start all Core Threads	true	false
Keep Alive Time	10.000 seconds	100 ms
Queueing Strategy	UNBOUNDED QUEUES	UNBOUNDED QUEUES
Specified Processing Time	50 ms to 500 ms in steps of 50 ms	50 ms
Inter-arrival Time	180 ms (mean)	30 ms (mean)

Table 7.2.: Thread Pool experiment configuration.

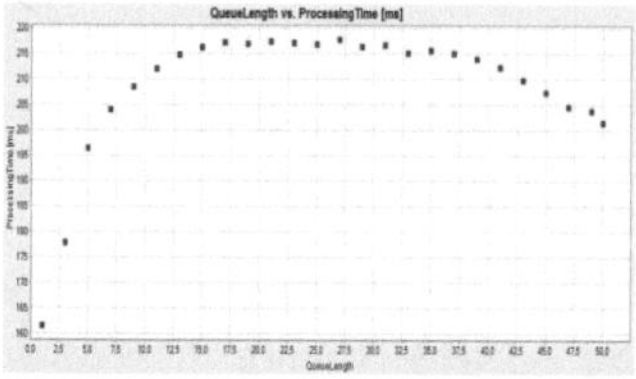

(a) Queue Length vs. Processing Time.

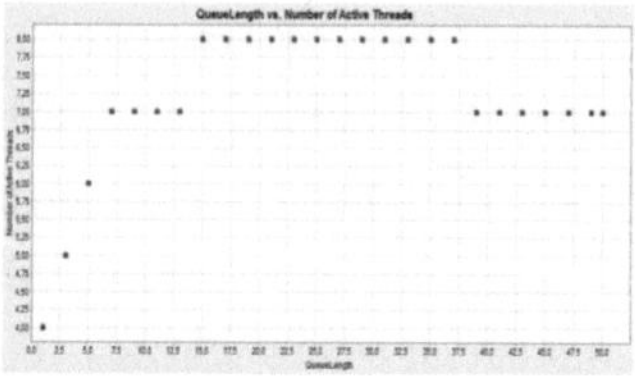

(b) Queue Length vs. Number Of Active Threads.

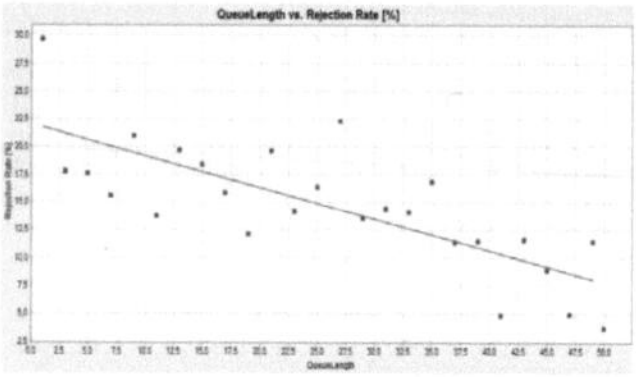

(c) Queue Length vs. Rejection Rate.

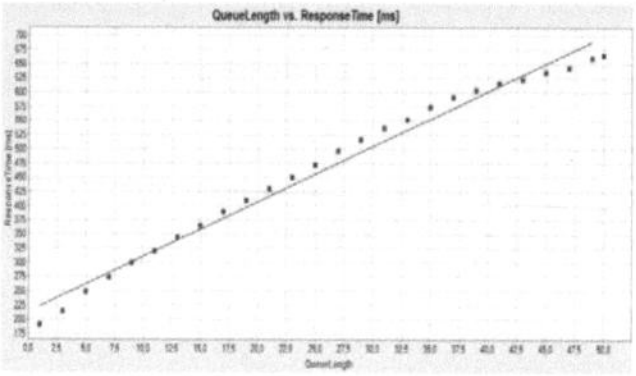

(d) Queue Length vs. Response Time.

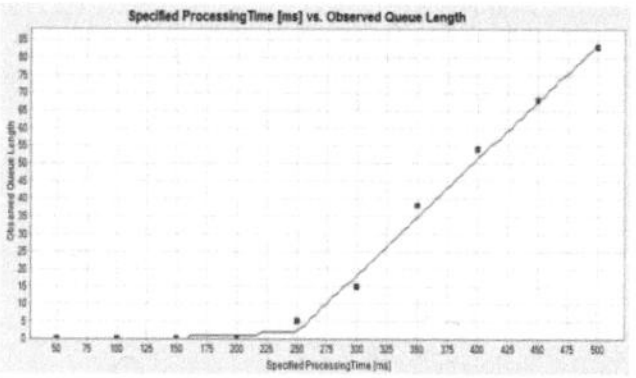

(e) Specified Processing Time vs. Observed Queue Length.

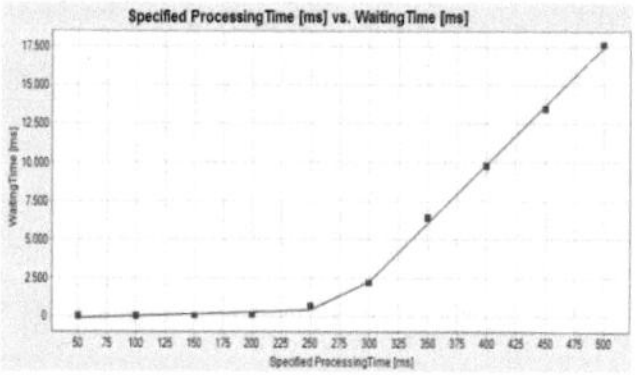

(f) Specified Processing Time vs. Waiting Time.

Figure 7.14.: Thread Pool completion: Calibration Data.

Results The configuration of the experiments is summarized in Tables 7.2 and 7.3. For the Core Pool Size experiment the pool is 'cold' at the beginning meaning that it has not been used before to process any jobs. Otherwise, we cannot observe the influence of the core pool size as it has already been dynamically adjusted by the `ThreadPoolExecutor`.

The comparison (cf. Figure 7.15) between the measurement and prediction shows the accuracy of the prediction. The model predicted the observed behaviour very accurately. We observed that by maximal pool size of 4 the observed number of threads in pool was in both of the experiments equal 3, thus $n+1$ for the used dual-core processor. The completed model manifested the same behaviour. Furthermore, the predicted processing time before the queue overflow is very accurate by value of 3,444s which corresponds to the observed processing time 3,763s in a first experiment. The predicted response time of 3,558s corresponds to the observed 3,975s, too. However, the completed model provided prediction with the error less than 8% for our experiments, the results start to significantly deviate after the queue overflow is observed. This deviation is visible on the right-hand side graph in Figure 7.15. Moreover, the queue overflow is observed $\approx 100ms$ later as measured in a real system. We discuss this observed effects further in the following section.

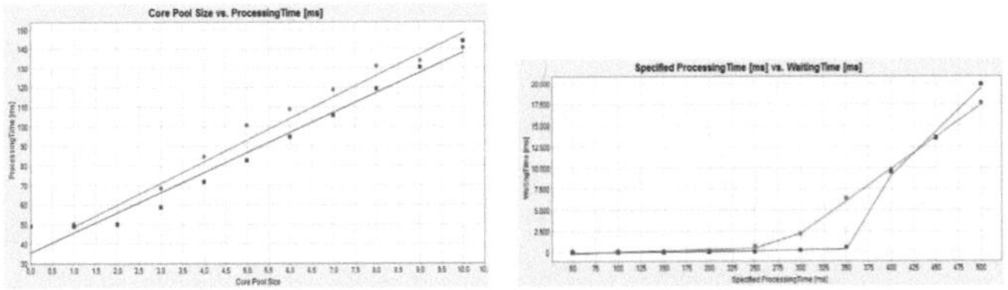

(a) Core Pool Size vs. Processing Time. (b) Processing Time vs. Waiting Time.

Figure 7.15.: Thread Pool completion: Comparison of prediction (BLUE) and measurements (RED).

DISCUSSION The results of the previous experiments demonstrated that, after the queue overflow is observed, the prediction is not accurate any more. The cause of the deviation is shown in Figure 7.16(b) where the queue overflow in the simulation is depicted. Figure 7.16(a) further illustrates this effect. The red curve shows the results of the same simulation only left to run longer as the blue one. It is clear from this graphs that after the queue overflow, results of the simulation are very sensitve to small changes. However, in this scenario, the absolute values are of minor interest. The fact that the queue is growing constantly if the processing time of a job exceeds 250 ms is predicted correctly.

The model presented here does currently not model bounded queues. However, a State Manager for keeping track of the queue length could solve a part of this problem (similar to the transactions in Section 7.2.1.1). Depending on the jobs currently waiting in the queue and the maximal queue length, the simulation can reflect the actual behaviour of the ThreadPoolExecutor. If the limit is reached further jobs can be rejected. However, this behaviour requires a combination of realibility and state that is currently not available in the PCM.

Experiment	**Queue Length**
Core Pool Size	4
Maximum Pool Size	10
Pre-start all Core Threads	false
Keep Alive Time	100 ms
Queueing Strategy	BOUNDED_QUEUES
Queue Length	1 to 50 in steps of 2
Specified Processing Time	50 ms
Inter-arrival Time	30 ms (mean)

Table 7.3.: Thread Pool experiment configuration for the Queue Length.

Figure 7.16(c) depicts additional difficulties for performance prediction using thread pools. In this graph, the red dots represent prediction results, the blue is based on measurements of a cold pool, and the green on measurements of a hot pool. Before the pool size reaches 2 (n for dual-core) the number of threads is smaller than number of CPUs, which results in resource contention. Thus, we can observe a decrease in the response time until n is reached. After this point the resource contention is not observed any more, there are enough threads created to process the requests. The prediction model manifests an utilisation of CPU $\approx 80\%$, which is in theory correct as the utilisation could be computed as follows:

$$cpuDemand.VALUE/numberOfReplicas/interArrivalTime.VALUE * 100$$

This formuly yield a utilisation of 83% ($= 50ms/2/30ms * 100$ for our third experiment. However, we observed a CPU utilisation of $\approx 100\%$ during the experiments. In the measurement results (cf. Figure 7.16(c) blue and green curve), a delay of at least 3s is visible. Most likely the arrival-rate and/or CPU demands are not close enough to the behviour of the real system. These additional delays could come from the operating system overhead (such as scheduling) or other services of the system. To provide more accurate predictions in such situations completions rely on the more detailed resource models, which model particular resources in more detail. Currently, this is a subject of research by Michael Hauck [80] in his PhD thesis.

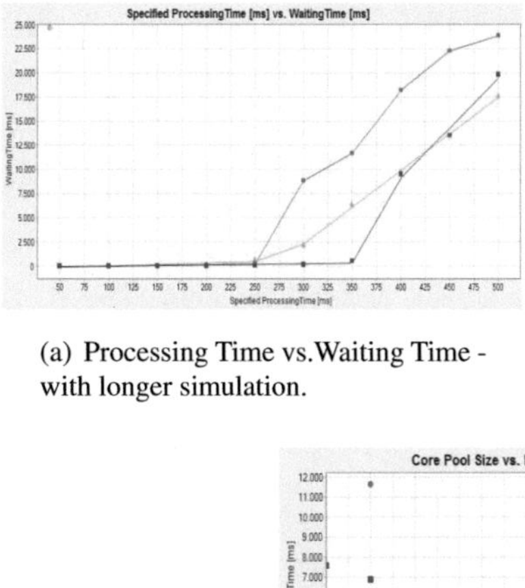

(a) Processing Time vs.Waiting Time - with longer simulation.

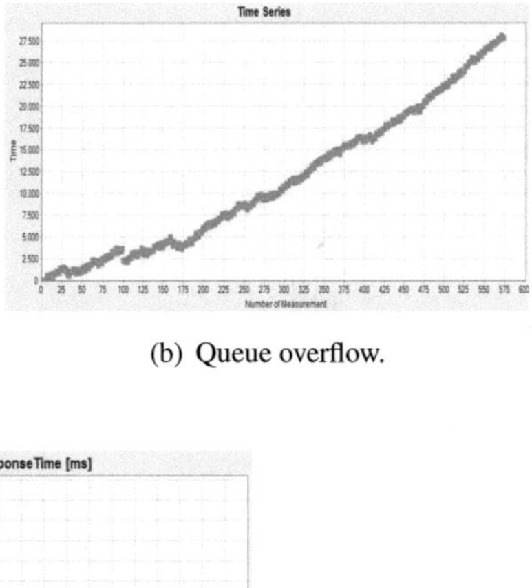

(b) Queue overflow.

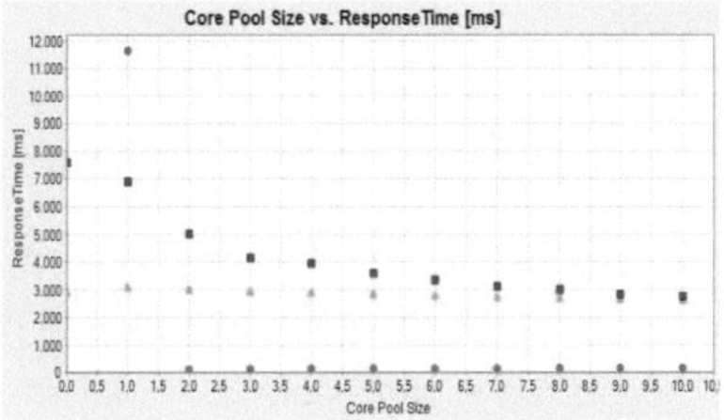

(c) Core Pool Size vs. Response Time.

Figure 7.16.: Observation of the queue overflow.

7.2.2. Type I: Completion Composition and Ordering

In this section, we address first the question *Q*2 regarding the prediction accuracy when using multiple completions:

Q2: Can models be automatically completed using a multiple completions to provide more accurate performance predictions?

In the following sections, we evaluate the composition of completions and their order. We implement and validate all completions used in this case study in isolation. Resulting completions are then composed to build more complex systems.

First, in this section, we introduce a scenario used to evaluate the basic concept of cutting the task of the connector down to separate individual steps. Furthermore, the effects of the composition of completions in connectors are explained. We demonstrate how completions based on concurrency patterns can be used to efficiently model software systems and evaluate performance. In a second step, we illustrate the applicability of our approach for partial completion ordering and conflict resolution. For this purpose, we present a case study of a *Supply Chain Management (SCM)* for supermarkets. In particular, we are interested in the performance of a *Business Reporting System (BRS)* for a subset of supermarkets. The BRS supports users by retrieving reports and statistical data about running business processes from databases of different supermarkets. This scenario is based on a real system by Wu and Woodside in [174].

Figure 7.17 shows the part of the system architecture relevant for business reporting. The main part of the business reporting is running on the HQ's server system. The data is distributed among the company's supermarkets and managed by *Data Managers*. In order to generate a report for a particular set of supermarkets, the business reporting sends a request to the supermarkets of interest. The data managers of each supermarket retrieve the necessary data and send it back to the HQ, when data from all

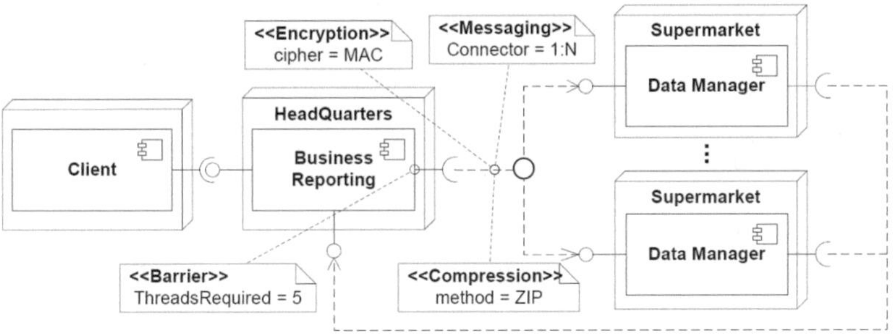

Figure 7.17.: Relevant part of the SCM architecture for BRS with annotations.

supermarkets are collected. As soon as all data is available, the *Business Reporting* generates the report and returns it to the client.

The presented case study consists of three levels:

1. In the first step of this case study, the HQ component is annotated with a *Barrier* pattern and the connector to supermarkets is annotated with *MOM* configuration. This case study demonstrates the application of completions and their effect on performance.

2. To illustrate the compositionality of completions, we implemented and validated *Compression* and *Decompression* completions in isolation. These completions are then composed together to build a connector abstraction.

3. To illustrate our approach for conflict resolution, we add further annotations for *Encryption* and *Compression* to the connector (see Figure 7.17). We apply our approach for conflict resolution to identify a locally optimal execution order for the completions applied to the connector.

7.2.2.1. Validation: Completion Composition

In the following, we describe a component completion applied on the Business Reporting component. The application of the `Barrier` [51] completion is illustrated in Figure 7.18 that shows the behaviour of the methods `generateReport` and `uploadData`, which realise a large part of the `Business Reporting`'s functionality. The Figure 7.18) contains two extensions that describe how these patterns are to be integrated into the software system in order to generate the business report from a number of supermarkets in a correct way.

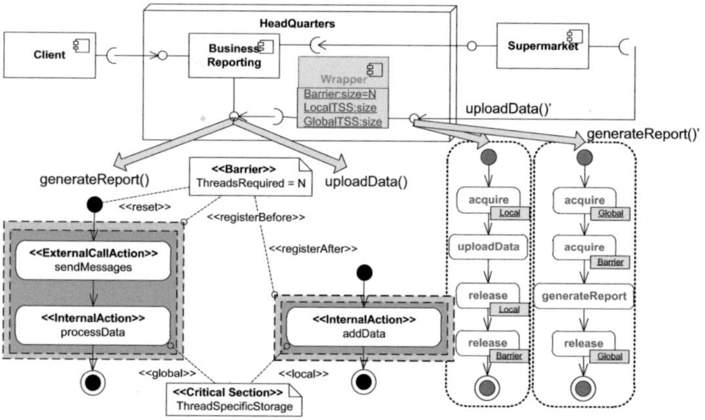

Figure 7.18.: Behaviour of the `Business Reporting` including annotations.

Communication between HQ and the supermarkets is realised by messages, to simultaneously collect data from all supermarkets. This requires the `Business Reporting` to block until the results of all supermarkets arrived. A barrier, modelled by an annotation of the outer scope of methods `generateReport()` and `uploadData()` including the actions `processData` and `addData`, ensures that the generation of the business report is deferred until all data is available. For report generation, this blocking is achieved by registering at the barrier before processing the data (`registerBefore`). During the upload of data, the supermarkets register at the barrier after they added the data (`registerAfter`). This behaviour signals the barrier that new data is available now. The data itself must be protected by a critical section in order to avoid lost updates or race conditions. For this case study, we used a thread-specific storage to reach this aim. We distinguish accesses to the `local` data of a single thread and `global` data of all threads. In general, the annotation `critical section` realises a strategized lock, i.e., the locking strategy can be exchanged by whatever seems appropriate. The complexity of the barrier is hidden in an external `Wrapper` component added to the system.

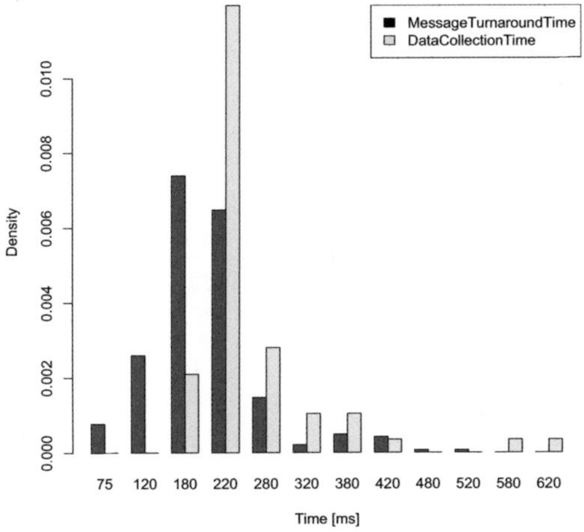

Figure 7.19.: Distribution of the turn-around time and data collection time.

We implemented the business reporting scenario using JBOSS 6.1 and message-driven beans for the message-based communication. For the measurements, we set up the system in a distributed environment with one client, one HQ, and five supermarkets each running on a separate machine. Figure 7.19 shows the probability distribution of the turn-around time of a message (i.e., the time from when the message is send until an answer of a supermarket arrives) and the data collection time (i.e., the total time from sending a message to all supermarkets until all answers arrived). As to be expected, the distribution of the data collection time represents a probabilistic lower bound of the turnaround time. Mathematically, it is the maximum turnaround time of five messages send in parallel. Sending a message to five supermarkets (publish-subscribe) took 16 ms only. The delivery of the message return took 158 ms on average. This strong difference is mainly caused by the different message sizes. The messages send back to HQ are much larger than the messages send by HQ since they contain the data requested. Finally, the JNDI-look up of the topic for sending the message took 116 ms and the report generation (after all messages have been received) 260 ms. The total processing time to generate a report was 522 ms.

In the following, we extend this system and apply additional processing steps in the connector. Thus, we evaluate the composition of a multiple completions in one connector.

SETTING: QUESTION, METRICS, ASSUMPTIONS We identified three different dimensions in the configuration of the completions which impact performance:

1. The *use of asynchronous calls* is introduced, which speeds up the simulation of procedure calls, that can be processed asynchronously.

2. Due to the capacity restraints the *capacity of concurrency* can be configured. This includes pile up effects in the connector and can be used to conduct bottleneck analysis.

3. The resource demands (e.g. required number of CPU cycles) for each of the *processing steps* can be specified.

In the remainder of this section, we deal with the issue of finding proper resource demands and separating the individual processing steps in the connector correctly. The process of finding proper (in some cases parametrised) resource demands is part of the completion development and results in the platform-specific completion definition. The separating of individual processing steps is the basis to support completion variability. We have to evaluate if these steps can be composed correctly.

IMPLEMENTATION The case study scenario consists of multiple `Data Managers` which generate great amounts of data that are requested by the `Business Reporting` component. Each `Data Manager` serves one supermarket. To preserve network bandwidth, the data is compressed before network transfer and decompressed afterwards, this does already reflect the steps in which the overall task of the connector is going to be cut down. The scenario is implemented in Java using the *GZIPStreams* and *Socket* communication. In our scenario, we use two machines, each with one core, similar processing rate and memory. All `Data Managers` run on one machine, while the server runs on the other.

To adapt models corresponding to the real system, we implemented a transformation realizing connector completions and composing them from basic elements. It is a model-to-model transformation using QVT Relational [72]. The tool used to run the transformation is Medini QVT Engine. As shown in Figure 7.20 the transformation can be divided into a number of basic steps.

As a first step in the transformation, the source model has to be copied completely into the target model, but without the annotated *AssemblyConnectors* (which are replaced by the transformation). The transformation copying the model is generated using the Routine HOT. Then the *Connectors* have to be created. The creation of a *Connector* can be divided into the following steps: (a) find elements in the target model, (b) create new elements, (c) connect elements, (d) allocate elements, and (e) place elements. First, the location (*pivot element*) and the elements that are directly connected to this location, where the *Connector* has to be inserted into the copied system, have to be identified. The new elements and their inter-

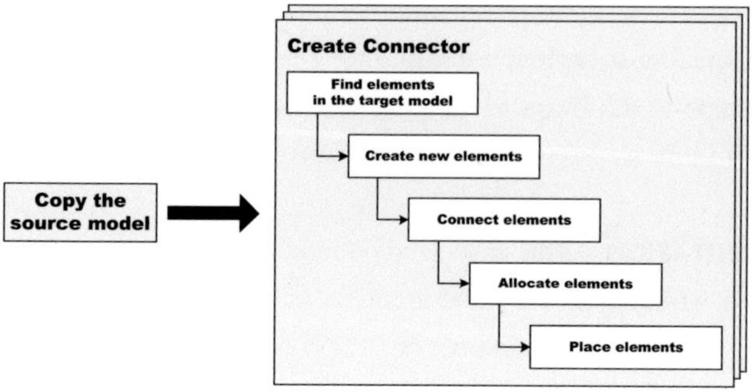

Figure 7.20.: Approach for executing a transformation.

connections are defined by the completion feature diagram and its feature effects. For each completion, a completion transformation is generated. Second, this transformation is executed and all the new elements that are part of the connector are generated. Then all the elements get allocated to hardware resources depending on the allocation in the source model. At the end all created elements have to be placed inside the system or allocation element to be at the right place in the PCM model. Resulting transformation completed prediction model in single steps integrating in each step an abstraction of single connector part (e.g., Compression/Decompression in a first step, MOM in a second step, etc.). If the completion created a 'coupled' sets of elements (i.e. subsystems), such as Compression/Decompression, the elements get connected by ab *AssemblyConnector*. This connector is then the pivot element for the next completion, in our case the MOM completion. When the completions do not create 'coupled' subsystems, the next completion is applied on the first *AssemblyConnector* after location of the by previous completion created subsystem. Thus, it is possible to compose a number of processing steps in connectors.

RESULTS To create the prediction model and to configure the components for processing steps, the response time of compression, socket trans-

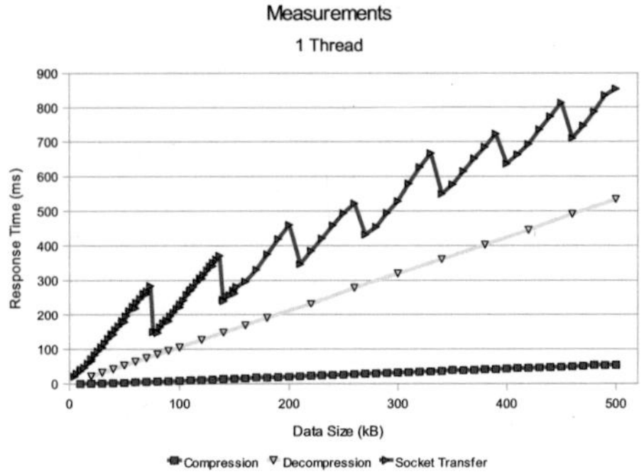

Figure 7.21.: Measurement Results: Overview.

mission and decompression has been measured independently. We focused on data sizes up to 0.5 MB and only a few concurrent threads to minimize trashing, we expect the server to run at moderate utilisation. The data is structured and thereby has a compression rate of 70%. We noticed, that the duration does not only depend on data size but also on the compression rate achieved for that data, thus we used only data with that constant compression rate.

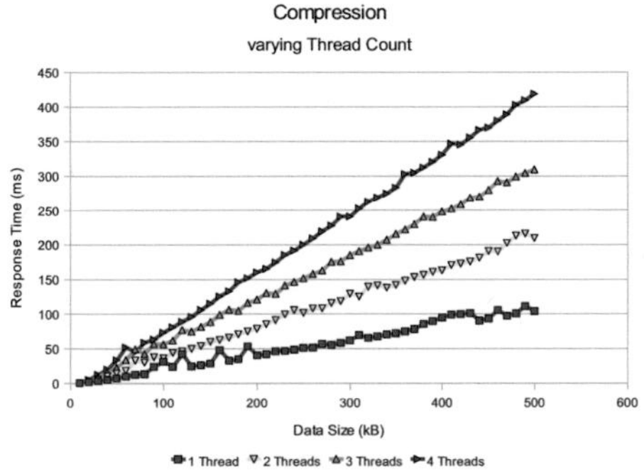

Figure 7.22.: Measurement Results: Compression.

The results for the duration of all three processing steps executed by one thread are shown in Figure 7.21. The compression and decompression clearly adhere to a linear behaviour, while the socket transmission show a periodically partial-linear nature. Please note, that the values for decompression do not relate to the response time from the data size as indicated by the x axis, but instead to the response time required to decompress to the indicated data size. This is done for illustration purposes, so that one can read on hand of one x value how long it takes to compress data, and for the same x value the decompression graph shows how long it takes to decompress that same data, although the input data sizes differ due to the compression.

Also, if there is more than one thread, the behavior scales additively as long as there is no trashing. Meaning that the duration of 4 threads doing one package of work is approximately the same, as one thread doing 4 packages of work. This is shown in Figure 7.22 in the case of compression. Note, that this only holds, if there is no blocking involved like from file IO or excessive paging, which is not the case here. Within this case study, we focused either on one or three `Data Managers` (i.e. threads). In case of `Data Managers` sensors the level of concurrency is configured through the think time of the `Data Managers`.

Another effect we experienced in the measurement of the overall scenario was that it did not relate to the sum of the individual measurements. This was caused by the fact that the decompression could already start, before the transmission of the whole data was finished. To simplify the scenario, we deployed a buffer in which the data is written and which is not decompressed until all data has been received via the socket connection.

The capacity of the worker pool of the decompressor has to be set to one, because the socket server accepts only one incoming connection at a time and accepts no new connection until the current is done processing. The model uses synchronous call mode to enable predictions of the overall response time. From the measurements of the processing steps we created regression lines to use them for the resource demands of the component's SEFFs.

The prediction achieved good results (<3% error) when only one `Data Manager` was used.With three active supermarket sensors (Figure 7.23) the prediction error was less than 3%, when the inter-arrival time was either very high or very low. The results deviated more with the inter-arrival time in middle values (approximately half of the execution time), although even for these cases the error went only up to 4%. What could be explained by repeated garbage collection activity by higher utilisation.

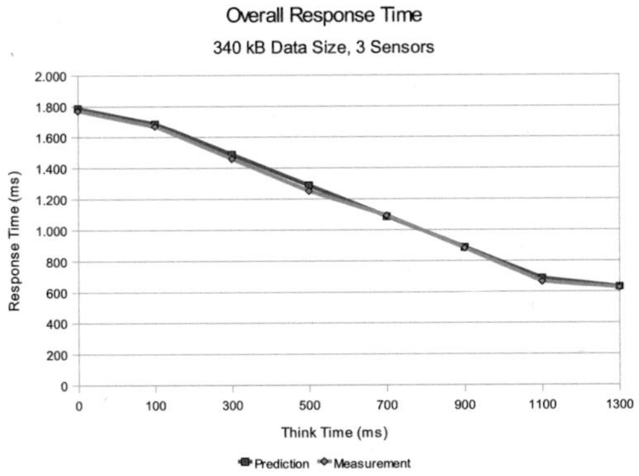

Figure 7.23.: Measurement vs. Prediction Results.

DISCUSSION This part of the case study showed that even a composition of multiple completions measured and calibrated in isolation provides accurate predictions. There are, however, still open questions. In this case study, some factors were simplified. Those factors are predestined to be focus of future studies. For example, streaming requires further investigation. One possible solution to model this is to split up the data into several small packages after the compression and process them asynchronously. Furthermore, varying compression rates should be supported. Together with varying degree of concurrency and data size, this turns into a multidimensional problem. This can be mastered by utilising Software Performance Cockpit [77], which had not suitable tool support at this point.

Additionally, the experiment can be also conducted on multi-core CPUs. The scenario can be enhanced by passive resources (e.g. semaphores, locks for critical sections) to validate the passive resource model and new features can be added.

7.2.2.2. Validation: Completion Ordering

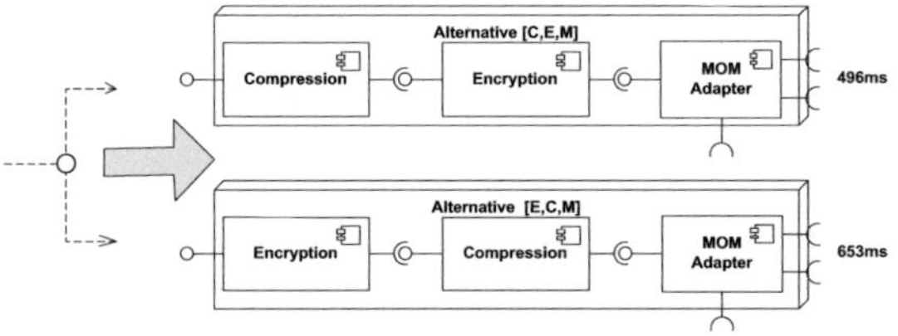

Figure 7.24.: Completion Alternatives.

Figure 7.17 shows the part of the system's architecture relevant for business reporting. In this architecture, one component, the `HQ Business Reporting`, is annotated by a `Barrier` pattern configuration. This is a completion annotating component, thus in a responsibility of component developer. Because it is a single completion having impact on this component, the conflict does not appear. More interesting is one connector (line connecting required interface of a HQ to provided interfaces of supermarkets) annotated by three completions: firstly, as `Messaging` connector, secondly, by `Encryption`, and thirdly, by `Compression`. All of these completion annotations refine the performance prediction model with certain properties. The sequence of completion execution affects the model structure and its validity. In the illustrated example, the completion execution order results in different semantic for the `Barrier` completion. Correctly is a barrier implemented as a part of an intern functionality of a component, thus the 'Barrier component' is located before the beginning of the connector chain. However, when the 'Barrier component' would be applied at the end of this chain after the MOMAdapter the model would be semantically invalid. In a first case, the 'Barrier component' waits for a number of replies from different Data Managers. By changed order the 'Barrier component' waits for replies from one Data Manager. Additionally, the results of performance prediction could be influenced as illustrated by our example (cf. Figure 7.24) for the connector chain. To identify a valid completion execution order in such complex system is a non-trivial task.

In the following, we demonstrate how conflicts of multiple completions can be resolved. It is possible that not all of the permutations in the completion sequence are valid, the reasons for it are different: some of the sequences could be structurally or semantically invalid, other one are not possible because of the middleware implementation that has a fixed sequence of the services. We do not consider these cases, in this part of the case study we focus only on the third dimension in completion conflict, thus, the performance dimension. We analyse the impact of completion order on performance and ability of our approach to help completion user identify suitable variants from performance point of view.

For the sequence of Messaging,Encryption, and Compression are all the possible permutations structurally valid. However, semantically does not make sense, for example, to both compress and decompress before or after sending the message. In reality such possibilities do not occur. For the purpose of this case study, we modelled all these permutations and applied our quality heuristics for conflict resolution.

In the presented example, the sequence of completion execution should result in the full architecture model illustrated in Figure 7.25 (e.g., with applied $[C,E,M]$ completion sequence). Using the method introduced in Section 5.2.3 we illustrate the reduction of conflicts in completion executions order. This way the sequence of completion execution can be implicitly defined.

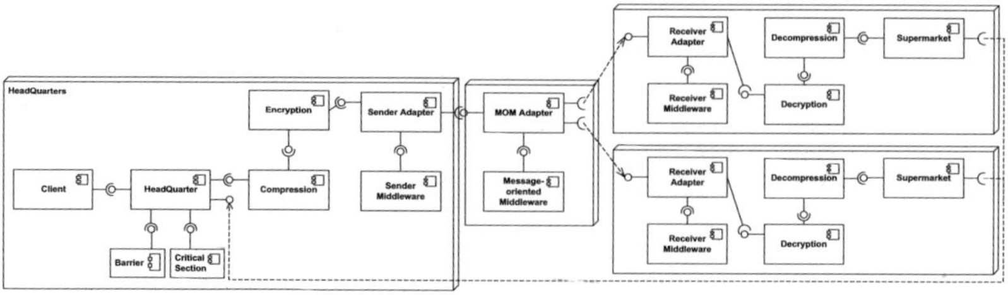

Figure 7.25.: Resulting Architecture.

	$[C,E,M]$	$[E,C,M]$	$[E,M,C]$	$[C,M,E]$	$[M,C,E]$	$[M,E,C]$
$rt(link)$	496 ms	653 ms	1137 ms	676 ms	1130 ms	1574 ms
$thp(link)$	115 msg/s	72.5 msg/s	39 msg/s	70 msg/s	39 msg/s	26 msg/s
$Q(e)$	4.3	9.0	29.1	9.6	28.9	60.5

Table 7.4.: Quality evaluation for all valid completion chains.

RESULTS As expected, the completion set applied to the connector is conflicting, producing significantly different results for different completion chains. To resolve the conflict, we analysed the application of all completion chains over the completion set $CS = \{M,E,C\}$. The set of all valid completion chains is $\{[C,E,M],[E,C,M],[E,M,C],[C,M,E],[M,C,E],[M,E,C]\}$. Based on the heuristics for order resolution we identified the most optimal completion order as $[C,E,M]$. The measured performance of E and M decreases with growing size of input data. The C completion decreases the data size and therefore should be the first in a sequence. The C is followed by E and by M as shown by quality function results. We modelled all alternative architectures in the *Palladio Component Model (PCM)*. To validate our approach, we developed a semi-automatic extension of the *PCM Bench* [18] that analyses the conflict location in isolation using our heuristics. The PCM Bench allows the specification of component-based software architectures and the analysis of their performance properties such as response time, throughput, and resource utilisation.

The order in which completions are applied heavily influences the response time and throughput of the connector. Table 7.4 lists the response time, throughput, and the computed results of local quality functions $Q(e)$ for all different permutations. In addition, Figure 7.26 shows the cumulative distribution functions for the response time of all permutations.

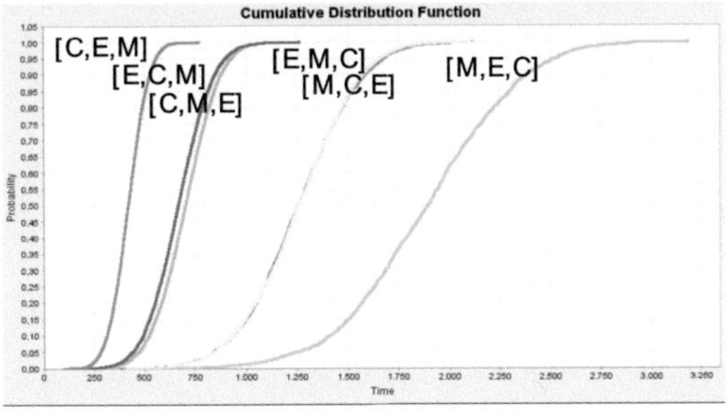

Figure 7.26.: Distribution of the response time for refined connector (based on all valid completion chains).

For the best permutation, we get a mean response time of 496 ms and a maximal throughput of 115 messages per second. This yields a value of 4.3 for our quality heuristics. By contrast, the worst combination results in a mean response time of 1574 ms and a maximal throughput of 26 messages per second. Consequently, the value of our quality heuristic is much larger (60.5). The results demonstrate how the quality heuristics further emphasises the differences between the permutations. While the response time of the best and worst permutation differs "only" by a factory of three, the results of the quality function differ by a factor of 14. Thus, the quality heuristic clearly select the permutation $[C,E,M]$ as the best alternative (cf. Figure 7.27).

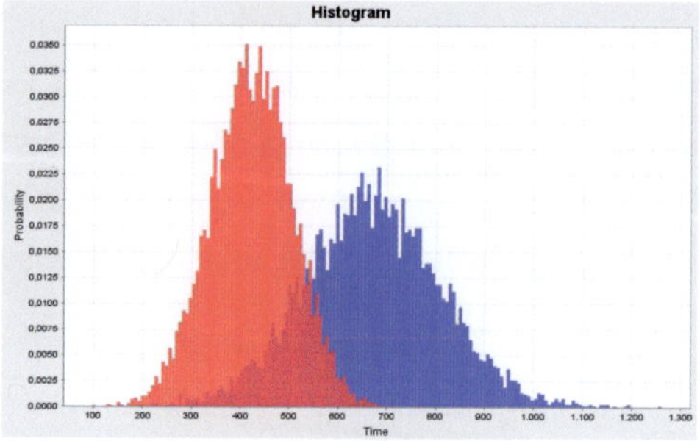

Figure 7.27.: Comparison of the overall response time distribution for the [C,E,M](RED) and [E,C,M](BLUE) alternatives.

DISCUSSION We shown that the proposed method for reduction and resolution of conflicts can give the completion user an indication of the best alternative. The exact results for the subsystems tested by this method in isolation do not correspond the exact values for the subsystem used as a part of a complex system with other usage profile, the pattern in results is, however, an indicator that remains. As such could be used to build a knowledge about the completions registered in library and give recommendations for best practices for the developers.

7.2.3. Type II Validation: Applicability Evaluation

In this section, we demonstrate how the introduced metrics give insight into the quality of transformations. We illustrate the applicability of our approach and discuss the results. For this purpose, we present a case study based on an evaluation of different types of transformations.

7.2.3.1. Maintainability Comparison

We address first the question *Q*3 regarding the maintainability of completion transformations:

Q3: What are the quality, especially maintainability, properties of used transformations?

SETTINGS In our case study, we evaluate following transformations:

MOM (Message-oriented-Middleware) Completion Transformation This transformation integrates performance-relevant details into software architectural models, it is a completion transformation. This type of transformations is a special type of customisation. The details are woven as additional subsystems into the model of architecture, thus the source model has to be copied first. The MOM completion transformation is dependent on the input from a configuration model that configures how the actual architecture model should be refined. Thus for each variant of this transformation the copier part is the same. The difference is in actual description of completed subsystem. We evaluate two different implementation of this transformation:

- `MARK_MOM` - **MOM mark transformation**: The configuration, defined by the mark model, provides the variability to the transformation. For example, if a connector is to be completed by message-passing, the mark model can provide information about the type of messaging channel, e.g., using guaranteed delivery. The disadvantage of such implementation is that the completion developer has to develop a overall transformation that produces a valid result for each combination of configuration options. Thus, such transformation has to read directly the configuration model and implement a huge 'switch'-like constructs to react on the read configuration correctly.

- `COMP_MOM` - **MOM completion transformation**: This transformation does not know about the configuration at all. It is generated using a composition (by the Composite HOT) of feature effects developed in isolation for each feature. Moreover, this transformation includes copy relations for all metamodel elements, these relations are generated by the Routine HOT.

We analyse both of these variants to get a feeling for the complexity of these transformation types. The source and target model of these transformations are based on an underlying component-based metamodel of 'core' PCM with the size of 290 classes. As such, these transformations are representatives of the group of quite complex and variable transformations.

`R_HOT` - **Routine HOT Transformation** This transformation is a Higher-Order Transformation (HOT), as it generates another transformation. This specific HOT is used to generate a default copy transformation for a given metamodel by producing a copy relation for each class and each property of the given metamodel. This is required because there is no copy operator in QVT Relational. The source model of this transformation is the `Ecore` metamodel having 31 classes and target metamodel is the QVT Relations metamodel itself with the size of 110 classes. This transformation is used as a representative of the group of medium-complex transformations.

`TRAN_T` - **Translation Transformation** This transformation is presented in the QVT specification as an example relational transformation [72]. In this case study, it serves as a reference example. The translation transformation only translate model instances of one metamodel language to another metamodel language. This translation transformation maps UML class models to RDBMS tables. The minimum UML source metamodel contains 6 classes and the target RDBMS metamodel has a size of 18 classes. This transformation is used as a representative of the group of simple transformations.

We applied the maintainability metrics introduced in Chapter 6 to evaluate maintainability of these transformations. The results were collected automatically using the Analysis HOT pattern. In the following section, we discuss the results of this evaluation.

RESULTS The results (cf. Table 7.5) of this case study have shown that the completion transformation (`COMP_MOM`) in contrast to the transformation without the generated parts (`MARK_MOM`) has a higher number of smaller relations. The relations in `COMP_MOM` are in average less complex. The decrease in complexity originates in the less complex match patterns, because the complexity of pattern matching is distributed on a number of relations.

Completion transformations show that usually the number of domains used is two, one for target and one for the source. In manually programmed transformations it can be observed, that more complex matching pattern are used and include several domains. Thus, the relations are bigger, but the number of relations is smaller comparing to generated transformation. This is visible on the graph 'Pattern Node Complexity' in Figure 7.29, where we see how the rate of domain pattern nodes per relation decreases significantly if the simple copy rules are added. Moreover, no additional local variables are necessary. In this graph is visible that the `MARK_MOM` transformation consists of the most complex relations.

The transformation `COMP_MOM`, intuitively categorised as a complex transformation, shows much higher values in average domain pattern tree depth as well as the average number of domains and `when`-predicates per relation (cf., Figure 7.29). Interestingly, the number of `where`-predicates increases diametrically opposed. This may indicate that different approaches for defining the overall transformation have been employed. Moreover, `where`-predicates indicate a somehow "forward" (thus also more imperative) executed transformation whereas more `when`- predicates indicates a more declarative way of the whole transformation design. The tendency to use more declarative constructs instead of imperative once is even visible by per-hand developed `MARK_MOM`, which was implemented by developers used to the concepts of functional programming. Which of these designs is more maintainable remains to be evaluated. However, using these metrics a connection between these findings could be underlined.

Moreover, on the last two graphs in Figure 7.29 we can observe that in a simple transformations such as TRAN_T usually one predicate depends on one variable only. However, in more complex transformations the number of variables in predicates grows. The most complex variable dependencies could be observed for the MARK_MOM transformation. Similarly, in the case of R_HOT the complexity of predicates is high, this transformation is an generator that is not variable and is implemented only once. As such, the higher complexity is reasonable.

Furthermore, generated transformations show an equal ratio of when- to where-predicates (cf. Figure 7.29). This means that a fulfilment of every relation is a precondition of as many relations as it depends on. This tendency is not visible in a manually programmed transformations. On the other hand, an increase in the usage of where- clauses is visible, because it is easier to think in the forward transformation direction. However, the tendency to use more when- predicates increases with the complexity of the transformation as shown for the MARK_MOM.

The ratio between the number of top level relations and non-top level relations (cf. Figure 7.28) is the smallest in case of the generated transformation (1:1). This means a higher utilisation of top level relations. The generated transformation takes an advantage from a higher number of execution paths possible in the transformation and is not tuned to limit the number of starts in order to support maintainability. This also makes sense as the parts generated for the copy transformations are not intended to be maintained manually anyway.

In general, our observation is that in a manually developed transformations roughly half of the relations are top-level relations. We can distinguish a pattern showing that a transformation was written manually by a human based on the number of starts as it seems natural for a human mind to consider only one execution path.

	COMP_MOM	MARK_MOM	R_HOT	TRAN_T
Lines of Code	7582	6875	473	239
Clean code	5789	6074	416	181
Comments	220	165	13	4
Number of relations	488	313	17	8
Number of top level relations	330	22	8	3
Number of starts	99	1	1	1
Number of OCL queries	20	21	1	1
Number of when-predicates	233	113	9	5
Number of where-predicates	221	90	12	13
Number of metamodels in transformation	2	3	3	2
Average number of domains per relation	2	4.65	2.76	2.5
Average number of domain pattern nodes per relation	2	14.78	11.53	2
Average number of when-predicates per relation	0.9	1.78	1	0.63
Average number of where-predicates per relation	0.49	0.87	1.82	1.63
Average number of local variables per relation	0.001	0.48	1.05	2.38
Val-in per relation	2.63	14.78	11.53	2
Val-out per relation	2.3	4.45	3.66	3.12
Fan-in per relation	1.12	1.67	1.34	0.78
Fan-out per relation	1.02	1.34	1.2	0.7
Average number of checkonly domains per relation	1.04	2.09	0.71	1
Average number of enforce domains per relation	1.08	2.57	2.47	1

Table 7.5.: Automatically calculated metrics.

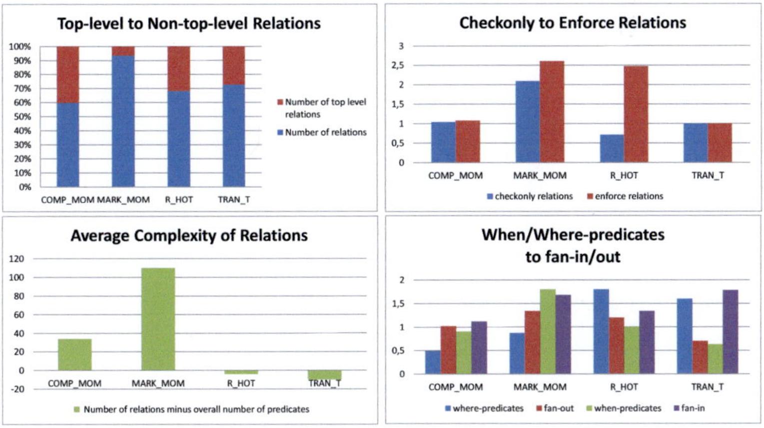

Figure 7.28.: Results: Transformation Complexity.

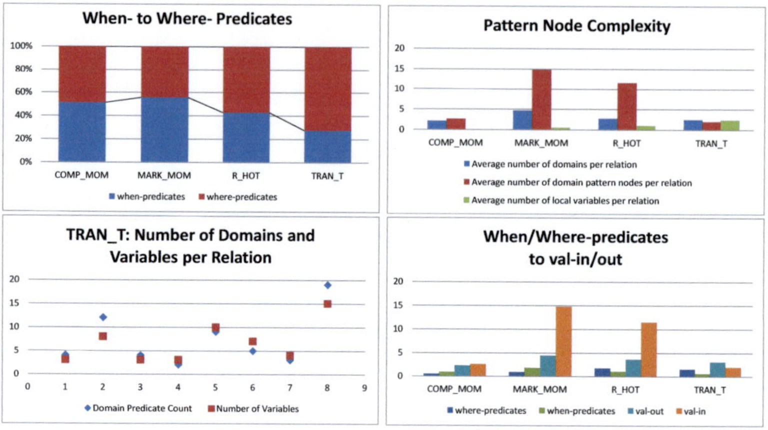

Figure 7.29.: Results: Relations Dependencies.

Additionally, the difference between the number of relations and number of predicates is negative for simple transformations, it is an indicator of average complexity of relations (cf. Figure 7.28). It indicates that in one relation developers used higher number of predicates. Together with the knowledge about the overall number of relations it shows that developer can do this only because they still have a quite good overview about the whole transformation in this cases. On the other hand, for complex transformations this indicator is positive, the higher the value of this indicator is, the more complex the relations are. The high average number of domain patterns and domain pattern nodes in the `MARK_MOM` shows that some the relations have to be even more complex (have more predicates) and some do not have predicates at all. The relations without predicates are so called 'helper' relations that are used to ensure validity of the target model or read configuration models. The `MARK_MOM` transformations has the highest number of these 'helper' relations. Which is an indicator that it was difficult for the developer to get an overview about the overall functionality of transformation. This could originate in complex dependencies between relations that are visible on results for the fan-in/fan-out metrics.

The R_HOT manifest very interesting ration between the checkonly and enforce domains. The number of enforce domains is significantly higher as the number of checkonly domains. This ratio shows that it is a generator type of transformation. Similarly, the 1:1 ratio in the case of TRAN_T indicates the translational type of transformation.

DISCUSSION The presented results illustrate how software architects can evaluate the maintainability of their model transformations. Our experience shows that the developers implementing one feature at the time focus on one aspect and thus the relations are less complex and focused, too. To generate or compose transformations from parts it is the best approach to implement a lot of small and focused relations. On the other hand, the implementation of mark transformation manifested increase in the relation size, especially in the domain pattern complexity. Moreover, the code was polluted with the 'helper' relations used to read the configuration model.

7.2.3.2. Complexity Comparison

In this section, we address the last validation question *Q4* regarding the complexity of feature effects development:

Q4: Is the complexity of transformations decreased by separation of concerns in feature-related transformation fragments?

SETTINGS To give an indicator of the transformation complexity decreased by our approach, we provide an experiment based on comparison between a generated completion and a manually written mark transformation. This illustrates that the separation of concerns decreases the transformation complexity and that mark transformations include a lot of infrastructure code (e.g., helpers). This infrastructure code is could be avoided or generated as well. Additionally, as we shown in previous section, generated transformations are more structured and therefore better understandable.

In this experiment, we evaluate the Thread Pool completion which integrates performance-relevant details about the Thread Pool design pattern into software architectural models. We compare following two implementation of this transformations:

- `MARK_TP` - **Thread Pool mark transformation**
- `COMP_TP` - **Thread Pool completion transformation**

We analyse both of these variants, MARK_TP implemented manually and COMP_TP generated (i.e., composed from transformation fragments), considering the extendibility and ability to debug the resulting transformation. Both of these transformations were developed for the PCM metamodel with the size of 290 classes.

RESULTS The main advantage of our approach is that developers can focus on effect of one selected feature at time and develop relations for this feature only, they are not concerned with all feature combinations and their dependencies. In the mark transformation, the developer has to consider all the possible configuration combinations and check the state of features (selected or eliminated) by accessing additional model (e.g., feature model) from relations in the mark transformation. Even later in development, the dependencies (`where`- and `when`- predicates) between the relations need to be resolved manually. These dependencies are solved in our approach by the Composite HOT using the constraints for the transformation composition. Table 7.6 gives numbers of generated lines of transformation code in comparison to lines of manually written mark transformation code. The transformation frame consists of a generated copy transformation (using Routine HOT), which is used by both manual and automatic fragment integration. We extracted this part of both transformations and focused comparison only on the customisation relations implementing the functionality presented in the running example 3.3.1 and the configuration presented in Section 3.3.3. The input model to be completed is a simple client-server application and the completion skeleton that is injected into the model is described in Section 3.3.2.4.

As shown in this comparison, the generated customisation part of the transformation consist of 7 relations in 3 fragments, these fragments could be reused in a case of an another feature combination. In a case of the mark implementation without reusable fragments, we have to implement a new transformation for each feature combination. For the chosen feature configuration, the transformation consists of 8 relations.

Complexity of the model	
290	metamodel elements
11	model elements
21	to be added/completed elements in the model
18	features in the feature model
4	chosen features in the feature configuration
1008	possible feature combinations
Generated transformation frame	
450	copy relations in the transformation
5850	lines of code implementing the copy relations
`COMP_TP` - **Thread Pool completion transformation**	
3	transformation reusable fragments
7	relations in the transformation fragments
195	lines of code implementing the relations
`MARK_TP` - **Thread Pool mark transformation**	
8	relations for one combination
250	lines of code implementing the relations

Table 7.6.: Comparison of completion versus mark transformation for one feature combination.

The results (cf., Table 7.6) show that, to realise feature effects for the 4 chosen features, we have to implement:

- `ThreadPool` feature effect: one fragment for the root feature `ThreadPool` consisting of one top-level relation and two normal relations.

- `Static` feature effect: one fragment for the `Static` feature consisting of three relations. The feature `OptimisationProperties` does not have feature effect, because of the mandatory choice of one of the child features.

- `PoolSize` feature effect: one fragment for the leaf feature `PoolSize` consisting of one relation.

For the mark transformation, we implemented 8 relations to achieve the same functionality. Each relation has to implement two input domains (i.e., source and configuration model) and one target domain. The additional relation is a 'helper' relation. Moreover, this simple mark transformation has already 55 lines of code more as the fragment-based implementation. This is an indication that the size and complexity of this transformation will grow significantly if the other valid configuration options would be considered (i.e., 1008 valid options).

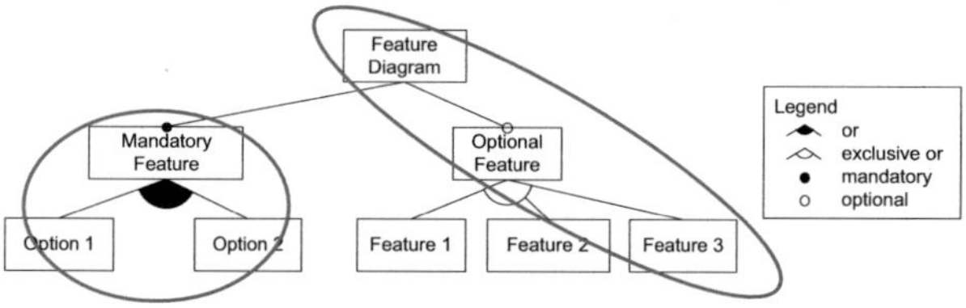

Figure 7.30.: Dependencies to other features for the `Feature 3`.

Furthermore, the separation of concerns based on feature diagrams (cf., Figure 7.30) helps even by extending of the configuration by a new feature or debugging the transformation. When adding a new feature in the mark transformation, we have to check the dependencies to the each relation having or calling a relation that has the configuration model as its input domain. In such cases, the structure of feature model gives an navigation to the feature effects that have to be updated. That are, for example, for each leaf feature all the feature effects on the direct path to the root feature and all mandatory features in the feature tree. Additionally, all the features possibly referenced by `depends` constraint have to by considered.

DISCUSSION The presented experiment shown that focused development using feature model is an advantage. Especially, the additional information about the dependencies between feature effects intuitively hidden into the structure of the feature tree supports completion developers. However, further empirical evaluation of the usability properties would be necessary to get quantifiable results.

7.3. Summary

This chapter presented the validation of completion-based improvement method for the accuracy of performance prediction. We structured the validation according to two main goals: First, we studied the accuracy of the completions them self. Second, we evaluated the quality characteristics of the main elements supporting the automated completion-based MDSPE: the model transformations.

With respect to the first goal, we found that:

- Completed models correspond better to the reality and can predict systems behaviour with a very high accuracy. The accuracy of prediction depends strongly on the modelled completion. In complex cases some influences (e.g., Virtual Machine optimisations) could not be modelled with 100% accuracy to the reality, what could result in a strong deviation. However, in other cases the calibrated model for a platform can provide predictions with an error of less than 3%.

- Using completion-based models we can predict not only the response time or throughput with high accuracy, but even the complex effects resulting from state-dependency.

- Even multiple completions used on one model element provide accurate predictions in the composition. Moreover, the order of completion execution in a sequence could be evaluated using performance prediction with our quality heuristics and help to identify the most advantageous sequence.
- The quality heuristics are suitable to provide indications about an order in a sequence of completions .

With respect to the second goal, we found that:

- The evaluation results show that completion transformations are more focused and consist of smaller relations mapping mostly only one model element at time. Thus, transformation developers could easily identify relations impacting one model element type. This gives an indication that completion transformations are better readable and understandable, because of lower complexity of domain patterns, stronger modularisation and less complex interdependencies between relations in transformations. We use established evaluation techniques using code metrics indicating the applicability of our approach.
- The feature model structure supports developers when introducing new features and extending completion transformation. It focuses the development effort through separation of concerns.

In addition, the possible topics for future work are mentioned throughout this chapter. The most important of them is the empirical validation of the used techniques, especially the evaluation of the ability of developers to take advantage of declarative constructs and implement transformations more in relational as operational way.

8. Related Work

In this chapter, we summarise the state-of-art of model-driven software development and performance evaluation both with respect to variability of models. There are other approaches dealing with similar challenges as this thesis, even though in different contexts and for different application domains. In this chapter, we compare the solution introduced by this thesis to some of these approaches. With this objective, we divide and list them in different groups discussed in separate subsections. Some of the approaches are, however, not dealing with the core problem that we want to solve, but they analyse and propose solutions for other related or partial goals of our approach. Numerous approaches could be discussed here, however, to focus our discussion we analyse methods that are applicable at the abstraction level of software architecture, and thus we exclude more low-level approaches that deal with variability and refinement of code.

The approaches related to the results of in this thesis can be classified into two main areas. The first area, discussed in Section 8.1, consists of MDSD approaches dealing with management of variability in transformations and quality metrics for transformations. The second area, discussed in Section 8.2, covers approaches that explicitly utilise model-driven software development techniques, similar to completions, for software performance predictions. The last Section 8.3 summarizes and compares the most important of the discussed approaches to the results of this thesis.

8.1. Model Transformation Engineering

The first area of the related work compares approaches that are similar to the main contributions of this thesis: (i) model completions and their realisation as an SPL for transformations built by HOT patterns; and (ii) quality metrics for transformations. To reduce development effort and to increase the maintainability of transformations, the transformation languages and tools have to support mechanisms for creating as well as integrating reusable transformation artefacts. Thus, the related work for the first contribution can be divided into two subgroups. The first group (see Section 8.1.1) includes methods for development of transformations for reuse and the second group (see Section 8.1.2) contains methods for development transformations with reuse.

8.1.1. Development of Transformations for Reuse

To create reusable transformation artefacts, the level of abstraction is essential. Current approaches are focused on reusing single rules of transformations or on reusing whole patterns or transformation fragments. Transformation reuse at rule-level has been addressed by several transformation language specifications, such as ATL [90], QVT [72] or VIATRA [5]. This kind of reuse is very fine-grained and focused on the reuse of separate mapping rules. QVT, which is used to implement our approach and as such we inherit its reuse mechanism, provides reuse mechanism at rule-level based on rule inheritance [72]. The oAW's Xtend language [166] is an imperative transformation language, which includes explicit code-level support for transformation aspects. This mechanism is effective to avoid common parts in code and structure the implementation, however, for the coarse-grained reuse using patterns and templates it is not suitable.

Typically, model transformation languages, e.g., ATL [90] and QVT [72], allow to define transformation rules based on types of the corresponding metamodels. However, such model transformations are not reusable for different metamodels and must be defined from scratch again and again. Such language definitions do not allow metamodel variation. For example, ATL requires to specify the metamodel package name as part of the mapping classifier. One exception is the approach of Varró et al. [5] who define a notion of generic transformations within their VIATRA2 framework. This framework in fact resembles the concept of templates in C++ or generics in Java. Therefore, VIATRA2 provides a way to implement reusable model transformations and could be principally used to implement our templates or feature effects in a metamodel-independent way. Metamodel-independent definition of feature effects is mentioned as one of the possible future work directions in Chapter 9. Nevertheless, they do not foster a general template instantiation technique as it is proposed in our approach based on HOTs in Section 4.6.

The coarse-grained reuse based on transformation patterns and parametrised templates, which is supported by our approach as described in Sections 4.4 and 4.6, has not been extensively treated yet. We can distinguish to types of approaches for coarse-grained reuse: (i) template-based and (ii) pattern-based approaches.

Template-based approaches: Czarnecki and Antkiewicz [44] propose a template-based approach for mapping feature models to concise representations of model variabilities. Allowed configuration combinations depend on the existence of suitable model templates that are bases for model instantiation. Our approach is not template-based in the sense that templates and feature models are an additional input for the transformation. We rather lift the template instantiation up to the transformation creation itself. We configure templates and instantiate them into the final product, which is again a transformation defined by feature model and a set of instantiated templates. The templates define independent transformation primitives. Because templates are used to implement feature effects in our approach, the complexity of handling all possible feature combinations within the transformations is decreased and is made explicit through the structure of the feature model. Furthermore, we define a general template instantiation mechanism and use templates to implement parametrised artefacts instead of reusing them directly.

Pattern-based approaches: The reuse of transformations in the form of transformation patterns is still in its infancy. A first list of patterns in the context of graph transformations has been proposed by Agrawal et al. [2]. Moreover, they introduce a graph transformation language named GREAT and a set of patterns for graph transformations. The introduced patterns are structurally similarly complex than the patterns used for definition of CBSE templates in Section 4.6. The difference to our approach is that these patterns are defined for graph transformations and a general instantiation mechanism is missing. Another initial list of patterns originating from QVT Relations specifications has been collected by Iacob et al. [87]. Iacob et al. introduced an initial set of design patterns for transformation specification. This set of patterns act as an input of the Routine HOT pattern in Section 4.4 that generates transformations implementing the chosen pattern.

In our approach, we provide support for both fine-grained (inherited from QVT and using Composition HOT pattern) and coarse-grained (using Routine and Template Instantiation HOT pattern) reuse. The focus of our work is not on a definition of new patterns, but more on the general MDSD structures used to instantiate, integrate, and resolve parametrisations and to compose existing patterns or templates that are specific for handling of design decisions integrating domain-specific aspects. We identified a general MDSD patterns in Chapter 4, so called HOT patterns, used to instantiate transformation templates and design patterns and we automatically generate transformations realising these patterns.

8.1.2. Development of Transformations with Reuse

In the MDSD context the reuse of transformations is one of the principal software quality factors and a key to achieve higher productivity. In the domains of model transformation languages, however, transformation generation, transformation composition, template definition for model transformations, and application of HOTs for the reusability goals are relatively new. In the following, we discuss the most important approaches in this area with special focus on the applications of HOTs.

8.1.2.1. Generative Approaches for Transformations

A very important answer to the demand of automated model refinement is *Model-Driven Development (MDD)*, which employs model-to-model transformations to refine system models. Czarnecki and Eisenecker introduced generator options in their book on Generative Programming [46] which is a predecessor of today's MDD paradigm. They used feature diagrams to capture different variants in the possible output of code generators. Feature diagrams model all valid combinations of a set of features called (feature) configuration where a single feature stands for a certain option in the respective input domain. Similarly, MDD employs feature diagrams as an additional input into the transformations to mark activation of transformation parts for a particular input model. Such transformations are so called *mark transformations* [11]. In our case, the choice of active features is woven into the transformation by a HOT. Thus, the concept of mark transformations is the same as ours, but we raise the level of abstraction a bit further.

Another generative approach, an automated framework DUALLY [111], aims to answer the issues concerning the interoperability of tools and languages. This approach introduces the concept of transformation generation with the purpose of translating model specifications from one language to another. The transformation generation is based on a mapping between these languages. The resulting transformation is generated based on the mapping model. The generated transformations serve as translation mechanism for models from one metamodel language to other. In current state it is not possible to generate customisation (or completion) transformations that introduce new domain-specific model elements.

The most related approach is the ATLAS Model Weaver (AMW) [47, 48] that offers abstraction mechanisms for definition of simple weaving operators (mappings) describing correspondence between two metamodels. This process can be done manually or semi-automatically. The result is called a weaving model. The weaving model is an input for the higher-order transformation (HOT) that generates model transformations. The AMW approach is implemented using Atlas Transformation Language (ATL), which is a mixture of declarative and imperative constructs. Because of the imperative constructs, the traces between the weaving operators and resulting transformation are hard to follow in AMW and for each new operator the whole HOT has to be adapted. Thus, the HOT is not general for all the operators, as in our approach, and the separation of concerns between the implementation of HOT and weaving operators is unclear. Finally, a weaving operator always connects source metamodel elements to target metamodel elements, so it is not possible to realize complex transformation logic or introduction of new domain-specific elements as by completions.

Lately, Herrmannsdoerfer et al. introduced a language for Coupled Evolution of Metamodels and Models COPE [84]. COPE is proposed as a solution to the problems that arise due to metamodel evolution and the resulting necessary model migration to a corresponding newer version of the metamodel. This approach is based on a reusable migration transaction library that is used for migration transformation generation. Although, it provides advanced means for reuse of migration transactions and migration transformations, it is not suitable to express the variabilities of application families based on metamodel-independent feature configurations.

Transformation Composition approaches: The composition of transformations causes additional problems and is subject to many currently running research initiatives. We can distinguish two types of transformation composition: internal and external. Internal composition consists of rule-based analysis, location of rule conflicts and scheduling of transformation rules, with the goal to merge two transformations into one.

One internal composition approaches is [168] which proposes a superimposition composition technique for ATL and QVT Relations. Superimposition is a white-box mechanism that allows to merge several transformations in a final transformation containing union of all transformation rules and helpers. Other works [130] and [114] investigate possibilities of composing complex transformations from atomic transformation definitions. Our approach is different to these composition methods, because it is based on a predefined structure (i.e. the feature model) that guides the transformation composition. Furthermore, our focus is on metamodel-specific transformation generation and not generic composition techniques. Therefore, many problems that arise when trying to compose arbitrary atomic transformation parts are avoided.

An intuitive example for external transformation composition is MDD, the transformations are applied in layers, in an a-priori defined order, hence not addressing possible conflicts in execution order. This is natural due to the nature of MDD refinements, which are very general constructs. The information that could lead an automatic conflict identification and resolution is hardly generalizable under their setting. This type of composition is called external composition where a sequence of transformation is created, thus the output of one transformation is an input for the next one in a sequence.

Among the external transformation composition approaches, feature-oriented programming approaches like AHEAD [8] allow only sequences of independent transformations and do not consider any feature dependencies. In our work, we compose externally a number of completions applied to the same model. Our approach is using the package structure of the metamodel to identify independent transformations which are easily composed externally. However, as discussed in Chapter 5, not all completions are independent and require further conflict resolution mechanism. A related approach of model-driven development for non-functional properties based on transformations [142] also does not consider transformation sequences. Some prior work has been done in the area of transformation sequences by Cooper et al. [39] with focus on searching for sequences of compiler optimisation transformations using random sampling. A line of related research can be identified in design-pattern integration [54] where the conflicts in integration order are also very likely. However, the studied integration processes are not quality-driven, and hence have different criteria that drive the decision on the optimal execution order. Approaches trying to identify an valid order of transformation in a sequence deal mostly with the structural conflict and do not consider the quality conflict as our approach does.

Other Transformation Variability approaches: Vara et al. [162] propose a method for model configuration by annotations. The annotations are drivers that specify the configuration of variable model elements. This process is manual and the method targets the context of databases and schema transformations. The usage of annotations is, however, very similar to our approach.

8.1.2.2. Software Product Lines for Transformations

In the area of product lines, several works [154, 70, 89] propose a mapping between features and model structure elements. These works proposed support for automated derivation of product line members based on a feature-driven development method. The expressiveness of these methods depends on composability of the mapped structural model fragments.

In the work of Garces et al. [60] an approach for variability management in model-driven SPL (MD-SPL) was introduced. The advantage of this approach is that it offers a possibility to introduce custom rules, implemented in ATL, to handle feature model-based variability. The rules then define a specific pattern in ATL language itself, however, the transformation definition becomes more complex and more imperative. This approach does not separate between variability definition and transformation definition. Our approach is different in this point, we reuse variability definition and provide more declarative transformation definition with better quality properties.

Voelter and Grober [71] combine the practices of model-driven and aspect-oriented software development (AOP-MD-SPL) to manage variability in a whole development cycle. The approach uses aspect weaving to integrate feature-model based variability into the target models. This approach allows to have a separate feature model, specifying cross-cutting variability, to configure the input model. The developers have the possibility to implement variability as aspects on multiple levels of the transformation sequence (i.e. in models, model-to-model, or model-to-text transformations). Variants are described on the model-level. A disadvantage of this approach is a limited support of weaving, which allows only additive weaving without updates or overrides of model elements. Moreover, this approach does not propose solution for transformation languages such as ATL or QVT. The aspect-orientation can be not only used to generate products, but even transformers and generators. However, our approach does not use aspect orientation, it provides mapping mechanism between feature diagram and its realisation using elements of the target metamodel. Our approach defines variability on a level of higher abstraction, as we do not define aspects on the code level but on the metamodel level, so that our approach lowers the learning curve for developers. Additionally, the distinctive feature of our approach is parametrisation of features with the goal to systematically improve the purpose completeness of the models (i.e. performance prediction). To allow reuse of existing tools, our approach transforms into the same metamodel, which is not the goal of aspect orientation.

Another very interesting approach by Morin et al. [121] develops product lines for Domain-Specific Modelling Languages (DSMLs) (DSML-SPL). This approach generates a modelling language with variability management capabilities. Similar to our approach, the variability aspects are woven into the domain metamodel at the level of higher abstraction and extend metamodel language. The significant difference is, however, that the resulting metamodel is not the same language as the input; moreover, it is a composition of two metamodels. Therefore, the tools implemented for the original metamodel are not reusable anymore. Additionally, their introduced approach does not provide any description of automated support, using HOTs or other generative approach.

8.1.2.3. Applications of Higher-Order Transformations

The continuous growth of complexity, which can be noticed for transformations, and which has only recently been addressed by researchers, is already being investigated for models for several years. In his report [153] on industrial experiences with structuring large scale domain models, Störrle strongly suggests to reconsider the notions and experiences from the era of structured analysis, as many model types and disciplines developed in the past are a perfect match for the architectural abstraction level of very large-scale modelling (VLSM) projects. Czarnecki's well-known paper [45] surveys transformation languages and presents a classification scheme for transformation language properties supported by feature diagrams. He describes higher-order rules as rules taking other rules as parameters. Higher-order rules are mentioned as one of three techniques which allow transformations to be parametrisable, the others being control parameters and generics.

Bézivin et al. [24] differentiate between two views on transformations: the textual concrete syntax of some transformation language (implementation view), and a semantically equivalent representation as a model (specification view). According to the authors, HOTs provide the following benefits: Abstraction from concrete implementations, languages, and their constraints (synthesis), refinement and refactoring (rewriting/modification), validation and formal reasoning, e. g. compatibility checks (analysis), and formal description of syntax and semantics of modelling languages through transformation models. Further use cases of HOTs are not discussed. In this work, we provide a set of solutions using HOTs for more complex goals and investigate the applicability of HOTs for product line variability.

Varró and Pataricza [163] point out the importance of non-functional properties of transformation languages, like compactness, reusability, and maintainability. By allowing transformation languages to compute on models of their own language, *generic transformations* (parametrisable transformations in our terminology), as well as *meta-transformations* (predominantly called HOTs by now) are specifiable. In analogy to higher-order-logics, generic transformations have decidability and performance problems. These problems may be overcome by using meta-transformations to reduce generic transformations to non-generic transformations.

Tisi et al. [158] provide a survey of different approaches using HOTs and propose a coarse classification of HOTs, called base patterns. These patterns are primitives consisting of analysis, synthesis, modification and (de)composition. Subsequently, they try to give an overview on existing HOTs. The overview is not intended to be complete, it merely lists publications known to the authors where HOTs written in the widespread ATL have been used in various areas. These HOTs are studied to support the proposed finer-grained classification. Further classification attempts or surveys are not known as the field of transformations and HOTs in particular is still immature. However, approaches implemented in QVT are not surveyed, and the need for improvement of current transformation languages for higher-order implementations is not pointed out. The difference between base patterns and our HOT patterns is that we propose generic patterns to solve particular problems, such as feature model-based transformation composition or template instantiation. HOT patterns are composite patterns which employ base patterns for partial task to achieve their overall goal. We define HOT patterns as building blocks that support generic model-driven transformation generation architecture, where each of the patterns encapsulates specific concern (e.g. weaving, model-to-model transformation, template instantiation or model-to-text transformation).

Furthermore, an example of HOT is synthesis of transformation from a source other as transformation, as applied by Goldschmidt et al. in [68]. He creates a HOT to generate transformation rules to copy model elements. Input for the HOT in solution of Goldchmidt et al. is the QVT metamodel. However, he does not generalise the HOT definition and only describes initial implementation. His implementation was inspiration for the *HOT Routine* pattern introduced in Section 4.4 and is an example of *Copying and Marking* version of this pattern.

8.1.3. Quality Metrics for Model Transformations

Quality metrics have been studied already to measure quality (software quality was defined by [26]) of object-oriented software [56, 83, 141] and software architectures [13, 151]. Metrics to estimate the maintainability of software are mostly based on measuring the size and complexity of code. Depending on the employed programming languages (functional, imperative, etc.) different metrics need to be employed for this task. Numerous analysis techniques exist to assess quality (e.g. maintainability) of traditional software artefacts. However, this is not the case towards analysing model transformations. The work of Anastasakis et al. [3] recognised that quality, especially maintainability, of model transformations is crucial for the success of MDSD. In their approach a transformation is considered to be a model and as such existing model analysis techniques for maintainability can be applied (i.e., transforming transformations into the Alloy models and simulating using existing tools).

The most relevant group of metrics for our approach is derived from related work in the area of functional languages, such as the metrics defined by Harrison et al. in [78]. The group of relational transformation languages is related to functional programming languages, therefore we can reuse the existing functional metrics, similar to [160], in combination with some metrics used for object-oriented languages. However, Amstel et al. [160] focuses on model transformations created using the ASF+SDF transformation language. Most of these metrics are, however, quite generic and could be applied to nearly arbitrary functional programming languages. Nevertheless they do not take into account the special character of relational transformations, such as their strong alignment to the source and target metamodels. Still, some of these metrics can be used to measure certain aspects of model transformations written in QVT Relations. We adapted some of the metrics to the special requirements of the QVT Relations transformation language and extended them by the addition of more specific metrics (especially the group of manual metrics). Furthermore, we automated the gathering of the majority of the metrics presented in this paper.

In [66] initial considerations for transformation metrics based on a classification of transformation features [46] and a goal-question-metric plan were presented. However, these ideas were still in a very early stage and were not elaborated down to the special needs of different groups of transformation, such as relational transformations.

Reynoso et al. [139] analysed how the complexity of OCL expressions impacts the analysability and understandability of UML models. As OCL is also part of QVT-R these findings are relevant for our approach. However, the remaining part of relational transformations, apart from OCL expressions, cannot be analysed using this approach.

A special way of gathering a maintainability metric based on the occurrence of frequent patterns within a model or transformation was presented in [105]. The presented metric is based on a pattern mining approach that detects the most frequently occurring constructs. The assumption made in that paper is based on cognitive psychology, which says that the human brain works like a giant pattern matching machine and therefore can process things that re-occur often more easily. Thus, we incorporated this metric into our suite.

Using OCL for the definition of metrics was introduced by Abreu in [52]. However, the approach presented there did not cope with metrics concerning the maintainability of transformations at all.

8.2. Platform Completions for Software Performance Engineering

The second area of the related work compares related approaches to the completions for SPE, as described in Chapter 5. The problem of adding performance abstractions of domain-specific aspects into the models (i.e., performance models) has been handled by using annotations only, or by injecting substructures depicting missing aspect. The majority of the approaches use only annotations to complete the model, for example to add measured overheads, etc. As we show for completions in Chapter 3, the injected aspects and their structure may be very variable. However, the common deficiency of existing approaches is no (or only partial) support for configurability of modelled aspects. Moreover, most of the approaches completely lack tool-supported automation. In the following, we discuss related approaches in more detail.

Woodside et al.: Performance-related Completions for Software Specifications [173] The initial work on completions is based on a simplistic definition of a completion as a quality-related annotation of a system model (e.g., with results of performance measurements). Woodside et al. [173] envisioned the concept of completions in order to supply additional information not needed for functional specification but required for performance prediction. They proposed performance-related completions to close the gap between abstract architectural models and required low-level details. The previously calibrated sub-models (or completions) are then added into to system models. The use of completions adds performance influences of a system's infrastructure to prediction models and, thus, increase prediction accuracy. In the original approach of Woodside et al. [174], performance completions have to be added manually to the prediction model. In [174] they planned a library of components for example database, middleware, or file system. Using a set of rules, completions build by these components should be added into the models. They point out that this should be done automatically.

The difficulty of automation is a result of the flexibility and variability required for performance completions. This difficulty was identified later by Woodside in [172] as a practical obstacle which kept off wider acceptance of completions. Since the completions, as viewed by initial simplistic definition, are not expected to introduce variable structural changes to the model and the conflicts of different execution orders is not of high interest, there is a little research on how the initial completion idea should be realised and supported. In order to provide tool support and to apply performance completions, we have to address the problem of variability. Model-driven development can provide the needed automation by means of model transformations, as we introduced in this work.

In the work of Woodside, completions are injected as a part of transformations transforming directly into the prediction model (e.g., Layered Queueing Networks). Thus, target models are on a less abstract level. In a case when we would have to transform into more than one prediction model (e.g., Layered Queueing Networks, Coloured Petri Nets) we would have to adapt all these transformations to know each possible completion. In our approach, we use model-to-model transformations that maintain the level of abstraction. As such, the transformation from the component-based model (e.g., PCM) into the prediction model (e.g., Layered Queueing Networks) does not know about the completion and, thus, it is a simple translation that can be fully reused. Completions are then applied before the translation and result of completion transformation is an input for a transformation into the prediction model.

Another important difference is the understanding of completions. Woodside et al. understands completions as sub-models that are not part of the product, but represent parts of its environment, such as middleware, file systems, databases or web services used by the product. We consider completions as a mean to include environment details but also design decisions that are a part of the product, such as design patterns or parallelisation of different application parts. Moreover, we do not use completions to include hardware related aspects such as storage models or virtualisation infrastructure, for this purpose we use special approaches, for example [81]. Moreover, we propose in Chapter 3 a structured process how to develop completions; in particular we introduce an application of automated measurements and experiments with the goal to calibrate resulting completions.

Happe et al.: A Pattern-Based Performance Completion for Message-Oriented Middleware [76] The authors of [76] analyse completion for Message-Oriented Middleware (MOM). The resulting MOM completion was implemented a number of times, first, using classical Java implementation, second, using mark transformation where configuration served as additional input for transformation, and third, using model-driven techniques introduced in this thesis . The MOM completion was additionally extended in this thesis, see Section 7.2.1.1. In this section, we discuss the deficiencies of integration approach used for MOM completion in work of Happe et al. [76].

Figure 8.1 illustrates the overview of completion concept used in [76]. They present an approach focused on the parametrisation of completions. The performance measurements using suitable test-drivers determine realistic resource demands for different platforms, like Java EE application servers. Moreover, test-drivers evaluate quantitative effects of different configuration combinations. In our approach, this evaluation is encapsulated in the domain analysis step (see Section 3.3.2) and automated using Software Performance Cockpit. In their approach, Happe et al. do not consider variability of the Completion Model Skeleton. Actually, their transformation integrates always the same subsystem with different calibration. However, this is not suitable when the subsystem should be variable too, for example because certain middleware services are not supported by a particular platform. Thus, the approach presented by Happe et al. does not consider variability of completions and do not provide an automated solution for their integration.

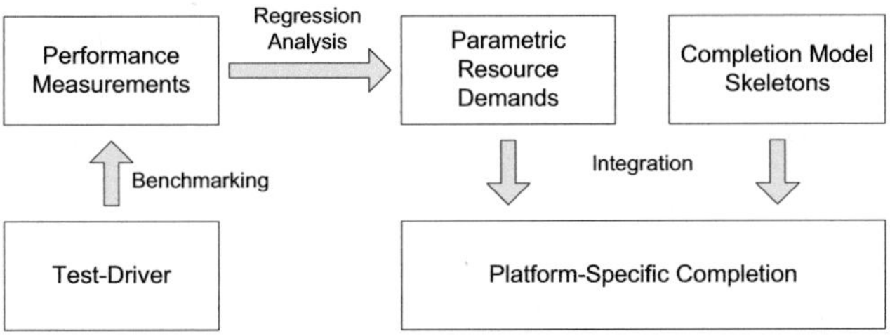

Figure 8.1.: Overview of the concept of parametric performance completions used in [76]

In our work, we focus on the creation of variable completion skeleton. Happe et al. use the selected combination of messaging patterns as configuration (mark model) for model-to-model transformations. We generate a completion transformation from the configuration for one variant only.

S. Becker: Coupled Model Transformations for QoS Enabled Component-Based Software Design [12] The coupled transformation concept is the inspiration for the HOT pattern described in Section B.1. In this section, we discuss coupled transformations [12] as a realisation of completion resulting in two different target models. Often starting with the same source model we generate not only prediction models, but even the implementation (or code).

Coupled transformations are actually mark transformations, which make the relationship between generated code and completion explicit. The implementation code in this approach is generated automatically using a model-to-text transformation. Injecting a completion into the model using mark transformation afterwards requires an adaptation of the code generation transformation, too. Coupled transformations, in this case, are two transformations, namely a model-to-model transformation (e.g., PCM to LQN) and a model-to-text transformation (e.g., PCM to EJB). Mark models then configure both transformations, the transformation to code as well as transformation to performance model. The models then consider the same information for prediction as used for generating code.

However, because the completion concept introduced in this thesis maintains the level of abstraction, we can simply execute in a sequence first the completion transformation and afterwards any other model-to-model or model-to-text transformation requiring the source model conform to the language on the same abstraction level as completion applied. This is possible, because the target model of completion is conform to the same metamodel as the source model. As such, all transformations applied after all necessary completions consider the same information, without necessity of their adaptation.

Furthermore, existing solutions [174, 76, 12] focus on the integration of only one completion with one configuration at a time. If more than one completion is applied to model element, conflicts between different completions are likely and have to be resolved. These scenarios are not discussed in any of the approaches [174, 76, 12].

Related Approaches employing Model-Driven Techniques In software performance engineering, several approaches use model transformations to derive prediction models (e.g., [115, 132, 49, 12]). Cortellessa et al. surveyed a number of performance meta-models in [40] leading to a general model-driven framework for analysis of extra-functional properties [42, 41]. In [42] they propose usage of reusable (but static) building blocks for platform models.

Other approaches (e.g., [69, 165]) extend this framework. Verdickt et al. [165] developed a framework to automatically inject a construct very similar to completion (but without configuration possibility) into the models. Their focus is on the impact of CORBA middleware on the performance of distributed systems. The provided vertical transformations decrease the level of abstraction, as they map high-level platform-independent UML models to other platform-specific UML models.

Grassi et al. provided a model-based approach for prediction model refinement using intermediate language KLAPER [69]. The transformations implemented in QVT Relations integrate the overhead caused by communication links into the models. They follow the same idea of using classical vertical refinements from model-driven technologies to integrate aspects of performance and reliability into the models. Although the approach uses model transformations, it does not support their configurability.

These approaches still neglect crucial issues that are an obstacle to their application in practice. First, support for structured increase of model completeness for the analysis of extra-functional properties is not considered. Thus, purpose-specific aspects cannot be integrated by configurable transformations and the model cannot be extended to fit particular purpose. Second, maintainability of the used model-driven framework and reusable configuration models is not discussed.

Related Design Pattern-based Performance Abstractions The idea of using pattern-based model enhancements for improving quality-prediction accuracy of component-based models has been discussed in the context of connectors between components [149] and component adaptors, used to bridge interoperability problems when composing components. Initial work has been done by compiling a classification of adaptation patterns by Becker et al. [14]. Additionally, Becker et al. sketch initial process to incorporate the patterns in a prediction process for extra-functional properties. Besides performance, we can analyse patterns for other quality properties, for example, there is also work looking at reliability prediction in the context of adaptation patterns by Reussner et al. [138].

Spitznagel et al. investigated the relationship of architectural connectors and common dependability techniques [149]. A special focus of their work was the composition of more than a single connector to combined connectors. However, their main interest has been to guarantee properties of systems like deadlock-freedom and not in the prediction of the extra-functional impact. Similarly, the work of T. Bures [28] analysed extra-functional properties of connectors, however, he does not provide calibrated models suitable for performance prediction and he does not use model-driven techniques. His work provides an initial input for domain analysis of connector completions in Section 5.3.4.

Performance Abstractions of Concurrency Design Patterns In the literature numerous approaches exist analysing parallel systems and the problems by design of parallel software. However, in case of concurrency, pattern modelling focuses mostly on functional properties or only make limited use of configuration options. Additionally, existing prediction approaches only provide basic modelling constructs for concurrency patterns modelling, leaving the creation of complex structures to software architects. Concurrent software systems are especially complex, hard to model and implement. Therefore, goal-oriented abstractions are desirable for such systems. Several approaches exist addressing these issues partially and we discuss these in more detail.

E. Lee proposed to use modelling constructs for concurrency patterns [107] to increase understandability of concurrency, communication, and synchronisation within a software architecture. He identified the thread-based models as a source for the difficult understandability of parallel software. As a solution to these problems he proposes language pragmatics that extend existing programming languages. The language pragmatics are defined in a form of a coordination language targeted to support developers when designing constructs for communication and synchronisation of components. He provesa major improvement of understandability of parallel software by using coordination pragmatics.

In the Ptolemy project [108], the same author proposed using reusable building blocks for communication composites based on the concurrency design patterns. Thus, using these abstractions they can introduce multi-threading in communication that is not already multi-threaded. Although it is a very promising approach, it neglects qualitative aspects, such as performance and reliability. Similarly, Spitznagel and Garlan [149] used connectors to extract communication aspects from components. However, both approaches focus on hard attributes, like deadlock-freedom , neglecting qualitative attributes, such as performance and reliability.

The performance engineering methods model concurrency, communication and synchronisation on very low abstraction level. A first step to model distributed systems on a higher level of abstraction is made Smith and Williams in [147]. They provide four communication and synchronisation patterns in a form of UML sequence diagrams. These patterns can be used to model interaction of components. In the area of performance prediction for component-based systems, Liu et al. [110] model architecture patterns for application servers. In the first step of their approach, developers have to create a general model of a component container for the application server. The second step is analysis and design of architecture patterns in a form of activity diagrams. In the third step, a parametrised performance model is created correspondingly to the previous general model. To provide accurate performance prediction, developers have to integrate the characteristics and demands of the platform. Therefore, in the last step, they use a test application to create a profile of the platform. All steps, integration of the platform profile and architecture patterns are manual, thus the development effort does not decrease.

8.3. Summary

The previous sections give an overview on the approaches closely related to this thesis. We have addressed approaches from two research areas, MDSD in Section 8.1 and CB-SPE in Section 8.2. The surveyed methods vary in scope and focus. In the following, we summarize the main findings and resulting deficiencies, which provide motivation for a more comprehensive approach. We provide two comparison studies of the most important approaches from both of the research areas: From MDSD approaches, we compare related approaches generating variable transformations and, from CB-SPE approaches, we discuss the scope of supported features of completions by the closest methods.

The first category of methods dealing with variability in the MDSD context provides specialised solutions to support model variability (cf. Table 8.1). In the comparison, we focus on comparing the generated artefacts and deficiencies. The approach DUALLY actually implements similar solution as is introduced by Routine HOT pattern for mappings. The AMW and AOP/MD-SPL employ mark transformations to support variability. The COPE approach supports external merge of transformations. The DSML-SPL merges two model instances into the target model that is conform to the merge of two source metamodels. The deficiencies of these approaches are summarized in Table 8.1.

	Generated	Deficiencies
DUALLY	Mapping rules used for translation between different metamodels.	Missing support for customisations and complex transformation logic.
AMW	Mapping rules between source model and target model. These rules are specified by an active weaving operator.	Mixture of imperative and declarative constructs. The HOT definition is not general, depends on existing weaving operators. Missing support for complex transformation logic and customisations.
COPE	Migration transformation which is an external composition of transactions from a library.	No support for variabilities, e.g. in application families or based on feature configurations.
DSML-SPL: *Morin et al.*	Transformation merging several metamodels.	Target metamodel changes, thus when the product is used for further analysis the tools are not reusable.
AOP-MD-SPL: *Garces et al.* *Grober et al.*	Variants of models based on feature-model-based variability definition.	No separation of concerns between variability definition and transformation definition. Variability definition is an input into the SPL. Only additive weaving no updates or overrides.

Table 8.1.: Comparison of related approaches from MDSD context.

In our approach, completions are realized by configurable model-to-model transformations. We present an approach to define domain-specific languages that capture the performance-relevant configurations of different implementation details. The configuration provides the necessary variability. The transformations are applied to model elements specified by the software architect. We realise the completions by means of model-to-model transformations. Depending on a given configuration, these transformations inject the completion's behaviour into performance models. Thus in our approach the transformation is specified by the configuration itself.

In the case of SPLs, the configuration happens on the lower level of abstraction, thus the variability is bound to model instance more tightly and can not be reused on the metamodel level. Furthermore, the changes of transformation in our solution can be both fine-grained and coarse-grained. Many SPLs support coarse-grained variability, where the whole methods are added. These methods encapsulating consistent fragment of functionality. Fine-grained extensions, where a parameter is updated, domain pattern of a mapping relation changed or a statement added in the middle of method, either require intricate workarounds or obfuscate the base code with annotations [95]. In our scenario, such fine-grained updates happen often. The classical SPL-based approach is limited to support such scenarios and produces often results of worse quality. Our approach reduces code replication and improves readability.

Moreover, in our solution the coupling between the features and the transformation fragments is more explicit than in classical SPLs. In many other SPL-based approaches the configuration describes the product itself not a way to the product as it is in our case. We rather lift the configuration up to the transformation creation itself. The configuration describes the transformation and thus we have described the product, too. This way the complexity of handling all possible feature combinations within the transformations is decreased and is made explicit through the structure of the configuration model.

The second category of methods deals with support for model completions in a context of MDSPE for component-based systems (cf. Table 8.2). In the comparison we focused on three closest approaches. First, we describe the criteria to compare these approaches: (i) the level of abstraction ("*Is the abstraction level maintained?*") , (ii) supported variability ("*Are completions configurable?*"), and (iii) automation ("*Is the integration of completions automated?*"). The first criterion is crucial for reuse of existing tools and transformations, because any change of target metamodel language limits the reusability of tools using the target model. The second and third criterion discuss the scope of variability support.

In case of platform completions and coupled transformation the annotation (or configuration) of models happens on higher level of abstraction as the resulting target model is located . In both cases the transformation decreasing level of abstraction (e.g. transformation from PCM to LQN) has to be adapted to handle the annotations and create the target model variant. Moreover, both approaches are realised by mark transformations However, usage of mark transformation has a clear disadvantage. It is a Y-

	Is the abstraction level maintained?	Are completions configurable?	Is the integration of variable completions automated?
Platform Completions: *Woodside et al.*	Annotations are on a higher-level of abstraction than the target model.	No support.	No automation.
MOM Completion: *Happe et al.*	Abstraction level is maintained.	Partially, only the resource demands, changes of the skeleton will result in highly-complex and un-maintainable transformations.	Mark transformation. Only single completion.
Coupled Transformations: *S. Becker*	Annotations are on a higher-level of abstraction than the target model.	Partially, the complexity of implementation allowed only partial variability support.	Mark transformation. Only single completion.

Figure 8.2.: Comparison of related approaches from MDSPE context.

transformation, which takes two input models, in this case model instance and annotation, and creates one output model. Thus, such transformation has to be adapted for each new annotation. Other previously discussed approaches by Grassi et al. and Verdickt et al. [69, 165] have further a disadvantage, they do not support flexible control of completions. This approaches provide an all-or-nothing method where for example all connectors in model are replaced by the same completion with the same configuration.

In this thesis, we have addressed the shortcomings of existing approaches and have proposed a method supporting variability of transformations by employing and composing HOT patterns (see Section 4) into the SPL for model-to-model transformations. The proposed method was applied to support model completions in MDSPE in Section 3. In addition, we have developed a structure completion library to reduce conflicts in application of multiple completions. At last, we introduced an initial set of completions that allow software architects to integrate different performance influences into the models. The creation of each completion is a research task on its own and includes discussion of related work for the particular modelled aspect. The discussion of related approaches for each completion is out of scope for this section, but it is a part of research in domain analysis by completion developer.

9. Conclusion

In this chapter, we summarize the contributions presented in this thesis (Section 9.1). Furthermore, we discuss achievements and current limitations of our main contribution, the CHILIES approach, and our additional contributions, the completion-based MDSPE, the structured completion library, and the maintainability metrics for transformations (Section 9.2). Section 9.3 presents open questions and visions for future research.

9.1. Summary

The presented approach is motivated by the requirement to improve the accuracy of performance prediction in MDSPE approaches, e.g. the PCM, through automated support of performance completions. However, we observed that model-driven approaches lack an applicable and suitable solution for managing variability, which is necessary to support completions. We had to deal with this challenge, thus, the main contribution of this thesis is located in the MDSD area. We introduced generalised concept of model completions and created automated support for them, which is based on HOT patterns. HOT patterns (CHILIES) are building blocks that can be composed together to form more complex model-driven architectures. In the next step, we applied our approach in the MDSPE domain to automate performance completions. For the PCM, a metamodel specially designed to support CBSE development and design-time performance prediction, we introduced a structured completion library with an initial set of performance completions for concurrency design patterns. Furthermore, to evaluate resulting model transformations, we created a set of maintainability metrics for relational transformations. To automatically collect the results of these metrics, we applied one of the presented HOT patterns, the Analysis HOT pattern.

In the following, we look back at the leading research questions and discuss how they are answered by this thesis. The research questions address limitations of existing approaches and were kept as general as possible. Thus, they lead to results applicable in other contexts as well.

Q1: *How to include purpose-specific aspects to models in an automated but adaptable manner inheriting its standard mechanisms and facilities, including transformations and tools?*

This question introduces three requirements on the resulting solution: *automation*, *adaptability*, and *reuse* of existing software artefacts, such as M2M/M2T transformations, EMF editors etc. We answered this question by introducing generalised model completions, which are (i) automated by generated completion (i.e. M2M) transformations, (ii) adaptable by the management of variability in completion transformations using feature diagrams, and (iii) allow reuse of existing tools due the maintained level of abstraction (i.e. metamodel language).

In our approach, we define model completions as horizontal specialisations of models for a certain domain to achieve a higher level of purpose-specific completeness. Completeness quantifies the level of model detail on which the ability of a model to serve its purpose depends. Each model is created to serve a certain purpose, in our application scenario it is performance prediction. As such, we can quantify the completeness for models as the ability to evaluate the performance of the modelled system with the desired accuracy. Because these necessary details (e.g. design patterns, middleware) are very variable, we defined model completions as configurable purpose-specific transformations. These transformations increase the level of model completeness while maintaining the language of the abstract level. This property of completions allows fully reusing existing MDSD tools, such as model transformations, without the need of any adaptations. Using completions, we maintain not only the original model language, but even the models are remaining in the responsibility of the same development role on the abstract level. In our application scenario, the performance knowledge is inherently fragmented. Not every role involved in the performance modelling process has the full knowledge of all performance properties of each aspect. Furthermore, these aspects appear in different contexts, applications or variants. The concept of model completions supports specification of reusable constructs that can be applied in different contexts. Thus, performance completions could be used to support a Performance Knowledge Base, as envisioned by Woodside et al. in [172]. In comparison to the Woodside's idea, the Completion Library is not only organised around results of analyses but even parametrised model fragments, expressed as completions, that are calibrated using measurement data.

Each completion is defined by two parts: *quantitative* and *structural* specification. The quantitative part require *calibrations* using results of measurements on real systems. The structural part is defined by a *configuration model*, i.e. a feature diagram, and *structural skeletons* that are expressed as a composition of feature effects (i.e., transformation fragments). As such, completions help to consolidate approaches based only on measurements, with those that exploit model-driven prediction techniques. Using completions a partial views on the black-box systems through measurement data such systems can be integrated into the models. The requirement to converge these two domains was identified already by Woodside et al. [172]. In this thesis, we contributed to the solution of challenges identified by Woodside et al. in his visionary big picture of SPE domain.

Moreover, we introduced an enhanced MDSPE process, where we illustrated the usage of completions to increase the effectiveness of model development. This process supports software architects in development of more accurate models that are so complex that it is not feasible to create them manually. Completion-based models are less complex and more understandable because of the encapsulation of the aspect's complexity in a form of simple configuration model. The completions decrease development efforts through automation and manageability of model complexity. Furthermore, completion-based development

- closes the semantic gap between an abstract model and low-level details (Chapter 3) that are in some cases necessary to fit the purpose of the model (e.g., performance prediction).
- hides the complexity of the purpose-specific aspect, allowing configuration of aspect variants and encapsulating domain-specific expert knowledge (Section 5.3).
- when applied to the MDSPE, increases the accuracy of performance predictions (Section 7.2.1).

Q2: *How to support configuration-based variability in model transformations?*

The answer to this question is the main contribution of this thesis. We created an automated support of completion transformations development using pre-processors and generators based on HOTs. Typically, variability solutions for MDSD or SPL deal with the variability of model instances. In our work, we recognized that dealing with the variability of models only, would not do the trick. The problem is that when going the classical way and using known MDSD and SPL paradigms, the transformations are growing in complexity, extensions of configurations are not feasible, and the maintainability of transformations quickly becomes a huge problem. Therefore, we decided to take an advantage of the abstraction levels in MDSD and move the management of variability to an higher abstraction level. In our approach, metamodels and transformations are subject to variability. Raising the level of abstraction enables to focus on individual aspects separately. Thus, the productivity of development is increased by modularisation and MDSD structures are more flexible. We introduced the CHILIES approach that builds on the definition of goal-specific MDSD building blocks which could be combined to chains of transformations with more complex goals. In our work, we identified a set of such building blocks using HOTs and targeting different goals, such as template instantiation or fragment composition. We compose these HOT patterns into the chains of HOTs to build complex MDSD structures.

In this thesis, we applied three HOT patterns to create an SPL for completion transformations. Using this approach completion developers can focus on one feature at time and do not need to implement an overall transformation that can handle all possible feature combinations. The resulting completion transformation is generated for one configuration instance only. We composed in an one SPL following HOT patterns:

- **Routine HOT pattern** generates frequently occurring patterns (e.g. copier) in transformations. The routine relation (e.g. copy relation) is generated for each metamodel element and can be used as a basis for more complex transformations (e.g. model customisations).
- **Composite HOT pattern** allows configuration-dependent transformation generation. The configuration happens on a higher level of abstraction. Thus, the configuration itself defines the transformation. The transformation is a composition of transformation fragments, which define the effects of configuration choices.
- **Template HOT pattern** uses parametrised transformation templates (as reusable transformation parts) and instantiates them into the transformation. Transformation templates allow modular definition of transformation which yields a simpler definition of transformation.

Using our approach, the completion transformation phase in the completion-based MDSPE is fully automated. The transformation definition is easily extendible with additional features. Moreover, the transformation and the configuration are loosely-coupled and the development of the configuration is separated from the transformation. Such separation of concerns allows reuse of completion definition, even easier implementation of completion in different language (e.g. ATL). Furthermore, we identified additional HOT patterns which are described in Appendix B.

Q3: *How to structure the Completion Library to reduce possible conflicts in an application of multiple completions?*

To answer this question, we created a library of completions structured according the development process and the roles appearing in this process. Our hypothesis is that the metamodel used to expressed models in this process maps the separation of responsibilities to different roles. Thus, it is possible to distinguish sets of elements in a responsibility of one development role. As such, completions working with these elements only impact elements in an independent cluster of the metamodel which contains all elements possibly adapted by the one development role. Thus, it is possible to identify sub-domains (i.e., independent metamodel clusters) which are solely affected by a change induced by a particular completion transformation and applied by a particular role. Based on this principle, we identified transformations which are independent and reduced potential conflicts of completions. Each role has only a small set of completions and can resolve remaining conflicts manually.

Additionally, the introduction of a new completion should be easily possible and conflict-free. Therefore, each new completion is registered with the Completion Library and categorised in three levels, which include its associated development role, the metamodel element type to which it can be applied, and the identification of dependencies to other completions of the same category.

Furthermore, we created a set of completions for concurrency design patterns. These completions are categorised in three groups: *Component*, *Connector* and *Infrastructure* completion. We introduced completions in each group:

- *Component Completion:* State Manager, Replication
- *Connector Completion:* Pipe&Filter Connector

- *Infrastructure Completion:* Thread Management

We analysed these completions and evaluated the prediction results using completed models. The resulting models reflect the real system behaviour more precisely leading to more accurate predictions. Therefore, performance completions allow a more realistic evaluation of different design decisions. Moreover, we observed a dependency of performance on the state of a component or a system. We analysed the impact of state on the performance and created a set of experiments that are summarized in Appendix A.

Q4: *How to analyse maintainability of relational transformations?*

In the development of HOTs and different versions of completion transformations, we identified a lack of metrics to evaluate the quality properties of relational transformations. We presented a set of code metrics to evaluate the maintainability of QVT Relational transformations. Such metrics can be applied to different relational transformations and they play important role when analysing completion transformations. We demonstrated the use of these metrics on a set of reference transformations.

The presented metrics help software architects to judge the maintainability of their model transformations. Based on these judgements, software architects can take corrective actions (like refactorings or code-reviews) whenever they identify a decay in maintainability of their transformations. This results in higher agility when changing metamodels of software architectures or their platforms, which together with metamodel build basis for transformation definition.

Validation We validate our contributions on two levels: A Type I validation shows that when completions are applied to a software performance model, the prediction accuracy can be increased significantly. We validate the prediction results by comparing them to measurements on a real implementation of the system. The prediction accuracy of a single completion is validated for two completions: the stateful case of Message-oriented

Middleware (MOM) (an extension of MOM completion in [76]), and the Thread Pool completion. Additionally, we evaluate prediction accuracy in a composition of a multiple completions in a Business Reporting System scenario (based on [174]). For this scenario, we discuss different permutations in sequences of completions and evaluated the best possible completion order. In the investigated cases, a significant correspondence with reality is achieved.

A Type II validation analyses the applicability of the model-driven approach using CHILIES. The main focus of this evaluation lies on the maintainability and complexity of used transformations. We evaluated the complexity of a number of completion transformations and HOT implementations. Furthermore, we compare the complexity between two different implementations of one completion, once implementing a mark transformation and once implementing a completion in a form of feature model with corresponding feature effects. This experiment discusses the advantages of separation of concerns using the feature effects.

9.2. Limitations

Limitations are discussed in particular chapters at the end of each contribution of this thesis. This section gives reference to the respective sections and summarizes the most important assumptions and limitations of our approach. Section 4.8 discusses various limitations and assumptions of CHILIES approach. Section 5.4 presents limitations and assumptions of completion library. Besides the overall limitation of completion library, each of the presented completions has its own assumptions and limitations that should be evaluated by completion developer in the domain analysis. Section 6.5 summarizes the limitations and assumptions of the introduced quality metrics for M2M transformations.

9.3. Open Questions and Future Work

This section gives an overview of open questions and possible areas of future research based on the results of this thesis. First, we discuss the open questions in the MDSPE domain. Second, we further evolve the usage of advanced model-driven techniques and discuss the open questions in the MDSD domain.

9.3.1. Future work in the MDSPE context

Automated Calibration of Completions Many completions are dependent on the deployment environment where they are applied, they are platform specific. The high complexity and diversity of middleware platforms make the design of completions cumbersome. The high effort for their development may void the benefit. Especially, the calibration of completions should happen automatically and the completion models should be able to be recalibrated for any platform. This calibration should be a black-box operation for the user. The idea is that the user chooses a platform and previously measured profile for this platform is loaded. Other possibility would be that user could chose his own computer as a platform to calibrate for, thus this platform should be automatically measured by previously defined experiment. At the time of writing, support for such operations is being developed for the Software Performance Cockpit [169]. The resulting tool will provide different adaptors for different platform and experiments. This tool than should be fully integrated into the tool support for completions.

Additional Concurrency Completions For the future, an extension of the approach to support a boarder set of concurrency patterns would be a natural endeavour. Here, one could focus especially on the accurate behaviour of these patterns, not the accurate calibration of them. Thus, the calibration should happen automatically the effort to get the accurate measurements manually would not be well spent. One may focus on the patterns in measurement and simulation results manifesting effects as state-dependency, usage of asynchronous calls, capacity restraints that restrain the level of concurrency, etc. Moreover, the clear separation of concurrency patterns as a processing steps is a question to research, as well.

Performance Tuning through Concurrency Today's trend of multi-core processors poses new challenges to software development. As the only reason to introduce concurrency is the performance, the natural idea for the future work is to use completions as automated tuning steps to find out if concurrency introduction would be of an advantage for a given system. These predefined completions should be automatically applied to a given system in different configurations, combinations and using different work-loads. Such analysis will help the developers to decide about the most effective concurrency solution. Based on provided results the unsuccessful development branches, where a high effort was spend to paralelise a system without awaited result, could be avoided.

Optimisation of Completion Configuration Optimisation approa-ches, such as PerOpteryx [113], could be used to automatically optimise the configuration of completions and the order in a sequence of completions for a better performance. The result of such automated optimisation would be a proposition of the most performant system configuration. For this goal, one would have to introduce the completion configuration as an additional degree of freedom in the PerOpteryx approach.

Completions for other Quality Attributes Furthermore, comple-tions for other quality properties such as reliability or security could be introduced. Having such completions will not only extend the completion library, but it would allow to reason about trade-off decisions between a number of quality attributes on a level of complex solutions for different, e.g. security vs. performance, problems.

9.3.2. Future work in the MDSD context

Necessity of Empirical Studies It is required to further evaluate empirically different aspects of MDSD. First, one would have to conduct an empirical study to explore the effects of modularisation on the system and transformation comprehension. It is accepted that reuse and automation is always for the better. However, to support this claim we have to use empirical methods. Especially, the usage of modularisation in a collaborative design and development is a challenging task. The ability of the developer to modularise and map partial changes to the features is a related aspect to the applicability of model completions. The participants of such empirical study would have to implement a transformation generating a completed model by two different approaches (i) once as a coherent transformation and (ii) once as a set of modules. The development effort, ability to modularise and transformation comprehension in both cases should be studied.

Second, the advantages of using relational instead of operational transformations have to be evaluated. There are many arguments in favour of both. Thus, we argue that empirical studies that incorporate developers using both of the language families are key to decide the fight. The quality metrics introduced in Chapter 6 could be used to evaluate the complexity of transformations developed by the participants. In addition, we think that the advantages (e.g. modularity and compositionality) of relational transformations have to be considered. The compositionality aspect could be studied by quantifying the amount of helper or service code needed.

Compositionality of Transformations The composition of transformations is a research field for itself. There are different approaches discussing this topic. To perform the composition of model transformations, which is needed after selecting required configuration in feature model, internal composition is used. Internal composition composes two model transformation definitions into one new model transformation, with a typically complex merge of the transformation rules. Internal composition, when performed by a model transformation, is a higher-order problem. We use internal composition to compose fragments of transformations. External composition consists of chaining separate model transformations and passing models from one transformation to another. We use external composition to create sequences of completions. In our approach the external composition of transformations could be abstracted as a composition of feature models. The composition of transformations on the level of feature models promises decrease of composition complexity, we plan to investigate this idea further in future.

Composition of model-to-model transformation should be guided by the purpose of the resulting transformation. In our approach, some parts of transformations provide a frame where customisations are injected. Thus, we think the transformation pattern-based frames composition with customisations should be analysed further.

Automated Extraction of Transformation Templates The automatic derivation of templates from example transformation models as it was proposed in [164] is interesting topic for future research. An automated extraction of templates could use pattern matching to identify common patterns in a set of transformation models. From the identified patterns one could derive templates with 'hooks' for parametrisation and register them in the template library. This would greatly ease the development of templates as the manual extraction from an instance model to the transformation can be shortened significantly.

General definition of HOTs and Transformation Templates Metamodel-independent definition of HOTs will ease their reuse to generate transformations in other transformation languages, not only QVT Relational. Moreover, the feature effects could be specified in metamodel-independent way to allow reuse of completions in other contexts, e.g. PCM, SOFA, etc. As a suitable language for metamodel-independent transformation specification we propose to use VIATRA [5].

View-based Model Development The completions allow to hide model details. With suitable tool support allowing to encapsulate and roll off chosen completions we can build a collaborative environment allowing developers to work on the same model, but with different level of detail. Moreover, purpose-specific views could be supported. Thus, developers could browse the model details and choose the level of completeness they need.

Model-driven Architecture Patterns The HOT patterns introduce complex structures in a model-driven architecture. We consider this group of patterns as 'model-driven architecture patterns', because they are reusable and goal-specific building blocks composed from different artefacts (such as models, metamodels, transformations). The introduced and upcoming HOT patterns need to be further formalised. HOTs, especially HOTs of multiple order are rare, the useful scenarios are still to be explored. Moreover, an experimental evaluation and efficiency study of some of the HOT application scenarios described in this work is planned for the future.

With the growing set of reusable building blocks in the model-driven world, it is more and more important to discuss the terms 'component' and 'architecture' in this context. We propose creation of component-based architecture models for MDSD. An architectural model will provide an appropriate mechanism to enable the modular and compositional specification of complex model transformation chains. Such models could support verification of complex MDSD systems and, moreover, allow to define a relation or their composition as an part of classical component-based software architectures.

Hots and Transformation Languages From our point of view the following topics could be addressed by HOTs in order to improve the applicability model transformations in general:

- Providing *parametrization* mechanisms directly, for example by providing new language constructs. This can be done using HOTs or language extensions.

- Supporting techniques to ensure the *correctness* of transformations. Design-by-Contract methods could be brought to the module-level, for example as OCL annotations. Heuristics to check such annotations formally or logic to generate test cases could be implemented as a HOT. Further, error-handling possibilities can be provided by transformation languages. Syriani et. al. are considering exception handling [156], these language constructs can only be provided by the transformation engine, whereas the higher-order level is insufficient.

- *Hybrid* transformation implementations, i.e., composition techniques, which permit mixing declarative (QVT Relational) and imperative (QVT Operational) code as tackled by approach [133]. Such mixing of declarative with operational code is already possible in ATL. Composition of rules or modules of operational or functional style can be implemented as a HOT.

- Supplying developers with better *tooling* is crucial for more complex implementations. Additionally, conformance to standards is still not guaranteed, e. g. full support of QVT Relational.

Best-Practices for Metamodel Evolution We showed that the structure of the metamodel could be a source of certain advantages for the future usage of metamodels in model-driven systems. In the PCM metamodel, we can distinguish disjunct clusters of metamodel elements. This metamodel clustering maps the separation of concerns between the roles in the development process. Intuitively, we propose to introduce an metamodel specification process, which considers the structure and roles in development process it will be used in. We think that the introduction of best practices for metamodel design considering future development of transformations will contribute significantly to the correctness of transformations and decrease their complexity.

Metamodel Coverage of Transformations The dependency between transformation and metamodel is very promising target for further analysis. Analysis of the metamodel coverage by a set of transformations helps to resolve conflicts in transformation execution. Additionally, debugging tools visualising this dependency and illustrating when the borders of a cluster in metamodel were crossed by a transformation could support composition and chaining of transformations. It will help to identify and reduce conflicts in transformation execution. This way developers could identify parts of functionality that could be developed in separation or that have to be merged. This will increase the productivity in development of complex MDSD architectures. Moreover, it will open possibilities to optimise execution in transformation chains through identification of transformations that are independent already on metamodel level so they can be executed in parallel.

Quality Metrics for Transformations The necessity of empirical studies for MDSD and any metrics for transformations is a clear issue. Additionally, the techniques evaluating presented metrics should be embedded in model transformation tools. The conducted studies showed that the metrics proved as useful for increasing the understanding of model transformations. This is a promising perspective, however, experiments should be conducted to empirically validate the benefits of the proposed techniques. Furthermore, the performance of transformations is an another quality attribute that should be further investigated.

An obvious point for future work is generalisation of the presented techniques for quality metrics, transformation composition from fragments, template instantiation or routine pre processors even further. All techniques introduced in this thesis were implemented in QVT Relational, as they use concept of relations and as such are suitable for any relational language, the extension of these techniques for other relational language (e.g. ATL) is simple implementation task. However, the extension of these techniques for other language families (imperative, QVT Operational) has to be further investigated.

Final Remark The work presented in this thesis is a step towards further automation of software engineering processes. It helps software developers (i) by reducing development efforts for manually implementing transformations, especially when variability of transformations is required, (ii) by defining a structured process for purpose-specific model completion, and (iii) by providing an automated transformation generation framework, called CHILIES, applicable in different practical contexts. In this thesis, we applied the CHILIES framework to the area of CB-SPE developing an extensible support for performance engineers. Our Performance Knowledge Base (i.e., Completion Library) enables reuse of expert knowledge to improve the accuracy of performance predictions. In addition, our approach contributes to the state-of-art in model-driven software development. (i) It is the first approach introducing enhanced scenarios and patterns for transformation generation. (ii) It clarifies the requirements for transformation variability and provides a flexible solution for transformation variability. (iii) It is the first method demonstrating how purpose-specific completeness can be increased in a systematic, incremental and traceable way.

A. State Dependence in Software Performance Evaluation

In this chapter, we discuss effective state abstraction in component-based performance models. Our previous work on this topic was published in [94]. In addition, this discussion is an extension and motivation of the domain analysis for the State Manager completion introduced in Section 5.3.3.2.

During the last years, many approaches dealing with performance prediction and measurement have been introduced. In the area of Component-Based Software Engineering (CBSE), systems are build out of reusable black-box components (implementing sets of services) interconnected to a component architecture. Specialised component performance prediction and measurement approaches introduce modelling languages with the aim to understand the performance (i.e., response time, throughput, resource utilisation) of a full architecture based on code-specific performance properties of individual components.

It is generally accepted that performance is a pervasive quality of software systems. Everything affects it, from the software itself to all underlying layers, such as operating system, middleware, hardware, communication networks, etc. [172]. The factors influencing the performance of a software component are difficult to analyse because they depend not only on the component implementation, but also on its usage, deployment and environmental context of the component (see Figure A.1), and occur at different stages of component and system life cycle.

Moreover, the difficulty of understanding system performance comes from the propagation of the effects of these factors throughout system con-

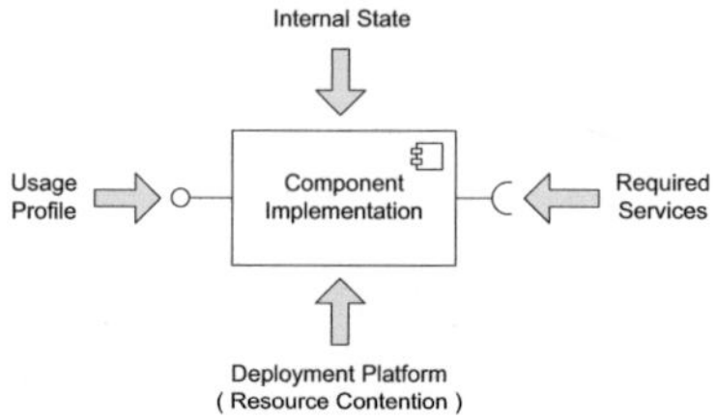

Figure A.1.: Performance-influencing factors.

trol flow, including the influence of the usage profile and history-dependent information defining system state. Besides these influential forces on their own, the difficulty of understanding system performance comes from the variability introduced by the factors and propagated throughout the system. This includes the variability in system control flow due to the propagation of system usage profile and influence of system internal states, and subsequent variability in resource demands awakened by the control flow, which results in complex sequences of resource requests and potential resource deadlocks. While the influence of usage profile on system control flow and subsequent performance has been studied and is commonly understood [97], not much attention has been paid to the influence of system stateful information.

When speaking about a state, we mean a context or history-dependent information remembered inside a component, system, or associate with a user, and employed to coordinate system behaviour. The state of a component or system can originate from its initialisation or previous executions, and can be changed at different stages of system life cycle, including system initialization, deployment or runtime. The state associated with a user uses to be quite stable along system execution and is typically used to customize system behaviour for a particular user type (i.e., standard or premium customer). Only a few performance prediction approaches deal with the modelling of states in component-based systems. Currently, there is no consensus in the definition and method to model stateful information in component-based systems and its performance impact, which limits the accuracy of existing performance models [99, 98].

A.0.3. Challenges of Stateful Analysis

The question that rises for current performance models is how to include the stateful software application properties in a performance model, and how to build more accurate and expressive models of stateful component-based systems. In this respect, we can identify four main issues.

- **State definition:** The property of statefulness can be identified in various artifacts of component-based systems, varying over several system life-cycle stages. Existing literature lacks the localization of state-holding information identifiable in component-based systems [16, 98, 172], and their classification into a transparent set of categories. Available surveys consider the capability to model state only partially or not at all. In this work introduced evaluation focuses especially on this property of performance prediction models (see section A.2.1).

- **Performance impact:** The benefits of state modelling include increased expressive power of the models and higher accuracy of predictions. It is however not well studied, as observed by a number of authors [98, 18, 172], what is the increase of prediction accuracy achieved by state modelling, especially in comparison to the increased effort for modelling and analysis. More important there is no consensus in understanding of the state definition and its impact on performance at all [98]. A discussion on how the existing performance-driven models deal with the interpretation and analysis of stateful prediction models is elaborated in section A.2.1.

- **Prediction difficulty:** The balance between expressiveness (state modelling) and complexity (model size increase) is a challenging research question. Only when it is understood what costs need to be paid for the increase in prediction accuracy, we can competently decide on the suitable abstraction of state modelling (to what extent we aim to include stateful information present in the analysed system).

- **State support in component models:** The lack of work addressing the discussed issues can be explained by insufficient support of stateful information in existing performance-prediction models. Industrial models (like EJB, CCM or Corba) have been designed to support internal state, since it is one of the crucial implementation details, but lack the support of broad analysis capabilities with respect to system properties. Academic research-oriented stateful component models (like SOFA [29]) are often accompanied with a special analysis method for a set of functional system properties (model checking), but not for performance, which is of our interest. The performance-driven research-oriented component models (see detailed survey in section A.2.1) either lack support for state modelling or model state only partially (see Table A.2). Additionally when they support state modelling the performance impact of the state is unclear, as shown in the Table A.2. Consequently, because of missing support for state modelling in the existing prediction methods the analysis of state dependency and related costs is not provided.

It is important to understand the state definition and its impact on the performance predictions. As mentioned by many works from performance prediction community, for example [98, 18, 172], there is a need for deeper analysis of component/system state, its impact on performance and situations when is needed to model the component state for accurate predictions. The purpose of this work is to address some of the challenges of state modelling in performance prediction models.

Missing research on performance influence of stateful information in component-based systems makes performance prediction for the majority of industrial component models (e.g., EJB) difficult and limited. In the component models, such as EJB, CCM, and COM, components are similar to object-oriented classes in the sense that they can be instantiated and that their instances can be stateful. Existing component models oriented on functionality and model checking (e.g., FRACTAL, SOFA) have support to model component internal state. However, the impact of component internal state on performance (or reliability) is not evaluated. Component models oriented on performance prediction have no notion of internal state, or they support internal state modelling and analysis only partially [98]. To build better models and their solvers, we need to think about component state introduction [172]. To reach this goal in the existing performance prediction models, we deal with two kinds of problems. Firstly, these models depend in many cases on assumptions, e.g. with the assumption of exponential service demand we need a significant effort to find a probability of timeout [172] (as such the probabilistic approximation of internal state is very difficult). Secondly, analytic performance models based directly on states and transitions deal with state space explosion problem [172]. To overcome this issues we propose performance-model-suitable state approximations and guidelines for their introduction in the architecture model.

This thesis addresses the challenges via three main contributions: (i) identification of stateful information in component-based systems and their classification into a set of categories, (ii) critical evaluation of state modelling in current performance prediction models, and an extension of a chosen performance-prediction language to provide sufficient state-modelling capability, and (iii) state-dependency analysis evaluating the performance impact of the identified state classes together with the discussion of the increase in the prediction difficulty introduced by state modelling.

The chapter is organized as follows. Section A.0.4 realizes the first contribution. It identifies and discusses state-specific properties of component-based systems, localizes stateful information, and classifies it along two dimensions into a categorization. Section A.2 realizes the second contribution. It surveys existing performance-driven component-based models with respect to state support, and extends one of the models, Palladio Component Model (PCM), to sufficiently support the identified state categories, as already discussed in Section 5.3.3.2. Sections A.3 and A.4 elaborate the third contribution by introducing an approach supporting software engineers with the information about performance impact and model-size costs of the individual state categories. In particular, Section A.3 outlines the approach and discusses its foundations, while Section A.4 presents the concrete observations from a set of experiments performed on both stateful and stateless PCM models for individual state categories, and formulates them into a set of heuristics navigating software engineers in the decisions on an appropriate state abstraction in their models.

A.0.4. Stateful Component-Based Systems (SCBSs)

In this work, we understand the state as an information remembered inside the system. A state is typically context or history-dependent, and is used to navigate system behaviour depending on the current state value. Therefore, a state influences system control flow, which propagates into resource-demand sequences, and finally to performance properties (such as response time, throughput, and resource utilisation). A typical example of a state is an attribute of an object in object-oriented programming, which is used to store information (updated by methods of the object) and which is employed for customizing object's response to incoming calls.

In literature, two main streams of understanding a state can be found. In the first one [98, 73, 85], the authors attach a state as an additional information to behavioural models. A state can be used in behavioural decisions. The behavioural models set and read state explicitly. In the second one [29], a state is encoded implicitly in the current position in system execution (behaviour). The main difference between the two is that in the first case, an update of a state is possible, and can be used to adapt the behaviour of the element. In the second case, the state cannot be changed explicitly. When we assume that a system comprises of interacting components, the impact of the state rises in the case of parallel usage of components, when all users share the same stateful information coordinating their behaviour.

A.0.5. Specifics of CBSs with Respect to a State

The state-relevant information influencing system performance can be found at different stages of system life cycle. As distinct to classic software systems, the life cycle of a component-based system constitutes of two separate abstraction lines—life cycle of a component and life cycle of a composite system [31, 157]. Moreover, components can be of two types: primitive and composite. Primitive components directly encapsulate implemented functionality, and are typically viewed as black boxes. Composite components are constituted by a composition of existing components, and are often viewed as grey boxes. In a similar fashion, we assume that the state of a composite component is simply a composition (an ordered n-tuple) of the states of its sub-components. In this sense, a complete composite system has two kinds of states: (i) the implicit state inherited from the (primitive) components in the system, and (ii) an explicit state containing additional information specific to the full system.

Life-cycle stages of a component:

- **Specified component:** represents a component frame with known provided or required interfaces. The performance model of a specified component may include *performance requirements*, e.g. maximum response time is 15 ms.
- **Implemented component:** defines how the provided services of the implementation call the required services. Including the definition of performance model consisting of behaviour performance abstraction

and resource demands, e.g. amount of requested CPU, hard disk or memory. Here defined resource demand could depend on input values from usage profile or deployment platform.

- **Instantiated component:** is an identifiable component instance derived from the implemented component, and ready to be executed (in its initial configuration). In some component models, all components are instantiated before launching the system, in others, components can be instantiated at run-time.
- **Deployed component:** is a component instance allocated on a hardware. The performance model can now include resource demands of required services and properties of the component container, operating system and hardware.
- **Running component:** is an actually executed component that serves client requests (not necessarily in its initial configuration). At run time, components can have a state used in current models for checking the violations of valid protocol states. In the performance model, at this stage the workload (i.e. the number of clients calling the component), the input parameters and information about concurrently running processes are known.

Life-cycle stages of a composite system

- **Specified system:** is a frame of the system with known access points and services required from the environment.
- **Assembled system:** is an executable system assembled from implemented (instantiated) components, and ready to be launched (in its initial configuration).
- **Deployed system:** is an assembled system deployed on underlying software and hardware.

- **Running system:** is a system at any moment of its execution.

The responsibility to model stateful information and initialise suitable state abstraction is based on CBSE development process. We divide the responsibility to model the state between development roles considering the moment in the development when certain role has enough information to refine the model with required state definition. The overall development process, integrating the evolution on both component and system level can be understood in terms of involved developer roles, which are component developers, software architects, system deployers, and domain experts [102]. *Component developers (CD)* code the components, and annotate their interfaces with abstract behavioural specifications, to facilitate the usage by third parties. *Software architects (SA)* assemble selected components into architectures forming the system. *System deployers (SD)* design the resource environment (e.g. CPUs, network links), and allocate the components in the architecture to the resources. Finally, *domain analysts (DA)* communicate and specify the system-level usage profiles (call frequencies and expected input parameter values), which then can be employed in formal reasoning about system properties.

A.1. State Categorisation for CBSs

To find a definition of a state in the context of CBSs and performance predictions, we studied different categories of states in existing component-based systems and component models (see section A.2.1). We observed that the notion of component/system state involves various properties and is dependent on different execution processes in the system. With respect to these, we have identified two dimensions, along which we categorise observed state types.

(i) **Place dimension** answers the question: *Is the state proprietary to a component/system/user?*

(ii) **Time dimension** answers the question: *Is the state initialised or changed at run/deployment/instantiation time?*

Table A.1 outlines the identified state categories. Along the place dimension, it distinguishes *component-*, *system-* and *user-specific* states, all defined below. With respect to the time dimension, we studied all stages of component/system life cycle, and observed that a state is by nature a dynamic information that evolves independently for individual elements in the system. If it is fixed along a life cycle, it is not set before the element gains its identity (instantiation stage in case of a component, assembly stage in case of a system). We refer to this moment as *instantiation time*. The following moments are the *deployment time*, which corresponds to the deployment stage of the life cycle, and *run time*, which belongs to the run-time stage.

The rest of this section presents the identified state categories, structured to three sections along the place dimension, and for each category, it outlines a demonstrating example, and comments on its modelling.

	Run time	Deployment time	Instantiation time
Component	(a) Protocol state (b) Internal state	(c) Allocation state	(d) Configuration state
System	(e) Global state	(f) Allocation state	(g) Configuration state
User	(h) Session state (i) Persistent state		

Table A.1.: Identified state categories.

A.1.1. *Component-Specific State*

Component-specific state is an information remembered for each component, and used inside the component to adjust component's behaviour to incoming requests. Component state can be modified only by the services of the component, not by other components.

(a) Protocol State: This state holds an information about currently acceptable service calls of a component. It is typically part of an interface contract between service provider and its client [157].

- *Example:* Consider a component managing a file, which can be opened, modified and closed. The component is initially in the state when it accepts only the request for opening the file. After that, it moves to the state, where the file can be either modified or closed. Closing takes the component again to the initial state. The indication for a protocol state performance impact is, for example, rate of rejected requests (contenting the communication link). Analogically, the protocol state uses to be employed also for modelling component life cycle, including stages like inactive, initialised, replicated, or migrated component.

- *Modelling:* The protocol state uses to be identified by component developer, and attached to a component via a proxy, filtering the calls on component interfaces. Illegal calls are either dropped or returned to the caller with an exception.

(b) Internal State: This state holds an internal information set by the services of the component (at run time), and used to coordinate the behaviour of the component with respect to the current value of the state. Internal state is externally invisible, and externally unchangeable.

- *Example:* Consider a component that can be in either *full* or *compressed* mode, based on the remaining capacity of its database. If it is in the *compressed* mode, all insert queries on the database are additionally compressed.

- *Modelling:* The internal state is defined by component developer, and stored internally as a local variable of each component instance. To reflect the state in a component model, there must be a possibility to define such a local variable, set its value at run time, and query its current value.

(c) Allocation State: This state holds component properties specified at deployment time, based on the allocation environment of the component.

- *Example:* An example of a performance-relevant deployment property is for instance the maximal length of a queue used by the component. Such a property is set at deployment time, and remains fixed along the execution of a component.
- *Modelling:* The component-specific allocation state can be modelled with a static component parameter, and is identified and set by the system deployer role.

(d) Configuration State: This state holds instance-specific component properties, fixed during instantiation of the component.

- *Example:* The configuration state may specify a selected parallel-usage strategy (like rendezvous or barrier synchronization), which may differ for each component instance.
- *Modelling:* Similarly to the component allocation state, the configuration state can be modelled with a static component parameter. In this case, it is typically set by a software architect, who decides on the configuration of the primitive components forming the assembled architecture.

A.1.2. *System-Specific State*

System-specific state is an information remembered in one copy for the whole system, and used to customize or coordinate joint behaviour of individual components. This state abstraction gains on importance with analysing the state of virtualised systems, cloud computing or systems sharing deployment environment.

(e) Global State: This (run-time) state holds a global information shared and accessed by all components.

- *Example:* A typical example of this kind of state is a global counter, remembering for instance the number of service calls executed in the system since the last back-up of the system, and triggering the back-up process after a certain number is reached.
- *Modelling:* Global state is specified by a software architect during system assembly, in terms of a modifiable system attribute (global variable). It can be either managed directly by the execution environment, or be encapsulated within a component that manages it as its internal state, update its value on request, and answers the questions on its current value.

(f) Allocation State: This state holds deployment-specific information shared by all components in the system.

- *Example:* The examples include the availability of supportive services of the underlying infrastructure (e.g., middleware), parameters of employed thread pool, or selected communication or replication strategies.
- *Modelling:* The system-specific allocation state can be modelled with a static system parameter, and is identified and set by a system deployer.

(g) Configuration State: This state defines system configuration properties specified before launching the system.

- *Example:* This may be for example an upper bound on the number of component instances that may resist in the system at the same time. This is an information of a configuration character, and utilized by all components whenever a new component instance is to be created.

- *Modelling:* The system-specific configuration state can be modelled analogically to the configuration state, and is identified and set by a software architect.

A.1.3. *User-Specific State*

User-specific state is an information remembered for each user, and used to customize system behaviour to the user.

(h) Session State: This state holds a user-specific information for a single session. The information defining the state is forgotten when the session terminates.

- *Example:* A session can represent one sale performed in a supermarket system. Each sale may start with scanning a customer card, which then customizes system processing of the sale. The system may for instance dynamically recompute during the shopping process the prices of some products or their combination, which may be time consuming and can influence the system response time for a user.

- *Modelling:* This kind of state is derived from the information given by a domain analyst, and could be modelled by additional input parameter in usage model or by more specific component state parameters. The behaviour in system per user/session could depend on the history of actions in the session, this history information could be traced in component internal parameters, what builds together with the persistent state an overlap with component state definition.

(i) Persistent State: This state holds a user-specific information throughout the whole existence of user in the system, independently on an existence of a session belonging to the user.

- *Example:* Each user of an online Media Store has a different limit on data for download under full downloading speed. The system

Component Model	Design-time prediction models						Formal Specification Methods	Measurement Methods		Simulation Methods
State Category	CB-SPE	PALLADIO	PECT	CBML	PROCOM	COMQUAD	HAMLET	AQUA	NICTA	MIDAS
Component-specific										
(a) Protocol	n/a	Prov./req. protocols	Statecharts	CBML	n/a	Petri-nets	n/a	n/a	n/a	n/a
(b) Internal	n/a	n/a	n/a	n/a	n/a	?	?	n/a	n/a	n/a
(c) Allocation	RT-UML PA profile Annotation	Static parameter, Passive Resources	n/a	?	Static parameter	n/a	?	Static parameter	Static parameter	Static parameter
(d) Configuration			n/a	Static parameter		n/a	Additional input			
System-specific										
(e) Global	n/a	n/a	Statecharts	CBML	n/a	n/a	?	n/a	n/a	n/a
(f) Allocation	n/a	Static parameter, Passive Resources	n/a	n/a	n/a	n/a	n/a	?	?	Static parameter
(g) Configuration	n/a		n/a	n/a	n/a	n/a	n/a	?	?	
User-specific										
(h) Session	n/a	Input data	n/a	n/a	n/a	?	Additional input	Static parameter	?	?
(i) Persistent	n/a	n/a	n/a	n/a	n/a	n/a	n/a		?	?

Table A.2.: Component Performance Models Comparison.

needs to remember this information to control the attempts of users to download data over the limit, and regulate downloading speed accordingly.

- *Modelling:* The persistent state can be modelled analogical to the session state, with a persistent data store involved.

A.2. Performance Model for SCBSs

This section surveys existing performance-prediction component models with respect to their state-related capabilities, and summarizes their coverage of identified state categories in table A.2.

A.2.1. State of the Art Evaluation

Existing performance-driven component models can be based on their analytical methods classified into four main streams: design-time, formal-specification, measurement, and simulation models.

In the group of *design-time* performance prediction methods these are few that partially support state modelling. First of them is the CB-SPE approach by Bertolino and Mirandola [22] that uses UML extended with SPT annotations profile to model component state or configuration in a static way. The component model based on a proprietary metamodel Palladio Component Model (PCM) [18] builds on statical state abstractions too. Additionally this model allows to model session state through additional input data in an usage profile of a system. Despite of these state abstractions a need of further extensions for state modelling was identified in PCM [99]. The PECT model [85] deals with state modelling in a more detail and addresses the performance predictability properties of components with runtime system assembly variability. Even though the notion of state is partially included there is no full support for including of this state-based variability in performance predictions. This model builds on a Component Composition Language (CCL) that allows to model component behaviour based on statecharts. The performance impact of state is not further investigated, the focus of state modelling is directed on model checking of functional properties. Additionally, based on statecharts and certain behaviour claims, reliability of the system can be verified. Similarly, state is modelled in the Component-Based Modeling Language (CBML) with the possibility to statically configure component parameters. In the component model ProCom [146] designed for embedded systems, state is modelled only statically by a set of component parameters. Further, the component architecture of COMQUAD [118] is using Petri nets as a system behaviour model, however, the dependency of the service call on input data is ommited. A lot of other models claim an ability to express state changes but in many cases they refer to the behaviour protocol checking [85], state changes monitoring [122] or performance annotations based on measurements [21].

The *formal specification* model for testing of performance and reliability HAMLET [73] suggest to model state as an additional input (additional floating point external variables loaded in the time of component execution) and provide tests showing functional aspects of a state. The *measurement* approach called AQUA [50] inherently monitors state impact (component description is given by the specification of EJBs) and showed how important it is to understand how system state is interpreted. Another approach to measure EJB applications NICTA [110] provides benchmarking methods to get platform-independent information, such as thread pool size etc. The *simulation-based* approach MIDAS [4] determines performance characteristics of the system through state estimation or computation during simulation, for example queueing characteristics.

A.2.2. Palladio Component Model (PCM)

Based on the evaluation in section A.2.1 we decided to extend the Palladio Component Model (PCM) [18] with further capabilities to model stateful information. This extension is one of the contributions we introduce in Section 5.3.3.2. The advantage of this model is its component-based nature, already partial support for state modelling and possibility to model usage profile in detail.

In this section, we informally describe the features of the PCM metamodel and focus on its capabilities for state modelling. The division of work targeted by CBSE is enforced by the PCM, which structures the modelling task to four independent languages reflecting the responsibilities of the four different developer roles outlined already in section A.0.5. The PCM already provides certain abstractions or approximations to model state: (i) static component parameters (or properties) characterize the state of a component in an abstract and static way and hence offer a more flexible parameterization of the model. These parameters are propagated through development process differently, they are defined and initialized by a *component developer* and can not be changed at runtime. (ii) Limited passive resources, such as semaphores, threads from a pool, or memory buffers result in waiting delays and contentions due to concurrently executed services. (iii) Input data from usage profile allows to express session state. Table A.2 illustrates the capabilities of PCM to model identified state categories. In addition, the State Manager Completion extends the capabilities of PCM to model state as described in Section 5.3.3.2.

A.3. Outline of the Approach

After identifying state types in component-based systems, and extending the PCM performance-prediction model to support them, this section together with Section A.4 elaborates the third contribution of the thesis—a study of the performance impact of the identified state categories, and analysis of the influences that should drive the decision on the abstraction level of state modelling.

In design-time performance prediction, this issue has already been addressed for various different constructs, including service parameters, return values, or usage-profile propagation. Our approach gives an insight into the issue of state modelling, which has not been addressed so far, and tries to help the software engineers to find the balance between accuracy and complexity of models more competently.

In particular, the approach aims to help software engineers to assess if the increase in the prediction accuracy introduced by the state modelling outbalances the price that needs to be paid for the increased model complexity. To compare the two metrics, we first discuss the quantification of the performance impact (see Section A.3.1) and the model size cost (see Section A.3.2). Second, we discuss the similarities among some of the state categories (in Section A.3.3), and design four classes clustering the state categories that are similar with respect to our goal. Each of the classes is later analysed in Section A.4. For each class, we discuss the observations about its performance impact and model size cost and design a number of heuristics condensing the advises for the software engineers. Each heuristic is experimentally evaluated and the results of the evaluation summarized in the text.

A.3.1. Quantification of Performance Impact

The adopted Palladio Component Model (PCM) allows software architects to quantify three aspects of system performance: *response time* (of a component or system service), *throughput* (of a service or communication link), and *resource utilisation* (of a hardware resource). All the three metrics are reported as random variables with probability distribution over possible values together with their likelihood. The response time is expressed in given time units (e.g., seconds), throughput in number of service calls or data amount per time unit (e.g., kilobytes per second), and resource utilization in the number of jobs currently occupying the resource.

The three performance metrics for all the individual model elements are at the end all propagated to the *system response time*, which quantifies the response time of a given usage profile. The system response time is dependent on the response times of the user-called system services, which depend on the response times of component services included in the triggered control flow, resource utilization of the system hardware resources employed during service execution, and throughput of the utilized communication links (due to contention and overloading effects).

In this thesis, we are hence primarily interested in the impact of state modelling on the system response time, which can be additionally expressed with different abstractions, including best/worse time, mean time, and others. Since for each of the abstractions, the state-modelling advices could have different validity, we discuss all of them in Section A.4 although we focus primarily on the probability distribution, which is the default metric used in the PCM.

The individual metrics of system response time discussed in this thesis are: mean value, median value, best/worst case, variance, probability distribution, and time series. The first two metrics, the *mean* and *median* values, approximate the expected system response time. Although both are very popular in statistics, they use to be considered too coarse-grained for performance engineering. To make the response-time characterization more detailed, the *best* and *worst case* values use to be given. Together with the *variance*, these metrics already characterize the possible response time values quite concisely. However, if all these information is needed, the full *probability distribution* of the response-time values is often required, alternatively formulated as a *cumulative probability function*. The most detailed metric is the *time series* which reports possible response-time values of individual system services in connection to the time when the service execution has been started. The *time series* provides view of the evolution of the response-time over the time, which is a basis for transient analysis of systems, however *time series* is the most difficult to analyse.

A.3.2. Quantification of Model Complexity

The complexity of a model can be best understood when translated to a low-level formal language with clearly definable size. One of the formalisms most commonly employed for this purpose are labelled transition systems. In the case of component-based systems, different kinds of interacting automata [176, 175] use to be employed, which allow us to specify large labelled transition systems via composition of automata-based models of individual components. In [175], the inclusion of a stateful information in a model is studied in terms of *Component-Interaction Automata*. It is shown that a component/system state can be encoded as an automaton interacting with the automata for component services—answering their queries of its current value, and accepting their commands to change the value. The model of a system is then a composition of not only the models of individual services (implemented by the components), but includes also the models of all states (whose size corresponds to the number of possible state values).

Since the size of a composite component-interaction automaton is defined over a Cartesian product of the vertices of composed automata, the size of the composite model can be in the worst case a multiplication of the initial stateless model with the size of the internal-state model. However, our experience shows that not only that this case is very unlikely to occur, but the model that includes stateful information can be even smaller than the initial stateless model, due to a higher certainty about the future behaviour of the system. A more detailed discussion of this phenomenon can be found in the sub-sections of Section A.4.

A.3.3. Diversity Among State Categories

In section A.1 we have identified nine state categories. Though they all embody the same construct (defined in section A.0.4), their practically observed performance impact differs, and is influenced by different criteria. At the same time, however, one can also observe strong similarities among some of the categories.

- **Allocation vs. Configuration state:** Both the allocation and configuration state (consider the component-specific case for now) are fixed before the actual system execution. Thus from the performance point of view, both can be understood as fixed component parameters, often usable in an interchangeable way.

- **System vs. Component-specific state:** Even if the component-based system behaviour is encapsulated in components, and structured to architectures, its core is in the interaction of system services. If we abstract from component boundaries, we can find a strong analogy between component internal state and system global state, and between component- and system-specific allocation and configuration state.

- **Session vs. Persistent state:** From the point of view of performance analysis, the persistent state is analogical to a session state for one life-lasting session.

The identified similarities cluster the defined state categories into four classes: (1) protocol state, (2) internal and global state, (3) allocation and configuration state, and (4) session and persistent state.

A.4. State Dependency Analysis

For each of the four state classes identified in Section A.3.3, we performed a number of experiments and drew observations on the performance impact and costs of the state modelling, which we present in this section. For both the performance impact and the cost, we compared the stateful model of a PCM instance to the stateless model of the same example, where the state-dependent decisions are guarded by probabilities (estimated as precisely as possible). The observations are discussed for all the response-time metrics defined above, although the heuristics have been primarily defined for the probability distribution of the response-time values, which is the most commonly employed response-time metric.

A.4.1. Protocol State

The protocol state, which is the only state category included in this class, is used for a very specific purpose. It holds an information about currently acceptable service calls of a component.

STATEFUL VS. STATELESS MODEL: Recall the protocol-state example outlined in Section A.1. The protocol state in the example can have two values: *closed*, when the only acceptable call is `open()`, and *opened*, when the component can accept calls `modify()` and `close()`. Both the stateful and probabilistic model of the example in PCM consist of three SEFF models and one usage profile. Each SEFF starts with a branch condition deciding if the service is going to be executed or rejected (see Figure A.2). While in the stateful version, the branch is guarded by a current value of the protocol state, updated after executing `open()` and `close()`, the probabilistic

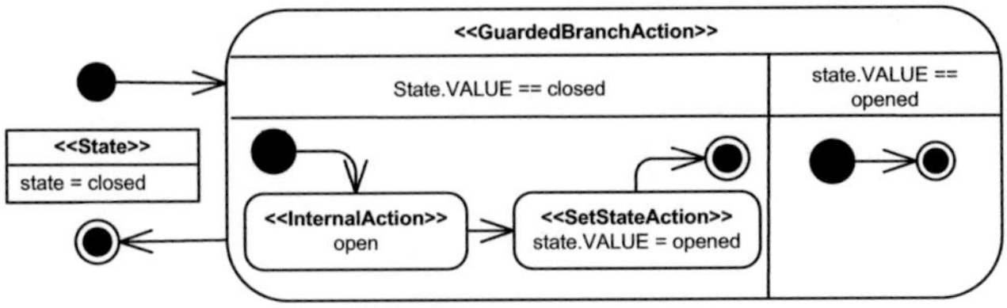

Figure A.2.: A SEFF of `open()`.

model fixes the probabilities of the branches based on expected likelihood of the alternatives.

PERFORMANCE IMPACT:

Observations: A number of performed experiments with different variations of the probabilistic model showed two main observations about the accuracy of the stateful model comparing to the stateless model.

Observation 1: The performance impact of the protocol-state modelling highly depends on the a-priori knowledge of the usage profile, which in general cannot be guaranteed since component behaviour and usage profile are typically defined independently by different developer roles.
Observation 2: Even if the usage profile is known, the actual probabilities of service execution depend on component's environment through which the usage profile is propagated, and thus can be very hard to quantify.

Heuristics: There are two heuristics that can be derived from the observations.
Heuristic 1: *The importance of protocol-state modelling raises with the lower knowledge of the usage profile.*
Experimental evaluation: Our experiments show that already a very lit-

tle inaccuracy in the usage profile may lead to a very imprecise stateless (i.e. probabilistic-abstraction) model, since the inaccuracies can be easily magnified by system control flow[1]. This is true for all the response-time metrics. There are two important arguments that justify the inclusion of the stateful information into the model in this case. First, significantly more effort is required in the stateless model to update its transition probabilities to a more accurate usage profile. Second, adaptation of the probabilities in the stateless model does not need to be sufficient to reflect the usage-profile change. A structural change of the model may be needed.

Heuristic 2: *The importance of protocol-state modelling raises with higher complexity of component's environment.*
Experimental evaluation: In some situations common in complex systems, it may be very hard or even impossible to estimate probabilities for the stateless model precisely. A simple exemplary model illustrating this phenomenon can be build on the fact that the probabilistic abstraction can hardly be foreseen in the models where the same service is called twice and each time behaves differently based on the actual protocol-state value that may change in the meantime. In such a case, two models of the same service would need to be present in the stateless system model to make it accurate. Otherwise, all the response-time characteristics of the probabilistic model (even the mean value, which uses to be very stable) may significantly deviate from the values of the more-precise stateful model.

MODEL-SIZE COSTS: The stateful model of each service has a unified form, having two independent alternatives: the first (complex one) if the service is executable, and the second (trivial one) if the call is rejected (see Figure A.2). In a stateful model of such a service, two sources of model-size increase can be observed.

[1] Note that the Palladio Component Model (PCM) supports value passing and value-guarded control-flow constructs, which implies that already a minor modification of an input value in the usage profile may influence system behaviour significantly.

Observation 1: *An increase due to state update after service execution.* The model-size increases with the higher number of state updates after service execution. The increase in this case is however negligible.

Observation 2: *An increase due to remembering the actual state value, and accordingly executing only the right alternative.* If the size of the model is understood in terms of a labelled transition system (a graph describing the paths of possible system behaviour), then the size remains unchanged as far as there is always only one state value for which each service can be executed. If a service can be executed in more than one values of the protocol state, the number of vertices in the model can be multiplied with the number of such state values. On the other hand, the complexity of the paths throughout the transition system remains unchanged.

A.4.2. Internal/Global State

The internal state, as well as the global state, holds local (resp. global) information used to coordinate the behaviour of the system or its components.

STATEFUL VS. STATELESS MODEL: Consider an example outlined in Figure A.3, with internal state *processed* remembering the amount of processed data, and coordinating a component to either process additional data or perform cleanup. A probabilistic model would be analogical, with the branches guarded with the probabilities of state values.

PERFORMANCE IMPACT:

Observations: The example outlined above was selected to disclose an additional influencing factor (besides the two identified for the protocol state), specific to this state category. It is connected to a possible correlation of state values in subsequent branches guarded by an internal state (typically with an additional execution in between of the branches).

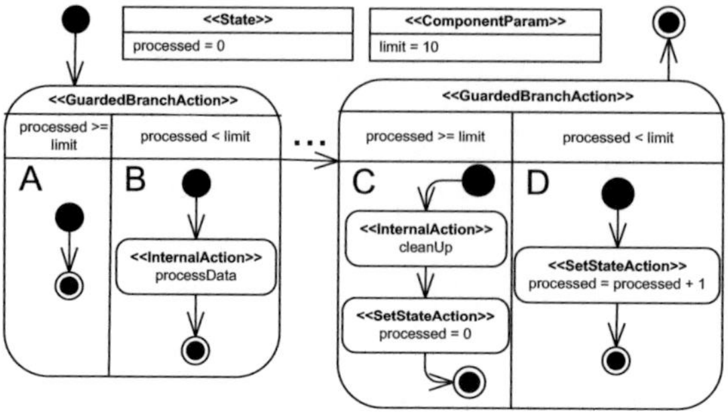

Figure A.3.: A SEFF of `processData()`.

Observation 1: Recall the example in Figure A.3 with strongly positively correlated branches (let us denote the alternatives in the first branch A and B, and in the second branch C and D). Note that while in the stateful model, there are only two possible service executions (either A followed by C, or B followed by D), in the probabilistic model, four alternatives are possible (both A and B can be followed by both C and D).

Heuristics: The observation can be summarized with the following heuristic.

Heuristic 3: *The importance of internal/global-state modelling raises with the higher correlation of subsequent state-driven decisions.*

Experimental evaluation: In the experimental evaluation, we used a number of models analogical to the example outlined above, with an internal action in between of the branches. The experiments for more details) have shown that even if the probabilities of the branches accurately reflect the usage profile, the results computed from the stateless model can be very imprecise. We have observed, that already in very simple models (one service with two or three branches), the probability distribution (mainly the variance and best/worst case) of the stateless-model results deviates significantly from the stateful-model distribution. The mean and median values tend to be quite stable for these simple examples, and start to deviate when more complexity is introduced into the models.

MODEL-SIZE COSTS: The model of a service involving an internal/-global state can have much more variability than in the case of a protocol state, since the state-guarded branches and state updates can be present anywhere in the model. This in the worst case implies multiplication of the model size with the size of the state (number of its possible values). In practice however, this case is very unlikely to occur. The likelihood is decreased by the factors summarized by the following observations.

Observation 1: *A high connection of component behaviour to a state value.* The model does not grow to the worst case if some of the behaviours are possible only under a particular state value. Then the combinations of these behaviours with the infeasible state values do not appear in the model and restrict the size increase (analogically to the argument for the protocol state).

Observation 2: *A low number of independent state-guarded branches.* Recall the example outlined above. While in the stateful model with dependent branches two behaviours were possible (A;C and B;D), if the branch conditions were independent, four behaviours would be possible (A;C, B;C, A;D and B;D). However, a high number of independent branches does not increase the number of vertices in the model. It only increases the number of transitions, and hence the number and complexity of behaviour-describing paths.

Observation 3: *A small number of state updates.* A smaller number of state updates implies a higher likelihood that some of the branch conditions will always (or at least often) be evaluated as false and the behaviours that follow them will be removed from the model.

A.4.3. Allocation/Configuration State

This class comprises of four state categories, in particular the component-specific and system-specific allocation and configuration state, all coordinating system behaviour according to a fixed (deployment or configuration) parameter.

STATEFUL VS. STATELESS MODEL: Recall the examples of these states outlined in Section A.1. The most important property shared by all the four state categories is that they are fixed before the execution and hence coordinate component or system behaviour in a unified way during system execution. Again, while in the stateful model, branches may be guarded with state values, in the stateless model, the same branches are guarded with probabilities (reflecting the likelihood of possible parameter values). If we are uncertain about the actual value also in the stateful model, we can include this uncertainty into the usage profile, which before triggering the system execution configures the parameters with the corresponding probabilities of their values and then uses them in a fixed way along system execution. On the other hand, if we have an absolute certainty about the value of the parameter, we can reduce the stateless model (and actually also the stateful model) to keep only the branch behaviours conforming to the actual value of the parameter.

PERFORMANCE IMPACT:

Observations: The above mentioned specifics imply two main observations influencing the effect of allocation/configuration-state modelling.

Observation 1: As distinct to so far discussed categories, the general influence of the allocation/configuration state to system performance is independent of the usage and the environment. For each service, the state-guarded branches are evaluated in a fixed way, irrespective of the service clients.

Observation 2: On the other hand, the prediction accuracy is highly dependent on the knowledge of deployment/configuration parameters, which allows the architect to cut off the behavioural branches in the stateless model that go against the expected value of the parameter. When such an information is not available to the component developer (since it is determined by a different role) and the uncertainty about the state value needs to be expressed with probabilities, the probabilistic model exhibits high inaccuracies.

Heuristics: The following heuristic can be derived from the observations.

Heuristic 4: *The importance of allocation/configuration-state modelling raises with the lower knowledge of deployment/configuration parameters.*
Experimental evaluation: The experimental evaluation reveals that whenever there is any uncertainty about the value of the parameters, which hence needs to be in the stateless model modelled with probabilities, the model may become very imprecise. The reason for this fact is that while in the stateful model, the parameter value for the whole system execution remains the same (the uncertainty about the parameter value is included on only one place, in the usage profile before triggering system execution), the stateless model includes also the behaviours reflecting the unrealistic cases of parameter changes during system execution (similarly to the phenomenon observed in Section A.4.2). Interestingly, the deviation of the stateless model from the stateful results tends to exhibit a common phenomenon regarding the probability distribution of the reported values. In particular, while the mean and the median of the results use to be the same (or very similar), the variance of the stateless results tends to be significantly higher, with much smaller best value (fastest response) and much higher worst value (slowest response) compared to the accurate results of the stateful model.

MODEL-SIZE COSTS: The model-size costs are influenced by the following observations about the expected sizes of the stateful and stateless model for the same system (or system element).

Observation 1: *Stateful model of a single system element uses to be larger than the stateless model of the same element.* This is the case whenever the architect of the stateless model cuts off those branch behaviours that go against the expected value of the parameter.

Observation 2: *In the case of aimed model reuse, the stateful model of a single system element uses to have the same size as the stateless model of the same element.* If we do not know the value of the deployment/configuration parameter in advance (typical in the case of aimed model reuse in different contexts), the stateless (probabilistic abstraction) model needs to include behaviours implied by all possible parameter values, and hence has the same complexity as the stateful model.

Observation 3: *System models resulting from the composition of individual stateful model elements are never larger than the stateless composite system models.* As the value of the allocation/configuration state does not change along system execution, there is no increase in model size, quite the contrary. Since all infeasible branches are never executed, the reachable space of the stateful model can even be smaller than in its probabilistic variant.

A.4.4. Session/Persistent State

The session state, as well as the persistent state, holds an information remembered for each individual user, and used to customize system behaviour accordingly.

STATEFUL VS. STATELESS MODEL: Consider the session-state example in Section A.1, with sessions connected to individual sales, parameterized by an information about the customer. The PCM model can be very simple, propagating the user-specific state in terms of an input value throughout the whole session. The component realizing the state then only checks the value and behaves accordingly. In the stateless model, the value-guarded decisions would again be replaced with probabilistic decisions. Any uncertainty about the parameter value would be expressed analogically to Section A.4.3.

PERFORMANCE IMPACT:

Observations: The session/persistent state exhibits some similarities, but also differences to all the state classes discussed above. It is very similar to the allocation/configuration state, but is not fixed along the whole execution (differs for individual sessions). It changes very rarely, and is updated only on a specific place (similarly to the protocol state). On the other hand, it may guard behavioural branches anywhere in the execution, as distinct to the protocol state but similarly to the internal/global state. This implies the following two observations.

Observation 1: First, the impact is not very dependent on the usage profile and environment, but highly dependent on the knowledge of the distribution of the state values (similarly to the knowledge of deployment parameters in case of the allocation/configuration state).
Observation 2: Second, since the subsequent queries on the state value are highly correlated, probabilistic models can hardly model session/persistent-state dependent behaviour faithfully (similarly to the internal/global state). This state class hence plays a significant role in the model, due to the implied strong correlation of subsequent state-guarded branches, and changeability of the state value along system execution.

Heuristics: There are two heuristics that can be derived from the observations.

Heuristic 5: *The importance of session/persistent-state modelling raises with the lower knowledge of the corresponding user-given parameter values.*
Experimental evaluation: The validity of this heuristic can be explained with the same reasoning that was used for Heuristic 4.

Heuristic 6: *The importance of session/persistent-state modelling raises with the higher correlation of subsequent state-driven decisions – which is typically very high.*
Experimental evaluation: The evaluation is built on a set of examples analogical to the set employed in the evaluation of Heuristic 3. Moreover, it demonstrates that the correlation can be very high, since the state value (for both the session and persistent state) is highly stable along system execution (i.e. also between the state-dependent decisions).

MODEL-SIZE COSTS: The experience learned about the size of the model can be summarized by the following observations.

Observation 1: *Connection of component behaviour to the state value.* The increase due to remembering the actual state value is similarly to the internal/global state dependent on the connection of component behaviour to the state value. The weaker the connection is, the closer the model can grow to the worst case.

Observation 2: *Correlation of subsequent branches.* Thanks to the correlation of subsequent branches, there is basically no complexity increase in terms of the behavioural paths.

Observation 3: *State update.* There is basically no size increase due to state update, since the state is not updated inside the system, and occurs very rarely.

A.5. Discussion

The decision about an appropriate abstraction of state modelling in component-based software systems is a very complex task. As we show, there are many aspects that influence the decision significantly. We have identified many situations when the probabilistic abstraction introduces high prediction inaccuracies, even if the transition probabilities are estimated as precisely as possible. At the same time, the expected increase in model size may anyway discourage software engineers from including the stateful information into their models.

In the following, we discuss the impact of explicit state models on analytical and simulation-based solution methods. Furthermore, we look at possibilities to approximate the influence state probabilistically. From a theoretical point of view, our explicit state model increases the state space of the underlying stochastic process. Consequently, the complexity grows for all analytical methods.

Although we have identified a number of aspects that indicate a low model-size increase in some situations, it is still very likely that stateful models have much higher complexity and size, which may complicate their analysis. Even if the models are not analysed fully, and are examined with simulation methods (like in the case of PCM), model complexity may have an impact on the time needed for sufficiently accurate performance prediction (duration of a simulation run). We have observed on many systems, that the results of stateful analysis tends to have much smaller variance, which also influences the time necessary to execute a simulation run. The higher variability of stateless models could be observed in the variance of the results. As a consequence it influences the number of measurements necessary to achieve results with a high confidence.However, explicit state models can, of course, influence the variance of resulting response time distributions and, thus, increase simulation time. But they enable the design of more realistic models that result in more accurate predictions. The increased prediction accuracy justifies the additional simulation effort. At the same time, even if the stateful model is significantly larger, the confidence about the correctness of predicted values will be higher if a low-coverage simulation is run on a more accurate (stateful) model, than if a high-coverage simulation is run on an unrealistic (stateless) model.

When studying the performance impact of state modelling in Section A.4, we have compared stateful models to their approximations with probabilistic models. As shown in the text, even if the probabilities in the stateless models reflect system usage and environment, the results of the performance evaluation may deviate significantly from the stateful models. The deviation is best visible on the probability distribution of the response-time values and the time series, which are the most fine-grained metrics. Also the variance and best/worse case are very different, with a higher variance of stateless models. On the other hand, the median and mean values use to be quite stable, deviating often only slightly from the stateful model.

There are many types of systems, where the probabilistic models can approximate the stateful models very closely. For example, the influence of transactions (described in Section 7.2.1.1) can be approximated probabilistically, if the waiting time of a message is known and modelled as an explicit delay that depends on the number of messages sent within the transaction. To achieve this, performance analysts have not only to know in advance the number (which is static and can not change at runtime) of messages in a transaction as well as the influence of a message on the transaction's delay (which needs to be adapted for each change in the transaction size to get accurate predictions).

A.6. Summary

This work addresses the challenges of performance prediction for stateful component-based software systems. To achieve this aim, we have accomplished a number of tasks. We investigated the requirements and the offered expressiveness of prediction models for stateful systems. We surveyed the state of the art and extracted a classification scheme of various state-defining and state-dependent model parameters. After that, we critically evaluated the possibility of modelling introduced categories using state abstractions in current performance prediction models. As a result, we extended the *Palladio Component Model* to provide sufficient state-modelling capability, and evaluated the benefits and costs it brings in a state-dependency analysis. In the state-dependency analysis, we further identified the similarities and differences of the individual state categories with respect to their performance impact and model-size increase, and introduced and evaluated a number of heuristics summarizing the advices to software engineers, and helping them to competently decide on the appropriate state abstraction in their models.

The future work includes further analysis of the individual heuristics and methods for their automatic evaluation on a system model. The first steps include decomposition of the heuristics to more concrete ones that define exact conditions to be checked on the analysed model. The automatization would also include employment of expert techniques to determine an appropriate abstraction on the state values, to keep the model size and model accuracy balanced. Another aim of our ongoing research is to examine the impact of the hardware-specific state categories, which may reflect the availability and speed (based on the actual workload) of system hardware resources. New challenges also rise from the introduction of dynamic architectures and support of virtualisation scenarios and dynamic allocation.

B. Further HOT patterns

In the following sections, we discuss additional HOT patterns for further scenarios. During our work, we developed an automated support for different goals and scenarios using advanced MDSD techniques, such as HOTs. We structured and extracted additional HOT patterns based on these scenarios. The extracted patterns provide support for *Shared Configurations*, *Retainment Policies*, *Model/View Synchronisation*, and *Transformation Analysis*.

B.1. *Shared Configuration* HOT Pattern

Shared Configuration pattern is based on the observation that transformations as a whole are also entities of reuse. Becker [11] first introduced very similar concept, so called *Coupled Transformations*, in order to factor out shared parts of transformations. This pattern try to give an answer to how transformation knowledge can be reused, and can be considered as an immediate application of Czarnecki's [46] Generative Programming methodology to the field of transformations.

B.1.1. Motivation:

In software development, refinement transformations are entities which encapsulate design decisions to be applied to an architectural model. Applying design decisions is leading to certain platform-dependencies, and finally results in an implementation model.

However, besides an implementation as one purpose, engineers could be interested in further transformation objectives, for example the perfor-

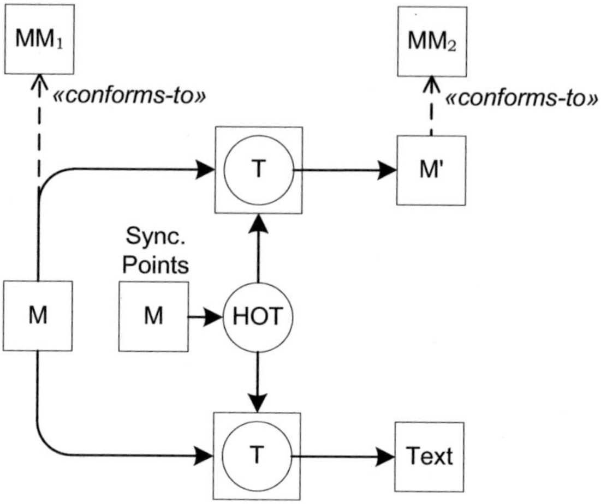

Figure B.1.: *Shared Configuration* pattern.

mance impact certain design decisions introduced into the model. In this setting we have a number of existing transformations towards different objectives. However, often the initial design decisions change during the development. After such a change, all existing transformations have to be adapted to correspond this new design decision. Instead of manually adapting each transformation, it is recommended to keep code for one design decision and different transformation objectives separated.

B.1.2. Implementation:

Figure B.1 depicts one HOT being able to automatically synchronise two transformations for the same configuration options (a shared synchronisation point), one targeting code, the other targeting for example performance aspects. As a result, the possible set of configuration options can be described in a single model.

Becker et al. originally implemented coupled transformations in Java, because no working implementation of a transformation engine was available back then. At that time, variability in configuration options had been limited on simple Boolean constants for the parameter values only.

B.1.3. Benefits and Drawbacks:

Shared Configuration pattern, implemented on the basis of HOTs, render code with higher reusability and provide better support for variability. On the negative side, it should be noted that transformation rules written on the meta-level, is harder to read and maintain through the inherent indirection introduced. However, if models are expected to be used for multiple purposes the increased effort should pay off.

B.2. *Retainment Policies* HOT pattern

The retainment policy approach introduced in [67] aims at the preservation of external changes in target models of transformations. To achieve this [67] introduced an annotation approach that allows transformation engineers to attach retainment policies to transformation rules. These policies then define how a re-executed transformation deals with external changes in target models, i.e., overwriting the change and resynchronising the target model according to the source model, or, keeping the external modification discarding updates from the source model. The paper also presented patterns on how the policies can be expressed in terms of QVT Relations. A HOT is then responsible for weaving these patterns into the annotated transformation, yielding a modified transformation that behaves like the original transformation but with the desired behaviour w.r.t. external changes to the target model.

B.2.1. Motivation:

For realising the retainment policy approach, two different possibilities exist. First, a library-driven approach, meaning that a reusable set of rules

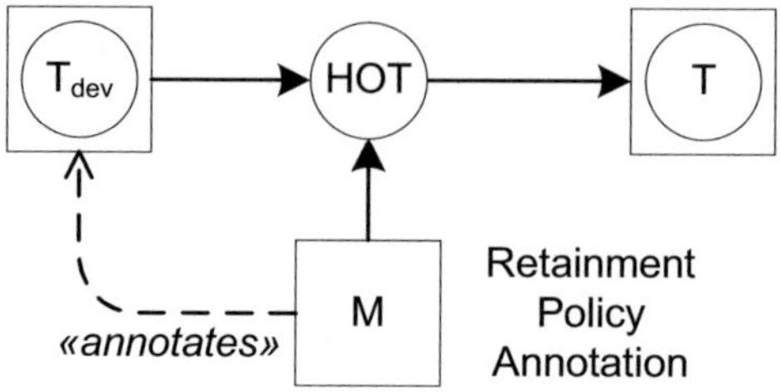

Figure B.2.: Retainment policies.

exist that implement each retainment policy. A transformation could use these generic rules to identify target changes and decide how to handle them. Second, the HOT approach which uses external annotations to the developed transformation and generates a new version of the transformation which incorporates the annotated retainment policies into the developed transformation.

We chose the latter option because we targeted QVT Relations as transformation language. The retainment policy approach is based on the information provided by the trace of the transformation. In the MediniQVT [88] implementation of QVT Relations the trace model is strongly typed with the actual domains employed in the transformation. Therefore, also the rules realising the retainment policies would have to be typed in that way. As we can determine this only when the transformation under development is available this decision needs to be deferred to a later point in time. Therefore, we used a HOT to weave in the retainment policies at build time of the transformation under development.

B.2.2. Implementation:

We implemented the HOT approach so that it uses the model of the transformation under development as well as the annotated retainment policies model as input as shown in Figure B.2. The output is then a modified source transformation incorporating additional parts and rules for handling the changes to the target model.

B.2.3. Benefits and Drawbacks:

Using the HOT approach in this scenario we did not only achieve the required later binding time of the retainment policies but also achieved a better separation of concerns. The retainment policies are now completely external to the transformation under development. Therefore, this transformation only contains domain-related information and is not polluted with technical concerns, i.e., the rules implementing the retainment policies.

However, applying HOT in this scenario has drawbacks as well. The major drawback is that debugging becomes more difficult. As the transformation that actually runs (the generated one) is different to the transformation the transformation engineer actually developed either he/she needs to have knowledge on how the code of retainment policies works or the transformation debugger needs to be modified in order to make the transformation modification transparent.

B.3. *Model/View Synchronization* HOT pattern

The synchronisation between model and views on that model has been investigated in several view-based modelling publications (e.g., [57, 61]). A special kind of view-based modelling is the area which merges textual modelling with the view-based modelling paradigm. In [64] was presented an approach that allows to create textual views on models based on a decorator approach comparable to the one used in graphical view-based modelling (see e.g., [53]). This textual decorator model is called TextBlocks-Model.

As both the TextBlocks-Model as well as the underlying domain model are subject to modifications, an incremental and bidirectional update approach is required. To achieve this transformation was a synchronisation approach [65] written in Java created. This approach works like an interpreter as it takes the view definition model into account when performing any synchronisation. However, this approach has several drawbacks w.r.t. debuggability and performance. Therefore, we investigated a HOT-based approach for realising the model/view synchronisation.

B.3.1. Motivation:

Having access to the view definition model which defines the mapping between textual view and the view's underlying model in a declarative, template-based manner served as an optimal starting point for employing a HOT based approach. The idea was to automatically generate model transformations from these view definitions that bidirectionally synchronise views and models. As both, the underlying model, as well as the textual view, in form of the TextBlocks-Model are available on model level, they can easily be accessed using model transformations. After having problems w.r.t. debuggability, due to the interpreter-based approach we decided to employ a HOT-based approach.

B.3.2. Implementation:

In this scenario, the HOT is employed as a means to bring the declarative, non-executable view definition to an executable level. If a declarative transformation language is used, the transformation itself is declarative as well. Therefore, as shown in Figure B.3, the input of the HOT is the view specification whereas the output is the synchronisation transformation.

B.3.3. Benefits and Drawbacks:

Using HOT-generated transformations in this scenario allows language developers to more easily debug the synchronisation process. The interpreter in the previous synchronisation approach required the developer to think on two parallel layers at the same time, i.e., the code of the interpreter as

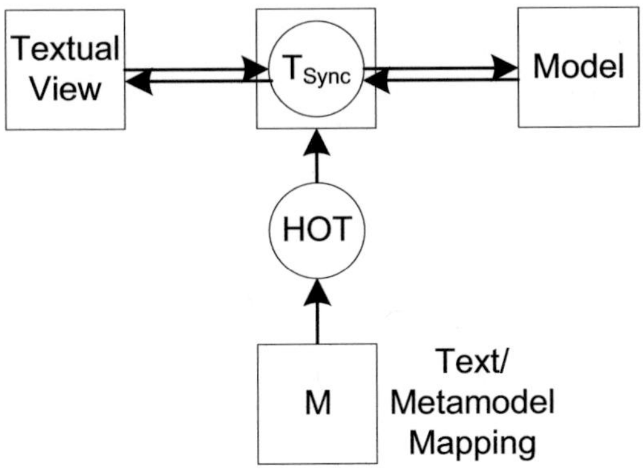

Figure B.3.: Model/view synchronization.

well as the mapping model that is currently interpreted. Instead, the developer can now focus on debugging a transformation. As the translation between a mapping and a transformation is a one-to-one relationship, also a simple debugger interface lifting debugging to the mapping level could be provided.

On the down side, using the HOT approach in this scenario adds complexity to the development. An additional artefact, i.e., the HOT has to be maintained and tested.

B.4. *Analysis* HOT pattern

Along with the wide acceptance of the MDE paradigm in the industry, a high number of transformation scripts need to be maintained in the foreseeable future. In order to guarantee high code quality, we require metrics to evaluate the quality of transformation scripts.

In [159], a collection of metrics has been elaborated and implemented as HOT in ATL. Additionally, the authors applied these metrics in a case study to judge the quality of example transformations bridging between technological spaces.

B.4.1. Motivation:

While metrics exist to judge about maintainability of imperative languages, there is a shortcoming of metrics which are focusing on declarative languages like QVT-R. In Section 6, we propose a set of metrics w.r. t. transformation size, fulfillment of relational properties, degree of consistency and level of inheritance.

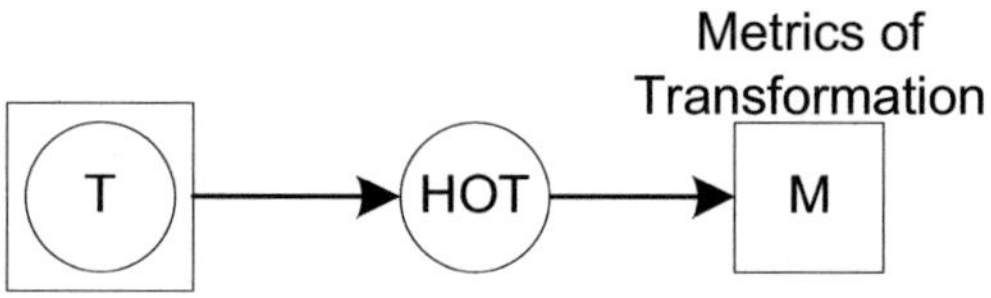

Figure B.4.: Transformation metrics.

B.4.2. Implementation:

As depicted in Figure B.4, we used OCL query functions, embedded into a HOT in QVT-R that transforms a QVT-R transformation into a special metrics model.

B.4.3. Benefits and Drawbacks:

Automatically computable metrics help to make quality assurance of software engineering ease-to-use. Although many metrics are easy to implement as a simple expression, some metrics exist, for which no efficient straight-forward algorithm is available. Among them are: the similarity of relations, the number of relations following a design pattern, or the rate of overlapping rules w. r. t. a transformation's source and target metamodels.

Further, a clear, formal definition of metrics and their computation make quality assurance a reproducible process. Because transformations are also models, it is a straightforward approach to analyse transformations based on their syntax tree. However, metrics based on the real sources are easier to write using the textual representation rather than the tree, for example the lines of code (LoC).

B.5. Future Scenarios

The open questions include of identification of further scenarios for application of HOTs. For example, the co-evolution of metamodels and transformations (cf., Figure B.5) could be one suitable scenario. The metamodels evolve over time, similarly as any other artefacts. We can distinguish different operation in evolution of metamodels, such as refactorings, construction or destruction of metamodel elements. These operations could be predefined as allowed as change operators. Based on the activation and configuration of such change scenarios could be metamodel and its transformations together updated to the required state.

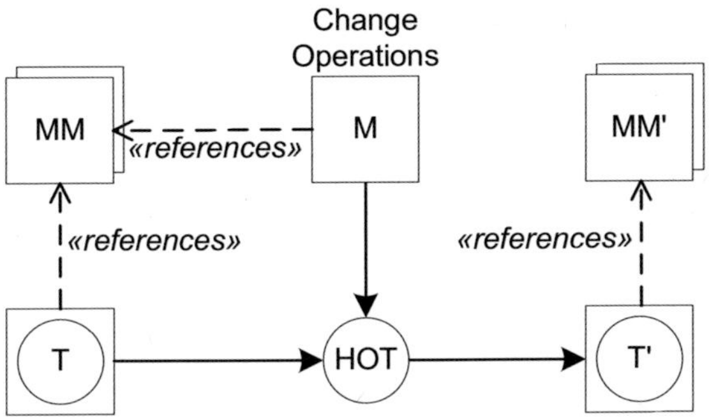

Figure B.5.: Co-evolution of metamodels and transformations.

Further scenarios could include, model merging or composition. In [168], Wagelaar augments ATL as well as QVT-R with new syntactical elements for a modularization mechanism he calls *module superimposition*. He incorporates HOTs as a means for defining semantics by reducing the widened syntax to already existing elements. [161] uses UML profiles to introduce one standardized metamodel for modelling the core features of Graph Transformations. Such core profile is extendable with new constructs. While new syntax may be specified in additional profiles, semantics are defined using HOTs based on the core metamodel of transformations normalizing added constructs back to core features. Such an approach relieves tool builders from integrating new language features as well as external language concepts. These scenarios could be basis to introduce further standardised HOT patterns.

The optimisation of transformations could be of interest as well. HOT could optimize a transformation by removing redundant code, replacing code with semantically identical code but better performance, for example by reordering instructions or lowering abstraction (behavior-preserving). Heuristics may be used to create mark models from transformations, which annotate code parts of input transformations with various informations. A HOT may analyse the performance of each rule for a rule-based transformation, and indicate possible problems and bugs where they might occur.

C. Examples of detailed QVT transformations

In the following, we provide two examples of completion transformations in the QVT graphical syntax. First, we describe relations of the MOM completion. Second, we illustrate the implementation of the Procedure Call connector.

C.1. *Message Oriented Middleware* Completion

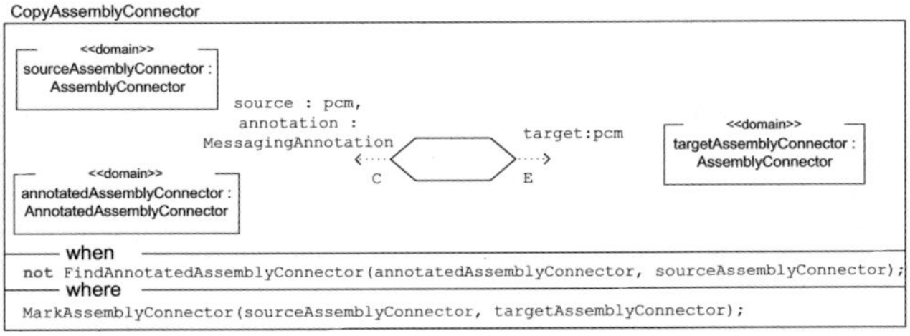

(a) Relation to remove assembly connector.

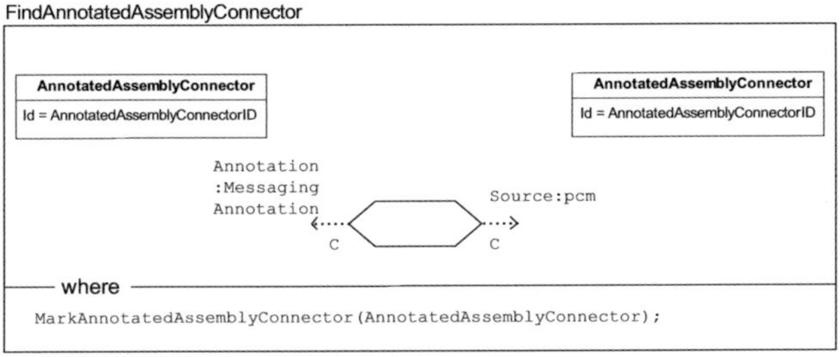

(b) Relation to identify the pivot element.

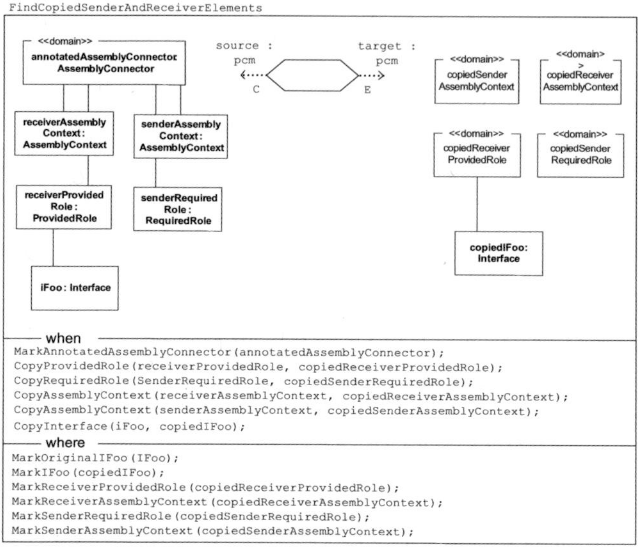

(c) Relation to find `Sender` and `Receiver` interfaces.

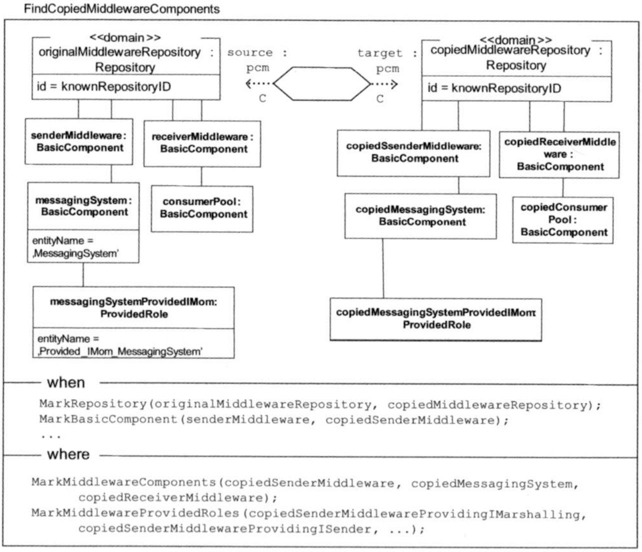

(d) Relation to identify `Middleware` components.

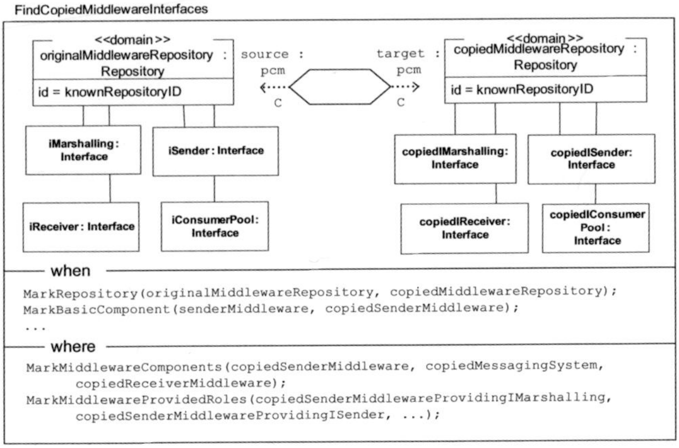

(e) Relation to bind the `Middleware` interfaces.

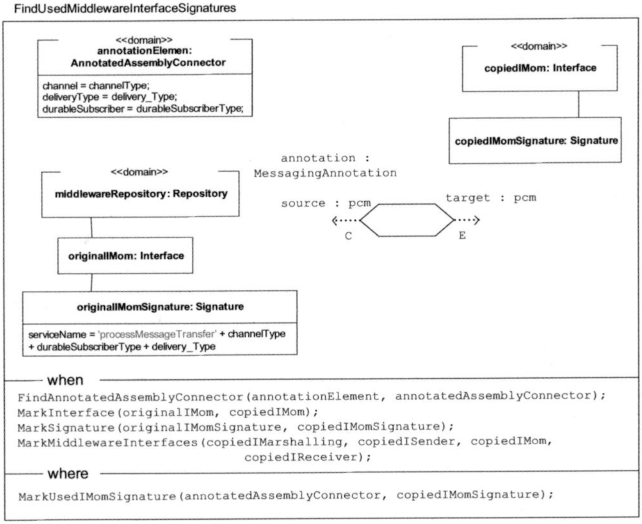

(f) Relation to identify the `Middleware` signatures.

FindSenderAndReceiverRessourceContainer

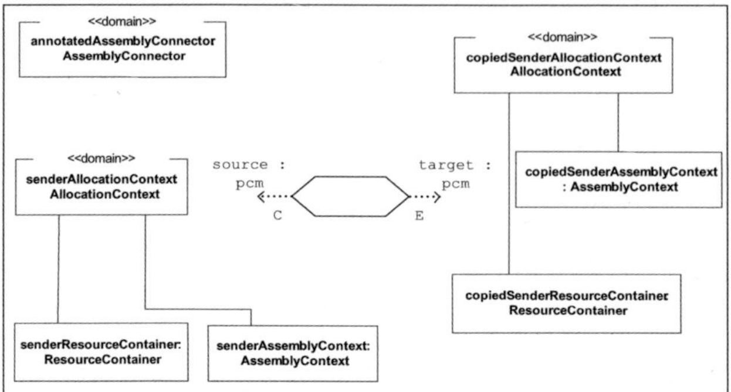

when

```
MarkAssemblyContext(senderAssemblyContext, senderAssemblyContext);
MarkResourceContainer(senderResourceContainer, senderResourceContainer);
MarkSenderAssemblyContext(annotatedAssemblyConnector,
      copiedSenderAssemblyContext);
```

where

```
MarkSenderResourceContainer(annotatedAssemblyConnector,
      senderResourceContainer);
```

(g) Relation to identify resource containers for `Adaptors`.

FindMiddlewareDeploymentElements

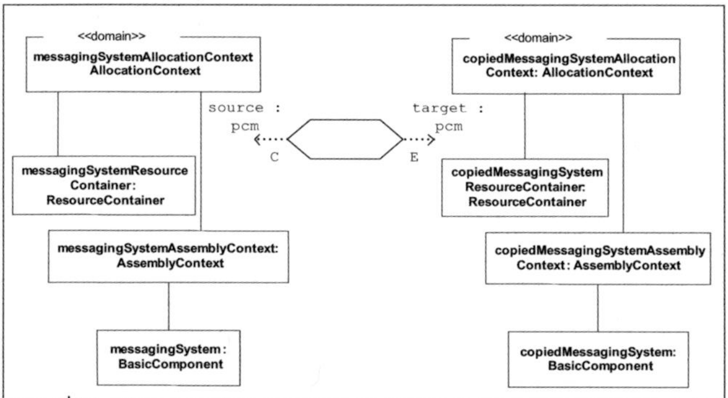

when

```
MarkMiddlewareComponents(..., messagingSystem, ...);
MarkAssemblyContext(messagingSystemAssemblyContext,
      copiedMessagingSystemAssemblyContext);
MarkAllocationContext(messagingSystemAllocationContext,
      copiedMessagingSystemAllocationContext);
MarkResourceContainer(messagingSystemResourceContainer,
      copiedMessagingSystemRessourceContainer);
MarkBasicComponent(messagingSystem, copiedMessagingSystem);
```

where

```
MarkMiddlewareAssemblyContexts(copiedMessagingSystemAssemblyContext);
MarkMiddlewareAllocationContexts(copiedMessagingSystemAllocationContext);
MarkMiddlewareResourceContainer(copiedMessagingSystemRessourceContainer);
```

(h) Relation to identify the `Middleware` deployment.

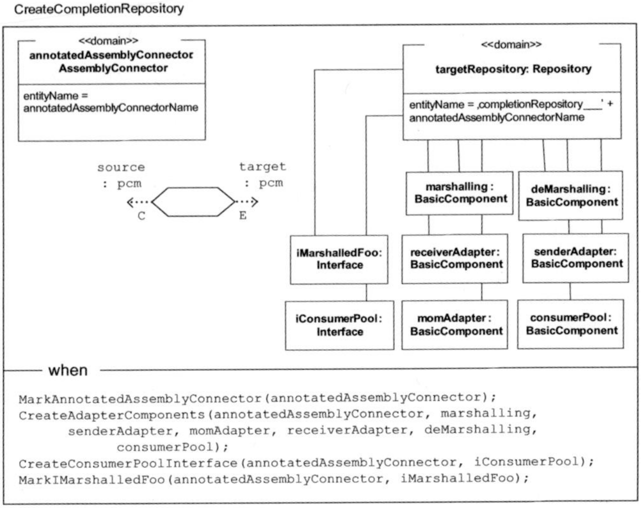

(i) Relation to create the `Repository` for components.

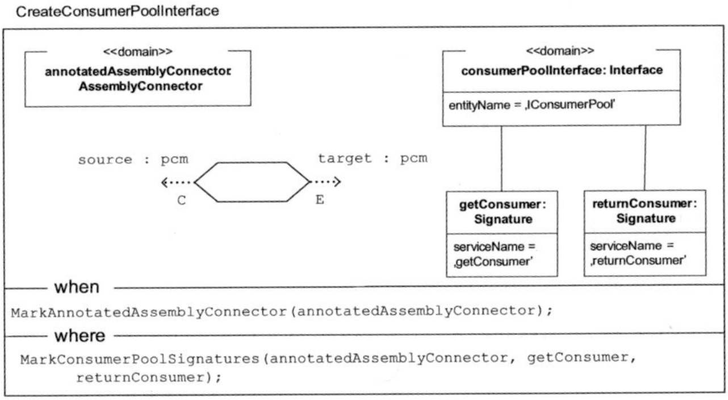

(j) Relation to create the `ConsumerPool` interface.

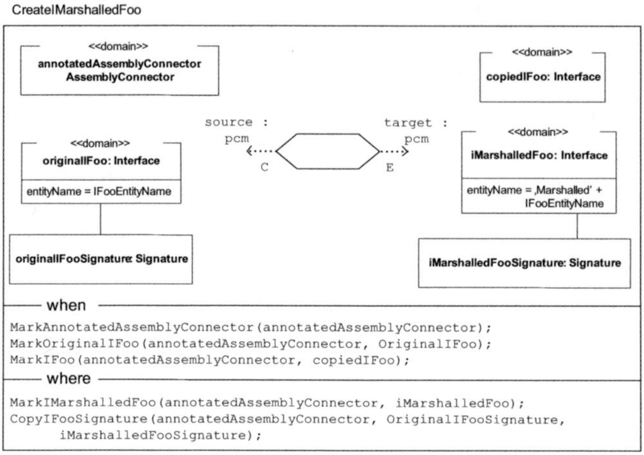

(k) Relation to create the original service interface.

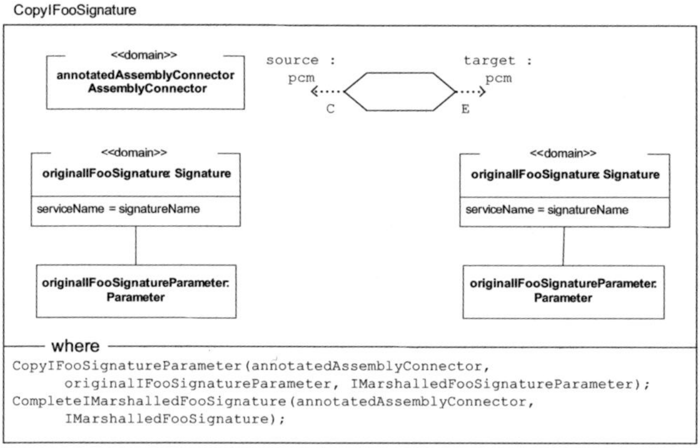

(l) Relation to complete the original service signature.

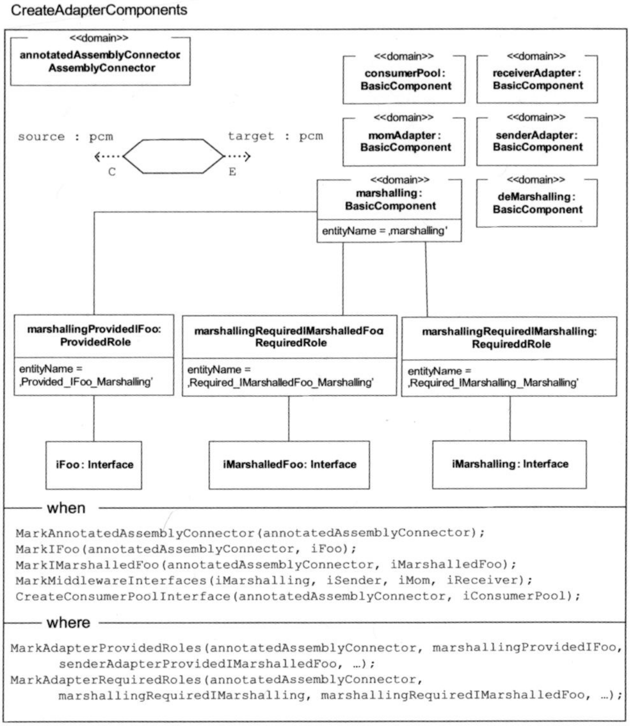

(m) Relation to create the `Adaptors`.

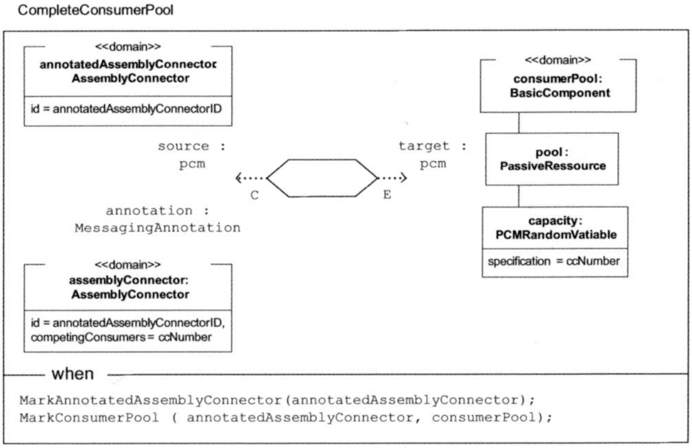

(n) Relation to create passive resources for the `ConsumerPool`.

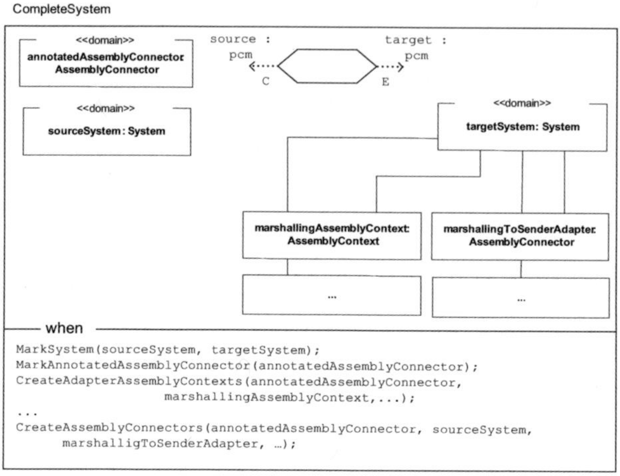

(o) Relation to create system elements.

Figure C.1.: *Message Oriented Middleware* Completion [35].

C.2. *Pipe & Filter Connector* Completion

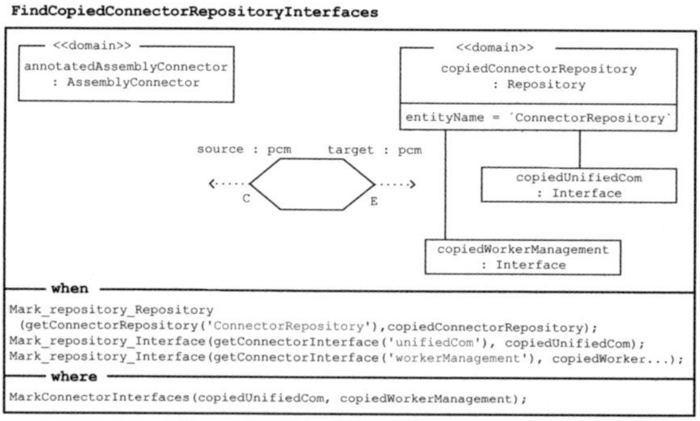

(a) Relation to mark all interfaces in the `ConnectorRepository`.

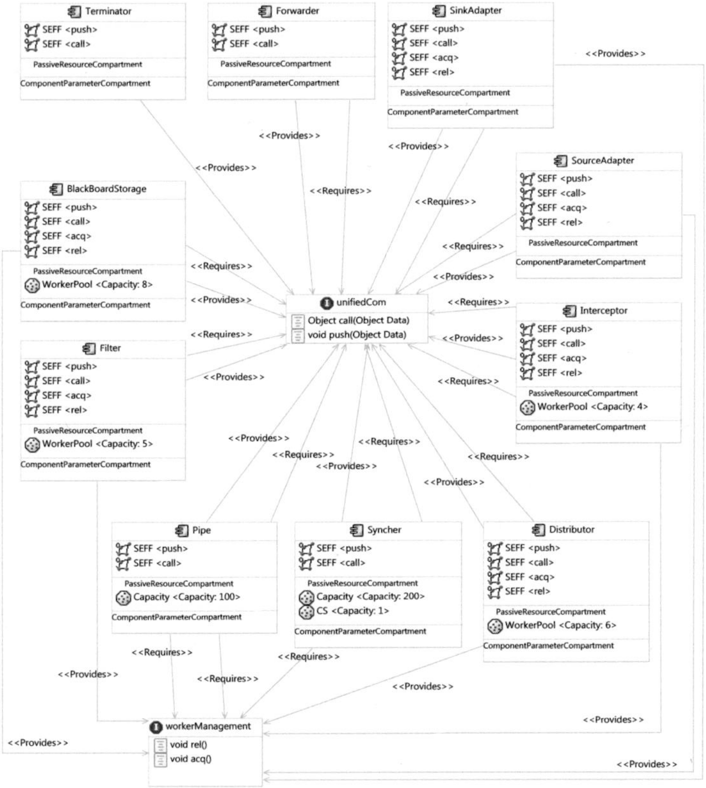

(b) The `ConnectorRepository`.

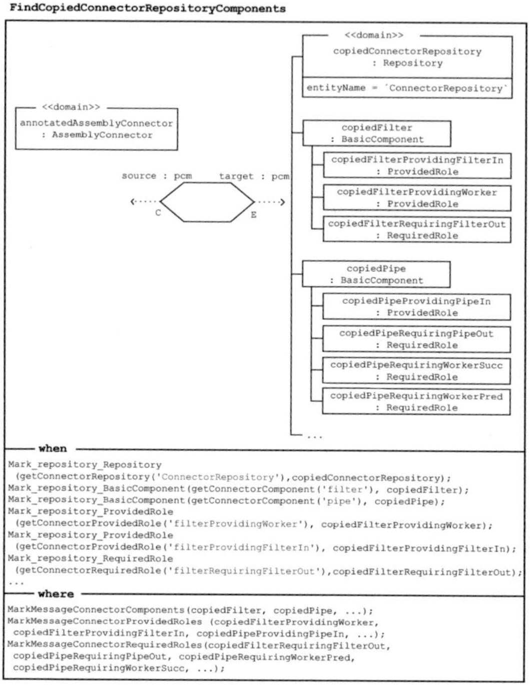

(c) Excerpt of the relation to mark all components in the `ConnectorRepository`.

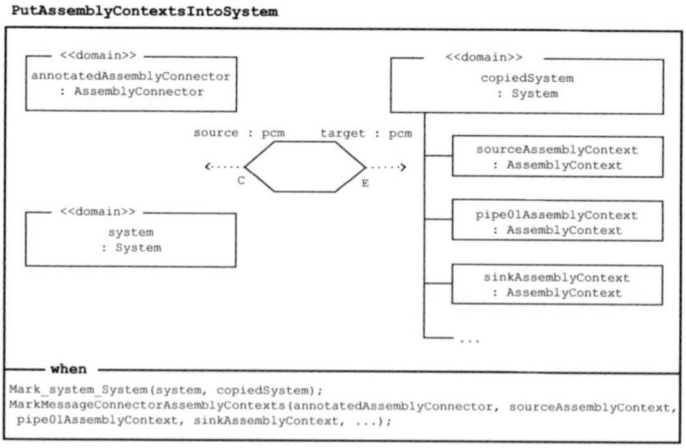

(d) Relation to place all `assemblyContexts` inside the system element.

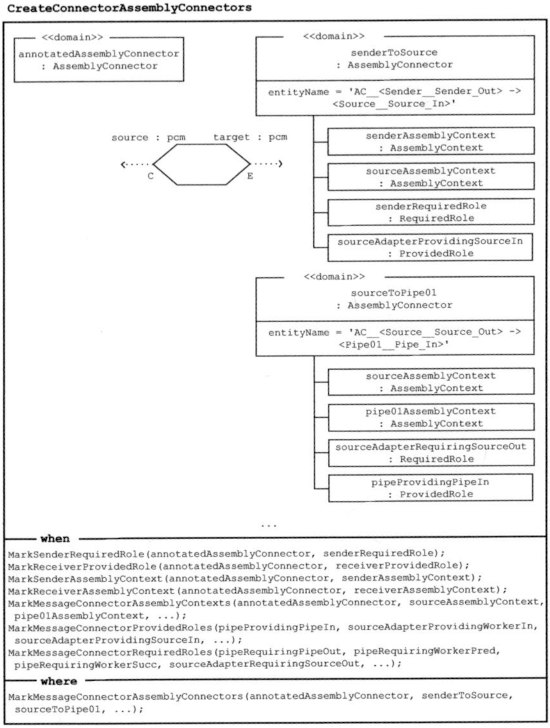

(e) Relation to create all `assemblyConnectors` for the `MessagingConnector`.

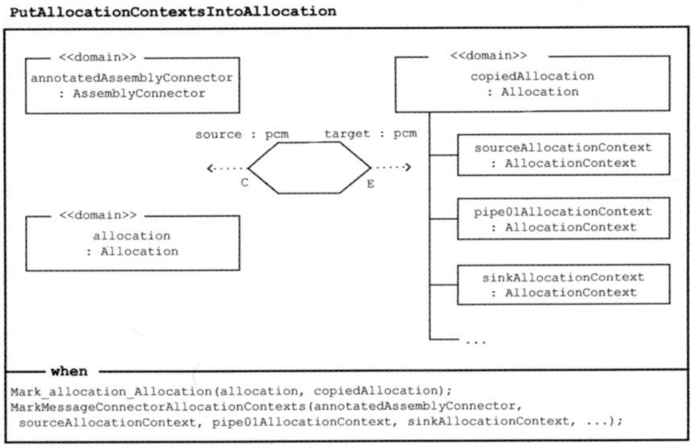

(f) Relation to place all `allocationContexts` inside the allocation element.

CreateConnectorAssemblyContexts

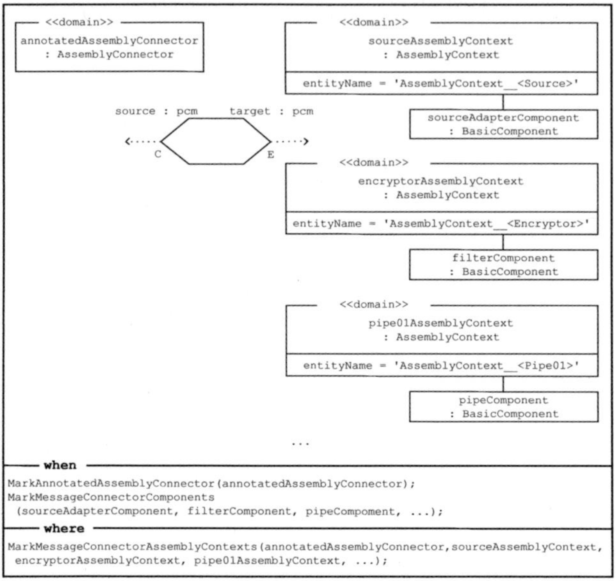

(g) Relation to create all `assemblyContexts` for the `MessagingConnector`.

AdoptSourceSinkInterfaces

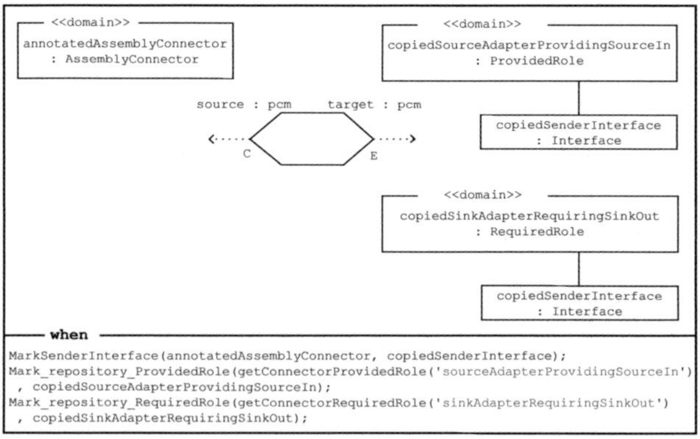

(h) Adoption of the interfaces of the `Source- & SinkAdapter` components.

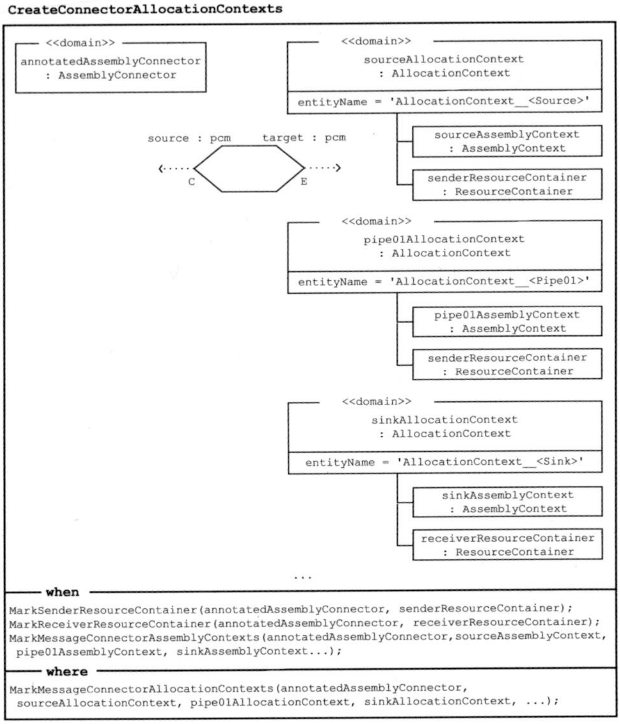

(i) Relation to create all `allocationContexts` for the `MessagingConnector`.

Figure C.2.: *Pipe & Filter Connector* Completion [36].

List of Figures

List of Tables

Bibliography

[1] "Java System Message Queue -Version 4.3," http://java.net/downloads/mq/-Open MQ 4.3 Related/MQ4.3_RelNotes_preFCS.pdf, last retrieved: July 2011.

[2] A. Agrawal, A. Vizhanyo, Z. Kalmar, F. Shi, A. Narayanan, and G. Karsai, "Great: Reusable idioms and patterns in graph transformation languages," in *GraBaTs*. Elsevier, 2004.

[3] K. Anastasakis, B. Bordbar, and J. Küster, "Analysis of model transformations via alloy," in *Proceedings of the 4th MoDeVVa workshop Model-Driven Engineering, Verification and Validation*. Citeseer, 2007, pp. 47–56.

[4] R. Bagrodia and C. Shen, "Midas: Integrated design and simulation of distributed systems," *IEEE Transactions on Software Engineering*, vol. 17, pp. 1042 – 1058, 1991.

[5] A. Balogh and D. Varró, "Advanced model transformation language constructs in the viatra2 framework," in *ACM symposium on Applied computing*, ser. SAC '06. New York, NY, USA: ACM, 2006, pp. 1280–1287. [Online]. Available: http://doi.acm.org/10.1145/1141277.1141575

[6] S. Balsamo, A. Di Marco, P. Inverardi, and M. Simeoni, "Model-Based Performance Prediction in Software Development: A Survey," *IEEE Transactions on Software Engineering*, vol. 30, no. 5, pp. 295–310, May 2004.

[7] V. R. Basili, G. Caldiera, and H. D. Rombach, "The Goal Question Metric Approach," in *Encyclopedia of Software Engineering - 2 Volume Set*, J. J. Marciniak, Ed. John Wiley & Sons, 1994, pp. 528–532.

[8] D. Batory, "Feature-oriented programming and the ahead tool suite," in *ICSE '04: Proceedings of the 26th International Conference on Software Engineering*. Washington, USA: IEEE Computer Society, 2004.

[9] ——, "Multilevel models in model-driven engineering, product lines, and metaprogramming," *IBM Systems Journal*, vol. 45, pp. 527–539, 2006.

[10] S. Becker, "Using Generated Design Patterns to Support QoS Prediction of Software Component Adaptation," in *Proceedings of the Second International Workshop on Coordination and Adaptation Techniques for Software Entities (WCAT 05)*, C. Canal, J. M. Murillo, and P. Poizat, Eds., 2005. [Online]. Available: http://sdqweb.ipd.uka.de/publications/pdfs/becker2005a.pdf

[11] ——, "Coupled model transformations," in *Proceedings of the 7th international workshop on Software and performance*. ACM, 2008, pp. 103–114.

[12] ——, "Coupled Model Transformations for QoS Enabled Component-Based Software Design," Ph.D. dissertation, University of Oldenburg, Germany, Mar. 2008.

[13] ——, *Dependability Metrics*, ser. Lecture Notes in Computer Science. Springer-Verlag Berlin Heidelberg, 2008, vol. 4909, ch. Quality of Service Modeling Language, pp. 43–47. [Online]. Available: http://www.springerlink.com/content/754u689927655237/fulltext.pdf

[14] S. Becker, A. Brogi, I. Gorton, S. Overhage, A. Romanovsky, and M. Tivoli, "Towards an Engineering Approach to Component Adaptation," in *Architecting Systems with Trustworthy Components*, ser. Lecture Notes in Computer Science. Springer, 2006.

[15] S. Becker, T. Dencker, and J. Happe, "Model-Driven Generation of Performance Prototypes," in *Performance Evaluation: Metrics, Models and Benchmarks (SIPEW 2008)*, vol. 5119, 2008, pp. 79–98. [Online]. Available: http://www.springerlink.com/content/62t1277642tt8676/fulltext.pdf

[16] S. Becker, J. Happe, and H. Koziolek, "Putting Components into Context: Supporting QoS-Predictions with an explicit Context Model," in *Proc. of Workshop on Component Oriented Programming (WCOP)*, 2006.

[17] S. Becker, M. Hauck, M. Trifu, K. Krogmann, and J. Kofroň, "Reverse Engineering Component Models for Quality Predictions," in *European Conference on Software Maintenance and Reengineering, European Projects Track*, 2010.

[18] S. Becker, H. Koziolek, and R. Reussner, "The palladio component model for model-driven performance prediction," *Journal of Systems and Software*, vol. 82, no. 1, pp. 3 – 22, 2009, special Issue: Software Performance - Modeling and Analysis.

[19] S. Becker, H. Koziolek, and R. H. Reussner, "Model-based Performance Prediction with the Palladio Component Model," in *WOSP '07: Proceedings of the 6th International Workshop on Software and performance*. New York, NY, USA: ACM, February 5–8 2007, pp. 54–65. [Online]. Available: http://sdqweb.ipd.uka.de/publications/pdfs/becker2007b.pdf

[20] M. Bernardo and J. Hillston, Eds., *Formal Methods for Performance Evaluation (7th International School on Formal Methods for the Design of Computer, Communication, and Software Systems, SFM2007)*, May 2007, vol. 4486.

[21] A. Bertolino and R. Mirandola, "Modeling and analysis of non-functional properties in component-based systems," in *Electronic Notes in Theoretical Computer Science*. Elsevier, 2003.

[22] ——, "Cb-spe tool: Putting component-based performance engineering into practice," in *Proc. 7th International Symposium on Component-Based Software Engineering (CBSE 2004*. Springer, 2004, pp. 233–248.

[23] J. Bézivin, "On the unification power of models," *Software and Systems Modeling*, vol. 4, no. 2, pp. 171–188, 2005.

[24] J. Bézivin, F. Büttner, M. Gogolla, F. Jouault, I. Kurtev, and A. Lindow, "Model transformations? transformation models!" *Model Driven Engineering Languages and Systems*, vol. Springer, pp. 440–453, 2006.

[25] M. Biehl, "Literature study on model transformations," Web site: [Last accessed Feb. 1, 2011] http://www.md.kth.se/~biehl/files/papers/mt.pdf, 2010.

[26] B. W. Boehm, J. R. Brown, and M. Lipow, "Quantitative evaluation of software quality," in *ICSE '76: Proceedings of the 2nd international conference on Software engineering*. Los Alamitos, CA, USA: IEEE Computer Society Press, 1976, pp. 592–605.

[27] R. Böhme and R. Reussner, *Dependability Metrics*, 2008, vol. 4909, ch. Validation of Predictions with Measurements, pp. 7–13. [Online]. Available: http://www.springerlink.com/content/662rn13014r46269/fulltext.pdf

[28] T. Bures, "Generating connectors for homogeneous and heterogeneous deployment,," Ph.D. dissertation, Charles University in Prague, 2006.

[29] T. Bures, P. Hnetynka, and F. Plasil, "Sofa 2.0: Balancing advanced features in a hierarchical component model," in *Proc. of Conference on Software Engineering Research, Management and Applications (SERA)*. IEEE, 2006.

[30] T. Bures, M. Malohlava, and P. Hnetynka, "Using DSL for Automatic Generation of Software Connectors," in *In Proceedings of ICCBSS 2008, Madrid, Spain*, Feb. 2008, pp. 138–147.

[31] J. Cheesman and J. Daniels, *UML Components: A Simple Process for Specifying Component-based Software*, 2000.

[32] S. Chen, I. Gorton, A. Liu, and Y. Liu, "Performance prediction of cots component-based enterprise applications," in *Electronic proceedings of 5th ICSE Workshop on Component-based Software Engineering Benchmarks*, ser. CBSE5, 2002.

[33] S. Chen, Y. Liu, I. Gorton, and A. Liu, "Performance Prediction of Component-based Applications," *Journal of Systems and Software*, vol. 74, pp. 35–43, 2005.

[34] L. K. Christian Harnisch, "Modelling parallel, component-based software architectures with design patterns - replication pattern," Study Thesis, University of Karlsruhe, 2010.

[35] L. K. Christian Heupel, "Automatisierte integration nachrichtenbasierter kommunikation in das pcm," Study Thesis, University of Karlsruhe, 2010.

[36] L. K. ChristianVogel, "Automated integration of connector abstractions in pcm," Study Thesis, University of Karlsruhe, 2010.

[37] P. Clements and L. Northrop, *Software product lines*. Addison-Wesley, 2001.

[38] P. Coad and E. Yourdon, *Object oriented design*. Prentice-Hall, 1991.

[39] K. D. Cooper, D. Subramanian, and L. Torczon, "Adaptive optimizing compilers for the 21st century," *J. Supercomput.*, vol. 23, no. 1, pp. 7–22, 2002.

[40] V. Cortellessa, "How far are we from the definition of a common software performance ontology?" in *WOSP '05: Proceedings of the 5th International Workshop on Software and Performance*. New York, NY, USA: ACM Press, 2005, pp. 195–204.

[41] V. Cortellessa, A. Di Marco, and P. Inverardi, "Integrating Performance and Reliability Analysis in a Non-Functional MDA Framework," in *Fundamental Approaches to Software Engineering, 10th International Conference, FASE 2007, Held as Part of the Joint European Conferences, on Theory and Practice of Software, ETAPS 2007, Braga, Portugal, March 24 - April 1, 2007, Proceedings*, ser. Lecture Notes in Computer Science, M. B. Dwyer and A. Lopes, Eds., vol. 4422. Springer, 2007, pp. 57–71.

[42] V. Cortellessa, P. Pierini, and D. Rossi, "Integrating Software Models and Platform Models for Performance Analysis," *IEEE Transactions on Software Engineering*, vol. 33, no. 6, pp. 385–401, June 2007.

[43] D. Cruz, R. Henriques, and J. Varanda, "Constructing program animations using a pattern based approach," *Computer Science and Information Systems*, vol. 4, no. 2, pp. 97–114, 2007.

[44] K. Czarnecki and M. Antkiewicz, "Mapping features to models: A template approach based on superimposed variants," in *GPCE'05: Proceedings of the Fourth International Conference on Generative Programming and Component Engineering*. Springer-Verlag, 2005.

[45] K. Czarnecki and S. Helsen, "Classification of model transformation approaches," in *Proceedings of the 2nd OOPSLA Workshop on Generative Techniques in the Context of the Model Driven Architecture*, 2003, pp. 1–17.

[46] K. Czarnecki and U. W. Eisenecker, *Generative Programming – Methods, Tools, and Applications*. Addison-Wesley Professional, 2000.

[47] M. D. Del Fabro and P. Valduriez, "Towards the efficient development of model transformations using model weaving and matching transformations," *Software and Systems Modeling*, vol. 8, pp. 305–324, 2009.

[48] M. Del Fabro and P. Valduriez, "Semi-automatic model integration using matching transformations and weaving models," in *Proceedings of the 2007 ACM symposium on Applied computing*. ACM, 2007, pp. 963–970.

[49] A. Di Marco and P. Inveradi, "Compositional Generation of Software Architecture Performance QN Models," in *Proceedings of WICSA 2004*, 2004, pp. 37–46.

[50] A. Diaconescu and J. Murphy, "Automating the performance management of component-based enterprise systems through the use of redundancy," in *Proc. of Conference on Automated software engineering (ASE)*. IEEE, 2005.

[51] B. P. Douglass, *Real-Time Design Patterns*, ser. Object Technology Series. Addison-Wesley Professional, 2002.

[52] F. B. e Abreu, "Using ocl to formalize object oriented metrics definitions," FCT/UNL and INSC, Tech. Rep., 2001.

[53] Eclipse Foundation, "Graphical Modeling Project Homepage," Web site: [Last accessed Feb. 11, 2011] http://www.eclipse.org/modeling/gmp/.

[54] A. Eden, A. Yehudai, and J. Gil, "Precise specification and automatic application of design patterns," *Automated Software Engineering, International Conference on*, vol. 0, p. 143, 1997.

[55] I. El-Oudghiri, "Evaluierung der leistungsfähigkeit von lastverteilern für java ee cluster," Study Thesis, University of Karlsruhe, 2008.

[56] N. E. Fenton, *Software Metrics: A Rigorous Approach*. London, UK, UK: Chapman & Hall, Ltd., 1991.

[57] J. Foster, M. Greenwald, J. Moore, B. Pierce, and A. Schmitt, "Combinators for bi-directional tree transformations: a linguistic approach to the view update problem," *ACM Transactions on Programming Languages and Systems*, vol. 40, no. 1, pp. 233–246, 2007.

[58] M. Fowler, K. Beck, J. Brant, W. Opdyke, and D. Roberts, *Refactoring: Improving the Design of Existing Code*, 1999.

[59] E. Gamma, R. Helm, R. Johnson, and J. Vlissides, *Design Patterns: Elements of Reusable Object-Oriented Software*. Addison-Wesley, 1995.

[60] K. Garces, C. Parra, H. Arboleda, A. Yie, and R. Casallas, "Variability management in a Model-Driven software product line," *Avances en Sistemas e Informática*, vol. 4, no. 2, pp. 3–12, 2007. [Online]. Available: http://pisis.unalmed.edu.co/avances/archivos/ediciones/Edicion\%20Avances\%202007\%202/01.pdf

[61] M. Garcia, "Bidirectional synchronization of multiple views of software models," in *Proceedings of the Workshop on Domain-Specific Modeling Languages*, ser. CEUR-WS, 2008.

[62] A. A. E. Ghazi, "Modellierung der performance von thread-pools mit modellierung der performance von thread-pools mit," Study Thesis at Karlsruhe Instute of Technology, 10 2007.

[63] M. Girschick, T. Kühne, and F. Klar, "Generating systems from multiple levels of abstraction," in *Conference on Trends in Enterprise Application Architecture*, 2006.

[64] T. Goldschmidt, S. Becker, and A. Uhl, "Textual views in model driven engineering," in *Proceedings of the 35th EUROMICRO Conference on Software Engineering and Advanced Applications*. IEEE, 2009.

[65] ——, "Incremental Updates for Textual Modeling of Large Scale Models," in *Proceedings of the 15th IEEE International Conference on Engineering of Complex Computer Systems - Poster Paper*, 2010.

[66] T. Goldschmidt and J. Kuebler, "Towards Evaluating Maintainability Within Model-Driven Environments," in *Software Engineering 2008, Workshop Modellgetriebene Softwarearchitektur - Evolution, Integration und Migration*, 2008.

[67] T. Goldschmidt and A. Uhl, "Retainment Rules for Model Transformations," in *Proceedings of the 1st International Workshop on Model Co-Evolution and Consistency Management*, 2008.

[68] T. Goldschmidt and G. Wachsmuth, "Refinement transformation support for QVT Relational transformations," in *Proceedings of the 3rd Workshop on Model Driven Software Engineering*, 2008.

[69] V. Grassi, R. Mirandola, and A. Sabetta, "A Model Transformation Approach for the Early Performance and Reliability Analysis of Component-

Based Systems," in *Component-Based Software Engineering, 9th International Symposium, CBSE 2006, Västerås, Sweden, June 29 - July 1, 2006, Proceedings*, ser. Lecture Notes in Computer Science, vol. 4063. Springer, 2006, pp. 270–284.

[70] I. Groher and M. Voelter, "Expressing feature-based variability in structural models," in *11th Software Product Line Conference (SPLC) - Proceedings of the Workshop on Managing Variability for Software Product Lines*, 2007.

[71] ——, "Aspect-oriented model-driven software product line engineering," *Transactions on Aspect-Oriented Software Development VI*, pp. 111–152, 2009.

[72] O. M. Group, *MOF 2.0 Query/View/Transformation, version 1.0*, O. document formal/08 04-03, Ed. OMG, 2008, no. OMG document formal/08-04-03. [Online]. Available: http://www.omg.org/spec/QVT/1.0/PDF/

[73] D. Hamlet, "Subdomain testing of units and systems with state," in *Proc. of symposium on Software testing and analysis (ISSTA)*. ACM, 2006.

[74] M. Hapner, R. Burridge, R. Sharma, J. Fialli, and K. Stout, "Java Message Service Specification -Version 1.1," http://www.oracle.com/technetwork/java/jms/index.html, last retrieved: July 2011.

[75] J. Happe, "Towards a Model of Fair and Unfair Semaphores in MoDeST," in *Proceedings of the 6th Workshop on Process Algebra and Stochastically Timed Activities*, 2007, pp. 51–55. [Online]. Available: http://pastaworkshop.org/2007/proceedings/fair-semaphores.pdf

[76] J. Happe, H. Friedrich, S. Becker, and R. H. Reussner, "A Pattern-Based Performance Completion for Message-Oriented Middleware," in *Proceedings of the 7th International Workshop on Software and Performance (WOSP '08)*. New York, NY, USA: ACM, 2008, pp. 165–176.

[77] J. Happe, D. Westermann, K. Sachs, and L. Kapova, "Statistical Inference of Software Performance Models for Parametric Performance Completions," in *Research into Practice - Reality and Gaps (Proceedings of QoSA 2010)*, ser. LNCS, G. Heineman, J. Kofron, and F. Plasil, Eds., vol. 6093. Springer-Verlag Berlin Heidelberg, 2010, pp. 20–35.

[78] R. Harrison, L. G. Samaraweera, M. R. Dobie, and P. H. Lewis, "Estimating the quality of functional programs: an empirical investigation," *Information and Software Technology*, vol. 37, no. 12, pp. 701 – 707, 1995. [Online]. Available: http://www.sciencedirect.com/science/article/B6V0B-3YS2CBK-6/2/903ab3819bd8fe854dc98ea24c213c0f

[79] T. Hastie, R. Tibshirani, J. Friedman, and J. Franklin, "The elements of statistical learning: data mining, inference and prediction," *The Mathematical Intelligencer*, vol. 27, no. 2, pp. 83–85, 2005.

[80] M. Hauck, J. Happe, and R. H. Reussner, "Automatic Derivation of Performance Prediction Models for Load-balancing Properties Based on Goal-oriented Measurements," in *Proceedings of the 18th IEEE International Symposium on Modeling, Analysis and Simulation of Computer and Telecommunication Systems (MASCOTS'10)*. IEEE Computer Society, 2010, pp. 361–369.

[81] M. Hauck, M. Kuperberg, N. Huber, and R. Reussner, "Ginpex: Deriving Performance-relevant Infrastructure Properties Through Goal-oriented Experiments," in *7th ACM SIGSOFT International Conference on the Quality of Software Architectures (QoSA 2011)*, Boulder, Colorado, USA, June 20-24 2011.

[82] F. Heidenreich, J. Kopcsek, and U. Aßmann, "Safe composition of transformations," in *Theory and Practice of Model Transformations*, ser. Lecture Notes in Computer Science, L. Tratt and M. Gogolla, Eds. Springer Berlin / Heidelberg, 2010, vol. 6142, pp. 108–122.

[83] B. Henderson-Sellers, *Object-oriented metrics: measures of complexity*. Upper Saddle River, NJ, USA: Prentice-Hall, Inc., 1996.

[84] M. Herrmannsdoerfer, S. Benz, and E. Juergens, "Cope: A language for the coupled evolution of metamodels and models," in *Proceedings of the 1st International Workshop on Model Co-Evolution and Consistency Management*, 2008.

[85] S. Hissam, G. Moreno, J. Stafford, and K. Wallnau, "Enabling predictable assembly," *Journal of Systems and Software*, vol. 65, pp. 185–198, March 2003. [Online]. Available: http://dl.acm.org/citation.cfm?id=860119.860122

[86] N. Huber, S. Becker, C. Rathfelder, J. Schweflinghaus, and R. Reussner, "Performance Modeling in Industry: A Case Study on Storage Virtualization," in *ACM/IEEE 32nd International Conference on Software Engineering, Software Engineering in Practice Track, Capetown, South Africa.* New York, NY, USA: ACM, 2010, pp. 1–10, acceptance Rate: 23% (16/71). [Online]. Available: http://sdqweb.ipd.uka.de/publications/pdfs/hubern2010.pdf

[87] M. Iacob, M. Steen, and L. Heerink, "Reusable model transformation patterns," in *Enterprise Distributed Object Computing Conference Workshops, 2008 12th.* IEEE, 2008, pp. 1–10.

[88] ikv++, "medini QVT," Web site: [Last accessed Jan. 6, 2011] http://www.ikv.de/.

[89] P. K. Jayaraman, J. Whittle, A. M. Elkhodary, and H. Gomaa, "Model composition in product lines and feature interaction detection using critical pair analysis," in *MoDELS*, 2007.

[90] F. Jouault, F. Allilaire, J. Bézivin, and I. Kurtev, "ATL: A model transformation tool," *Science of Computer Programming, Special Issue on Second issue of experimental software and toolkits*, vol. 72, pp. 31–39, 2008.

[91] L. Kapova, T. Goldschmidt, S. Becker, and J. Henss, "Evaluating Maintainability with Code Metrics for Model-to-Model Transformations," in *Research into Practice - Reality and Gaps (Proceeding of QoSA 2010)*, ser. LNCS, G. Heineman, J. Kofron, and F. Plasil, Eds., vol. 6093. Springer-Verlag Berlin Heidelberg, 2010, pp. 151–166, to appear.

[92] L. Kapova, T. Goldschmidt, J. Happe, and R. H. Reussner, "Domain-specific templates for refinement transformations," in *MDI '10: Proceedings of the First International Workshop on Model-Drive Interoperability.* New York, NY, USA: ACM, 2010, pp. 69–78.

[93] L. Kapova and R. Reussner, "Application of advanced model-driven techniques in performance engineering," in *Computer Performance Engineering*, ser. Lecture Notes in Computer Science, A. Aldini, M. Bernardo, L. Bononi, and V. Cortellessa, Eds., vol. 6342. Springer Berlin / Heidelberg, 2010, pp. 17–36.

[94] L. Kapova, B. Zimmerova, A. Martens, J. Happe, and R. H. Reussner, "State dependence in performance evaluation of component-based software systems," in *Proceedings of the 1st Joint WOSP/SIPEW International Conference on Performance Engineering (WOSP/SIPEW '10).* New York, NY, USA: ACM, 2010, pp. 37–48. [Online]. Available: http://sdqweb.ipd.uka.de/publications/pdfs/kapova2009b.pdf

[95] C. Kästner, S. Apel, and M. Kuhlemann, "Granularity in software product lines," in *Proceedings of the 30th international conference on Software engineering.* ACM, 2008, pp. 311–320.

[96] A. Koziolek, H. Koziolek, and R. Reussner, "Peropteryx: automated application of tactics in multi-objective software architecture optimization," in *Proceedings of the joint ACM SIGSOFT conference – QoSA and ACM SIGSOFT symposium – ISARCS on Quality of software architectures – QoSA and architecting critical systems – ISARCS*, ser. QoSA-ISARCS '11. New York, NY, USA: ACM, New York, NY, USA, 2011, pp. 33–42. [Online]. Available: http://qosa.ipd.kit.edu/qosa_2011/

[97] H. Koziolek, "Parameter Dependencies for Reusable Performance Specifications of Software Components," Ph.D. dissertation, University of Oldenburg, 2008.

[98] ——, "Performance Evaluation of Component-based Software Systems: A Survey," *Performance Evaluation*, vol. 67, no. 8, pp. 634–658, August 2010.

[99] H. Koziolek and S. Becker, "Transforming Operational Profiles of Software Components for Quality of Service Predictions," in *Proc. of Workshop on Component Oriented Programming (WCOP)*, 2005.

[100] H. Koziolek, S. Becker, J. Happe, and R. Reussner, *Model-Driven Software Development: Integrating Quality Assurance.* IDEA Group Inc., December 2008, ch. Evaluating Performance of Software Architecture Models with the Palladio Component Model, pp. 95–118.

[101] H. Koziolek and V. Firus, "Empirical Evaluation of Model-based Performance Predictions Methods in Software Development," in *Proceeding of the first International Conference on the Quality of Software Architectures (QoSA'05)*, R. H. Reussner, J. Mayer, J. A. Stafford, S. Overhage, S. Becker,

and P. J. Schroeder, Eds., vol. 3712, 2005, pp. 188–202. [Online]. Available: http://sdqweb.ipd.uka.de/publications/pdfs/koziolek2005b.pdf

[102] H. Koziolek and J. Happe, "A QoS Driven Development Process Model for Component-Based Software Systems," in *Proc. of Symposium on Component-Based Software Engineering (CBSE).* Springer, 2006.

[103] H. Koziolek, J. Happe, and S. Becker, "Parameter Dependent Performance Specification of Software Components," in *Proc. 2nd Int. Conf. on the Quality of Software Architectures (QoSA'06)*, C. Hofmeister, I. Crnkovic, R. H. Reussner, and S. Becker, Eds., vol. 4214, July 2006, pp. 163–179. [Online]. Available: http://sdqweb.ipd.uka.de/publications/pdfs/koziolek2006f.pdf

[104] K. Krogmann, "Reconstruction of software component architectures and behaviour models using static and dynamic analysis," Ph.D. dissertation, Karlsruhe Institute of Technology (KIT), Karlsruhe, Germany, 2010. [Online]. Available: http://digbib.ubka.uni-karlsruhe.de/volltexte/1000022278

[105] J. Kübler and T. Goldschmidt, "A Pattern Mining Approach Using QVT," in *Proceedings of the 5th European Conference on Model Driven Architecture - Foundations and Applications (ECMDA)*, ser. Lecture Notes in Computer Science. Springer-Verlag Berlin Heidelberg, 2009. [Online]. Available: http://sdqweb.ipd.uka.de/publications/pdfs/kuebler2009a.pdf

[106] M. Kuperberg and R. Reussner, "Analysing the Fidelity of Measurements Performed With Hardware Performance Counters," in *Proceedings of the International Conference on Software Engineering 2011 (ICPE'11), March 14–16, 2011, Karlsruhe, Germany*, 2011.

[107] E. A. Lee, "The Problem with Threads," *IEEE Computer*, vol. 39, no. 5, pp. 33–42, May 2006.

[108] ——, "Threadedcomposite: A mechanism for building concurrent and parallel ptolemy ii models," EECS Department, University of California, Berkeley, Tech. Rep. UCB/EECS-2008-151, Dec 2008. [Online]. Available: http://www.eecs.berkeley.edu/Pubs/TechRpts/2008/EECS-2008-151.html

[109] K. Lee, K. Kang, and J. Lee, "Concepts and guidelines of feature modeling for product line software engineering," *Software Reuse: Methods, Techniques, and Tools*, pp. 62–77, 2002.

[110] Y. Liu, A. Fekete, and I. Gorton, "Design-level performance prediction of component-based applications," *IEEE Transactions on Software Engineering*, pp. 928–941, 2005.

[111] I. Malavolta, H. Muccini, and P. Pelliccione, "Dually: A framework for architectural languages and tools interoperability," *23rd IEEE/ACM International Conference on Automated Software Engineering*, 2008.

[112] A. Martens, "Empirical Validation of the Model-driven Performance Prediction Approach Palladio," Master's thesis, Carl-von-Ossietzky Universität Oldenburg, Nov. 2007.

[113] A. Martens and H. Koziolek, "Automatic, model-based software performance improvement for component-based software designs," in *6th International Workshop on Formal Engineering approaches to Software Components and Architectures (FESCA)*, 2009, pp. 77–93. [Online]. Available: http://sdqweb.ipd.uka.de/publications/pdfs/martens2009a.pdf

[114] R. Marvie, "A transformation composition framework for model driven engineering," LIFL IRCICA University of Lille, Tech. Rep., 2004.

[115] M. Marzolla, "Simulation-based performance modeling of UML software architectures," PhD Thesis TD-2004-1, Dipartimento di Informatica, Università Ca' Foscari di Venezia, Mestre, Italy, Feb. 2004.

[116] D. Masak, *Legacysoftware*. Springer, 2005.

[117] metamodel.com, "Community site for meta-modelling and semantic modelling: What is metamodeling, and what is it good for?" 2009, last retrieved 2011-08-09. [Online]. Available: http://infogrid.org/wiki/Reference/WhatIsMetaModeling

[118] M. Meyerhöfer and K. Meyer-Wegener, "Estimating non-functional properties of component-based software based on resource consumption," *Electronic Notes in Theoretical Computer Science*, 2005.

[119] L. K. Misha Strittmatter, "Performance abstractions of communication patterns for connectors," Study Thesis, University of Karlsruhe, 2010.

[120] M. Moriconi, X. Qian, and R. A. Riemenschneider, "Correct architecture refinement," *IEEE Transactions on Software Engineering*, vol. 21, no. 4, pp. 356–372, 1995.

[121] B. Morin, G. Perrouin, P. Lahire, O. Barais, G. Vanwormhoudt, and J.-M. Jézéquel, "Weaving variability into domain metamodels," in *Proceedings of the 12th International Conference on Model Driven Engineering Languages and Systems*, ser. MODELS '09. Berlin, Heidelberg: Springer-Verlag, 2009, pp. 690–705. [Online]. Available: http://dx.doi.org/10.1007/978-3-642-04425-0_56

[122] A. Mos and J. Murphy, "Performance management in component-oriented systems using a model driven architecture approach," in *Proc. of Enterprise Distributed Object Computing Conference*. IEEE, 2002.

[123] D. Muthig, "A light-weight approach facilitating an evolutionary transition towards software product lines," Ph.D. dissertation, 2002.

[124] Object Management Group (OMG), "Unified Modeling Language Specification: Version 2, Revised Final Adopted Specification (ptc/04-10-02)," 2004. [Online]. Available: http://www.uml.org/\#UML2.0

[125] ——, "Model Driven Architecture - Specifications," Web site: [Last accessed Feb. 1, 2011] http://www.omg.org/mda/specs.htm, 2006.

[126] ——, "MOF 2.0 Core Specification (formal/2006-01-01)," 2006. [Online]. Available: http://www.omg.org/cgi-bin/doc?formal/2006-01-01

[127] ——, "Object Constraint Language, v2.0 (formal/06-05-01)," 2006. [Online]. Available: http://www.omg.org/cgi-bin/doc?formal/2006-05-01

[128] ——, "UML Profile for Modeling and Analysis of Real-Time and Embedded systems (MARTE) RFP (realtime/05-02-06)," 2006. [Online]. Available: http://www.omg.org/cgi-bin/doc?realtime/2005-2-6

[129] ——, "CORBA 3.0 - OMG IDL Syntax and Semantics chapter," 2007. [Online]. Available: http://www.omg.org/docs/formal/02-06-39.pdf

[130] J. Oldevik, "Transformation composition modelling framework," in *Distributed Applications and Interoperable Systems*, 2005, pp. 108– 114.

[131] Oracle Technology Network, "The JAVA homepage," http://www.oracle.com/technetwork/java/javase/overview/index.html.

[132] D. C. Petriu and X. Wang, "From UML description of high-level software architecture to LQN performance models," in *Proc. of AGTIVE'99 Kerkrade*, M. Nagl, A. Schürr, and M. Münch, Eds., vol. 1779. Springer, 2000.

[133] C. Pons, R. Giandini, G. Perez, and G. Baum, "A two-level calculus for composing hybrid QVT transformations," in *Proceedings of the 2009 International Conference of the Chilean Computer Science Society*, ser. SCCC. IEEE Computer Society, 2009.

[134] A. Rentschler, "Model-to-text transformation languages," in *Seminar: Modellgetriebene Software-Entwicklung Architekturen, Muster und Eclipse-basierte MDA*, 2006.

[135] R. H. Reussner, S. Becker, H. Koziolek, J. Happe, M. Kuperberg, and K. Krogmann, "The Palladio Component Model," Universität Karlsruhe (TH), Interner Bericht 2007-21, 2007, october 2007. [Online]. Available: http://sdqweb.ipd.uka.de/publications/pdfs/reussner2007a.pdf

[136] R. H. Reussner and W. Hasselbring, *Handbuch der Software-Architektur*. dPunkt.verlag, Heidelberg, 2006.

[137] ——, *Handbuch der Software-Architektur*, 2nd ed., December 2008.

[138] R. H. Reussner, H. W. Schmidt, and I. Poernomo, "Reliability Prediction for Component-Based Software Architectures," *Journal of Systems and Software – Special Issue of Software Architecture – Engineering Quality Attributes*, vol. 66, no. 3, pp. 241–252, 2003.

[139] L. Reynoso, M. Genero, M. Piattini, and E. Manso, "Assessing the impact of coupling on the understandability and modifiability of ocl expressions within uml/ocl combined models," in *Proceedings of the 11th IEEE International Software Metrics Symposium*. Washington, DC, USA: IEEE Computer Society, 2005, pp. 14–. [Online]. Available: http://dl.acm.org/citation.cfm?id=1090955.1092154

[140] T. Rohrberg, "Visualisierung von entscheidungshilfen für software-architektur-tradeoffs," Master's thesis, Karlsruhe Institute of Technology, 2010.

[141] R. J. Rubey and R. D. Hartwick, "Quantitative measurement of program quality," in *Proceedings of the 1968 23rd ACM national conference.* New York, NY, USA: ACM, 1968, pp. 671–677.

[142] S. Röttger and S. Zschaler, "Model-driven development for non-functional properties: Refinement through model transformation," in *In: Proc. UML Conference.* Springer, 2004, pp. 275–289.

[143] D. C. Schmidt, H. Rohnert, M. Stal, and D. Schultz, *Pattern-Oriented Software Architecture: Patterns for Concurrent and Networked Objects.* New York, NY, USA: John Wiley & Sons, Inc., 2000.

[144] A. Schürr, "Specification of Graph Translators with Triple Graph Grammars," in *21st International Conference on Graph-Theoretic Concepts in Computer Science*, 1995.

[145] M. Scott, *Programming language pragmatics.* Morgan Kaufmann Pub, 2000.

[146] S. Sentilles, A. Vulgarakis, T. Bureš, J. Carlson, and I. Crnković, "A component model for control-intensive distributed embedded systems," in *11th International Symposium on Component-Based Software Engineering (CBSE).* Springer, 2008.

[147] C. U. Smith and L. G. Williams, *Performance Solutions: A Practical Guide to Creating Responsive, Scalable Software.* Addison-Wesley, 2002.

[148] R. L. Solso, *Cognitive Psychology.* Allyn and Bacon, 2001.

[149] B. Spitznagel and D. Garlan, "A Compositional Formalization of Connector Wrappers," in *Proceedings of the 25th International Conference on Software Engineering, May 3-10, 2003, Portland, Oregon, USA*, IEEE, Ed. Los Alamitos, CA: IEEE Computer Society, May 2003, pp. 374–384.

[150] H. Stachowiak, "{Allgemeine Modelltheorie}," 1973.

[151] J. Stammel and R. Reussner, "Kamp: Karlsruhe architectural maintainability prediction," in *Proceedings of the 1. Workshop des GI-Arbeitskreises Langlebige Softwaresysteme (L2S2): "Design for Future - Langlebige Softwaresysteme"*, 2009, pp. 87–98.

[152] Standard Performance Evaluation Corp., "SPECjms2007 Benchmark," http://www.spec.org/jms2007/, last retrieved: July 2011, 2007.

[153] H. Störrle, "Structuring very large domain models: Experiences from industrial MDSD projects," in *Proceedings of the Fourth European Conference on Software Architecture: Companion Volume*, 2010.

[154] D. Streitferdt, "A component model for applications based on feature models," in *Proceedings of the 2nd Workshop on Software Variability Management - Software Product Families and PopulationsProceedings of the 2nd Workshop on Software Variability Management - Software Product Families and Populations*, December 2004.

[155] H. Sutter and J. Larus, "Software and the Concurrency Revolution," *ACM Queue*, vol. 3, no. 7, pp. 54–62, 2005.

[156] E. Syriani, J. Kienzle, and H. Vangheluwe, "Exceptional transformations," *Theory and Practice of Model Transformations*, vol. 6142, pp. 199–214, 2010.

[157] C. Szyperski, *Component Software – Beyond Object-Oriented Programming*. Addison-Wesley, 2002.

[158] M. Tisi, F. Jouault, P. Fraternali, S. Ceri, and J. Bézivin, "On the use of higher-order model transformations," in *Model Driven Architecture - Foundations and Applications*, ser. Lecture Notes in Computer Science. Springer Berlin / Heidelberg, 2009.

[159] J. B. Tolosa, O. Sanjuán-Martínez, V. García-Díaz, B. C. P. G-Bustelo, and J. M. C. Lovelle, "Towards the systematic measurement of ATL transformation models," *Software: Practice and Experience*, vol. 41, pp. 789–815, 2010.

[160] M. F. van Amstel, C. F. J. Lange, and M. G. J. van den Brand, "Metrics for analyzing the quality of model transformations," in *12th ECOOP Workshop on Quantitative Approaches in Object-Oriented Software Engineering (QAOOSE)*, 2008.

[161] P. Van Gorp, A. Keller, and D. Janssens, "Transformation language integration based on profiles and higher order transformations," in *Software Language Engineering*, ser. Lecture Notes in Computer Science. Springer Berlin / Heidelberg, 2009.

[162] J. Vara, V. Bollati, B. Vela, and E. Marcos, "Leveraging model transformations by means of annotation models," *Model Transformation with ATL*, p. 88, 2009.

[163] D. Varró and A. Pataricza, "Generic and meta-transformations for model transformation engineering," *The Unified Modelling Language*, vol. 3273, p. 290, 2004.

[164] D. Varró, "Model transformation by example," in *9th International Conference on Model Driven Engineering Languages and Systems (MODELS)*, 2006, pp. 410–424.

[165] T. Verdickt, B. Dhoedt, F. Gielen, and P. Demeester, "Automatic Inclusion of Middleware Performance Attributes into Architectural UML Software Models," *IEEE Transactions on Software Engineering*, vol. 31, no. 8, pp. 695–711, 2005.

[166] M. Voelter and I. Groher, "Handling variability in model transformations and generators," in *Proceedings of the 7th Workshop on Domain-Specific Modeling (DSM'07) at OOPSLA '07*, 2007.

[167] M. Völter and T. Stahl, *Model-Driven Software Development.* Wiley & Sons, New York, USA, 2006.

[168] D. Wagelaar, "Composition techniques for rule-based model transformation languages," in *Theory and Practice of Model Transformations*, ser. Lecture Notes in Computer Science. Springer Berlin / Heidelberg, 2008.

[169] D. Westermann, J. Happe, M. Hauck, and C. Heupel, "The performance cockpit approach: A framework for systematic performance evaluations," in *2010 36th EUROMICRO Conference on Software Engineering and Advanced Applications*. IEEE, 2010, pp. 31–38.

[170] L. G. Williams and C. U. Smith, "Making the Business Case for Software Performance Engineering," in *Proceedings of the 29th International Computer Measurement Group Conference, December 7-12, 2003, Dallas, Texas, USA*. Computer Measurement Group, 2003, pp. 349–358.

[171] E. D. Willink and P. J. Harris, "The side transformation pattern: Making transforms modular and re-usable," *ENTCS*, vol. 127, pp. 17–29, 2005.

[172] M. Woodside, G. Franks, and D. C. Petriu, "The Future of Software Performance Engineering," in *Proceedings of ICSE 2007, Future of SE.* IEEE Computer Society, Washington, DC, USA, 2007, pp. 171–187.

[173] M. Woodside, D. C. Petriu, and K. H. Siddiqui, "Performance-related Completions for Software Specifications." in *Proceedings of the 22rd International Conference on Software Engineering, ICSE 2002, 19-25 May 2002, Orlando, Florida, USA.* ACM, 2002, pp. 22–32.

[174] X. Wu and M. Woodside, "Performance modeling from software components," *SIGSOFT Software Engineering Notes*, vol. 29, pp. 290–301, 2004.

[175] B. Zimmerova, "Modelling and Formal Analysis of Component-Based Systems in View of Component Interaction," Ph.D. dissertation, Masaryk University, Czech Republic, 2008.

[176] B. Zimmerova et al., *The Common Component Modeling Example: Comparing Software Component Models*, ser. LNCS. Springer, 2008, ch. 7.